Tracking Deception

Bush Mid-East Policy

Tracking Deception

Bush Mid-East Policy

William A. Cook

A Dandelion Books Publication
Tempe, Arizona
www.dandelionbooks.net

Copyright, 2006 by William A. Cook

All rights exclusively reserved. No part of this book may be reproduced or translated into any language or utilized in any form or by any means, electronic or mechanical, including photocopying, recording or by any information storage and retrieval system, without permission in writing from the publisher.

A Dandelion Books Publication
Dandelion Books, LLC
Tempe, Arizona

Library of Congress Cataloging-in-Publication Data

Cook, William A.,
Tracking Deception: bush mid-east policy

Library of Congress Catalog Card Number 2005930386
ISBN 1-893302-83-0

Front cover art/concept/design and book design by Amnet Systems Private Limited
www.amnet-systems.com

Disclaimer and Reader Agreement

Under no circumstances will the publisher, Dandelion Books, LLC, or author be liable to any person or business entity for any direct, indirect, special, incidental, consequential, or other damages based on any use of this book or any other source to which it refers, including, without limitation, any lost profits, business interruption, or loss of programs or information.

Though due diligence has been used in researching and authenticating the information contained in this book, Dandelion Books, LLC and the author make no representations as to accuracy, completeness, currentness, suitability, or validity of any opinions expressed in this book. Neither Dandelion Books, LLC nor the author shall be liable for any accuracy, errors, adequacy or timeliness in the content, or for any actions taken in reliance thereon.

Reader Agreement for Accessing This Book

By reading this book, you, the reader, consent to bear sole responsibility for your own decisions to use or read any of this book's material. Dandelion Books, LLC and the author shall not be liable for any damages or costs of any type arising out of any action taken by you or others based upon reliance on any materials in this book.

Printed in the United States of America

Dandelion Books, LLC
www.dandelionbooks.net

I read each day the crippling accounts of soldiers caught in a maelstrom of unseen death lurking on roof tops, in narrow alleys, behind cement walls and black windows, beneath tires littering the streets. I see pictures of burned out buses, sidewalks and curbs bathed with blood, faces twisted in pain, bits and pieces of flesh scattered about like fallen leaves, blown helter-skelter by the wind. Faces, I see suffering on so many faces, mothers weeping over their dying children, old women and men huddled in the debris left of their bulldozed home, medics carrying the lifeless body of a man whose hand rests beside his face held there by the torn shred of his sleeve, his arm gone, his body black with grime...

This is a world gone mad, a madness on all sides, the madness of greed that sees in oil the riches of Sultans and Kings, the madness of arrogant pseudo-philosophers who conjure beliefs of personal superiority that gives them license to conquer and enslave, the madness of ancient minds that dreamt of power and glory in covenants with gods, the madness of fanatics that fabricate fantasy out of indecipherable images lodged in pages of metaphors, the madness of little minds that grab onto faith as the golden ring that will bring them salvation, the madness of those born again to the child's world of impossible dreams forgoing in their new world the reality of this.

Today I read of depleted uranium, 1000 metric tons made from the deadly U238 isotope dropped on America's killing fields, that wafts on the wind like aerosol spray, a toxic death that sticks in human lungs, bringing a slow and painful death. I saw pictures of new born children bloated and bruised by scars, eyes missing, a nose of scar tissue and nostrils, no lips, the detritus of our advanced civilization scattered on hospital beds in Baghdad. I read of soldiers twisted in mind and spirit by no visible symptom except the phantom of our cursed nuclear waste that encircles them in their tank and haunts them the remainder of their lives. Our young return from this nightmare of devastation devastated themselves, courtesy of our Commander-in-Chief.

And I read today that 24,010 Americans have been evacuated with wounds and injuries from our "war" zones, that 37,000 innocent men, women, and children in Afghanistan and Iraq have died and more than 500,000 have suffered wounds. And I hear the silence, the deafening silence of indifference that our compassionate conservative leader offers to those who suffer the consequence of his acts, and feel with them the utter helplessness of their plight.

I look in vain for this Christ in the Christianity practiced by the right wing, fanatical sects that preach the Book of Revelation, reveling in the glory they perceive to be their reward if they destroy the enemies they identify as the enemies of God. I wonder where in this acclaimed Christian land of TV Evangelists and literalist ministers is there a man who acts as Christ would act? I see none. I see only a God forsaken Tele-Evangelist land of vitriol and bigotry where none could say I "love the Lord my God with my whole heart and mind and soul, and my neighbor as myself." They have buried the teachings of Jesus in the quagmire of a malevolent and malicious God of the Old Testament, a God that would order one Semitic tribe to exterminate another. We have not moved beyond the racist hatred that blotted the landscape 2500 years ago.

—William A. Cook, from *Tracking Deception*

Dedication

I have always wanted to dedicate a book to those who strive, against formidable odds, to place principle before personal gain, prick power with profundity, and proffer peace with prudence and passion. My brother Jack belongs in this group; his dedication to the cause profoundly influenced me. Many have spent their lives selflessly devoted to a better way, influences all: Robert Fisk, Edward Said, Alex Cockburn, Jeffrey St. Clair, Teriq Ali, Saul Landau, Noam Chomsky, Howard Zinn, Ken Peerless, Michael Ortiz Hill, Uri Avnery, Gideon Levy and Lewis Lapham, to name a few. Thanks.

Notes

"The Destructive Power of Myth: Implications for 9/11" was written in the days following the President's address to the joint session of Congress, September 20, 2001 and submitted to *Crossings* in October. The Editorial Board of *Crossings: An Interdisciplinary Journal* published by SUNY, Binghamton, accepted it for publication in February, 2002. It appeared in a special double issue, No. 5/6, 2002-3. With the exception of chapters 13 and 17, all of the articles appeared in *Counterpunch* Internet Magazine. 13 and 17 appeared in Ken Peerless' *News From the Edge* Internet newspaper.

Preface

Deceit is the Devil that destroys Democracy and, like a corrosive acid, it is destroying America. The Bush administration, driven by the twin horses of the Apocalypse, the Evangelical Christian Zionists and the Neo-Con Zealots, pulls America ever closer to the brink of disaster by wielding whips of righteous prophecy and self-serving lies. The life-blood of Democracy is truth, and Bush has murdered truth! How ironic that the self-proclaimed righteous, the born again Christian Zionists and the Jewish Zionists wheedle their way into their respective governments, preaching the Devil's agenda, using superstition, deception and hypocrisy. In the process they destroy the true and permanent tenets of Christianity and the founding principles of Democracy.

The Founding Fathers rose in righteous indignation against a despotic King who attempted to impose his will and economic system on the Colonists by occupation and coercion. Now America, once the herald of individual rights, has metamorphosed into the despotic nation that coerces and occupies other nation states. It forces them to adopt a leader who accepts America's brand of Capitalistic control the better to serve the wealthy few even as they exploit the majority who live in poverty.

America, in 1776, declared the right of a people to disband the ties that bound them to a despotic King. But now it imposes despots who will do America's bidding, and calls it "advancing Democracy around the world." Bush cloaks America's imperialistic advance across the globe in hallowed terms. The red, white and blue vestments of "Democracy and Freedom are not America's gift to the world, but God's gift." He is only the humble minister of the Almighty christened at this moment in history to garb the world against the cold reality of despotic "evildoers."

Now is the time for Americans to return to their revolution, to rally 'round their principles, not their prevaricating President. Now is the time to remove the yoke of imperialist adventurism that has been thrust on their necks by this administration, to overturn the despot that forces his will on Americans through fear. We must protect the right of separation of church and state lest the self-proclaimed righteous shackle us to the cross of imposed dogma and doctrine, to restrict the insidious growth of militarism that threatens the power of the people. We must return our representatives to the will of the people lest they remain lackeys of corporate elites.

The principles that gave birth to unalienable rights through natural law have been eroded by this administration. We stand on the precipice Jefferson feared, threatened by the three forces that are anathema to Democracy: despotic rule, corporate power by a pseudo-aristoi, and organized religion. Now is the time to act.

This book tracks the deceit that characterizes the Bush administration. It surfaced in the speech he gave to the joint session of Congress in September 2001 in which he declared war on terror and avoided any reference whatsoever as to why that war should exist or how a nation fights a concept. That speech gave impetus to this book with Chapter 43, "The Destructive Power of Myth: Implications for 9/11," serving as a response and a foreshadowing of events yet to come. Although that chapter was written in late September of 2001, it presents a scholarly and extended argument about primary causes avoided by Bush when he began his crusade against the "terrorists." It appears toward the end of this volume because it offers an instructive way to perceive this most recent abuse of power in a historical context. It also demonstrates how deception is used to drive the desires of the few who control the many.

From September 2002, when the administration issued the National Security Strategy Report, a document prepared 10 years before and never brought for discussion or debate before our Congress or Senate, much less the people, this country has been on a trajectory that defies the Democratic principles that provide its foundation. It casts America as a pariah before the world, and lashes America to the corrupt and savage regimes of Ariel Sharon and dictators like Saddam Hussein who rule in Kazakhstan, Uzbekistan, and Turkmenistan. The people of the world see in Bush the greatest threat to world peace that currently rules a nation. They watch America recede from the community of nations, isolating itself by abandoning treaties that supported the environment, restricted proliferation of missiles and nuclear weaponry, and brought uniformity in justice through international courts. They stand in shock and awe at an America shamelessly becoming judge, jury, and executioner of individuals and nations as it moves ineluctably to world domination.

This America mirrors the consequences of arrogance that sees perfection in itself while it castigates its neighbors for harboring evil, projects its God protected beliefs on all the unbelievers in the world, presumes a holy covenant with God that proclaims His favoritism above all humankind, and assumes the judicial robe of righteousness. It willingly incarcerates individuals without charge or recourse to legal counsel, executes those it judges to be guilty without trial or presumption of innocence, and, finally, in all brazen hypocrisy, determines for the world what is good and what is evil.

America, in short, mirrors the arrogance of the Israeli state under Sharon and his right-wing Zionist religious groups that constitute his government. America has been reborn in the likeness of Sharon's Israel, and with Israel we are the twin demons of destruction that live in constant fear of all peoples who would rather die than be subjugated, exploited, or oppressed.

What America was, it is no longer. It stood once against the oppressor and now it is the oppressor. It began as a nation respectful of others' rights and now it determines for others what their rights will be. It designed a government tolerant of all beliefs, but now finds favor with an intolerant minority that proclaims to know the prophecies that are imbedded in ancient myth. It knew the hazards of militarism and imperialism; now it has become an imperial military dominance in the world. None of these realities is presented to the American people in these terms. They are couched in euphemisms, hypocrisy, and deception.

The chapters of this book follow Bush Mid-East policy from September 2002 to the present. That September, Bush abandoned the community of nations by declaring his intention to invade Iraq, hypocritically hiding his intention by offering a resolution to the United Nations Security Council. He deceptively proposed the need to support the UN by enforcing their resolutions against Iraq, thus making that organization meaningful while failing to mention the nation that most flagrantly violates UN resolutions: Israel. Bush presented the American people with his administration's Strategy Report without deliberation by their elected representatives; he made no reference to his imperialist agenda. And that was just September.

Month by month Bush duplicity and deception mounted. His administration took America to war against a nation that had no intention of harming America, no means to harm America, and offered no threat to America. Yet he claimed all three. He concocted lies that convinced the American people that it was under imminent threat from biological, chemical, and nuclear weaponry when none existed. He fabricated an enemy force of considerable might that would confront American troops once the invasion started—when in reality Iraq had been devastated by 12 years of sanctions and had no army to field.

Bush justified his invasion as a liberation of the Iraqi people who would throw flowers at our soldiers as they brought liberation. These were lies manufactured by those with the most to gain: the Neo-Con Cabal and the expatriate Iraqis. Bush deceptively proved connections between Saddam Hussein and al Qaeda, knowing full well that Saddam hated al Qaeda as much as al Qaeda hated Saddam.

So America went to "war" believing Bush's lies. The result: Saddam out of power, Iraq now an anarchistic state flowing with "terrorists" from many countries that have a grudge against America, and our soldiers sitting targets as they become the on-site symbol of America's oppression and collusion with Israel—which acts as consultant on how to occupy a foreign nation and control its people. Democracy in Iraq is a distant and hopeless dream as the various factions struggle to gain power—with the outcome a foregone conclusion—the creation of an Islamic "Democracy."

Bush claims even now that his "war" has brought more security for America, when he and the world know Iraq has become ground zero for terrorists, with Afghanistan rapidly returning to its state as a safe-haven. Bush defends his "war" as necessary to secure America against terrorists when he knows the expenditure of 150 billion dollars should have been used to deal with the causes of terrorist attacks. He belittles the intelligence of Americans by claiming the attackers "hated America's freedoms."

Bush's deception, like Pinocchio's nose, grew with each passing month. All members of his administration joined the lies: Rumsfeld, Powell, Cheney, Wolfowitz, Rice, Fleisher, Perle, Armitage, Abrams, Libby and all who worked for the administration or influenced the administration from the American Enterprise Institute and the Project for the New American Century. These men, almost all men, have subverted American Democracy, stolen the power of the people, and let personal gain and conflict of interest in their allegiance to Israel betray their positions as they effectively determined the fate of our soldiers who died. They also effectively determined the fate of innocent Iraqi civilians who died, the soldiers and civilians from coalition nations who died, and the devastation wrought on the countries of the Mid-East.

For these crimes they must be punished, preferably by impeachment in which a full disclosure of their evils can be spread before the American public and the world. Nothing short of this will compensate for the havoc they have wielded, the deaths they have caused, and the principles of Democracy they have decimated.

Contents

Contents

Introduction

Intolerable Opinions in an Age of Empire

Jeffrey St. Clair

In Love's free state all powers so levelled be
That them affection governs more than awe.
                                                    —William Davenant

In 1638, John Lilburne was put on secret trial by the Star Chamber of Charles I. His crime? The writing and distribution of seditious pamphlets that skewered the legitimacy of the monarchy and challenged the primacy of the high prelates of the Church of England. He was promptly convicted of publishing writing with "dangerous consequence and evil effect."

For these intolerable opinions, the royal tribunal sentenced him to be publicly flogged through the streets of London, from Fleet Prison, built on the tidal flats where Fleet Ditch spilled out London's sewage, to the Palace Yard at Westminster, then a public showground for weekly spectacles of humiliation and torture. By one account, Lilburne was whipped by the King's executioner more than 500 times, "causing his shoulders to swell almost as big as a penny loafe with the bruses of the knotted Cords."

The bloodied writer was then shackled to a pillory, where, to the amazement of the crowd of onlookers, he launched into an impassioned oration in defense of his friend, Dr. John Bastick, the Puritan physician and preacher. Only weeks before, Bastick's ears had been slashed off by the King's men as punishment for publishing an attack on the Archbishop of Canterbury, an essay that Lilburne had happily distributed far and wide.

Lilburne gushered forth about this barbaric injustice for a few moments, before his tormentors gagged his mouth with a urine-soaked rag. After enduring another two hours of torture, the guards dragged him behind a cart back to the Fleet, where he was confined in irons for the next two-and-a-half years. This was the first of "Free-Born" John Lilburne's many parries with the masters of Empire.

While in his foul cell in Fleet prison, Lilburne was kept in solitary confinement on orders of the Star Council, his lone visitor a maid named Katherine Hadley. Somehow the maid was able to sneak pen, paper and ink past the Fleet's guards to the young radical. According to Lilburne's own description, he was "lying day and night in Fetters of Iron, both hands and legges," when he began to write furiously, penning a gruesome account of his mock trial and torture, *The Work of the Beast*, and a scabrous assault on the Anglican bishops, *Come Out of Her, My People*. These pamphlets were smuggled out of Newgate, printed in the Low Lands and distributed through covert networks across England to popular acclaim and royal indignation.

Oliver Cromwell, then a Puritan leader in the House of Commons, took up Lilburne's cause, giving a stirring speech in defense of the imprisoned writer. It swayed Parliament, which voted to release Lilburne from jail. Lilburne emerged from the jail grateful to Cromwell, but not blind to the general's dictatorial ambitions. He would later pen savage attacks on Cromwell and his censorious functionaries.

Soon Lilburne joined the Parliamentary Army, fighting with distinction against the royal forces in numerous clashes, including the battle at the Edgehill, the first major encounter of the English Civil War, before being captured at Brentford on November 12, 1642. Once again he faced trial, this time at Oxford, for "taking up arms against the King." Lilburne was swiftly convicted and sentenced to death. But his friends in Parliament rose to his defense, threatening similar reprisals against Royalist prisoners. A prisoner exchange was arranged and Lilburne was on the loose again, leading soldiers into battle against the king's troops, eventually rising to the rank of Lieutenant-Colonel.

But in 1645, Lilburne abandoned Cromwell's New Model Army, known for singing the Psalms as they clamored into battle, after he was told that he must swear to the Solemn League and Covenant, Cromwell's equivalent of a religious loyalty oath to the Presbyterian church. Lilburne, an Independent, hated oaths and had defied the Star Chamber, in his first prosecution, by refusing to take the oath *ex officio*, which he argued violated the ancient right of *habeas corpus*.

But by now, Lilburne was plotting a more profound insurrection aimed at democratizing the army, as well as the rest of the nation. Why, he asked, should soldiers be expected to fight in a war declared by legislators for whom they could not vote? Why, he asked in the halls at Westminster, weren't the soldiers paid more? Why weren't the families of the slain compensated?

"Every free man of England, poor as well as rich, should have a vote in choosing those that are to make the law," Lilburne wrote. "All and every particular and individual man and woman, that ever breathed in the world, are by nature all equal and alike in their power, dignity, authority and majesty, none of them having (by nature) any authority, dominion or magisterial power one over or above another." Jefferson sounds cautious beside Lilburne's exuberant prose.

These were the opening shots of the Levellers, aimed, in the words of one observer, "to sett all things straight and rayse a parity and community in the kingdom." It would be, in Lilburne's view, a new kingdom, without a king or a House of Lords or even land lords.

The Leveller movement began as a rebellion within a rebellion, spreading from the Army to persecuted religious sects to farmers and working class people. It was a movement energized by writers, headlined by Lilburne, Richard Overton and William Walwyn, and the pamphlets flew off the presses, with more than 2,100 different tracts printed in 1645. This prompted the repressive acts known as the Ordinances, which suppressed public assemblies, outlawed meetings of Antinomians and Anabaptists, prohibited preaching by lay preachers, and imposed strict censorship of the press. Cromwell's notorious Committee of Examinations, essentially Parliament's version of the Star Chamber, was tasked with investigating "scandalous" writing, destroying independent presses and arresting writers, publishers and vendors of documents deemed seditious. These were the oppressive laws, which prompted Milton to write the "Areopagitica." Milton's passionate polemic, one of the great defenses of a free press, was mild compared to the furious denunciations that poured from Lilburne's pen.

These testy impertinences landed Lilburne in Newgate again, this time on charges of libel. But 2,000 leading Londoners signed a petition on his behalf and public riots in his defense prompted his quick release. The experience only served to sharpen his resistance to Cromwell, who he saw as a dictatorial sell-out to the forces of Empire (not unlike, say, John Kerry), and the leading agent of state oppression. He fired off a threatening public letter to Cromwell, which darkly concluded: "rest assured if ever my hand is upon you, it shall be when you are in your full glory."

Lilburne and his Leveller cohorts started an underground paper called *The Moderate*. The title was something of a joke. After all, the Leveller platform seems downright pinko by our constricted standards. They wanted to outlaw monopolies, eliminate taxes on the poor, impose term limits on members of Parliament, eliminate all restrictions on the press and religious worship, assure trial by juror for all defendants, and also assure universal suffrage.

But Lilburne was far from the most radical spirit in those topsy-turvy days. He was outflanked to his left by Gerrard Winstanley's Diggers and by the Seekers, Ranters, Antinomians and militant fen dwellers, the Earth Firsters of their time. Like Tom Paine, he opposed the death penalty, speaking out against the execution of Charles I. "I refused to be one of his (Charles I) judges," Lilburne wrote. "They were no better than murderers in taking away the King's life even though he was guilty of the crimes he was charged with. It is murder because it was done by a hand that had no authority to do it."

Cut to 1649. Lilburne is imprisoned once more in the Tower of London, along with four of his Leveller cohorts, including the brilliant polemicist Richard Overton. This time they'd attacked Cromwell head-on, accusing him of being a reactionary force roaming the land with secret police threatening all dissenters. "If our hearts were not over-charged with the sense of the present miseries and approaching dangers of the Nation, your small regard to our late serious apprehensions, would have kept us silent; but the misery, danger, and bondage threatened is so great, imminent, and apparent that whilst we have breath, and are not violently restrained, we cannot but speak, and even cry aloud, until you hear us, or God be pleased otherwise to relieve us." The charge was treason.

His wife Elizabeth, herself a forceful agitator for peace and the rights of women, wrote an urgent pamphlet in his defense, titled "A Petition of Women." The prose still resonates, perhaps more now than it has in 300 years. "Would you have us keep at home in our houses, when men of such faithfulness and integrity as the four prisoners, our friends in the Tower, are fetched out of their beds and forced from their houses by soldiers, to the affrighting and undoing of themselves, their wives, children, and families? Are not our husbands, our selves, our daughters and families, by the same rule as liable to the like unjust cruelties as they?" Elizabeth got 10,000 people to sign a petition on Lilburne's behalf.

He was soon released—but arrested again within the year, this time for denouncing Cromwell's genocidal raids on Ireland. But the jury refused to convict him and Cromwell had him banished from England. Lilburne spent a few months in Holland writing incendiary pamphlets before sneaking back into England. He was soon discovered and arrested on charges of treason once again. Again the jury refused to convict. But Cromwell refused to release him, shuttling Lilburne from the Tower, to the Mount Orgueil, a dank Norman castle in Guernsey, and finally to Dover castle. One of his guards described Lilburne as being tougher to handle than "ten Cavaliers."

While locked in Dover castle, Lilburne fell under the spell of the Quakers, and became a radical pacifist, writing that he had finished with "carnal sword fightings and fleshly bustlings and contests." His pen never stopped, though. The pamphlets continued to flow until his death in 1657. Lilburne refused to be a martyr. He faced the beast, endured prisons and tortures that would give even an inmate at Guantanamo the chills, and remained defiant and upbeat. He lived the life of an escape artist, who could talk himself into and out of trouble, almost effortlessly. His mind ran in overdrive and so, apparently, did his mouth. His friend Harry Marten, the regicide, quipped: "If the world was emptied of all but John Lilburne, Lilburne would quarrel with John and John with Lilburne." And so it should be.

I first encountered the writings of John Lilburne in 1981 during a series of lectures on Milton and the radicals of the English revolution delivered by the great British historian Christopher Hill, author of *The World Turned Upside Down*. Hill was stalking other game in those lectures, but his energetic asides on

Lilburne and his band of Levellers pricked my interest. Here were Puritans who detested imperial ambitions and believed in unfettered free speech and absolute equality—a far cry from Nathaniel Hawthorne's band of vicious prudes, not to mention the Neo-Puritans, like Falwell and Robertson, then in the ascendancy.

Lilburne had long fallen out of favor with American historians and his writings were difficult to track down. I ended up devouring them at the stark library of Georgetown University, overlooking the Potomac River and the gloom-stricken Lincoln Memorial. In those days, the chill shadow of Reagan loomed over the Republic and Lilburne's polemics on freedom and repression gripped me like an urgent voice from the grave.

It's strange, but perhaps instructive of our current historical amnesia, that Lilburne's reputation has fallen into such neglect in the US, for his anarchic style seems more in line with the rambunctious spirit that animated the American revolution than the dour pontifications of John Locke, whose writing gets all the press clips these days.

So why do I reprise the moldering life of John Lilburne now, at this perilous moment in the life of the Republic? Well, for starters, the forces that Lilburne confronted "with violent and bitter expressions" have coalesced once again (not that they ever really dissipated, mind you) and threaten to impose their preemptive will upon the living creatures of the world. What are these forces? Militarism, religious bigotry, official censorship, prosecutorial inquisitions and torture, imperial expansion, monopolists, land grabbers, misogynists and those who buy and sell the earth and humans, too. In short, the whole sick crew.

It strikes me that Bill Cook, whether he likes to admit it or not, comes out of that restless tradition, a vibrant spectrum of seditious writers stretching from Lilburne and Gerrard Winstanley, through William Godwin and Mary Wollstonecraft, Tom Paine, Jean-Paul Marat, and William Hazlitt, all the way to Twain, Gore Vidal and Jimmy Baldwin.

Cook lives high in the San Bernardino Mountains in southern California. He looks out over the smog-shrouded LA basin below every morning as he drives to work at the University of La Verne, nestled in the foothills below. From this prime aerie, Cook surveys the effluent of American culture at full-throttle, the cancerous sprawl, poisonous air, techno-fetishism, fretless narcissism and guiltlessly corrupt politics. Lesser minds might have fled for New Zealand or a cabin in the Midi-Pyrennes. But Cook chooses to stand his ground and do battle with the beast.

Like me, Bill Cook studied English literature, before the critical theorists muddied the waters, sucked all the fun out of reading and turned the art of prose writing into an exercise in vacant obscurantism. Cook is old school. He writes with vivid urgency as he excavates the Augean muck of the Bush years, subjecting the president and his gang to an excruciatingly tight close up, where every flaw, every imperfection, every touch up is exposed to all who dare to look.

Bill Cook's wife, D'Arcy, like Elizabeth Lilburne, is also an accomplished agitator, as well as a fine poet and playwright. These days you need the entire bag of tricks just to get through the week. In an age of remote control weaponry and long-distance death, where the images of destruction are cooled through the reassuring medium of cable TV, Cook compels us to confront the flesh and blood consequences of a government that has run amuck—our government, acting in our name, even if the current gang seized control of the White House through a kind of judicially-approved breaking-and-entering. Face it: America didn't become a global empire overnight. Go read Twain. Or ask any Filipino.

Most of the people of this world live on $2 a day, struggling against the odds to scrape together the bare necessities of life, day after day, with only faint hope of betterment for themselves or their children's children. Yet, again and again the managers of the American empire have sided against the poor and with their oppressors, from Indonesia to Haiti to Palestine to Oakland. We have become an empire without a heart, brokering IMF austerity measures, Frankenstein crops, privatization of natural resources, all backed up by cruise missiles and Stealth bombers. And some dare call it liberation.

Cook warns that this bullyish path toward global dominion has grave consequences. There are rhythms to history that it is foolhardy to ignore. Consult Gibbon on the fall of Rome. Look up the final chapter of Pasha Gordon's career in Sudan. This isn't prophecy, but a precise and meticulous reading of current events. The 9/11 attacks weren't bolts from the blue, but tragically predictable events, born out of a seething anger toward American imperialism that has been simmering in remote quadrants of the globe for decades. Sometime, somewhere, it was bound to happen. Blowback.

When you survey the wreckage of the Bush imperium, it's very easy to become overwhelmed by the darkness of the times, submerged by the remorseless riptide of blood and official violence. But Cook never surrenders to defeatism. His writing is infused with purpose. This is not a doomsday chronicle you hold in your hands, but a radiant call for global action, a last shot at redemption.

So savor Cook's essays. They are a fortifying antidote to the palsy of paranoia and panic that has shaken the republic under the grip of the new imperialists. At this point reading them is risk free. Acting on them, natch, may be another matter entirely. But after you lay this volume down I suspect that you'll feel that you have no choice. Then ask yourself: What would Lilburne do?

~

Jeffrey St. Clair is an investigative journalist, writer and co-editor of the political newsletter *Counterpunch* [*www.counterpunch.org*]. His recently published books include: *The Politics of Anti-Semitism* (co-edited Alexander Cockburn); *Been Brown So Long, It Looked Like Green to Me: The Politics of Nature*; and *Serpents in the Garden: Liaisons with Culture and Sex* (co-edited with Alexander Cockburn).

1

Yet Another Bush Doctrine

[September 8, 2002]

He said it and we must obey! "We (America) want the United Nations to be effective and respected and successful. We want (the) its resolutions... to be enforced." This is the third of Dubya's new foreign policy doctrines, each a furtherance of his unilateral approach to world domination.

Following September 11, the fledging President, whose foreign policy initiatives up to that date had been marked by retreat from international and global agreements in favor of isolationism, announced a declaration of war against the forces of evil that reside in the world. This Manichean perception of the world fit logically into his Puritan fundamentalist view that America represents the forces of good fighting against the forces of evil, the same America that had been directed to this new land by the Almighty and blessed with truth and righteousness.

"You are with us or against us," he declared on September 20. The authorities in power in 1636, the Puritan Divines, determined who was good and who was evil because they believed they were God's anointed. They determined that the Natives were "salvages" working for Satan and that gave them the right to exterminate the Pequot tribe in 1637. They praised God for permitting it and for making the slaughter so thorough! So today we have a President who believes he is born-again in Christ and can interpret His word as to who is good and who is evil.

Unfortunately, since terrorists cannot be defined as rulers of nation states as defined by the United States, he provided to the world's leaders an avenue of justification for their acts of occupation and slaughter of those opposed to their regimes or their desires. We have witnessed this in Russia's justification of the slaughter of the Chechnyans, Melosovic's defense that he was only subduing "terrorists" in his ethnic cleansing of the Muslims in Bosnia, Pakistan's and India's justification of their respective attacks against each other in Kashmir, and in Israel's defense of its occupation of Arab territory. The first Bush doctrine has opened the door for anarchy throughout the world as leader after leader justifies his actions against his enemies as a "war against terrorists."

But our President didn't stop there. He annunciated his second doctrine at the West Point military academy: the right of America to determine and execute "pre-emptive attacks" against perceived enemies. This doctrine effectively undermines international law and makes "irrelevant," to use a Sharon operative word, the United Nations. But it is worse than that. It also undermines the basic premises that have determined how the United States declares war: a determination that the United States has been attacked before it attacks. It also shifts responsibility for determination of such action from the Congress to the Executive branch if the reality of "pre-emptive" strike is to be effective. The second Bush doctrine augments the first by giving those in power another "right" to act without evidence of perceived intention or determination of "evil" by presentation of evidence before a court or a congressional or representational body.

Now we have Dubya's third doctrine: resolutions of the United Nations must be enforced; at least that is how Dubya defended his desire to bring about "regime change" in Iraq when he addressed the UN on the 12th. On the surface this would seem to be a desirable goal for international order. Unfortunately, neither Bush nor his administration mean what they say. If they did, they would apply the same doctrine to Israel. Consider the discrepancies: Iraq has broken UN resolutions since 1991 according to the President; Israel has broken UN resolutions since 1948. Bush claims that Saddam has defied the UN and thus "...is a threat to UN authority and to peace." He asks this question as he presents his arguments before the UN delegates: "Are UN resolutions to be honored and enforced or cast aside without consequence?" Will the UN become irrelevant if its resolutions are not obeyed? The answer applies, of course, only to Iraq. It is the only argument he could make at the UN.

He could not claim that the United States has authority to "go it alone" against his perceived "evildoer." He could not use the fabrication that Iraq, with only a third of its military intact following the other Iraqi war, and hobbled with a population that has suffered ten years of deprivation caused by the US-imposed sanctions, posed a threat to the US—unless they were to hand-deliver a weapon across 7,000 miles. So he resorts to this doctrine, trusting, I suspect, that no one would notice that Israel has defied over 55 UN resolutions since 1967, and others prior to that, reaching back to 1948. These resolutions condemn Israeli intransigence against implementation of fundamental human rights and illegal occupation of Arab territory.

Consider the wording of these resolutions and contrast them with the resolutions condemning Iraq. Resolution 194 (III), dating from 12/11/48, demands that Israel give refugees the right to return. That right has never been granted. Resolutions 237, dated 6/14/67, and Resolutions 2252, 2341B, Human Rights Resolution 6, and 1336 continue a string of UN resolutions against Israel demanding "Right of Return" calling "...upon the government of Israel to facilitate return of those inhabitants who have fled the area of military operations since the outbreak of hostilities." They further "expressed its [the UN] grave concern at the violation of human rights in Arab territories occupied by Israel." These resolutions "called upon the Government of Israel to desist forthwith from acts of destroying homes of the Arab civilian population inhabiting areas occupied by Israel and to respect and implement the Universal Declaration of Human Rights and the Geneva Convention of August 12, 1949 in occupied territories." Israel has defied the UN on each and every one of these resolutions.

But it gets worse. The UN Security Council passed resolutions 242, 338, 262, 267, 446, and 465, each stating substantially the same thing. Israel must vacate all their illegal settlements and provide "land for peace" for the Palestinians. Israel has defied every one of these resolutions. In wording resolution 56/59, dated December 10, 2001, the UN deplored "...those policies and practices of Israel which violate Human Rights..." Yet Bush has said nothing about Israel's disobedience, nor has he asserted that its defiance is a threat to the UN authority or to peace. What hypocrisy.

Bush condemned Iraq for defying the UN by not acquiescing to resolution 688 of 1991 concerning repression of minorities and the use of torture. Similar condemnations of Israel have been made by human rights organizations and accepted by the UN as fact in its resolutions. Why condemn one and not the other? Bush condemned Iraq for not returning 600 prisoners of war as demanded by UN Resolutions 686 and 687, but he said nothing of the many UN resolutions demanding that Israel permit Palestinians who number in the million to return to their homeland. Why? The answer is clear enough: Bush supports Israel and condemns Iraq. He determines who is good and who is evil. How else can he implement his first two doctrines?

Bush doctrines as noted provide a blueprint for US domination of the world agenda, regardless of the UN. If the US demands it, it must be done. It is not a question of equality of treatment; it's a question of who is with us (US) and who is not. It is a question of who determines who is good and who is evil!

2

What Bush Didn't Say to the UN: The Case against Israel

[October 10, 2002]

In his Cincinnati address, before an audience of 700 hand-selected yea-sayers, President Bush pushed once again his third foreign policy doctrine: the UN must enforce its resolutions or become irrelevant, leaving the correction of world problems to the Emperor of the only world super power, George the "Wunderkind." Since he was unable to provide any substantive evidence that would necessitate war with Iraq, the ostensible purpose of this speech, he had to rely on a rationale with substance. Indeed, Iraq has not complied with 16 UN resolutions and, therefore, must be forced to comply, with military force if necessary.

But Bush forgot to mention that almost all the resolutions are years old, deflating the immediacy of their enforcement now; that other nations including the US and Israel have not complied with UN resolutions; that the business of enforcement is the responsibility of the UN membership, not the prerogative of a single nation, super power or not; and that opening the door to resolution enforcement requires equity of treatment against all nations that have defied the UN. Extending logic that far would negate the purpose of Bush's talk, to convince the uninitiated that war is necessary.

This man has no shame. Having delivered the same meaningless message to the UN on September 12, he reiterates this beefless argument in his Cincinnati address to the citizens of America as he rushes to war stealing the Constitutional right of Congress to declare war and turn America from a peaceful nation to the preeminent warmonger in the world.

Consider the hypocrisy of the President's address to the UN concerning Iraq. His blistering diatribe against Saddam Hussein, delivered as he prepares America to launch yet another war against an Arab state, not only enunciated the latest Bush Doctrine (the enforcement of UN resolutions against rogue states that defy them) but accused Saddam of flagrant acts against humanity. At the same time, he hypocritically ignored his administration's support for a regime that makes Saddam look like the Archangel Michael, the regime of Ariel Sharon in Israel. Consider the points of grievance the President raised against Saddam and apply them to Israel.

1. **Iraq invaded Kuwait:** Israel has invaded and occupied territory owned by Lebanon, Syria, and Palestine against international law and countless UN resolutions dating back to 1948. Israel occupied most of the cities in Palestine before May 1948: Tiberias, Haifa, and Jaffa in April, and Beisan, Safad, and Acre in May. Israel now occupies 8 of the 9 principal cities in the Palestinian territories. Unlike the aggression in Kuwait, the US did not lead a coalition of nations against Israeli invasion and, consequently, the land now under Israeli dominance approximates 78% of the land formerly owned by the Palestinians. Ironically that resolution provided only 55% of the territory for the Israeli state.

2. **Iraq was poised to continue their march to seize other countries and resources and has failed to comply with UN imposed commitments following the Iraq War of 1991:** Iraq did not continue its march because of the 1991 war. Israel, however, did march against other countries in 1967 and has continued to defy UN resolutions to withdraw from those illegally occupied lands. Even more brazenly, it has established over 30 settlements since Sharon became Prime Minister, not counting those created before him, with populations now exceeding 400,000, all against international law. No coalition has attempted to stop Israel's aggression and occupation, nor has the President raised this defiance of UN resolutions as a threat to peace. Nor has he demanded that Israel comply with international law and cease occupation of illegally obtained land and remove the illegal settlements from Palestinian territory.

3. **Saddam has defied the UN by not complying with 16 UN resolutions:** Israel has defied the UN by not responding or complying with 68 resolutions, not counting the resolution imposed two weeks ago. The resolutions charged Saddam with repression of his people, especially minorities, and this threatens international peace and security in the region. Israel has been asked to "stop violating human rights in the Arab territories, desist from destroying homes of the Arab civilian population, and respect and implement the Universal Declaration of Human Rights and the Geneva Conventions of August 1949." Israel's defiance amounts to sadism. It even taxes the humanitarian supplies brought in to alleviate the suffering of the Palestinian people who are forced to stay inside their homes because of Israeli imposed curfews. Resolutions of like wording, including citation of torture, imprisonment, and wanton destruction of homes, continue to be issued by the UN even now; and Israel defies every one of them.

4. **Iraq has failed to return prisoners in numbers reaching approximately 600:** Israel has refused to allow the return of over one million Palestinian refugees to their homeland despite UN resolutions demanding that they do so.

The conclusion drawn from this defiance by Iraq is, according to the President, "a threat to the authority of the United Nations and to peace." Replace Iraq with Israel and the President's allegation carries more substance.

Despite the fact that Iraq no longer occupies territory owned by another state; despite the fact that its present military is considered to be one-third the size and power it maintained in 1991; despite the fact that the UN inspections removed up to 90% of its weapons capability by 1998; despite the fact that it does not possess nuclear weaponry while Iran and Israel do, the President demands that Iraq disarm unconditionally. Yet Israel has nuclear capability, has the fourth largest military operation in the world, and has actively occupied Palestinian territory while killing women and children in the vain attempt to stop suicide bombers. This demonstrates Israel's willingness to be an aggressor, even if it means mimicking the destruction of innocents caused by extremist groups like Hamas, and causes as a result the instability in the Mid-East. Even though this instability has overflowed into the terrorist acts visited upon the US, the President says nothing!

Perhaps if Israel does what the President demands of Iraq, peace will come to the Mid-East: return stolen property, cooperate with the international community to resolve the issues that divide, allow free movement of reporters throughout the territories, so a new openness and accountability will blossom, and create and abide by a constitution that guarantees freedom and equality for all who live within the state. Then perhaps the statement made by the President would have credibility: "Free societies do not intimidate through cruelty and conquest... the world must move deliberately and decisively to hold Israel to account... the Security Council resolutions will be enforced—the just demands of peace and security will be met. And a regime that has lost its legitimacy will also lose its power."

Can there be any doubt that the President's new Doctrine applies more credibly to Israel than it does to Iraq? Should the UN not demand that he level these charges equitably? What other resolution is there?

3

Blinded by the Right: America Stumbles into the Ditch

[November 11, 2002]

America stumbled yet further this week into the ditch of fanaticism, led by its blind President who is led by Ariel Sharon. With the exit of Binyamin Ben-Eliezer, leader of the Labor Party, from Sharon's coalition government, and with Sharon's appointment of Shaul Mofaz as Defense Minister, a hardliner who has directed the occupation of the Palestinians for the past two years, America's support for Israel drags it further into the morass of rabid fundamentalism. Following the exit, Sharon's coalition retains only 55 of 120 seats. He will turn to ultra-right and religious parties to garner the numbers he needs to retain control. Such a coalition will move Israel even further in the direction of eliminating the Palestinian right to a homeland. That in turn will drag the region further and further into chaos.

Mofaz's appointment already complements Sharon's drive to force religious fundamentalism on the people of Israel. As his cabinet moves to the extreme right, he ineluctably pushes his people to the fulfillment of ancient myths. More tellingly for America, President Bush's continuing capitulation to Ariel Sharon's deeply rooted desire to destroy any possibility of a Palestinian state yokes America's foreign policy to these same ancient myths that have tethered ultra-conservative Jews together for over 2500 years. Although the Zionist movement can be traced to 1885 when Nathan Birnbaum edited *Selbst-Emanzipation* and promulgated the ideas of the *Hovevei Zion* movement (The Jewish Agency for Israel, *www.us-israel.org*), the belief that God's chosen people had a right to "Judea and Samaria," the "Promised Land," goes back to Moses. Indeed, the American-Israeli Cooperative Enterprise asserts "some Religious Zionist Jews see the formation of the secular state as accelerating the process of *redemption, with themselves playing a major role in doing G-d's will by serving the state, whose creation is often seen as miraculous."* [Emphasis mine] [*www.us-israel.org*]

As Sharon's cabinet closes ranks around the right-wing Likud priorities, and with the entrance into that cabinet of Effi Eitam, head of the National Religious Party, the merger of Sharon's political agenda, the denial that the Palestinians have a right to a homeland, and the mythological beliefs of Eitam's expressed purpose for entering politics, the return of the Promised Land to God's chosen—Israeli policy toward the Palestinian people becomes mired in religious myths more than 2500 years old. These myths give the Jews authorization to destroy "... the experts of impurity, cursedness and evil," as Eitam characterizes the Palestinians. [*Los Angeles Times*, Sunday, 6/30/02, A11]

According to Eitam, the Palestinians are not ordinary people, but "uncircumcised," "little people," and "evil," by contrast with the Jews who are "the blessed," and who have "returned home for our rendezvous with the Lion of the World and the Lioness that is our nation." [*Los Angeles Times*] This man, who claims to bring morality back to politics, openly proclaims his policy toward the Palestinians: "And when we pounce on you (the Palestinians), and it will happen—when we come with vengeance against your terrible evil, woe will be unto you—we will make a reckoning with you." [*Los Angeles Times*] Here is a prophet of old speaking in the language of the Old Testament as though it were truth and the source of domestic and foreign policy in this new millennium.

Eitam is not alone in his expressed ideology. Gush Emunim rabbis, another right-wing religious group, have "reiterated that Jews who kill Arabs should be free from all punishment." They have gone further; they claim that Arabs living in Palestine are thieves because the land was Jewish and belongs to them. [Prof. Israel Shahak, *www.abbc.com*] These beliefs arise from adherence to centuries-old myths that have no relevance in today's world either politically or theologically, yet they persist despite our perspective on dramatically similar events in the past. Consider our enlightened view of the ancient "Crusades," those ushered in by Urban II and later by Innocent III, as they compare with the conflicts current in Palestine. Innocent gathered

50,000 troops to destroy the Cathars in the 13th century. The Cathars were a heretical sect that threatened the absolute authority of the Roman Catholic Church. The recounting of the slaughters of the heretics during the "Albigensian Crusade" by the monk of Vaux-Cernay concludes with the same phrase after each massacre: "and the pilgrims (crusaders) seizing nearly sixty heretics burned them *with infinite joy.*" [Sismondi 45] They, too, like Eitam, found joy in slaughtering those who God determined to be evil.

Indeed, the radical elite tend to enjoy fulfilling God's word as they have determined His meaning. Sismondi declares: "The more zealous they were for the glory of God, the more ardently they labored for the destruction of heretics, the better Christians they thought themselves." [31]

Now we have Eitam and Likud coupled with Sharon's personal drive to ensure that only the Jews possess what used to be Palestinian land. How similar the cries of praise to God of the Crusaders, "How glorious are the victors who return from battle! How blessed are the martyrs who die in battle." Compare this response to the conquering Jews after the 1982 war: "Oh Lord, Oh Lord, You have chosen us for conquest!" [Chomsky 96] All ruling elites use ancient myths to move their people to "take up the cross" against the impure so that sacred land given to them by God can be cleansed and returned to its rightful owners.

These myths lie deep in the psyche of the ultra-right and National Religious Party that Eitam heads. Perhaps the article by Mordechai Nisan, "Judaism and Politics" in the *Jerusalem Post* of Jan. 18, 1983, captures this thinking most graphically:

> At the dawn of Jewish history, contact with the Land of Israel established the principle that the presence of non-Jews in the country is morally and politically irrelevant to the national right of the Jews to settle and possess the Land... The Bible states the Jewish right regardless of non-Jewish presence... Dwelling in the Land is the Jewish priority and it is no way restricted, let alone nullified, by a non-Jewish majority population in any given part of the Land...
>
> —Chomsky 444

Nisan understands the dilemma this position causes in a democratic age, since it appears to be a non-democratic one. But his response is blatantly pro-Jewish: "...it is nowhere provided that non-Jews will enjoy full equal rights as a national community." The fact that "the Land is in the eternal possession of the Jewish people alone..." is not fully understood by other people because they have not recognized that Western liberal ideas are no longer sustainable in this modern age!

Chomsky offers this quote that references Maimonides: "There is no relation between the law of Israel [*Torat Yisrael*] and atheistic modern humanism... in a divinely-commanded war one must destroy, kill and eliminate men, women, and children."

Gush Emunim thinking and its counterparts among the growing elite that seem to have gained power in Israel in this last year fall prey to the malaise that inflicted Kurtz in Conrad's *Heart of Darkness*: the acceptance in themselves of absolute righteousness and self-perceived fulfillment resulting in the unquestioned need to wantonly slaughter innocents to achieve their own conception of their eminence... despite behavior that is barbaric, bestial, and inhumane.

Reaching this level of behavior requires dissembling rational thought, indeed a total rejection of it, blind adherence to beliefs that have no justification outside of the fanatical zealots' own cult, and an abhorrence of normal morality that applies to humans in favor of a morality that fulfills the cult's own perceived destiny. Ultimate depravity becomes the end product of God's commands.

The belief in the "unity of man," in the natural rights of men and women, has given way to the "unity of nations," specifically in this instance to the Israeli nation, the homeland of the Jewish race. This understanding places the elite, who interpret the Biblical stories, in a position of immense power. They have not only determined that God speaks, but that God has given a specific piece of geography to a specific people regardless of conditions that have existed for thousands of years. This understanding allows for, indeed demands, that international law, internationally determined human rights provisions, and the philosophical foundations of Western thought be abandoned in favor of God's directives as determined by a small segment of a small population as though they alone possess truth.

The President, a known born-again Christian, has ties to those fundamentalist denominations that support the Zionist aspirations to create a Jewish state, not because they favor Judaism, but because they believe in ancient myths as well: the necessity for the Jews to reoccupy Judea and Samaria if the Second Coming is to happen. Bush's linkage to these denominations and his dependence on the Israeli lobbyists in this country have governed his policy toward the conflicts in the Mid-East. His recent "vision" statement (an apt mythological appellation) on the conflict unites him ineluctably to Sharon. Nothing that he said forestalls or even minimizes the likelihood of complete Israeli control and occupation of the land formerly owned by the Palestinians.

In short, the President has linked America to those ancient myths, stories that compel one people to slaughter another because their God has given them the right to act. This thinking is no different than that used by Hamas authorities when they inculcate into their members the God given right to destroy the Jews because that is what God demanded in the Koran.

Would anyone have believed that in the year 2002 America would join ranks with fanatics driven by fabricated stories more than 2500 years old as the basis for foreign policy? Our acceptance of Sharon's administration and its savage policies also means we have accepted the fanatics of Islam who use the same God as the Israelis to justify their atrocities.

These mythologies become the motivating tools of those in power to justify their purpose. They grab at the opportunities present—fear inflicted by enemies of the people, righteous behavior demanded by their God, promise of rewards in the hereafter for those joining against the forces of evil, and ultimate victory for the myths that gave them purpose to carry out their desires. It is unfortunate that America has been hoodwinked into supporting beliefs that should have died a quiet death years and years ago. What a mockery of international law, of the Geneva Convention on Human Rights, and America's proclaimed belief in Democracy and the inherent rights guaranteed to all people, is our obeisance to the whims of those who would find recourse to oppression in the pages of a mythological text.

4

WWJS: What Would the Jews of Terezin Say?

[November 20, 2002]

I saw the pictures children drew at Terezin last March when I delivered a paper at a Prague conference. Yesterday I saw a picture of a Palestinian woman, old and bent, weeping as she watched Sharon's bulldozer demolish her home. The children's pictures jumped to mind; the thousands of drawings, hidden in Terezin, are the only evidence of their existence. Mothers, the old women lured to Terezin by the Nazis on the pretext that it was a care facility for the elderly, and the Nazi Commandery, allowed the children to draw, a way to express how they felt about being herded like cattle, crowded into dark attics and cellars, separated from their parents before they were transported to Izbice, Maly Trostinec, Sobibor, Majadanek, Treblinka or Auschwitz. For Terezin was a transport town.

It occurred to me that Sharon's savagery against the Palestinians mirrors the plight of the Jews in Terezin. Consider the woman weeping for her home. What would the women of Terezin say as they watched Sharon destroy this woman's home? How they would share the anguish of being driven from their home and confined, as was the Palestinian woman, in squalid conditions, in a refugee camp under the booted foot of their oppressor? What would the Jews of Terezin say as they watched their sons, daughters, nieces, and nephews corral the indigenous people of Palestine into ghettos, packed into cement bunkers not unlike the cells at Terezin—or crammed into ancient towns where the walls are falling down or bulldozed into oblivion?

What would the Jews of Terezin say as they watched Sharon build walls around the ghettos? How like the walls of Terezin that rose before those locked in, waiting the day they would be transported to their death! How like the Gestapo the IDF looms before the Palestinians as they crouch locked in their homes under curfew, unable to get to the market, unable to play in the streets, unable to work; dependent on the oppressor's will to get to UN food supplies, the only defense against their impending death.

What would the Jews of Terezin say as they watched Sharon circle their temporary homes with search lights from towers and trucks, hemming them in behind barbed wire, suffering the indignity of caged animals? What would they say as they watched the Palestinian family wait hours in line before they could pass through the gate, derided and mocked by the soldiers who laughed at their plight? What would the Jews at Terezin say as they witnessed their own kin steal land and homes from those who owned them on the pretext that they were animals and did not deserve the land given to Sharon by G-d? Had they not lost all to their oppressors?

What would the Jews at Terezin say to those imprisoned behind the walls unable to till the fields taken from them, unable to move from one city to another to visit relatives, friends, neighbors—unable to survive without the largesse from nations beyond the walls? Would they not understand those who tried to resist? Had they not tried to resist? Would they not understand that what desperation breeds is desperation? Had they not seen themselves as David against Goliath? Would they not see this David, the imprisoned Palestinian, as their brothers and sisters throwing stones at tanks weighing tons, scattering shells from Kalashnikov rifles at F-16 Fighter Jets and Apache Helicopters, and standing defiantly in front of bulldozers while Goliath dispatches some of his 134,000 troops into the ghettos, sends a few of his 32,000 air force to shell homes and factories, and drives his 3,900 tanks into the ghetto cities and refugee camps?

Would they not grasp the metaphor of the Biblical story that graphically illustrates the consequences of the strong, willingly and mercilessly, attempting to destroy the weak? And would they not know that David will triumph because David has nothing to lose, his cause is just, and his God has promised him victory? But the strong have everything to lose, and the fear that they will lose it. As Israeli Professor Martin Van Crevold stated: "He who is wise should never engage the weak for any length of time."

When at Terezin, I saw the drawing of a hearse, the only means of transportation in the ghetto, by Ferdinand Bloch, Alfred Kantor's picture of a police patrol controlling women returning from work, and Bedrich Fritta's black drawing of cramped life in the attic, and others, by children. I thought of the old woman kneeling in the street watching her home demolished. That, too, is a drawing that captures forever the fear of those who live without hope, without dignity, without respect. What would the Jews of Terezin say? Perhaps they would speak through me:

THE GHOSTS OF TEREZIN

I saw the pictures children drew at Terezin
As they clustered in the attic's closing darkness—
Pictures of the sun beyond the rain,
Of Mothers muffled in scarves and solemn dress,
Of Fathers proud beneath their *yarmulkas*—
All waiting patiently the promised day
When they would board the silver train
And flee to the Holy City.

And I wept at their plight,
The silent, unknown, gnawing fright
That burned within their Ghetto of sin,
This Terezin.
And then before my eyes there came
Another scene, so strange, as if incarnate in the first
That burst untimely before my weeping heart;
A scene more ravaged than Terezin,
Of streets and alleys swamped in sewage and despair
Where children breathed the fetid air of hate
That smoldered like steaming ashes there.

Suddenly appeared above the graves, the ghosts of Terezin,
Arising like mist around the crematorium;
Fathers and Mothers, in their promised land at last,
Grasping children to their breasts.
Silent as sentinels they stood,

And there they wept as they watched in vain
The wardens wander through the camps
Like Gestapo agents of old,
Stark, cold, indifferent to the pain
Of those who huddled beneath the tin roofs,
Encased like the dead in cement boxes
As the acrid stench of lingering sewage
Flowed through the alleys and the homes.

They saw the tanks rattle through the streets
With ranks of soldiers scurrying behind,
Seeking the vermin that infested this place—
Homeless, nameless, without a face—
Sneaking through this ghetto in the dark of night
To drive the children from this transport town,
This resurrected refugee camp, this new Terezin,
Where the new Jew wanders the world
Like the Jews of Terezin,
Joined in their loneliness and despair
As they watch their children there
Become the walls of Terezin!

5

A World-Wide Intifada? Why?

[December 7, 2002]

A satellite view of attacks against western interests spotlights the reality that a worldwide intifada against the "developed" nations of the west and their allies is already underway. Russian apartment houses and, recently, a theater, the Twin Towers in New York, two Bali discos, a French super tanker blown up off the coast of Yemen, an Israeli hotel destroyed in Kenya, a failed missile shot at an Israeli passenger plane off the coast of Africa, and others too numerous to mention—demonstrate the magnitude of the effort underway to wake up the west to the consequences of its dominance over the lives and interests of peoples throughout the world.

Recent events, coupled with the investigations of Jean-Louis Bruguiere, the French Judge who has been tracking terrorist acts for two decades, forces us to grapple with why this is happening. Bruguiere recently warned that France is one of the two or three countries "most at risk of attack due to its historic links to Algeria."

"Islamic extremism," he noted, "is breeding like a virus in Europe." [World-Reuters, Sunday, Dec. 1, 2002]

What conditions prefigure the coming "Intifada" against the United States and the west? The first is misunderstanding of the deprived and displaced people of the world, a subject far too broad to cover in this chapter. Let us concentrate on what Bin Laden told us was the most egregious cause: "You attacked us in Palestine. Palestine, which has sunk under military occupation for more than 80 years. The British handed over Palestine, with your (US) help and your support, to the Jews, who have occupied it for more than 50 years; years overflowing with oppression, tyranny, crimes, killing, expulsion, destruction and devastation." [Bin Laden, "Letter to America," 11/24/02] Harley Sorensen pointed out, tellingly, that Osama's letter had virtually no publicity in the American Press; America's corporate press does not want Americans to know why they are hated. [*San Francisco Gate*, Dec. 2, 2002]

Most citizens in the west, and certainly American citizens, do not understand the Palestinian people, their history, and their perception of the existence that has been thrust upon them, what I will label as "The Stolen Homeland"; the second is consciousness of the disparity that exists between the Palestinians and the Israelis and the reluctance of the state of Israel and its major supporter in the west, the United States, to engage that disparity, which results from the economic controls, the indignity and disrespect engendered by the Ultra-Orthodox Right-Wing Likud and the military. This I label "The Chasm of Indifference and Desperation." Finally, the third is the corrosive destruction of a culture by brute force in the bulldozing of their memory and the destructive power implicitly present in globalization that impacts the uniqueness of a people's culture, its economic structures, and its values—what can only be labeled "Ethnic Erasure by Globalized Capitalism."

In many ways, these three form a complex interwoven fabric that makes it difficult if not impossible to see each clearly. Yet, unless we make the attempt, we are doomed to find ourselves constrained to our homes through fear of the unknown individual(s) who must resort to self-sacrifice as the last resort to rectify the unacceptable disparity that allows no alternative.

The Stolen Homeland

Most Americans know nothing about the way in which Israel was created. They do not know that Britain turned Palestine over to the UN for resolution because it could not continue its governance in light of the rising tensions that existed between Zionists and Palestinians. In 1947 the UN General Assembly resolved by a two-thirds vote to endorse the partition of Palestine into a Jewish and an Arab state (Resolution No. 181). The Palestinians did not accept that resolution, yet the partition went forward even though the General Assembly had no legal authority to divide a country—especially through the process of endorsing a Resolution. The proposed partition called for 55%

of the Palestinian area to be given to the Israelis, yet they comprised slightly more than 30% of the population and owned only 6% of the land. The Jewish population was composed mostly of foreign-born immigrants, only one-third of whom had acquired Palestinian citizenship. In addition, the territory allocated to the Jews comprised the coastal plain from Akka to Ashdod and other fertile lands. The Palestinians were left with mainly mountainous areas and arid regions.

Americans receive most of their information regarding the Israeli/Palestinian conflict from corporate controlled, politically manipulated mainstream media. Few have the opportunity to scrutinize the reality of the history that has resulted in the tensions that exist in the Mid-East. Few know that Palestinians are, in all legitimate ways, the indigenous population of the area; that the land now occupied by the Israelis was owned by the Palestinians; that in 1870, 98% of the population was Arab and only 2% Jewish; that in 1940, Palestinians accounted for 69% of the population even as Jews thronged to the area from Europe in an attempt to escape the Nazis; that in 1947, the year the UN created Israel without the approval of the indigenous population, the Palestinians represented 65% and the Israelis less than 35% of the 1,845,000 who lived there; that Israel now occupies all but 22% of the Palestinian land, having taken it in the 1967 war and consistently refusing to return it to its proper owners. This is in direct refutation of UN resolutions demanding its return. Few know that Israel has created illegal settlements in Palestinian areas, with a population in excess of 400,000, taking land and aquifers from the Palestinians, 34 of those settlements created during the two-year Prime Ministry of Ariel Sharon, and in direct violation of UN mandates.

Is it surprising that the Palestinians have rejected the existence of a state imposed upon its population by foreign powers? Is it surprising that it has rejected the Oslo Agreement when its full implementation was not part of the "final" settlement and provided no resolution of the refugee problem? Is it surprising that a people occupied by a state supported by the world's greatest military power which supplies the Israeli people with more than 3 billion dollars for military hardware a year—more than any other nation receives from the US—finds itself oppressed and humiliated?

The Chasm of Indifference and Desperation

On May 4, 2002, the *New York Times* reported "it is safe to
say that the infrastructure of life itself and of any future
Palestinian state—roads, schools, electricity pylons, water pipes,
telephone lines—has been devastated." The most recent estimate of the infrastructure damage alone by the UN and the
World Bank comes to over 361 million dollars. The totality of
Sharon's destruction can never be known because Sharon
refused to admit the United Nations to inspect the carnage. But
it is safe to say that if we limit our focus to the Human Rights
Watch reports alone, the savagery is more than terrorism; it is
barbaric. Palestinians, especially the families who suffered
immediate devastation of homes and family members, cannot
but perceive the dehumanization of their lot by the Israelis.
HRW reports that 22 civilians in the Jenin refugee camp "were
killed willfully or unlawfully" [5/3/02], civilians were used as
human shields, medical personnel were killed, and civilian
homes became military targets. Yet no one cared.

Perhaps nothing is so incomprehensible to the deprived as the
indifference of those who are responsible for the deprivation.
Nothing is more devastating to human dignity than to be
ignored. Nothing is more destructive to communication among
people than the hypocrisy of "developed," "democratic," and
"Judaic-Christian" nations exploiting "under-developed," non-
Democratic, and non-Christian nations.

The United States, led by a "reborn" Christian, supported by a
fundamentalist Attorney General and by fundamentalist denominations like Pat Robertson's, rally behind support of Israel
because they believe their God has determined that the Jews must
be resident in "Judea" if they are to be converted to the one true
faith, Christianity. They willingly accept the necessity of Sharon's
slaughter of the Palestinians to accomplish that goal. It matters
not that Christ said you should not take up the sword; the myths
of the Old Testament shall carry the day, "An eye for an eye, a
tooth for a tooth." These are the Christians who support the
right-wing elements among the Jews who call Palestinians "two-
legged vermin" (former Prime Minister Golda Meir) and
"drugged roaches in a bottle" (former Prime Minister Begin).

These are bloodthirsty Christians unwilling to give their cloak
to the beggar, unwilling to give shelter to the homeless, unwilling

to give food to the hungry, unwilling to succor the weak and the dying. These are the Americans willing to provide on average $500.00 per Israeli citizen per year beyond that provided for the military, but unwilling to provide comparably for the Palestinians. This is the born again President who extols Sharon, a man condemned by an Israeli court for allowing the wanton slaughter of thousands at Shabra, as a "man of peace."

Considering the slave-like conditions imposed on the Palestinians by the Israelis, it might be instructive to hear the thoughts of the former slave Frederick Douglas as he contemplated his condition: "I loathed them [my oppressors] as being the meanest as well as the most wicked of men." And that inner anger tormented him day and night: "I saw nothing without seeing it, I heard nothing without hearing it, and felt nothing without feeling it... I found myself... wishing myself dead..."

Here is an explanation for the "suicide bombers," intolerable indignities and humiliations inflicted by those who are the chosen of God. They are acts of absolute desperation wrought by futility as Daoud abu Sway's family suggested, as they attempted to explain why a father of eight would detonate himself: "That he did so illustrates the depths to which people caught up in this conflict are sinking." [*Los Angeles Times*, 12/9/01]

Consider the slave-like conditions we as Americans have imposed on the deprived of the world to fuel our economy at home, and we can understand how desperation will seek its solace in destruction through sacrifice. Such people need only a bin Laden, a man driven by hatred of the perceived oppressors, to bring the requisite money to achieve his ends, and the future state of fear for America becomes immediately apparent. Israel's oppression of the Palestinians mirrors how the deprived of the world perceive America, a land that could receive the same condemnation from Hosea in 800 BC: "Sins of greed are compounded by Israel's arrogance."

Ethnic Erasure by Globalized Capitalism

Beyond America's image as overseer of Israel and protector of her right to exist, is the image created by America as the protector of transnational corporations. This image coupled with the

presence of America's military negatively portrays the US as the
perpetrator of Third World exploitation, the destroyer of
forests, minerals, metal resources, land, and people. And the
people of these poor nations must live with the environmental
disasters, soil erosion, pollution, poisonings from toxic waste,
and industrial accidents. With only 5% of the world's population America emits 1.5 billion tons per year of carbon dioxide,
a quarter of the world's total.

Hatred of America grows with each passing day. The most
recent Pew Foundation Report detailing that dislike came out
this week and shows that European as well as Arab states have
the same loathing. People feel deprived, taken advantage of, and
ignored. They see the disparate conditions because the west has
made available, through satellite communications, the viewing
of the standard of living available in the west, particularly in the
US, since its programming dominates the airwaves. They understand that Americans and Europeans spend 17 billion a year on
pet food, 4 billion more than the estimated annual additional
total needed to provide basic health and nutrition for everyone
in the world. [UN Human Development Report, 1997]

The excessive use of natural resources in the US, resources
taken from Third World countries, explodes visually on the TV
screen even in the worst of hovels in Africa, South and Central
America, Asia, and the Mid-East. These are the deprived who
have nothing to lose and much to hate. These are the people the
CIA and the FBI talk about when they warn Americans of future
"terrorist" acts. As this anger erupts, America will live in the
same atmosphere of fear that envelops Israel.

Consider the reality of this "Ethnic Erasure by Globalized
Capitalism." Consider the perceptions and reactions it causes in
the minds and hearts of the deprived as it prefigures attitudes
and behaviors in lands beyond Palestine impacted by the west,
and particularly the United States. As transnational corporations spread their tentacles around the world, they create stran-
gleholds on local governments, forcing them to concede
relaxation of tax income, release of land areas for industrial
development, sale of natural resources, and exploitation of citizens. Martin Khor has noted how transnational corporations
have moved their operations to Third World countries
"... where safety and environmental regulations are either lax or

nonexistent." The result is exposure for Third World citizens to hazardous products, toxic or dangerous technologies, crippling drugs, pesticides and the like. [*Global Economy and the Third World*]

The introduction of global agreements that benefit transnationals has negated the standards forced upon these corporations in the United States, standards that require regulations to protect against child labor, that regulate safety conditions, and protect workers' health. Neither NAFTA nor GATT imposes regulations that ensure worker protection in these areas. Sunday's *Los Angeles Times* [December 1, 2002] carried a magazine story detailing the end of Levi Strauss Company's production in America. Levi had to resort to production abroad because it is caught in the web of competition and must "chase low-cost labor." These wages reflect the full exploitation of people in "underdeveloped" countries: Guatemala, 37 cents per hour; China, 28 cents; Nicaragua, 23 cents; Bangladesh, 13 to 20 cents.

The transnationals have deforested more than half of the forest area in developing nations, created large infrastructures to support industrial projects and built huge steel plants, cement plants, vast highways and bridges. All of these require enormous land holdings taken out of the control of the weak nation states. All need energy resulting in hydroelectric dams and nuclear power stations. These conditions lead to displacement of thousands of people, the crowding of populations into cramped quarters in urban areas, sanitation problems, homelessness and poverty.

The chasm of disparity glares through the statistics: the richest fifth of the world's population receives 86% of global income while 1.2 billion live on the equivalent of less than a dollar a day. Edward Goldsmith explains the situation in these terms: "Even strong national governments are no longer able to exert any sort of control over TNCs [Transnationals]... Indeed, TNCs are now free to scour the globe and establish themselves wherever labor is the cheapest, environmental laws are the laxest, fiscal regimes are the least onerous, and subsidies are the most generous." [*Development as Colonialism*] Documentation of human exploitation in Indonesia, Vietnam, China, Malaysia, and Mexico is readily available. What is not available, then, is an understanding of the feelings that gnaw at the souls of the deprived: the sense of hopelessness, indignity, lack of respect and dehumanization. In addition, the United States military presence in a hundred and fifty nations, ostensibly for the protection of US interests, results in huge areas owned and/or controlled by a foreign power. As the US pours millions of dollars into the economy of these countries, the benefits are seen by the local population as going to the local power elite, as is evident most recently in the case of Saudi Arabia. But the same conditions have resulted in flare-ups in Japan, Korea, and Greece (until the US was expelled under the Papandreou regime in the early '90s). In short, the people of these countries are at odds with their rulers. This has been painfully evident in recent months as even Kuwait citizens have demonstrated against their government and the US.

As a result of America's monetary support since its founding in 1947, Israel has prospered militarily and economically at a rate far greater and faster than any other nation anywhere. The US has poured more than 3 billion a year into the Israeli military since 1947. Considering that this investment ensures the continuation of the military-industrial complex in the US, since Israel is required, by the agreement that provides this support, to buy three-quarters of its equipment and technology from US firms, it is crystal clear why the corporate elite desire to maintain Israel's dominance in the Mid-East. Israeli allegiance to US interests ensures that the oil needed by the US will continue to flow. But Israel can demand a heavy price for their collusion with the US, and hence their defiance of Bush's demands that they withdraw from the West Bank.

The US's support for Sharon's government is touted throughout the world without regard for its consequences by Senate and Congressional resolutions; the standard of living in Israel which is a mirror image of its host, the United States, stands in mocking contrast to the squalor of the refugee camps and the sewage infested alleys of the Palestinians who are crammed into miniscule segments of land surrounded by their oppressors. The oppressors' army controls Palestinian movement through heavily guarded positions with towers, barbed wire fences, and crossing guards whose attitude toward the Palestinian is one of hatred and disdain. These conditions give rise to jealousy, hatred, vengeance, despair, retaliation, and sacrifice against the enemy; conditions every Israeli should understand from their own unfortunate history. How many Jews offered themselves for sacrifice against the Nazi forces during the war and against the British when the Israelis were attempting to establish a Jewish state in Palestine?

In their drive to own and control all of Palestine, the right-wing Likud party and the Ultra Orthodox look only to the Old Testament, a text 2500 years old that does not reflect the reality of the past two thousand years. Yet their absolute commitment to these ancient myths legitimizes their actions to suppress the Palestinians. They encouraged, nay they forced Sharon to bulldoze whole sections of ancient cities sacred to the Palestinians, demolish mosques so even the memory of their existence would be forgotten. They destroyed documents that established ownership of properties and the personal identities of Palestinian citizens as though through that destruction they could erase the memory of a people. How ironic that this was the purpose of the Nazi regime's eradication of the Jews.

They are indifferent to the plight of those who have been driven from their homeland penniless, uncompensated for the homes they have lost, who wait the day when they can return after fifty years in refugee camps in foreign lands. They are indifferent to the rampant poverty that sits next to them in Jenin, Ramallah, or Rafah. They do not see or want to see the wastelands that the tanks and bulldozers have created in Rafah as they smashed hundreds of homes, dozens of shops, leaving hundreds homeless, a scene repeated over and over again throughout Palestine.

Yet these are the religious of Israel, those who claim to believe in the one true God, a God who willingly allows the destruction and slaughter of thousands of defenseless women and children. But, blinded by their ambition to claim once again God's Promised Land, they overlook the reality of what they have created: a people more defiant then ever, a people who have endured and will continue to endure even if that be their only lasting claim to their humanity. The Palestinians are a people filled with patience, lacking hope, but determined to be a people, to retain a culture, to love a God, to share what little they have with those worse off than themselves.

The above scenario plays throughout the world in those nations labeled underdeveloped. The deprivation and poverty have been created by Capitalism's global thrust and by the indifference of its corporate elite who have only their investments to protect and the ultimate fulfillment of their faith's ultimate promise: globalized markets where products can be manufactured at the lowest possible cost and return the greatest profit for the investor—regardless of the consequences to the workers, the natural resources, or the cultures that are destroyed in the process. Islamic fundamentalism has become the "repository of a passion for pure belonging, a passion exacerbated by the unsettlements of globalization," according to Todd Gitlin in a review of *In the Name of Identity*. [*Los Angeles Times Book Review*, 9/23/01]. Gitlin's point refers to the helpless state of those deprived throughout the world; Islamic fundamentalists capture only a small percentage of those deprived. He cautions that we must understand the hatred that drives the terrorist, for they are neither a god nor an animal. They are wounded persons touched by a community of wounded people, among whom arises an agitator "who promises victory or vengeance" against those who deserve it; and they slip imperceptibly from denouncing injustice to perpetrating it.

Unless the US and the west recognize the inherent and explosive consequences generated by their indifference to the plight of those exploited; unless sincere attempts are made to realign the disparity between the haves and the have-nots; unless the arrogance of the elite changes to empathy for the deprived, the vicious and insidious behaviors of the fanatics, the desperate, and the powerful will explode throughout America.

6

An Open Letter to Osama bin Laden

[December 10, 2002]

Dear Osama,

Your "letter to the American people" arrived on the 24 of November via a translation provided by the *Observer* in Britain. I had not seen a copy of it in the American press although Mr. Sorensen wrote a column about it in the *San Francisco Gate* remarking about its absence in our corporate papers. My apologies for not responding before this, but I'm sure you understand.

Please don't assume that I write this response on behalf of all Americans; each of us cherishes our right to speak for ourselves though relatively few take advantage of that right. If they do, however, they may find it difficult to gain access to the corporate media where they might be heard by their fellow citizens. But I do write from my heart with all the sincerity I can muster because your letter deserves a response, if only because you took the time to inform us of your grievances. Let's hope a dialogue can ensue that might bring an end to retaliation and vengeance executed in the name of God, but serves only to breed devastation, deprivation and despair for the innocent even as those who inflict their will on others reap the harvest of their greed and lust for power. As a man of self-determined moral stature, I assume you will agree.

I find three areas of concern expressed in your letter: the first focuses on the past 50 years of "oppression" in Palestine; the second on the United States' support of governments, in both Arab and non-Arab countries, that bow before American power—thereby suppressing and humiliating their own people and/or capitulating to American interests that exploit their people and their natural resources.

The third area of concern is your contention that Americans should submit to your understanding of the Quran since Allah's command that you cannot fail will result in America's destruction. I will attempt to respond to each of these concerns.

Let me begin with your point regarding Palestine: "... that the Jews have a historical right to Palestine." "... this is one of the most fallacious, widely-circulated fabrications in history. The people of Palestine are pure Arabs and original Semites. It is the Muslims who are the inheritors of Moses..." Your contention rests on the proposition that the Semites are the true owners of Palestine. The origin of the word 'Semite' can be traced back to the peoples that inhabited the lands around the Euphrates and Tigris rivers, Ethiopia, Arabia, Palestine, Phoenicia, and Syria. The term refers to the descendants of Noah's son Shem. These people were nomadic, moving around from the Mediterranean to Egypt. They include tribes that belonged to the Hebrew group of the Semites, the Habiru. Much more could be said about this affiliation of tribes that constitutes the Semites, but I think the point is clear: you and the Israelis are brothers and sisters; you are all Semites.

As brothers and sisters from the same family, wouldn't it make sense to join together to form a nation-state that incorporates all as citizens with equal rights for all, with shared resources and mutual goals, bonded in love, peace and aspirations? Wasn't this in fact the way Muslims and Jews lived together for decades upon decades before the advent of Nazi Germany's attempt to exterminate the Jews? Wasn't that in fact the desire of most of the world's Jews as their numbers increased in Palestine as a result of the escape from Europe? Wasn't that the expectation of most of the world's population before Resolution 181was passed by the UN General Assembly that proposed splitting the land into two? Can we not resolve the horrendous conflict that has erupted between brothers and sisters where internecine warfare cripples families that should be living as neighbors? If Jews and Arabs attended their respective temples and mosques in peace in times past, why not now, when we purportedly have risen in civilized stature? The question should not be, "Should there be an Israel or should there be a Palestine?" The question should be, "How can we bring our respective families together to enjoy the fruits of the earth in harmony, mutual respect, and dignity?"

Let's turn now to your second concern: American domination of nation-states and the consequences of that control. Nowhere in your statement do you grapple with why America dominates these nations; nowhere do you differentiate among Americans who condone practices that result in that domination and those who do not; and nowhere do you offer alternatives to America's willingness to use its power to control. Rather, you undertake to justify your use of the same means to accomplish your end. Is not this a mirror image of the hypocrisy you level at the United States?

If we do not lead by moral force, we are by acquiescence the followers of those who fail to act, and subjects of those who impose their will. That statement may be leveled at you as well as George Bush. But there are those who refuse to submit to your dictates, as there are those who refuse to accept what the Bush administration does in their name. You need only read the hundreds of books and countless articles, watch the marchers who refuse to submit to their government's dictates, check the jail roles to see who would suffer rather than acquiesce to know that Americans are not of one mind when it comes to submission to their government's actions. Should you assert the right to kill any American, you offer this regime in America the right to slaughter civilians indiscriminately. Neither logic nor morality can stand against this reality.

The issue cannot rest on retaliation. We must address why America has determined that it can lord it over other nations and bend them to its will. This issue cannot be addressed to the American people; they are ignorant of its cause. Government in America has become the victim of its own system. Freedom to acquire wealth, freedom to buy communication of one's values and ideas, freedom to support those who run for office gives to those who have the wealth and drive to power, the means to control the Democracy.

Over the past 50 years, corporations have evolved into transnational entities that use America as a base of operations even as they locate their headquarters offshore in tax-free places like the Cayman Islands. They enforce their will through legislation controlled by those they have put into office. They create International Monetary Funds and impose World Bank regulations on nations to ensure their continued growth and profit. They are able to eradicate laws that protect workers and

investors by creating trade agreements like NAFTA and GATT
that contain no regulations that protect against child labor, or
protect workers against risk or health hazards, and they provide
no means to ensure continuation of employment or care for
retirement.

These companies move from country to country seeking the
lowest paying wages to ensure the highest profit. They are par-
asites on humanity. These powerful corporations use American
military might to protect their interests even as they gain
increased wealth through the increase in military expenditure.

Can any American believe that this country has to fear
another nation in this world? Why then do we have troops in
150 nations around the world? Because the corporate interests
demand that we protect their investments. They are not there to
protect Americans. How do you resolve this issue? By force
against a far superior force? I don't think so. Force inflicted, by
terrorist acts or any other means, guarantees only retaliation,
increased suppression of freedoms around the globe, and
increased force by those already in power.

Would it not make more sense to bring all the nations together
that are victims of this worldwide industrial revolution with its
concomitant abuses inflicted on the poor of the world to stand
against the trans-nationals? Why after three major industrial revolutions in England, Europe, and America do we stand by and
let the trans-nationals tell us that these "underdeveloped" countries must endure the heartache, deprivation, poverty, disease,
pollution, dangers, and uncertainties of the industrial revolutions
just as England, Europe, and America had to? Haven't we in the
"developed" west put legislation in place to protect our workers,
to protect our futures, to protect our natural resources and the
environment? Why deny that protection to the new industrial
nations? Why pay pennies per hour to workers? Why offer no
health protection? Why pollute their streams and cast smog over
their people and the land? Why allow these corporations to create hatred for America for profit?

Can't all of those who abhor this exploitation—Mexicans,
Americans, Indonesians, Chinese, Vietnamese, Cambodians,
and those in Bangladesh—gather together to present to the UN,
to the whole world, the disparity that is inflicted on our communities by those few who possess the wealth? This may take

marching in the streets, it may take years to accomplish, but it will bring about a peaceful resolution to the issue—not a continuation of the slaughter of the innocents.

Do not preach that God demands that the oppressed have a right to return the aggression. What God commands those He has created, to destroy their brothers and sisters? Unite to win, don't destroy. Proclaim the need to share the wealth of the world with all its inhabitants, not provide for the few; argue the need for compassion for those who have nothing; condemn power for the elite; extol those who share their time, their resources, their love with the deprived and destitute of the world, and decry those who hoard, inflict usury, and relish their selfishness.

Americans who loathe the power these corporations have over their Democracy, speak out against it. They follow the path of Henry David Thoreau and stand against the government when it acts contrary to what is right. Join with them and with your brothers and sisters in nations across the globe to protest the inequity of the distribution of the world's resources. You and all those who are against oppression, fight against a new colonialism, one dominated and enforced by the few over the many, by control of the governments of nation states rather than by occupation, but with the same results—control of the masses and the resources. But the people of the world stood peacefully in past ages against colonialism and oppression: Gandhi in India, Martin Luther King and Malcolm X in America, Mandela in South Africa, the Muslims in Algeria, and in other places around the globe. It can be done peacefully again.

Let me now move to your third concern. Your belief that you must impose your religion on America repeats what Urban II attempted to inflict on Muslims and Jews in the creation of the crusades in the 10th and 11th centuries. He, too, cried out "God wills it!" He, too, was wrong! Now we have Christian fundamentalists raising the cry that God wills the second coming, requiring that the Jews be reinstated in Judea-Samaria while Ultra-Right Orthodox Jews proclaim that God has bestowed Judea back to them through Abraham. But each group reads from a different book, *Genesis* or *Revelations*, and each arrives at a different understanding of why God wants the Jews in Judea.

Which group has God's ear and knows with certainty what He commands? Does Eitam in Israel? Does Falwell in America? No, none do; nor do you. Neither you nor any man can inflict your will on another and have him accept it in his heart; nor can you legislate belief in another's soul. Indeed, what you claim America does to the peoples of the world, you would proclaim you have a right to do! You do not have that right; America does not have that right.

There are over 6 billion people in the world; they behave in multitudinous ways because they are each distinct in nature, temperament, personality, local customs, beliefs, and mores. How can one person or one group legislate how all will behave or believe? What utter nonsense to assume that would be possible or desirable. Diversity is the nourishment of the global community; it enriches our souls, our minds, and our hearts. We must relish that, nurture it, delight in it. We don't need one righteous religion imposed like a monolith on our communities, whether it be fundamentalist Christian or fundamentalist Islamic. We need, rather, tolerance, compassion, love, and mercy. Let's accept the reality of our errors, but not condemn; let's reach out for unity the better to bring about change without retaliation or vengeance; let's seek equity through peaceful means that all may find peace in life and hope for the future.

Let me close now, Osama, with this thought: vengeance is a disease that multiplies, divides, and becomes the scourge of humankind; it is anathema to creation because it destroys what exists. We must, together, give the living a chance so that our children and their children can experience the fruits of this earth and share them with their brothers and sisters. Peace to you and to all whom you love.

7

US vs. Iraq, the Tale of the Tape: The Road to Basra and Back

[December 23, 2002]

As the US military sets up offices in Qatar and prepares for war, I thought it might be an interesting exercise to compare the combatants. As a kid, I'd come home from the last days of elementary school in June ready to listen to the Louis/Conn fights on the radio. My Dad would set up a gambling pool of winner rounds selected by chance from slips of paper taken from a hat. He'd then show us the "Tale of the Tape." I remember the importance of the comparison of the fighters as a measure of the fairness of the fight. So what does the "Tale of the Tape" tell us about the Iraq vs. US combatants?

It was fairly easy to find figures on the US forces from the Department of Defense. In addition, CNN.com "In Depth Specials" provides Gulf War Facts for the first war against Iraq and the *Washington Post* offers a site that gives figures for US strength in the Persian Gulf in 1998. The most recent 2002 figures are not readily available, since that might disclose current strength and positions to the enemy. Statistics for Iraq are not quite so available although I was able to find figures for Iraq's military through the International Institute for Strategic Studies and supplementary material on *www.alertnet.org*. In addition, *www.Seattlepi.com* has a special Iraq facts report that provides demographic information. *World Factbook* has alternative information on Iraq military power.

We have heard from the likes of Richard Perle (American Enterprise Institute) that Iraq's forces are about a third of what they were in 1991 as a result of coalition destruction of their military. We also know the sanctions have devastated the civilian population's health and wealth. The UN has marked the estimated number of children dead as a result of the sanctions, thus reducing the number of potential recruits reaching enlistment age. But Iraq, we are told, still poses a threat and must be dealt with immediately. The CNN report tabulates the number of Iraqi soldiers in the 1991 war as follows: 100,000 Iraqi soldiers died (Human Rights groups tabulate more than that), 300,000 wounded, 150,000 deserted and 60,000 taken prisoner. Baghdad lists 35,000 civilians killed.

Those figures are not easy to read. Do we subtract the 150,000 deserters and the 60,000 prisoners from the 300,000 wounded? Would that mean that Iraq's military forces amounted to 400,000 total? Let's assume that is so; we now must reduce that number by two-thirds to meet the estimate provided by Perle or roughly 130,000. One is tempted to hope they are from the deserter pool!

Now as we draw the comparison with American and coalition forces in that first war, we find the following: the US had more than 500,000 troops in the War and non-US forces added up to an additional 160,000. US wounded tallied 467, British 24, French 2. US casualties were 148 battle deaths and 145 non-battle deaths, and allied Arab casualties numbered 39. That means the US suffered 293 deaths to Iraq's 100,000, not counting the 35,000 civilians killed, or less than one percent of Iraqis dead.

Before and during the brief war, the US flew more than 116,000 air sorties losing 75 aircraft. Iraq on the other hand lost 36 fixed wing aircraft, 6 helicopters, 87 aircraft lost on the ground, 3,700 tanks, 2,400 assorted armored vehicles, 19 naval ships sunk, 42 divisions made combat-ineffective, and 2,600 artillery pieces destroyed. Aside from aircraft losses, the US lists no other equipment losses. Since the Iraqi forces consisted, at the time, of 4,280 tanks reduced to 580, and 2,870 assorted vehicles reduced to 471, and 3,110 artillery pieces reduced to 510, the available hardware for this upcoming war appears rather thin. However, Iraq does have the potential, perhaps, to recover 137 aircraft flown to Iran, although the reason they left Iraq appears to be that they could not compete with US and British aircraft. However one looks at it, Iraq has about 15% of its former ordinance to hurl against the current US forces.

That update brings us to today. How do these two Goliaths compare? IISS reports the total armed forces in active service in Iraq numbers 424,000. There are an additional 650,000 reservists. The Army has 375,000 including 100,000 recalled reserves with, perhaps, 2200 main battle tanks. The Navy has an overwhelming force of 2000 men overseeing a fleet of 1 frigate, 5 patrol and coastal vessels, and 3 mine sweepers! The Air Force has 30,000 men with about 6 bombers and about 316 fighter aircraft. The Air Force Command has an additional 17,000 personnel.

By contrast, if the US deployed the same number of troops as it did in 1991, they would outnumber the Iraqi forces by 236,000. Eleven years ago the US had 100 strike aircraft equipped with precision-guided bombs and an unidentified number of aircraft with conventional bombs. The *Washington Post* reported on Tuesday, December 10, 2002 that the aircraft carrier *USS Harry Truman* "left Virginia last week... at the head of a naval group. The *Truman* carries about 70 strike jets. The group has a supplement of three other battle groups, each with carriers holding 70 aircraft. That's a total of 210 aircraft on its way to Iraq, not including the numbers that are already stationed in the vicinity.

In a December 8, 2002 report the *Post* provided some troop numbers available for service should war come. "About 55,000 soldiers, sailors and Air Force personnel are within striking distance of Iraq..." But that number does not include the forces on board the ships at sea; each carrier carries about 5,000 sailors and personnel or an additional 15,000. But the 5th fleet is currently deployed in the Persian Gulf with a listing of sailors and marines that exceeds 20,000. These behemoths of the sea carry more than 4.6 million pounds of air launched missiles, laser-guided bombs, general purpose bombs, and ammunition. [*Washington Post*, "US Strength in the Persian Gulf"] That same report lists 8,000 Air Force personnel and over 100 aircraft based in Saudi Arabia, two dozen fighter jets in Bahrain, 12 F-117 stealth fighter jets in Kuwait, 3 bombers in Bahrain, and 14 B-52 bombers at the island of Diego Garcia. These figures do not include support ordinance.

If we assume the US intends to match its numbers from 1991 to invade Iraq, it would deploy 236,000 more troops than its foe; it will have available from the 5th fleet (in information reported in February of 1998 by the *Washington Post*) the *USS Washington, USS Independence, USS Harry Truman,* 2 Cruisers, 5 Destroyers, 3 Guided Missile Frigates, 2 Attack Submarines, 3 Fast Combat Support Ships, 2 Mine Countermeasure Ships, the *USS Guam* Amphibious Ready Group of 3 additional ships; it will have over 8,000 Air Force personnel from Jabir Air Base in Kuwait with 36 aircraft, Incirlik Air base in Turkey with 24, Sheik Isa Airfield in Bahrain with 40, and about 100 aircraft in Saudi Arabia; it will also have Army personnel, some 7,000 stationed at Kuwait plus the untold numbers being deployed from bases around the world. That puts potential US naval personnel at approximately 18,760... enough personnel to subdue the 2000 sailors that Saddam will deploy, one would hope.

Finally, a few figures on the relative size of the combatants: Iraq land area amounts to 167,000 square miles with a population of approximately 23 million. The US by contrast contains 3,537,438 square miles, or to put this point into greater resolution, New York City has 119.6 square miles of area with population density exceeding 25,000, and a 2000 population count that approximates 280 million. Iraq's population is about 8% the size of the US population. But that does not tell the whole story. US Armed Forces strength as of September 30, 2002 totals 1,385,116 not including the Coast Guard. The US has a larger Army than Iraq has total forces: 480,801 to 400,000. Indeed, the US Navy has almost as many forces, 377,810 and the Air Force is not far behind at 353,571 [DOD]. Iraq's forces are approximately 3% the size of the US forces.

That is the "Tale of the Tape." Once again the US takes on the worst threats to America: Nicaragua, Granada, Kadafi's Castle, and now Iraq. It reminds one of the elephant and the flea. Considering how the US and its allies defeated Iraq eleven years ago in 90 days with a total death count of 293 (many killed by friendly fire), decimated the Iraqi Air Force, wiped out its supply of tanks and armored personnel carriers, and, in the process, effected one of the worst slaughters ever recorded at the "Highway of Death," one would think that a wounded Iraq would be no match for the new Empire of the World. What does the behemoth fear? Or is all this just practice for the future when some upstart nation decides that it, too, would like more military toys—when the President will have to kick in his International Strategy Policy Report to curb their desires and we reduce that nation to rubble? Or is this action against Iraq a showpiece of US might to demonstrate to the world that no one had better "Mess with Texas"? Whatever its purpose, it will inscribe for all the world, not least the Iraqi people, how the US and its citizens comport themselves against a helpless nation.

Let's consider how this nation comported itself in 1991 and hope beyond all hope that we do not repeat that behavior. Following is a passage from Jack Barnes' work, *The Opening Guns of World War III: Washington's Assault on Iraq*:

> The most concentrated single bloodletting was organized by the US command in the final forty-eight hours of the invasion, as Iraqi soldiers fled Kuwait along the roads to Basra... Washington ordered that tens of thousands of fleeing Iraqi soldiers be targeted for wave after wave of bombing, strafing, and shelling. These were people who were putting up no resistance, many with no weapons... leaving in cars, trucks, carts, and on foot. Many civilians from Iraq, Kuwait, and immigrant workers from other countries were killed at the same time as they tried to flee.
>
> The US armed forces bombed one end of the main highway from Kuwait city to Basra, sealing it off. They bombed the other end of the highway and sealed it off. They positioned mechanized artillery units on the hills overlooking it. And then, from the air and from the land they simply massacred every living thing on the road. Fighter bombers, helicopter gunships, and armored battalions poured merciless firepower on traffic jams backed up for as much as twenty miles. When the traffic became gridlocked, the B-52s were sent in for carpet bombing.

Our forces did not wait for the fleeing people to surrender. They did not surround them and force them to surrender; they just exterminated them. Americans never heard about the "Highway of Death"; they just paid for it, a slaughter that, in Barnes' words "ranks among the great atrocities of modern warfare."

Given the forces being assembled to destroy Iraq, the probability of our forces again using such devastating tactics against the weakest of enemies is all too likely. That possibility alone should deter us from allowing this President, son of the man who made possible the "Highway of Death," to carry out his vengeance in our name.

8

Israeli Democracy: Fact or Fiction?

[January 25, 2003]

Israel's bulldozing of 62 shops in the village of Nazkt Issa, north of Tulkarem next to the West Bank line with Israel on Tuesday, and its refusal to allow International and Israeli peace activists to witness the devastation, illustrates the total control of the military in what is supposed to be a democratic state. Americans saw and heard little of this action except that it was caused by the illegal establishment of the shops by Palestinians. In a democratic state, the alleged "illegality" would be dealt with in a court of law, not by an army protecting bulldozers from citizens throwing stones. But Americans hear only what Sharon allows the corporate media in America to receive from his minions as he prevents outsiders from witnessing the demolition.

The impending Israeli elections and the plethora of commentary that touts Israel as the only bastion of Democracy in the Mid-East warrants consideration of the truth of the claim in light of Tuesday's devastation. It would appear that the American public accepts the reality of Israel as a democratic state and finds comfort in its compatibility with American values. That comfort translates into approximately three billion dollars per year for Israel, more aid than any other country receives.

A true Democracy must meet two criteria: one philosophical that presents the logic of its argument in a declaration and/or constitution; the other practical that demonstrates how the Democracy implements legislation, distributes resources, and makes equitable all policies and procedures for all its citizens.

Democracy is first and foremost a concept, a philosophical understanding concerning the rights of humans relative to the government that acts in their name. A democratic government serves through the manifest consent of the governed. That government receives its authority through the citizens in whom the right resides. Inherent in this philosophical understanding is the acceptance of the rights of all citizens that reside in a state: each and every citizen possesses the right to consent to the legitimacy of those who govern, and each and every citizen must receive equal treatment before the law.

For a state to claim a democratic form of government, it must have an established geographic area accepted by other nations as legitimate and defined. The need for established borders is both obvious and necessary, with necessity arising out of the obvious. Without borders, there can be no absolute determination of citizenry, and, therefore, no way to fulfill the establishment of the rights noted above.

What has this to do with the democratic state of Israel? Everything.

Israel has no accepted legitimate borders other than those provided to it by Resolution 181, according to Anthony D'Amato, Leighton Professor of Law at Northwestern University, in his brief "The Legal Boundaries of Israel in International Law": "The legal boundaries of Israel and Palestine were delimited in Resolution 181."

Since the 1967 war, the borders of the current area controlled by Israel exceed those outlined by the UN in Resolution 181 of 1948, as the current incident in Nazkt Issa illustrates. Despite numerous resolutions from the UN demanding that Israel return to its proper borders, especially Resolution 242, Israel defies the world body continuing to retain land illegally held. The reality of this dilemma is most manifest in the settlements. Here, Jews residing in Palestinian areas continue to vote while Palestinians literally surround them and cannot vote. Where is the state of Israel? A look at a map would make it appear that Israel has the spotted coloration of a Dalmatian. Clearly, those living under Israeli domination are not considered citizens of the state of Israel even though they reside within parameters controlled by Israel. Since they are not citizens of Israel, and since there is no Palestinian state, these people are without a country and, therefore, without rights. This is an untenable position for any people that is recognized as a distinct governing group by the UN through its election of the Palestinian Authority as its governing body. That election followed democratic procedures, including the creation of a constitution and the international monitoring of the election process.

A democratic state must declare the premises of its existence in a document or documents that present to the world the logic of its right to govern. That usually comes in the form of a constitution. Unlike the Palestinians, Israel has no constitution. Chuck Chriss, President of JIA writes, "Israel has no written constitution, unlike the United States and most other democracies. There was supposed to be one. The Proclamation of Independence of the State of Israel calls for the preparation of a constitution, but it was never done."

It has been more than 50 years since that "call." Why has Israel demurred on the creation of a constitution? Both Chriss in his article and Daniel J. Elazar, writing in "The Constitution of the State of Israel," point to the same dilemma: how to reconcile the secular and religious forces in Israel. Elazar states:

> Israel has been unable to adopt a constitution full blown, not because it does not share the new society understanding of constitution as fundamental law, but because of a conflict over what constitutes fundamental law within Israeli society. Many religious Jews hold that the only real constitution for a Jewish state is the Torah and the Jewish law that flows from it. They not only see no need for a modern secular constitution, but even see in such a document a threat to the supremacy of the Torah...

The consequences of this divide can be seen in the discrepancies that exist in practice in Israel. Although "the State of Israel is described in the Proclamation of Independence as both a Jewish State and a Democracy with equal rights for all its citizens," the Foundation Law of 1980 makes clear that Israeli courts "shall decide [a case] in the light of the principles of freedom, justice, equity and peace of Israel's heritage." Without a written constitution, Israel relies on a set of laws encased in Israel's heritage, "some blatantly racist in their assignment of privilege based on religion," according to Tarif Abboushi writing in Counterpunch in June of 2002.

But the structure of Israel's governing process that depends on a Knesset is also flawed. According to Chriss, "Members of the

Knesset are elected from lists proposed by the parties on a national basis. Following the election, the parties get to assign seats in the Knesset based on their proportion of the national vote, drawing from the party list...Thus, individual *MKs owe allegiance to the party chiefs and not directly to the electorate.*" [Emphasis mine] He further states: "This political system has resulted in some distortions in which Israeli law and government do not reflect the actual wishes of the voting population."

For a state to claim a Democratic form of government, it must accept the equality of all residents within its borders as legitimate citizens regardless of race, ethnicity, creed, religion, political belief, or gender. For a state to claim it is Democratic and reserve the rights of citizenship to a select group, negates its claim. It is an oxymoron to limit citizenship rights to Jews alone and call the state democratic. As Joel Kovel has stated in *Tikkun*: "A democracy that is only to be for a certain people cannot exist, for the elementary reason that the modern democratic state is defined by its claims of universality." Yet this inherent contradiction exists in Israel. And this brings us from the philosophical phase to the practical one.

Daniel Elazar, reflecting on this conundrum in the postmodern era, notes that this "makes it impossible for the State to distinguish between the entitlements of Jewish citizens and others based upon obligations and performance; i.e., more benefits if one does military service than if one does not."

How does Israel implement the Democracy it claims to possess? First, any Jew from anywhere in the world can come to Israel and receive citizenship by virtue of their Jewishness. By contrast, a Muslim or Christian Palestinian living in exile because of the 1948 war cannot claim citizenship even though they were indigenous to the area, nor can their descendents claim citizenship. Second, ninety percent of the land in Israel is held in restrictive covenants—land initially owned by Palestinians for the most part—covenants that bar non-Jews from ownership, including the Palestinians, who hold a limited version of Israeli citizenship. Third, Israeli citizens who are Muslim or Christian do not share the rights accorded Jews who serve in the military, nor do they receive the benefits extended to those who serve in the military. Non-Jews are taxed differently than Israeli citizens and the neighborhoods in which they live receive less support. As recently as June 12, 2002, Paul Martin writing for the *Washington Times* noted, "Israeli Arabs are trying to strike down a new law reducing family benefits, arguing that it has deliberately been drafted in a way that will affect Arabs more harshly than Jews."

Although Arabs constitute 20% of the population within Israel, their voice in government is limited. Recently, an "expert" working for the General Security Service submitted his "expert opinion" to the Central Election Committee that undertook to disqualify Azmi Bishara and other Arab MKs from taking part in the election. This action would have deprived the Arabs of a voice in the Knesset if the Israeli court had not overturned it. The reality of Israeli political parties virtually assures non-representation of the Palestinians in the governing process. Even with Bishara permitted to run, the voice of the Palestinians is muted.

As Uri Avnery noted recently: "One glance at the political map shows that without the Arab votes, no left-wing coalition has any chance of forming a government—not today, nor in the foreseeable future... This means that without the Arabs, the Left cannot even dictate terms for its participation in a coalition dominated by the Right."

Perhaps the most graphic illustration of the non-Democracy that exists in Israel comes from Human Rights Watch and the US State Department reports published in *Jurist Law*. The range of abuses listed by the State Department includes detainees beaten by police, poor prison conditions that did not meet international standards, detainees held without charge, holding of detainees as bargaining chips, refusal to allow access to Obeid by the Red Cross, imposition of heavier sentences on Arabs than Jews, interference with private rights, etc., and finally, "Trafficking in women for the purpose of forced prostitution is a continuing problem."

Human Rights Watch offers a litany of abuses, many more serious than those proffered by the Department of State: Israel has maintained the "liquidation" policy, targeting individuals without trial by jury, lack of investigations to determine responsibility for killings and shootings, increased use of heavy weaponry, including F-16 fighter jets, etc., against "Palestinian police stations, security offices, prisons, and other installations."

HRW also references the Israeli Information Center for Human Rights in the occupied Territories for the wanton killing of civilians by settlers. The listing is too extensive to offer in its totality here.

As I mentioned at the outset of this article, the American public hears constant reference to Israel as the only democratic nation in the Mid-East. They receive little or no information about the accuracy of that statement. Yet Americans accept this administration's and past administrations' support of Israel in large measure because they believe it reflects the ideals expressed in the American Constitution, and they are willing to spend their tax dollars in support of those ideals. In reality, American Democracy and Israeli Democracy are decidedly distinct.

Democracy cannot exist in ignorance of policies, processes, and actions undertaken on behalf of the people, including the refusal to admit citizens to areas like Nazkt Issa where non-democratic action exists. Silence by the peoples' representatives concerning reasons for actions taken in their name corrodes Democracy. Americans have not been told, for example, that American authorities removed 8000 pages of information from the 12,000 provided by the Iraqi government to the UN Inspectors, according to former MP Anthony Wedgewood Benn in an interview on BBC January 12. These pages were removed to protect corporations that provided Iraq with chemicals and other material that could be used to develop WMD.

Die Tageszeitung, a Berlin daily newspaper, reported the names of the corporations that acted with the government's approval through the '80s and up to 1991 supplying Saddam with nuclear, chemical, biological and missile technology. An extensive report on the chemicals sent to Iraq by the US was disclosed in the *Sunday Herald* by Neil Mackay and Felicity Arbuthnot, but received little press beyond this paper. How can the American people respond intelligently to the designs of this administration against Iraq without knowing how Iraq obtained its capability to develop WMD and the reasons for developing them?

Similarly, Israel cannot restrict its citizens, including peace activists, or its American supporters, from knowing how it acts relative to Palestinians by preventing reporters or activists from describing what is done in their name. Preventing the UN investigation of the Jenin "massacre" is only one example. Restricting journalists from occupied territory is another. Preventing Israeli and international peace activists from Nazkt Issa is the most recent.

Although the founding fathers verbalized the concepts and ideals that are the foundation of American Democracy in the Declaration of Independence and the Constitution, the full implementation of those ideals took many years to bring to fruition: a Civil War that freed slaves more than 70 years after the creation of the nation, Women's Rights more than 120 years after the founding, and the Civil Rights Acts of the '50s and '60s more than 150 years after its birth. That, however, is not a reason for Israel, or any nation moving toward a democratic status, to delay implementation of equal rights for all of their citizens. Rather, it is a demonstration of the necessity to introduce and ensure equity from the outset.

9

Armageddon Anxiety:
Evil on the Way

[February 22, 2003]

Bob Woodward's deferent, perhaps even obeisant homage to "Dubya" in his recent book, *Bush at War*, contains this troubling observation: "The President was casting his mission and that of the country in the grand vision of God's Master Plan." Woodward reinforced this frightening perception when he closed his book with this quote taken from those acting for the Administration: "We will export death and violence to the four corners of the earth in defense of this great country... and rid the world of evil."

Considering how Bush, Jr. grew up beneath the Reagan/Bush *baldachino* and then helped guide his father's ascension to the throne, his connections with the Christian Right have a long and deep history, including familiarity with the pseudo-prophet, Hal Lindsey, a frequent visitor to the Reagan White House.

Lindsey, the *New York Times* "Best Selling Author" of the past three decades, author of at least 20 books like *The Late Great Planet Earth*, and influential Father of Christian Zionism, foresees the imminent and unavoidable great battle of Armageddon, the fulfillment of John's prophecy in the *Book of Revelation*, the cataclysmic conflict between the forces of Good against the forces of Evil, climaxing in our lifetime. Jesus Christ, King of the Jews, will return to rule the world from the rebuilt temple in the reclaimed nation of Israel according to the prophecies, and we will witness the inevitable suffering and global holocaust. Lindsey proclaims deliverance from Armageddon depends on understanding God's purposes for the Jews, including the restoration of Israel as a nation in the land of Judea and Samaria.

Lindsey also proclaims that he purposefully writes these books to shock people into believing in Jesus Christ as their

Lord and Savior. And like any good insurance salesman, he instills fear as he threatens his customers with the plagues revealed in the Acts of the Apostles and the Book of Revelation: "...The sun shall be turned into darkness, and the moon into blood.... With Justice he judges and makes war... He is dressed in a robe dipped in blood and his name is the word of God... Out of his mouth comes a sharp sword with which to strike down nations... so you may eat the flesh of kings, generals, and mighty men, of horses and their riders, and the flesh of all people, free and slave, small and great." The Messiah slays the Antichrist and "creates a new heaven and a new earth" and He judges the dead, saves the Christians, and casts the rest into eternal perdition.

Lindsey accepts as reality that his interpretations of the prophecies come directly to him from God: "I believe that the Spirit of God gave me a special insight, not only into how John described what he actually experienced, but also into how this whole phenomenon encoded the prophecies so that they could be fully understood only when their fulfillment drew near... I prayerfully sought for a confirmation for my apocalypse code theory..."

This self-proclaimed, God inspired interpreter of the Bible has had a profound influence on American and British Christians and Jews. Since Ronald Reagan's Christian-based regime of the '80s, which included access to the President by not only Lindsey, but Jerry Falwell and the Christian Zionist televangelist Mike Evans, the interests of Zionism as an integral component of prophetic lure have been central in policy formation toward Israel in particular and the Mid-East generally, in both America and the United Kingdom.

The current administration, even more so than Reagan's, is rife with right-wing reliance on the coming revival predicted in the *Book of Revelation*. Consider observations made by Paul Krugman of the *New York Times* December 18, 2002: "Tom DeLay soon to be House majority leader, told a church group that: 'Only Christianity offers a way to live in response to the realities that we find in this world—only Christianity.' He also said he was on a mission from God to promote a 'biblical worldview' in American politics." This from the most powerful man in the Congress! And he is not alone.

According to Krugman, many leading Congressional Republicans belong to the "secretive" Council for National Policy, an organization founded by Tim LaHaye, co-author of the apocalyptic *Left Behind* novels. Members include Pat Robertson, Ralph Reed, Sen. Jesse Helms, Congressman Dick Armey and Tom DeLay of Texas, Howard Phillips, and many, many others. This fundamentalist group listens, in private, to none other than the self-proclaimed "Born Again" Christian, George W. Bush. Consider also the appointment of John Ashcroft to the position of Attorney General, a vocal Christian fundamentalist who "gives every appearance of placing his biblical worldview above secular concerns..."

Add to this the Neo-Cons in the administration like Rumsfeld, Cheney, Wolfowitz, Perle, Feith, and many others, and one understands that the ties that bind the Neo-Con Christian right, read Christian Zionists, to the Zionist Orthodox Jew, cement mentalities that embrace myths as truth and behavior directed by superstitious beliefs, regardless of those who do not share their zeal.

I believe the views expressed by Hal Lindsey (reflective of beliefs held by "Dominionists," including Dr. Tony Evans, founder of Promise Keepers, Dr. Martin Hawkins, Assistant to Evans, James Ryle of the Vineyard Movement among others) permeate the Bush administration's major figures, especially the President. They guide their approach to foreign policy, and transform their perception of themselves as executers of God's will. The potential destructive power inherent in this mentality, that accepts as truth interpretations of mythological stories or willingly uses those interpretations to exhort others to action, can be understood and thwarted before such devastation occurs.

That conclusion we can draw from history should we consider the destructive power of myth as it was wielded by Urban II as he inaugurated the Crusades to liberate Jerusalem, Innocent III when he and his successors exterminated the Cathar sect in the 13th and 14th centuries, the Puritan divines when they slaughtered the Pequot Indians in 1636-37, and the elimination of the beliefs extant in northern Europe before the onslaught of Christianity in the Middle Ages—to offer a few examples. When the elite few who gain power in a country or over a group of people accept myths as truth, or when they insidiously and ruthlessly use the beliefs people hold to affect their ends, devastation follows. An enlightened American public can thwart the myth-driven elite.

Michael Ortiz Hill, author of *Dreaming the End of the World*, characterizes Bush, in his essay in Counterpunch, January 4, 2003, as "...delusional and the shape of his delusion is specifically apocalyptical in belief and intent." By apocalyptical, Hill means that "all systems are supposed to go down so the Messiah can come and Bush, seemingly, has taken on the role of the one who brings this to pass."

"God sovereignly controls all aspects of life," according to this view, and that understanding is inherent in the teachings of the Promise Keepers Movement and its founder, Dr. Tony Evans, and the perspective of Billy Graham, two of the prominent right-wing Christians who have influenced Bush. Graham is credited with Bush's rebirth in Christ and Dr. Tony Evans is pastor of a large Dallas church where Bush heard a great deal about "how the world should be seen from a divine viewpoint," according to Dr. Martin Hawkins, assistant to Evans. [Hill]

Both the Promise Keepers and the Vineyard Movements, according to Gary Gilley in *The Vineyard Movement*, accept the doctrine of "end time" or "dominionism," i.e., that there will be a seizure of earthly power by God's people (read Christians) to restore the earth to God's control. Dominion theology teaches that Christ restored dominion over life to the followers of Christ, but the church now has the obligation of redeeming society in order to bring about the Second Coming. They also contend that the kingdom of God is now and they have the responsibility to manifest God's power before the entire world. Taking control of the earth must happen before Christ will return to usher in the physical kingdom on earth over which He will reign.

But Christian Zionists also believe before Christ can return, the Jews must return to Israel. Many evangelical Christians cite Genesis 12 and 13 to demonstrate that "the Jews have title deed to Israel and the land must not be given back to the Palestinians," according to Thomas Williamson in his article "To Whom Does the Land of Palestine Belong?"

Christian Zionists, according to Williamson, "regard God's covenant with Abraham, including the land grant, as an unconditional covenant." More frighteningly, "Every act taken by

Israel is orchestrated by God, and should be condoned, supported, and even praised by the rest of us," notes Grace Halsell in her article, "Israeli Extremists and Christian Fundamentalists: The Alliance." Not all Christians accept this interpretation, but for those who do, the reestablishment of Israel in 1948 ushered in the conditions necessary to bring about the rapture: Jewish control of Jerusalem and rebuilding the temple. Then and only then can the final, great battle called Armageddon begin. Estimates vary, but Halsell claims "10 to 40 million Americans believe Palestine is God's chosen land for the Jews." Maintenance of Israel as a nation becomes an obligation on the part of Christian Zionists if Biblical prophecy is to be fulfilled.

That places George W. Bush in a unique position as a leader of the world's mightiest military power: to bring about the fulfillment of God's prophecy. Hill claims that Bush has accepted this eschatology through which he sees himself "as an agent of God who has been called by him to 'restore the earth to God's control.'" S.R. Shearer of Antipas Ministries, notes Hill, calls this delusional. Hill refers to Bob Woodward's new book, *Bush at War*, to give substance to this Messianic view of the President. Woodward observes "the President was casting his mission and that of the country in the grand vision of God's Master Plan."

Add to these comments the closing sentence of his 2003 State of the Union Speech: "The liberty we prize is not America's gift to the world, it is God's gift to humanity," and we can sense his Messianic fervor as he leads the world against the "man-made" forces of evil.

Unfortunately, the determination of that evil resides in the beliefs of those interpreting the "prophecies" and who accept those interpretations as truth. For Lindsey and the Vineyard ministers, God's covenant with the Jews is truth and it translates, according to Stephen R. Sizer, into the need for America to "continue military and economic funding of Israel," for Israel to "resist negotiating land for peace," "maintain their apartheid policies," and incite fundamentalist groups to destroy the Dome of the Rock so the new temple can be built.

Lindsey accuses those who refuse to accept this eschatology as anti-Semitic. This transition from biblical prophecy to current events translates myth into international policy, emphasizing the potential destructive power of mythology. Who are these self-appointed servants of the Almighty who give direction to Israeli and US leaders regarding the establishment of nation states, the conception and determination of evil, and the righteousness of actions taken on behalf of their interpretation of God's word?

Lindsey believes, as we have noted, that the Spirit of God has given him special insight "into how this whole phenomenon encoded the prophecies." Others like James Ryle of Promise Keepers find God giving revelation through dreams and visions; in *Hippo in the Garden*, he notes that he was called to preach through a prophetic word situation. In either case, their interpretations come from an indeterminable source, yet a source of vast power and consequence. Lindsey writes: "Only now, as mankind approaches the third millennium, do I feel like the Holy Spirit has provided me with the proper perspective—the Big Picture, so to speak—on the mind blowing experiences of the modern world." [*Planet Earth*, 2000 A.D.]

And what are those "mind blowing experiences"? "I am certain The Second Advent will occur in the next few years—probably in your lifetime." And, "the greatest threat to freedom and world peace today—is Islamic fundamentalism" [*The Final Battle*]. Acceptance of these modern-day prophets and their beliefs by the elite in power portends disaster for American policy in the Mid-East in particular, and for American interests generally. But, as we have seen, these ministers of God have the ear of those in power in the current administration.

Two issues arise immediately: why should America determine its future course based on interpretations of God's word as contained in documents 2500 years old, designed and written for civilizations long dead? And, second, what is the evil that these modernday prophets determine as the threat against God's predictions?

Plainly, the Books of *Genesis*, *Daniel*, and *Revelation*, the primary sources for "end-time theology," for "Dominionism," for the Apocalyptic perspective, and for Armageddon, while accepted by literalists as the word of God, are in fact derivatives of stories and ideas from other cultures that anti-date Moses by hundreds of years and John, the purported author of *Revelation*, by more than 1700 years.

How then can they be the word of God? How can Americans take seriously the interpretations of pseudo-prophets who claim to know the meaning of prophecies when they are only the latest in a series of such claimants that date back to Joachim of Fiore, an Italian monk of the 12th century, Christopher Columbus in the early 1500s, Martin Luther, Thomas Muentzer in the 16th century, the Puritans in America, the interpretations arising out of Nazism and Marxism, William Miller and John Darby... to mention a few who appeared before the most recent group headed by Lindsey? [PBS]

There can be no doubt that the *Book of Revelation* has had a searing impact on the American conscience that dates back to the establishment of God's "city on a hill" given to the Puritans by God Himself. The absolute acceptance of the forces of good and evil as extant and operative in the world, concepts that date back to influences from ancient Greece and Persia in the 5th to 3rd centuries before Christ, existed without question in the Puritan mind. Hope in the eventual victory of the forces of good over evil, however, existed long before the 5th century BCE in the "Enuma and Elish" stories of the struggles between chaos and order that date to 1780 BCE in Mesopotamia. These myths tell of Marduk, the God of light, struggling against Tiamat, the force of evil, to bring order out of chaos and peace to the world. [*www.gatewaystobabylon.com*] The influence of these myths on the *Book of Genesis*, purportedly written by Moses who was born circa 1571 BCE, is unmistakable and conveyed directly in Psalm 74:14, 15, 16.

But Marduk is not Yahweh, yet current pseudo-prophets will declare the accuracy of their visions as direct from God who speaks to humankind from the pages of the Old and New Testaments. They fail to account for the origins of God's word that comes from non-Jewish sources. Many ancient myths influenced the Bible: the burning of the world by the Hindu God, Shiva; the Akkadian prophecies from Mesopotamia; the messiah-like king that takes over the world, rewards the just, and rules forever from the Uruk Prophecy; and the judgment of the dead by the Egyptian god Maat for the good and evil they performed in their lifetime. [Patricia Eddy, "The Persian Connection: the End of the World Begins"]

Judaism also borrowed "angels, the holy spirit, paradise in heaven, eternal life, Judgment Day, the resurrection of the dead, a fiery hell, a messianic savior, and man's personal responsibility to do God's will" from Persia. [*www.alsopreview.com*] These same concepts exist in Zoroaster's faith that prevailed in the 6th century BCE. He designed a monotheistic God, Ahura Mazda, considered by some as a precursor of the God of the Judaic Bible. Zoroaster's last battle between the forces of good and evil, the biblical Armageddon, is headed by a messiah known as Saoshyant. Upon victory, he would herald in a millennium of peace and plenty. An apocalypse preceded that last battle to gain the attention of the people. Indeed, the *Book of Revelation* enlarges upon Zoroaster's end of the world concepts as do sections in the Dead Sea Scrolls discovered in 1947 at Nag Hammadi, and date to the 1st and 2nd centuries CE.

Unfortunately, Christians reading this literature have focused on the necessary and inevitable return of the Jews to Judea-Samaria as conveyed in one source written by a monk in 950 CE, Adso of Montier-En-Der, at the request of Queen Gerbera of France as he interpreted biblical passages. He also noted there would arise "the Last World Emperor" who would unite Christianity and defeat Muslims before the Antichrist arises [PBS]. This Christian Zionist focus that requires the fulfillment of the covenant between God and His chosen people arises from two broad predictions in the Old Testament: predictions of a return to Palestine from the Babylonian exile and promises of Palestine as the land given by God to the Jews.

Scholars argue about these predictions, some claiming that God fulfilled His promises when the Jews returned to Palestine, rebuilt the Temple and the Walls of Jerusalem, and restored the religious life of the community under the Maccabees; others disagree. [*www.users.cloud9.net*] Citations of God's promises to "the descendants of Abraham" for land appear in Genesis 12:7, 13:15, 15:18, 28:13-14 among others. The dispute caused by these passages has to do with the "seed" to which God promised the land. Zionists argue that God's promise was to Jews only; others argue that the seed of Abraham includes Arabs. [*www.mideastfacts.com*]

Regardless of these indeterminable disputes, "prominent evangelists preach to their followers that God never fulfilled His promise of giving all the land of Palestine to the Jews" [*www.mideastfacts.com*] and, consequently, support "**whatever action necessary, even nuclear war, to obtain Arab lands in** the **Middle East and give them to Jews.**" [emphasis mine] [*www.mideastfacts.com*] Obviously, such interpretations bring the world to the brink of nuclear holocaust and represent to many in the Christian community a backward step in theology.

Is it possible to believe in the 21st century that a God, designed by a small tribe of nomadic Semites 3200 years ago from stories and myths that existed centuries before in the literatures of Mesopotamia, Persia, Egypt, Canaan, and elsewhere, could dictate to Americans how they should conduct foreign policy? Myths, after all, are stories that explain for a people how they perceive their existence in a world filled with mystery and awe. They create reference points for the people to see connections between their condition and forces greater than themselves, or to understand how they must relate to the society that surrounds them, or to grapple with the internal energies that reside within themselves.

Yet we have in the union of Christian Zionists and Jewish Zionists mentalities that find absolute truth in these myths and willingly inflict them on the American populace. These beliefs bring ancient prophecies from myths into today's political arena as this comment from Lindsey's *Planet* makes all too clear: "The dispute to trigger the war of Armageddon will arise between the Arabs and Israelis over the Temple Mount and Old Jerusalem [Zachariah 12:2-3], the most contested and strategic piece of real estate in the world... Two religions, Judaism and Islam, thus are on a collision course with global and heavenly repercussions. Islam will never accept Jerusalem as the undivided capital of the Jewish state, and Israel will never agree to give it up..." [p.155]

Consider the comments of Margot Patterson in the *National Catholic Reporter*, October 11, 2002: "Thousands of Christian Zionists met in Jerusalem for the Jewish holiday of Sukkot to cheer Sharon and to declare their unconditional support for the state of Israel." These people embrace "end-time" theology and are supported in turn by right-wing Israelis who like the economic and political support they bring to the Israeli cause. Christian fundamentalists and Jewish Messianic settlers, according to Patterson, promise formation of a "Greater Israel" that will usher in Armageddon. They, too, see war between Muslims and Jews as bringing about the Second Coming.

Patterson quotes a variety of sources to enforce her perception of the political impact these interpreters of God's word
have on America's policies toward Israel and Palestine. James
Zogby, President of the Arab American Institute, argues:
"Despite disclaimers to the contrary, the US is waging a war on
Islam at home and abroad even as it tacitly supports extremist
settlers in the occupied territories Israel controls."

Lewis Roth, President of Americans for Peace Now, says:
"You have a number of very conservative Christian groups that
support settlements because they see this as a way of strength-
ening Jewish hold on the land of Israel because in their mind
this is important for end-of-time theology and part of hastening
the Second Coming and the conversion of the Jews..." Since
Jews have their own Messianic reading of the biblical sources,
different from the Christian Zionists except in the necessity of
fulfilling God's covenant to return the Jews to Judea-Samaria,
they find support of the Christian Zionists helpful in bringing
about the creation of Greater Israel that would include not only
the borders of the present state but the entire land of Israel
described in the Hebrew Scriptures.

Consider as well Robert Kaiser's February 9, 2003 article,
"Bush and Sharon Nearly Identical on Mideast Policy" in the
Washington Post. Kaiser quotes Richard Perle, chairman of the
Pentagon's Defense Policy Board: "Israel should insist on Arab
recognition of its claim to the biblical land of Israel... and should
focus on removing Saddam Hussein from power in Iraq"; this
despite multiple UNSC resolutions that declare Israel in defiance
of international law by holding on to these lands. But there's
more! Douglas Feith, undersecretary of defense for policy, has
written extensively on Israeli-Arab issues, and argues, according
to Kaiser, "that Israel has as legitimate a claim to the West Bank
territories seized after the Six-Day War as it has to the land that
was part of the U.N. mandated Israel created in 1948."

Indeed, Donald Rumsfeld has made the same claim even as he
demands that the UN force nations that defy UN resolutions to
comply: "...There was a war... and they (neighboring countries)
lost a lot of real estate to Israel because Israel prevailed in that
conflict." Here are America's Defense Department spokesmen
directly contradicting the UN resolutions demanding that Israel
comply with international law and the Geneva Conventions.

Why do these individuals speak for America in this manner? Kaiser quotes a senior official of the first Bush administration as saying: "Sharon played the president like a violin: 'I'm fighting your war, terrorism is terrorism,' and so on, Sharon did a masterful job." Rabbi Yechiel Eckstein, also quoted by Kaiser, claims "President Bush's policy stems from his core as a Christian, his perceptions of right and wrong, good and evil, and of the need to stand up and fight against evil... I personally believe it is very personal, not a political maneuver on his part." Rev. Richard Land of the Southern Baptist Convention echoed those sentiments when he noted how important evangelical support for the president is, and claimed, "We need to bless Israel more than America needs Israel's blessing because Israel has a far greater ally than the United States of America, God Almighty."

That observation, you will recall, ended the President's State of the Union address as quoted above. In short, America has at its helm a man who understands his role in God's plan and is determined to carry forward, regardless of the views of world leaders or the American people. As Dr. Lower points out in *Counterpunch*:

> Bush's war version of God "has two dangerous implications." One is that those who have lost their lives in service to God and country [Astronauts] "weren't actually taking risks or showing bravery... because their fate was in God's hands." The other implication is that "tragedies are God's will." This is in the tradition of Pat Robertson and Jerry Falwell, who suggested that the September 11 tragedy happened because God had removed his active protection from an immoral United States.

Bush is furthered in his drive to Armageddon by those who surround him, both secular zealots intent on ensuring Israel's expansion to the biblical lands given it by the covenant, or by the religious right that supports Sharon and controls great Jewish influence in America. Perhaps the most recent evidence of this control on America's Mid-East policy comes in the person of Elliott Abrams, the recently appointed director of Mid-East Affairs for the National Security Council. Abrams has stated categorically: "The Palestinian leadership does not want peace with Israel, and there will be no peace."

Given his current position, we know the future of American policy in Palestine. Abrams' prophecy of no peace allows the Christian Zionists and the Jewish Zionists to usher in the forces of their perceived good against the forces of their perceived evil, the Muslims. All of which makes possible the scenario prophesied by Hal Lindsey in *The Final Battle*, making fiction truth and truth fiction.

10

When Logics Die: Rage against the Regime!

[March 13, 2003]

I went for a walk around Lake Gregory this past Sunday afternoon searching for peace, the freedom that comes with peace of mind. The sun's heat spread through the cobalt blue sky over this lake that sits five thousand feet up in the San Bernardino Mountains east of Los Angeles, while sparklets of light glistened on the lake's surface that nibbled slowly at the shore... a glorious day in mid-March here in the mountains.

I went to the lake to find peace. This was the week the president gave one of his rare prime time press conferences, the only opportunity we, the public, get to see him perform. It is also the week America goes to war. I went to the lake to find peace of mind, the ultimate state that comes with freedom, the state of being that is the primary goal of all religions, the end mystics dream of achieving and eastern faiths call Nirvana.

I went to the lake to find the freedom Dubya claims others want to take from me, the freedom promised in the Constitution and the Bill of Rights: freedom to believe as my conscience dictates, freedom to accept the beliefs of others, especially those who differ with me, freedom to pursue my talents and respect the right of others to pursue theirs, freedom to live a healthful life, to speak freely, to learn, and to seek just protection before the law.

I went to find freedom; I found none. I found no peace of mind.

As I walked around the lake, I could not help but think that this was Sunday, the day God rested from His labors. Three faiths worship that God of Abraham, including 90% of Americans; some are Jews, some Christians, and some Muslims. In a few years, more Americans will declare their book of faith to be the Koran than those who declare it to be the Torah. With all these people worshiping the same God, why do we have such division in this country?

As I walked the path around the lake, it occurred to me that it's the leaders who cause the problems. Consider Jerry Falwell, Pat Robertson, Hal Lindsey, Dale Evans, Franklin Graham and his father Billy (to name a few), who deride the prophet Mohammad and declare the Muslim faith to be one of violence. Consider also how they use the Jews to bring about their belief in the *Book of Revelation*, needing the Jews to establish themselves in Israel if the Second Coming is to happen. Consider how they call upon the Christians of the world to unite to fulfill God's master plan even if it means a nuclear holocaust. These are the weapons of mass destruction! Minds filled with the certitude that only belief in myth can allow.

And Sunday is the day Christians set aside to worship that God. This Christian God, this Jesus, asked His followers to "turn the other cheek," to perform the spiritual and corporal works of mercy, in short to care for all God's creatures. Yet this Sunday as I walked about the lake watching children toss their fishing lines out from shore, as others played "T" ball in the park, as young lovers cooed by the side of the lake, as the old and infirm watched from their bench above the path, I heard the whistle of the missiles slam into Baghdad. And I saw the mothers grasp their children to their breasts as they fled in horror at the searing flames; I saw the walls of their homes shatter before their eyes.

I saw this born-again Christian president order American boys and girls to "take up the cross" in defense of their homeland: to defend America against those who have inflicted no harm on America; who have in 12 years not molested any nation; who have claimed they possess no WMD and no nuclear capability verified by international inspectors to be the case; who occupy no other people's lands; who have been subjugated to eleven years of deprivation by a coalition of nations that deprive them of basic medical, sanitation, health and economic necessities; who live in daily fear of American and British war planes that arbitrarily destroy their defenses and kill innocent civilians; and who are surrounded by the greatest massed force of destruction ever assembled in the history of humankind.

This president claims he will bring freedom to the Iraqi people, not America's gift of freedom, but God's! This president will liberate the Iraqi people even as he slaughters an inestimable number of innocents, a liberation of questionable value one suspects. This president will bring Democracy to Iraq whether they want it or not, a gift that Americans don't even enjoy when he is president by selection of five judges! This president will decide the conscience of the American people, since he disregards their voice both at the voting booth and in the streets. This president elevated Iraq to the stage of enemy number one by claiming it had connections with the terrorists that caused 9/11, a contention that proved to be a lie.

This president claimed Iraq had biological weapons of mass destruction, but failed to tell the American people his own father sold Saddam those weapons illegally and surreptitiously. This president claimed Saddam gassed his own people, the Kurds and Iranians, against international law and the Geneva Conventions, but failed to tell the American people that the government at the time, the Reagan/Bush government, not only did not object to this action but provided the means to do it.

This president claimed that Saddam did not comply with Resolution 1441 when he submitted a 12,000-page report, but failed to tell the American people that his administration removed 8,000 pages from that document—pages that contained sensitive material, including the names of American, British, and German firms that supplied Saddam with the chemicals and equipment needed to produce WMD. This president claimed Iraq was in a position to acquire nuclear arms within a few months, a potential threat to America, but failed to tell the American people that he would disregard other nations that possessed or would soon possess nuclear arms including two nations of the three that he called the "Axis of evil": Iran and North Korea.

This president claimed Saddam was a vicious dictator who used torture, oppression of women and the jailing of dissidents to stay in power, but failed to tell the American people that his own father let Saddam stay in power because he was a known quantity and any replacement would not necessarily follow America's orders. Nor did he tell the American people he would authorize torture if done by another nation for America; or that he would incarcerate people without access to lawyers, trial, or jury—indeed, without even a charge of criminal conduct.

And, finally, this president claimed Iraq must be taken down by force because it defied the 17 UN resolutions that called upon it to disarm and respond to human rights violations, an action that if not taken, would result in making the UN irrelevant, but he failed to tell the American people that America supports the state of Israel that has defied 155 UNGA resolutions since 1948, and 69 UNSC resolutions (28 vetoed by the US) since the 1967 war—a defiance that far overshadows the 17 resolutions Iraq has defied. How irrelevant can the UN be if this is the criterion?

What power does the UN possess to enforce its resolutions? Only the moral will of its members. It has no army; it has only the willing acceptance of the rights of all humans to life, liberty, respect, and dignity as determined by its member states. Thus when the most powerful member state disregards the moral stand of that bodies' membership, when it resorts to bribes and coercion to have its way, it denies the only strength the UN can bring to bear on wayward nations. The claim of UN irrelevancy is specious. Indeed, each and every contention made by this president has been shown to be demonstratively false. When logics die, leaders lie!

Patriotic platitudes, vapid values, and incongruous ideals cascade from our leaders' mouths like waters over the cliffs of Niagara. Witness the recent babbling of Blair, Bush, Powell, Rumsfeld and Rice as they resort to condemnation of Iraq for defying the 17 resolutions passed by the UN. This defiance castrates the authority of the UN and cries for resolution by force, regardless of the effectiveness of inspections or the will of the world community.

Witness their despair that Iraq, after eleven years, will ever succumb to the will of the nations that passed these resolutions. Witness their declamations that the security of the US and UK depends on immediate action against the treacherous dictator who gassed his own people 15 years ago (without objection by the US or the UK) and carried forth this same warfare against the Iranians with full approval of the US and the UK, indeed to the supplying of the materials.

Witness their lamentations over those citizens who would object to a war that would instill "shock and awe" in this terrible enemy even as it liberates an estimated half million Iraqis by slaughtering them—saving them from continued oppression by Saddam. Witness their invoking the twin absolutes of freedom and Democracy that will be the offspring of this war even as they prepare to occupy a foreign nation-state and force their will on its people; thus making moot the meaning of Freedom and Democracy. When logics die, what hypocrisy!

I have waited anxiously for a reporter to question these men and this woman about their resolve to hold Iraq to the authority of the UN resolutions. Why Iraq only? Why now? Why not other countries? Why not Israel and Palestine, for example, since most world leaders and the majority of the people in the nations around the world seem to find the Israeli/Palestinian crisis of greater consequence to peace in the Mid-East? Do we not raise the specter of Israeli occupation and aggression against the Palestinians before the world body because we will be condemned as anti-Semitic? Do we not raise the issue of the Palestinian people resorting to suicide bombers because it casts condemnation on the members of the UN for allowing this crisis to continue for over fifty years?

When will we invoke the authority of the UN to make both the Israelis and the Palestinians meet the demands of the international community and international law? When will we declare the hypocrisy of our stance before the world that the US and the UK believe wholeheartedly in the ideals of the world body and its authority in matters of international conflict? When logics die, leaders lie.

Lies, deceit, hypocrisy couched in euphemisms as evidence, security concerns, and ideals beneficial to the international community about the imminent threat posed by Iraq dominate the mainstream media, effectively hiding the reality of the savagery being waged in Israel and Palestine. Beyond the lies uttered without shame by Blair and Powell justifying war are those lies of omission that force Iraq to prominence now to hide the administration's acceptance of Sharon's war against the Palestinians.

Why blanket the truth? Why not speak straightforwardly to the American people? This administration has capitulated to Sharon's demands even as he cloaks his actions in Bush's own terms, "defense against terrorists." As Sharon has told the Knesset, "Don't worry about American pressure on Israel; we, the Jewish people control America, and the Americans know it."

Why hide the truth? Tell it like it is: a war against Iraq can bury what is happening in Israel; a war against Iraq will bury the new Sharon coalition that depends on 13 members who are adamantly opposed to the creation of a Palestinian state. A war against Iraq will hide the request by Israel to have the US cover 15 billion in loans and grants to bail out their floundering economy even as the US states fall deeper and deeper into the ditch of debt. When logics die, leaders lie!

Contrast the demand that Iraq surrender to UN resolutions with the silence that greets the question, "Why not Israel?" Israel has defied the UN for 55 years, Iraq for 12. Israel has invaded and continues to hold illegally land that belongs to Palestinians, defying UN resolutions for 35 years to return the land. Iraq invaded Kuwait 12 years ago with CIA collusion and went to war with Iran 15 years ago with US approval and support. It occupies no foreign land now and is not considered a threat by its neighbors. Israel continues to defy not only UN resolutions that it abide by the Geneva Conventions to protect human rights, but spurns all Human Rights Watch Reports that request investigations into behavior that demeans human dignity and defies international law. Iraq has been forced to release control of its northern territories occupied principally by Kurds, and to give up absolute control in the south, a "no fly zone" controlled by the US and the UK.

Israel has used the "war on terror" to define the Palestinian people, thus giving them absolute right to determine who is a criminal and who will die, without trial by jury, without the right to a lawyer, and without appeal. All of these actions are in defiance of international law. The Iraqi people are victims of this same logic that provides for the use of seven times the destruction visited upon Hiroshima to be visited upon the Iraqi people to catch one man. Israel has WMD and openly admits this fact. It also has nuclear weapons and, in the words of one Israeli Professor, will use them on European capitals as well as against Iraq, if needed to ensure the existence of Israel. It also occupies and suppresses Palestinians using tanks and bulldozers to destroy property not belonging to them. They also use the third largest military force in the world against a people that have no defense except old rifles, missiles and stones.

Iraq has no comparable WMD, nor does it have nuclear capability. It does not occupy any territory owned by another nation and hasn't in the past 12 years. Its military forces are a third of what they were in 1991, and incapable of defending the nation against the might of the US.

Israel has visited terror of an indescribable nature on a defenseless people, from refugee camps surrounded by dozens of tanks, thousands of foot soldiers, Apache helicopters, F-16 fighter jets, and the latest in state-of-the-art technology to subdue the defiant few who will use their life as a weapon in a futile effort to turn the tide. Israel creates these suicide bombers by using vengeance to impregnate the deprived and the hopeless.

America supports this state run terror with our tax money and our military hardware, thus ensuring that America becomes a silent victim of Israeli vengeance. Why Iraq? Why now? Why not line up all who defy UN resolutions and force them to abide by UN authority after we have forced this on Iraq, including US defiance of such resolutions? When logics die, leaders lie!

As I walked around the lake on this Sunday before America slips ineluctably into chaos, I could find no sense of freedom here in America. I have as much chance of defying Bush as an Iraqi citizen has of deposing Saddam. I am a victim of a man who can use my tax dollars to do whatever he wishes, whether that be to support Sharon's savagery or inflict devastation on Iraq. Freedom to speak is no freedom if those in authority defy the voice of the people. Freedom to representative government is no freedom if our representatives abdicate their responsibility under the Constitution. We do not elect another person's conscience when we enter the voting booth; we must stand against those who ignore the people even as they march in the streets and declare their desires before the world.

There is no freedom if there is no Democracy, if the voices of the people are overridden by the corporate voice, the voice of the military/industrial powers, and the wealthy elite who buy their freedom of speech. There is no Democracy if we force it in name on other nations of the world because we demand that they "accept God's gift" regardless of their beliefs—and force America's gift of consumerism on other nations because it is the way to provide heaven on earth. Ultimately, the Presidency of a Democracy must be the laws of the land, not a man who willingly twists the laws to his own end.

I could find no freedom, no peace of mind as I walked about the lake because the Constitution of the United States has been stolen by this administration to be used as a document to control, because it has subverted the freedoms guaranteed in that document and placed our freedom in the hands of a religious zealot that by definition does not accept freedom. It has preempted freedom by adopting a policy of preemptive strike based on the belief of evil determined by one fanatical man sitting illegally in the White House. I could find no freedom because this administration is oblivious to the plight of the unemployed, the homeless, the elderly, single mothers, and the sick and the dying.

I have lived through half a century of slaughter, witnessed America defy itself as it languished in segregation, oppression of women, and governmental inquisition under McCarthy; I have witnessed it justify non-intrusion into genocidal savagery, accept without question the need to carpet bomb whole cities in the cause of peace, and add collateral damage to the lexicon of euphemisms that give credibility to slaughter. But I have always lived with the hope that America's acceptance of a world court, of values inherent in the Nuremberg trials, of mutual cooperation with other nations would lead to a 21st century of peace and equanimity throughout the world.

When logics die, cynicism thrives.

11

Would You Have Sent Your Son (or Daughter) to War If...?

[April 5, 2003]

American families have always responded to the call of their President to send their sons and daughters to fight on behalf of the country. The cries of alarm resound over the years: "Remember the Alamo," "Remember the *Maine*," "Remember Pearl Harbor," "Remember the Gulf of Tonkin." Although it's true that some of these alarms have turned out to be fabricated cries that covered the true intentions of the government at the time, such as the most devastating lie that gave rise to the "Gulf of Tonkin," the American people have shown remarkable trust in their leaders. They believed the values expressed in the Constitution must be upheld.

In making this sacrifice on behalf of the Democracy that grants them freedoms they hold sacred, American families depend primarily on the availability of information supplied by the mainstream media, both print and television. If Americans knew at the time that the *Maine* blew up from an internal explosion and not an unprovoked attack by Spain, they would not have supported going to war against Spain. If McNamara had made available to the press what he knew about the situation in Vietnam, 58,000 lives would not have been lost.

There can be little question that accurate, informed, and honest information should and must be supplied to the American public. But that is not the case, as the brouhaha in the White House Press Corp makes perfectly clear. When reporters need to have their reports checked by the very people they are reporting about, when CNN demands of its press corps that they can print nothing that is not reviewed by central headquarters in Virginia, when NBC, owned by one of the major suppliers of military hardware in the country GE, fires Peter Arnett for making a news analysis report on Iraqi TV, the free press in America no longer exists. This accounts for the relatively strong support the President has received from the American people. They are the silent victims of the controlled news coverage available in the major newspapers like the administration's own voice, the *Washington Times*, and the corporate controlled speaking heads on TV: the Kudlows and Kramers, O'Reillys and Savages. What would be the situation if Americans knew the truth? Let's ask the question.

Would you have sent your son or daughter to war if you knew that, as the Canadian Broadcasting Corporation news reported, "Law experts around the world have condemned the war as illegal"? Would you want to jeopardize your offspring to the potential of a war crimes trial not unlike that at Nuremberg?

Would you have sent your son or daughter to war if you knew the plans for this war were laid out in special reports that date back to 1992? The Cheney Defense Department designed the Defense Policy Guidance Report in the waning days of the first Bush administration. This report, with input from Paul Wolfowitz and Richard Perle among others, became the basis for another document, "A Clean Break: A New Strategy for Securing the Realm," that was prepared for Benjamin Netanyahu as a guide for Israeli foreign policy development by Richard Perle and Douglas Feith, among others. These same figures, now all holding major policy positions in the Bush Junior administration, brought their recommendations to Clinton in 1997/8. He refused to consider them.

This means, in effect, that the reasons for going to war now— the imminent danger Saddam poses, the Iraqi connection with al Qaeda, the threat to America of weapons of mass destruction, the failure of Iraq to comply with UN resolutions—are fabrications to provide a basis for war against Iraq as a means of achieving what these men considered to be advantageous to Israel; yet using the American military as proxy to accomplish their goals.

Would you have sent your son or daughter to war if you had known that it negates Article 51 of the UN Charter, that requires a nation to be invaded before it can go to war against another country—or it must have compelling evidence that the country intends to attack it, e.g., proximity of that nation's forces to its borders? By negating the UN Charter, the United States opens the door for any nation to do the same. Witness the provocative behavior of North Korea. Without the UN, and without the United States accepting the decisions of the UN, the people of this nation put themselves at risk and open the door to anarchy throughout the world.

Would you have sent your son or daughter to war if you knew the Iraqi people had no intentions of throwing roses in front of our liberating tanks? Would you have sent your son or daughter to war if you knew the Iraqi people held dear their nation state and would look upon America's entrance across their borders as a hostile act, not an act of salvation? Yet our soldiers were brainwashed to believe they would be received as liberators—as many have told the imbedded reporters in question and answer sessions.

Why were these deceptions perpetrated on the American people?

Would you have sent your son or daughter to war if you knew the military planning was being done by chicken hawks (i.e., Rumsfeld, Cheney, Perle, and Feith) who had to overrule real military planners when conceiving the Iraq war plan? Would you have sent your son or daughter to war if you knew the brilliant plan touted as "Shock and Awe" had the potential to achieve the opposite? That politics would alter its approach in order to minimize world reaction? That the combination of the myths of Iraqi love for the US invaders and the "Shock and Awe" treatment would solidify Arab opinion against this Anglo-American intrusion and ensure weeks and months of mayhem and death?

Would you have sent your son or daughter to war if you knew that Bush Senior supplied Saddam with the very weapons of mass destruction that we now seek? If the nation's press had published the information in Alan Friedman's book, *A Spider's Web*, written in 1993, the American public would know the junior Bush is out to protect his father from censure for forwarding cluster bombs and missile technology through Pinochet to Saddam illegally. They would have been reminded or have learned for the first time that George H.W. Bush sent over 5 billion of our tax dollars to Saddam with full knowledge of the CIA, an outfit Bush, Sr. had formerly headed.

Would you have sent your son or daughter to war if you knew the vast majority of countries around the world are adamantly against the invasion? If you knew the "coalition of the willing" includes the UK, although its citizens are 80% against the war? That Australia has supplied 2000 troops, even though its population is over 90% against the war? That others have been bribed or coerced into allowing their names to be put on the list? That some, like Slovenia, did not know their country had been placed on the list?

Would you have sent your son or daughter to war if you knew that Cheney's former company, Halliburton, from which he receives a million per year in compensation even after his resignation, had already signed contracts for itself and its subsidiaries for contracting work in Iraq, before the war started? Would you have sent your son or daughter to war if you knew Bechtel, Fluor, Parsons, the Washington Group among others had also received similar contracts, all without a public bid process and all without consideration of existing Iraqi firms who are to be liberated by our forces? Would you believe all these companies are major financial supporters of the Republican Party? Would you believe these contract negotiations began as early as 1997?

Would you have sent your son or daughter to war if you knew that Richard Perle had arranged for his own company to gain contracts in Saudi Arabia and Iraq to ensure security strategies there, even as America was preparing for war and as he served as Chairman of the Defense Policy Board? Would you have problems with those in charge of defense policy working out deals that would benefit them personally because of the actions they were proposing—and because of their influential positions and prior knowledge? Is this what your son or daughter is defending and dying for?

Would you have sent your son or daughter to war if you knew Richard Perle and Douglas Feith, in their 1996 report to secure the "realm" for Israel, a realm that includes the land it now holds (and more by implication: "Our claim to the land—to which we have clung for hope for 2000 years—is legitimate and noble") defies the many UN resolutions demanding that Israel return the lands it captured in 1967? Perhaps this will force the US to bring Israel before the UN to ensure that it complies with its resolutions. Would knowledge that this same report calls for Israeli troops to give "hot pursuit" into all Palestinian areas, to actively destabilize Iraq even to the "redefining" of it? That this report further calls for Israeli troops to strike Syrian military targets in Lebanon with the use of "proxy forces," and to establish a policy of "preemptive" strike that ensures Israeli dominance in the Mid-East—all efforts that require US financial and military support? Would that knowledge give pause in sending sons and daughters to war?

Would you have sent your son or daughter to war if you knew Colin Powell used plagiarized material to make his case for war before the UN? Would you have sent your son or daughter to war if you knew Blair's document detailing Saddam's WMD was fabricated as well? Would this knowledge have caused you to pause and question everything this administration says?

Would you have sent your son or daughter to war if you knew the President has pretensions to be an executer of God's Master Plan? That he sees himself as an instrument in bringing about the prophecies described in the Book of Revelation? That both the Iraqi population and the American people are his to use as he fulfills this mythological vision? Would you want your children fighting in a war that is the brainchild of right-wing Christian zealots and Israeli Zionists?

Would you have sent your son or daughter to war if you knew Donald Rumsfeld's righteous indignation at Iraq's alleged abuses of the Geneva Convention Protocols failed to mention that the United States did not sign Protocol 1 of 1977, a Protocol added to the original human rights documents of the Geneva Accords? This Protocal provides for Protection of Victims of International Armed Conflict. Indeed, Rumsfeld had been chastised by the Commission on Human Rights for US abuses to the Geneva Convention protection relative to the prisoners held in Guantanamo in a statement that noted, "The Secretary seems unaware of the requirements of international humanitarian law." In short, the US does not abide by the principles that protect prisoners, yet cries foul when another state, that also failed to sign the Protocol, doesn't play according to the rules.

This litany of failures to the American people demonstrates how great is the failure of the American press. What had been an objective instrument to bring information and analysis to the people is now in the hands of corporate interests whose profits are dependent on ensuring acceptance of policies and legislation that will increase their power and wealth. The American Democracy has been bought. Freedom of speech is possible for those with the wealth to assert it in the media they control.

The majority of Americans depend on the mainstream media for their information, both newspapers and TV. But as one can see from the above, they cannot find the truth there. American Democracy depends on a free flow of information to inform the citizenry. Absent accurate information, citizens become puppets of those willing to control. The magnitude of this issue cannot be overstated. American families have sent their children to war believing in their leaders as honest and trustworthy men. They are not. The United States has become an invading power of a nation that did not attack or provoke it. It has done so against the deliberative judgment of all the world's communities and has become the dominant force in the world—willing to determine who should rule and willing to inflict its judgment on all. This posture was conceived by a handful of men who have gained control of the American government and forced it to their will. These same men have personal fortunes to gain as a direct result of their influence. Clearly, the America that was defined by the Constitution no longer exists.

The media's responsibility is to search out the truth and present it to the public. When it does not, it has committed the sin of omission. When it allows the people to believe the lies perpetrated by this administration, to have them believe in the righteousness of its policies, it has become the very embodiment of evil.

12

Sharon Recruits US Mercenaries Against Syria: Of Pariahs and Pre-emptive Strikes

[April 26, 2003]

Even before the "victory" in Iraq had been declared, Administration officials began leveling accusations at Syria that sounded strangely familiar, something like a regurgitation of the lies that had propelled our forces into the "war that wasn't." Predictably, that series of accusations was followed by Sharon's demands of its mercenary forces, the US military, that they undertake five goals desired by Israel. These demands represent the next step in Israel's fulfillment of the Wolfowitz/ Perle design to achieve "The New Strategy for Securing the Realm," the report they prepared for the Israeli right wing Likud party in 1996.

Ha'aretz listed Sharon's demands in its April 16 edition, demands uttered only two days earlier by Israeli Defense Minister Shaul Mofaz:

1. The removal and dismantling of Palestinian terrorist organizations operating out of Damascus—Hamas and Islamic Jihad;
2. The ouster of Iranian Revolutionary Guards from Lebanon's Bekaa Valley;
3. An end to Syrian cooperation with Iran, including attempts to transfer arms to the Palestinian Authority and incite Israeli Arabs;

4. The deployment of the Lebanese Army along Lebanon's border with Israel, and the ouster of Hezbollah from the area;

5. The dismantling of the surface-to-surface missile network that Israel charges Hezbollah has built in Southern Lebanon.

Sharon added that President Pashar Assad "is dangerous. His judgment is impaired." Like Saddam, Israel and America are confronted once again with a dangerous threat in the form of a dictator.

Obviously, Sharon has no qualms about making such demands; he has already made it known to his Cabinet and to the Israeli public via radio that Jews run the US and we here in America know it. He does not fear the Israeli academics or peace groups in the homeland or the American Jews who recoil at his policies toward the Palestinians—groups like Jews for Peace in Palestine and the many who have affiliated with *Tikkun* magazine in its efforts to bring a peaceful resolution to the crisis.

These actions are seen in the Arab world as portending Mid-East domination by Israel. Kamal Kharrazi, Iranian Foreign Minister, stated that United States actions are done to allow Israel domination in the Mid-East. A Syrian Cabinet report notes that US statements regarding Syria are a "stimulus and a service to Israel's goals and expansion greed..." In a similar vein, AIPAC's recent invitation to Intifad Qanbar of the Iraqi National Congress to attend its conference, one of the primary Iraqi figures expected to play a major role in the "new" Iraq, reflects Israel's links to pro-Israel Iraqi groups as a "democratic" Iraq emerges.

AIPAC has had ongoing meetings with Ahmed Chalabi, founder of that organization, personal friend of Rumsfeld, and self-proclaimed future leader of Iraq. Add to this Israeli/Iraq connection the imposition of General Garner as "pro-consul" of Iraq and sympathizer with the tribulations of Ariel Sharon, the off-hand dismissal of the UN as a participant in the reconstruction of the new Iraq, and the distribution of reconstruction contracts to corporations tied to the "pro-Israeli clique"—and it is no wonder the Arab world fears the rising power of Israel in the Mid-East.

A recent article suggests that America's preemptive role in the Mid-East can be linked to the influence of the Wolfowitz/Perle duo and their emergence into positions of prominence in the Bush administration. Michael Lind's article in *The New Statesman* focuses on a core clique of influential men in the Bush administration who have co-opted control of America's foreign policy. There can be no question that they are linked to the 1991/2 "Defense Policy Guidance Report" prepared for Dick Cheney and Daddy Bush. That document brought the concept of "preemptive" strikes into vogue as a premise for safeguarding America's superiority in military power.

Subsequently that document became the basis for the 1996 report prepared for the Likud right wing. The Institute for Advanced Strategic and Political Studies prepared the report, "A Clean Break: A New Strategy for Securing the Realm." The main ideas for the report came from "prominent opinion makers" Richard Perle, James Colbert, and Douglas Feith, among others. Of all the recommendations presented in that report, the most pertinent to this paper is this statement: "Israel can shape its strategic environment, in cooperation with Turkey and Jordan, by weakening, containing, and even rolling back Syria. This effort can focus on removing Saddam Hussein from power in Iraq—an important Israeli strategic objective in its own right—as a means of foiling Syria's regional ambitions."

That strategic objective, removing Saddam from power, has now been achieved through the use of the US military. While Saddam may have appeared to be a threat to Israel some years ago, in recent years, since the first Gulf war, he was not perceived as such by Israel's military or the nations immediately surrounding Iraq, including Kuwait—although, for reasons unknown, he was a threat to America according to our President. One wonders, therefore, why Perle would make this observation in the 1996 report. The answer is in the immediate access Israel has to Iraqi oil now that it is under US occupation. The pipeline through Jordan will be reopened, providing cheaper oil to Israel. In addition, US troops present in Iraq and Kuwait offer strategic support to the continued existence of the Israeli state and rearrange the strategic balance in the Middle East in favor of Israel. Neither of these reasons could be declared publicly.

Having achieved one objective, Perle can now look to the second: "foiling Syria's regional ambitions." To bring focus to the threat Syria poses for the United States and its alleged desire to create democracies in the Mid-East, Israel can turn to the "Securing the Realm" report for arguments: "It is dangerous for Israel to deal naïvely with a regime murderous of its own people, openly aggressive toward its neighbors, criminally involved with international drug traffickers and counterfeiters, and supportive of the most deadly terrorist organizations." Substitute the United States for Israel in the above quote and you have the arguments being offered to America to take out Syria. Once again, the United States becomes Israel's proxy army.

Since Perle and Wolfowitz have transferred their presence to the new administration, having been out of power during the Clinton years, they can now resurrect the essential points of their old 1991/2 report in the form of the September 2002 National Security Strategy Policy Report that calls upon the US to adopt "the principle of preemption," as outlined in their report and made a part of the Israeli 1996 study. Indeed, that principle served as the basis for attacking Iraq. Now it can serve to invade Syria. All that is needed is the threat as outlined above. Congressmen friendly to Israel, including Rep. Eliot L. Engel, D-NY, Senators Rick Santorum (PA) and Barbara Boxer (CA) are already moving to force sanctions on Syria, a first step in the acceptance of the arguments that allow for a preemptive strike. The simple arrangement of an "unprovoked" attack by Syria against Israel or an Israeli interest will be stimulus enough to "justify" invasion.

In a letter to the President, dated April 3, 2002, five months before the National Security Strategy Policy Report was issued as the guiding document for the Bush administration's foreign policy, Perle, Daniel Pipes, Norman Podhoretz, William Kristol, William Bennett and many others from the New American Century Project, wrote:

> No one should doubt that the United States and Israel share a common enemy. We are both targets of what you have correctly called an "Axis of Evil." Israel is targeted in part because it is our friend, and in part because it is an island of liberal, democratic [sic] principles—American principles—in a sea of tyranny, intolerance, and hatred.

As Secretary of Defense Rumsfeld has pointed out, Iran, Iraq, and Syria are all engaged in "inspiring and financing a culture of political murder and suicide bombing" against Israel, just as they have aided campaigns of terrorism against the United States over the past two decades. You have declared war on international terrorism, Mr. President, Israel is fighting the same war.

Even if we overlook the obsequious drivel in this letter and the omitted realities of Israeli behavior under Sharon, who has made a hallmark of state-run terrorism, we can see that Israel's interests as promulgated by Perle and Wolfowitz have been transferred to America. Indeed, Israel is being targeted for terrorist actions precisely because it is a friend of the US. Therefore, it follows that the US has a responsibility for defending Israel. To that end, Perle and company demanded that "...the United States should lend its full support to Israel...(and) we urge you to accelerate plans for removing Saddam Hussein from power in Iraq."

Nowhere do these Israeli advocates mention that Israel alone in the Mid-East has known weapons of mass destruction including Lithium-6 or nuclear capability in the neighborhood of 200 bombs. Nowhere do they mention that the argument against Iraq for defying UN resolutions can be leveled as well at Israel, including the most recent resolution of this month, voted 50-1 with the US voting against the resolution, condemning Israel for "mass killing" of Palestinians and for its settlement policy. Nowhere do they tell the truth about Israeli Democracy that exists for Jews but not to the same extent for Arabs and certainly not for Palestinians. Nowhere do they explain that America's forces, its sons and daughters and American tax dollars, are being used to effect Israel's interests as laid out in the "Securing the Realm" report. Nowhere do they mention that it is Sharon's savage policies that have made America a pariah in the Arab world because of its unswerving support for his vengeful, retaliatory attacks against incarcerated Palestinians in refugee camps surrounded by tanks and barbed wire.

In brief, the Wolfowitz/Perle coalition have managed to have the United States achieve the first of their desired goals for Israel: the elimination of Saddam Hussein. Israel seems prepared to use

US forces again to remove Syria and then Iran. For the US to become a mercenary force for Israel because a few persistent Neo-Con fanatics have managed to corral America's foreign policy, threatens the very premise of our Democracy just as it threatens the security of our citizens who become the victims of those who decry the imperialist direction the current administration has designed for America.

13

The Star-Crossed Lives of Ali Abbas and Donald Rumsfeld

[May 7, 2003]

"War causes many mysterious things, unexplainable by Rabbis, Priests, or Kings."

In 1991, Ismaeel and Azhar Abbas celebrated the birth of their first son, Ali Ismaeel, an event that had great significance in their lives. The proud parents could now look to a future that held great promise, since the Gulf War had ended on March 3, and Azhar's pregnancy had survived the bombing; she brought forth a healthy and beautiful boy. They named him Ali, a name that commemorated the great Shi'ite prophet and honored Azhar's family, since it was her family's surname. He was given his father's name as well, Ismaeel, which means "God heareth," after the son of Abraham and Hagar, the father of all Semites. Ismaeel was the son who wandered into foreign lands and went to the place where Mecca was to rise, and where his descendants flourished throughout Arabia.

Ali, of course, knew nothing of the Gulf War or the 40 days of bombing or the sanctions that gripped his country during the first decade of his life. His family, like 60% of the Iraqi people, depended on UN humanitarian aid to survive. But his father and mother kept these humiliations from him since they wanted him to flourish and succeed as he grew into manhood. Ali played in the streets outside his home in the small town of Al Zafariya, a short distance from the capital, Baghdad. He yearned to be a soldier when he grew up, the way many young boys in every country desire to don the brass buttoned uniform bedecked with ribbons and medals and epaulets.

That same year, 1991, 6,000 miles away, in Washington DC, Donald Rumsfeld, Paul Wolfowitz, and Richard Perle worked assiduously on a report for their boss, the Secretary of Defense, Dick Cheney. That document, the Defense Policy Guidance Report, was prepared for the President of the United States, George H. W. Bush, who, unfortunately, never had an opportunity to adopt it since he lost the 1992 election to Bill Clinton. But the report did not molder on a shelf in some Defense Department office; it became the National Strategy Policy Report of the second Bush administration in September of 2002. The document contained unique ideas, at least unique for a democratic government, since it advocated, indeed assumed as a right, the use of preemptive strikes against any nation determined by the administration to be a "threat" to America whether or not that nation had taken any belligerent action against the US and whether or not the administration could produce evidence of such intent.

The report listed Iraq as a nation that posed such a threat. Hence, as soon as the Bush Junior administration received appointment to the Presidency by the Supreme Court, it moved to take action against Iraq. However, until the atrocity of 9/11, the administration could not muster interest in the Congress or in the military for such preemptive action. Following 9/11, and following the aborted attempt to capture those truly guilty of that devastation, the administration turned its full attention to Iraq. Fearing a crucial loss at the polls in the fall of 2002, Karl Rove forced the administration to resurrect the lie that Iraq had connections to Al Qaeda and Osama bin Laden. The second war against Iraq was underway.

During the Clinton years, little Ali grew up in the dusty streets, attended school where he excelled in geography, went with his parents to the Mosque, played soccer, hassled his younger brother, and was spoiled by his sisters. As he ran to school, the neighbors marveled at how nimbly he moved with his black curly hair flying in the wind, his deep brown eyes sparkling in the sunlight, his arms waving at his friends, and his voice filled with joy and merriment. Many of his friends, the schoolmates of those early years, disappeared; he did not know why. But we know why. These were the years of US-led sanctions that prevented medical and food supplies from reaching the Iraqi people. A half million children died as a consequence. But Ali survived and his parents were proud.

Back in Washington, Donald Rumsfeld went to war. He headed the Department of Defense, and he and his colleagues Perle, Wolfowitz, and Cheney, were determined to attack Iraq. They needed no reason other than their determination to act. They did not need UN authorization, and they did not need the approval of the people's representatives or the people. They had designed and written the new American foreign policy and they were in power. They took to the airways to assert their pseudo-evidence; they issued commands to the mainstream media about how to present the lies they advanced; they forced a compliant Congress to stifle civil liberties. They bought or coerced any government too small to object, and they mocked both the UN and any significant government that objected to their war. It was their way or no way. The UN was cast aside. Pan America was on the move. Iraq became the Poland of the Bush regime; it suffered "shock and awe" as the *blitzkrieg* moved ineluctably to devastate that crippled nation. The wave of bombings, greater by far than that hurtled at Iraq in 1991, the year Ali was born, began and has not stopped to this day.

On March 30, at 1 AM, a missile slammed through the door of Ali's home. He had been put to sleep that night by his mother who feared, even as she tucked the blanket around his small frame, that the bombs could come closer to Al Zafariya any time now, since the roar of the planes and the movement of the ground had intensified with each night of bombing. But she also knew the Americans claimed they were targeting only military sites and not civilians. She knew and felt Ali's fear as she kissed him that night and left him in the hands of Allah.

At his daily news conference, daily since the war began, Donald Rumsfeld, touted as the "Rock idol" of the Bush administration, the "sex symbol, the new hunk of home-front airtime" moved swiftly, confidently to the podium with his puppet, General Myers, in tow. He delivered prepared remarks noting how "surgical" the precision bombing of this campaign had been to date, how few civilians had been killed by contrast with other wars, and how actual numbers of civilian deaths were impossible to come by. Then he took questions from the assembled reporters, refusing to answer some of the questions because, as he noted, "I could, but I won't"; his engaging squinty-eyed grin declaring his superiority as he toyed with his audience.

Ali woke briefly that morning hearing the strident voice of his Aunt Jameira calling for help, and then all was silence until he woke the next day in the Al Kindi Hospital. Dr. Rahim Methaur al Kinat and Chief Surgeon Mowafak Gabrielle had to explain to Ali what had happened. But how do you tell a child that his mother and father, and his younger brother, had all been killed when that missile blew into their home and incinerated all inside? How do you tell the child that he no longer has arms or hands? How do you explain the crushing feel of his body that clamps down on his small frame because he has no skin left, that it has been burned off like an apple peel? How do you tell him how he is to live tomorrow without the hands and arms that were to carry the rifle or make the salute as he stood in that radiant uniform he had dreamt about just the other night? How do you look into those deep brown eyes that glowed with joy just yesterday, and tell him he is an orphan and all his dreams and hopes and expectations were obliterated by that same bomb that burned his parents and his brother? How do you explain to him, as Omar Ocean of Tunbridge Wells, Kent wrote, "How can we explain to this innocent child that it was for his own good his family has been taken away from him, and his life destroyed?"

Who will tell Donald Rumsfeld that his war, planned in 1991, snuffed out the family of an innocent boy who had done him no harm, had threatened him no ill will, had lived, and dreamed and prayed that their son might thrive in a world better than the one they had endured? How do you tell Donald Rumsfeld that he snuffed out the expectations of life for a boy who had never left the confines of his home town, who knew nothing of the Donald Rumsfeld who destroyed his life, who did not know this same Donald Rumsfeld had been a partner of Saddam Hussein, the demon dictator he now decried, as he prepared for war against his neighbor Iran?

How do you tell Donald Rumsfeld that his privileged life left him blind to human feeling, that his cold, calculating intellect has turned him to stone as Hawthorne has described of those who lose feeling for their fellow humans and calculate their life as statistics to be placed in the collateral damage column? How do you tell Donald Rumsfeld that his expressed regret for civilian casualties and the efforts taken to avoid them are so many words devoid of meaning to those who walk the streets on crutches or stumble blindly through the rest of their days or beg for others to feed them since they have no arms or hands to care for themselves?

How do you explain to the Donald Rumsfelds of the world that they create the star-crossed lives emblazoned in Ali's pathetic plight, that the meetings they hold to design their world obliterates the world for people they have never met? How do you explain to those so arrogant they know only of their own superior might, that all who walk this earth have equal rights to bathe in the heat of the sun and share the bounty of its harvest? How do you explain to the Rumsfelds of the world that they cannot uphold the values of the Constitution by obliterating it with thousands upon thousands of bombs, by isolating America from the community of nations, and by forcing a personal and distorted vision on all the peoples of the earth?

So may we ask as Robert Frost did of the spider and the moth: What had Ali to do with Rummy's war against the ancient land of Ismaeel, God's own? What brought these two together from so far; what but design of darkness to appall?

War causes many mysterious things, unexplainable by Rabbis, Priests, or Kings.

14

Road to Nowhere: The US Is Not a Neutral Party

[May 24, 2003]

As Colin Powell shuttles from place to place and person to person around the Mid-East, as he qualifies more and more the details and purpose of the touted roadmap to peace in Israel and Palestine, as he runs into ruts and berms, snubbing and insults, it becomes obvious that the roadmap is flawed, the touted peace a mirage, and its true purpose a rouse to make evident the need for total military control of the area.

The cartographer's craft exists to provide a clear rendering of a geographic area that enables users to find their way. A roadmap makes movement from one point to another obvious. It removes uncertainty, avoids obstacles to progress, and identifies the final goal. The roadmap Colin Powell carries in his pocket, coffee stained, wrinkled and torn, does none of these things. No end goal is identified; no obstacle is avoided; no certainty exists. It unfolds a road to nowhere.

The Bush roadmap makes two things very clear (and it makes this clear to Arab and European countries if not to the US): solving the crisis in Palestine must take priority over all other foreign policy matters, and all attempts to solve the crisis through the current Israeli government and the Palestinian Authority are doomed to failure.

The current crisis in Palestine exists because of events that transpired in 1947 and prior to that date leading to the partitioning of Palestine by UN Resolution and the failure of the British Mandate. One could argue the crisis can be traced to the political Zionist movement created in 1897, an effort to design and implement a Jewish State in all of Palestine, South Lebanon and the Golan Heights. To affect this goal an ethnic cleansing would have to be undertaken. The first serious effort to achieve that goal happened in 1947/8 when more than 700,000 Palestinians had to flee their homes; that group and their descendants, now numbering over a million, have yet to return.

For Arabs, this Palestinian Diaspora and the subsequent homelessness for the people for over fifty years, the lopsided financial and military support of the United States for Israel, averaging (according to Richard Curtiss in "Washington Reports on Middle East Affairs") approximately $23,240.00 dollars per American taxpayer each year, the invasion of Afghanistan and Iraq, the storage of US military hardware in Saudi Arabia and Kuwait, the American armed forces presence in these Arab countries, the presence of Sharon who is remembered for his massacre of the inhabitants of Kibbya in 1953 and subsequent atrocities against Arabs, and the threats implicit in the "New American Century Project Report" and "The National Security Strategy Policy Report" of September 2002—both of which contain implied invasions of Syria and Iran and the forceful removal of Hamas and Hizballah from Palestine and Lebanon—the potential control of the Mid-East, through the domination of US forces and Israeli presence, is inevitable and ultimately destructive of their existence.

The European community of nations, observing this same scenario, sees the control of energy sources that will fuel their economy in the future under the jurisdiction of America and Israel. That threatens not only their independence economically, but puts the dollar and the euro on a collision course. The disequilibria created by the American presence in the Mid-East and the aggressive nature of the Sharon government towards Syria and Iran as that government, through its Ambassador Daniel Ayalon in Washington last month, asserts the need for regime change in these countries because they are a threat to Israel, causes Europeans to find the resulting uncertainty unacceptable to their future interests. Add to this the Asian perspective that sees the American and Israeli dominance in the Mid-East a threat to their hegemony and future growth, and the need to immediately address the Israeli/Palestinian crisis is evident.

But the roadmap calls for Israel and the Palestinian Authority to work out the solution despite the reality that Israel distrusts the Europeans and the Palestinians distrust the Americans. The roadmap avoids all reference to the causes of the conflict and thereby avoids solving them; in that reality lies its deception and its demise. Consider the causes: 55% of the land occupied by an indigenous population of Arabs for over a thousand years given by an external organization, the UN through a non-binding General Assembly Resolution, to a predominantly immigrant group belonging to the same religion and, purportedly descendents of Abraham, without the acceptance of that resolution by the indigenous population; the forceful eviction by fear or arms of more than 700,000 of that population in 1947/8, making them refugees in other lands; the non-payment of recompense to those so deposed and no acknowledgement of their rights of return which are guaranteed by the Universal Declaration of Human Rights and Resolution of 1948; the forceful occupation of all but 22% of the indigenous population land area after the 1967 war; and the confinement of the majority of the population into two areas, the West Bank and Gaza—where they must live under the occupation of the Israeli military.

If these are the reasons why the roadmap is doomed to fail from the perspective of the Palestinians, and these reasons do not include the devastation and havoc that have been the hallmark of these last two years of invasion and occupation by the Sharon government, then the recent remarks by Benyamin Elon, a minister in Ariel Sharon's government, should make clear that Israel has no intentions of abiding by the roadmap. Speaking in Washington and reported in the *New York Times* May 18, Elon argued that Palestinians must be convinced that the proper place for a Palestinian State is in Jordan and that all of Palestine properly belongs to the Jews because they were given the land by God.

Considering that Sharon's current government hinges on two religious parties that proclaim openly their refusal to permit the existence of a Palestinian State, it does not take a genius to understand that this is not the government that can bring peace to Palestine.

It should be evident that peace cannot come through the roadmap or through the control of the process by the Bush administration, or through the cooperative efforts of Sharon and a shill appointed for the Palestinian Authority acceptable to Sharon.

The recent spurt of terrorist activity in Israel, Morocco, Chechnya, and Iraq suggests not only the resurrection of an active Al-Qaeda but the intensification of the forces allied against the touted roadmap for peace—fabricated by a coalition of outsiders that has no ostensible authority to hobble together a plan for those under the boot of an occupying force or the occupiers. Putting aside the mythological rationale that has emerged from the Christian and Jewish Zionists that grants all of Judea and Samaria to the Jews through a covenant with Yahweh, the reality of the current Jewish State is a creation of the United Nations in consort with the United States principally, and, politically through Harry Truman, who could count on Jewish votes but had no expectation of Palestinian ones. In short, it is the UN's responsibility to address the crisis, not that of the United States or Russia or Europe.

On what basis can this be done? We have the precedent: nation states that defy UN resolutions must be brought before the UNSC to account for their defiance. Both Israel and Palestine, through UN recognition of the Palestinian Authority, have defied UN resolutions, including the most recent passed 50-1 in April of this year, and more than the number defied by Iraq. Indeed, many of the UNSC and UNGA resolutions call upon Israel to return to the pre-1967 borders and for the Palestinians to recognize the rights of Israelis. Many of these resolutions require that both sides accept the Human Rights provisions of the Geneva Accords that they have flaunted for many years. Many condemn the incessant mass killings of innocent civilians by both sides.

In short, the proper authority and appropriate process already exist to bring this crisis to a halt. The introduction of UN forces between the antagonists would be the first step. It would remove the US as the dominant but flawed power because it is aligned with one of the antagonists and seen, by Palestinians and Arabs alike, as an enemy of the other. It would remove both competing powers, the Sharon government and the administration of Arafat, from futile attempts to determine who goes first, who determines when violence has ceased, who ratifies that step one has been completed and its time to move on to step two, and what compromises need to be cobbled together to create an impossible peace.

The Sharon government has adamantly refused to let the UN become involved. One can understand why: Sharon has no desire or intent to return any of the land taken by Israel in the '67 war; indeed, it would seem from the remarks made by Elon that Israel's intent is to take all the lands identified by the Bible as belonging to the Jews, and, hence extra judicial and "accidental" killings of innocent Palestinians will continue indefinitely. Israel, for example, continues its aggressive pace against the Palestinians, especially in its demolition program that has displaced more than 12,737 people since September of 2000 while the killing rate has increased to 2350. Recognizing the political power that the Christian Zionists hold over the Bush administration and their alignment with the Jewish Zionists, the probability that the Bush administration could force the divestment of these lands or stop the military occupation and slaughter of the Palestinians is beyond credibility.

Conversely, any expectation that Hamas or Hizballah will relinquish their embedded desires to reclaim the lands of their forefathers and, consequently, force the removal of the Israeli State, is equally remote. The continued harassment and wanton slaughter of innocent Israeli citizens will continue indefinitely. The struggle seen from the eyes of the Palestinian fanatic turns on the same spit as that which drives the fanatical right in Israel, a righteous and violent interpretation of their respective scriptures. Mustapha Mohammed quotes the Qur'an 5:82, "You will surely find that the people with the most hatred and enmity toward the believers are the Jews and the Polytheists..." And he goes on to say, "Don't you realize what Allah is telling you? Don't you realize that our struggle against the Zionist is a struggle of religious identity?"

Here is a call to arms to aid the helpless brothers and sisters and children "buried under the rubble of their demolished homes with American weapons." How can an "Authority" stop this insane drive to destruction?

If the primary causes of this prolonged and agonizing crisis are to be addressed, the nations of the world through the UN must step in and assert control. This effort must begin with all the nations of the world in the General Assembly, then move to France and China with the support of the EU and the Arab states in the Security Council. The United States must be removed from the process as a principal because it lacks credibility as a disinterested party. In addition, the United States is currently under the control of a few men who have hijacked its Democracy. They seek nothing less than universal control of the world that will be governed according to the dictates of this "cabal." They have no desire to bring an end to their "age of endless war." The means to accomplish this goal resides in "The National Security Strategy Policy Report," the guiding foreign policy document of the Bush administration. Both Israel and the Palestinian Authority, acting on behalf of the Palestinian people, must also be removed as parties responsible for bringing about a solution because both have defied UN resolutions and both continue to demonstrate no desire to relinquish their destructive ends toward each other.

Only the principal power that brought the crisis to a head, then subsequently removed itself from engagement in the area, can alleviate the causes that have devastated so many lives and threaten the continued destruction of many more. Only the UN is in a position to bring stability to this area of the world and bring the "peace that passeth understanding" to those who worship the one god who, in their mythical stories, gives meaning to this land. Only the UN can prevent the powerful and divisive special interests from selfishly devastating a land so vital to all nations and all peoples.

15

Defining Terrorism from the Top Down: Bush and Sharon as Terrorists

[June 16, 2003]

Blair's refusal to acquiesce to Sharon's demands to sideline Arafat, signals a recognition that sidelining one terrorist who has limited capacity to stop Hamas, pales by comparison with Sharon's total control of the IOF and other renegade Israeli terrorist groups. Sharon's current trip to visit Blair and Bush, a calculated attempt to needle his bedfellows to control European governments' recognition of Arafat, is designed to force them to snub the democratically elected Arafat who is preventing the implementation of the roadmap while Sharon appears to be the man of peace. Needless to say, Sharon's insidious support of the settlements and his terrorist acts as he removes troops from the occupied territories stamps him as the obstacle in the road to peace. Sharon's trip follows President Bush's recent demand made to the EU ministers in Washington, that they declare Hamas a terrorist organization and take action to interrupt its economic activities—a demand that found little support among EU representatives.

The issue is complex because the definition of 'terrorist' is not precise. Indeed, the very actions condemned by Bush about Hamas are actions that other nations find condemnatory about Bush. Terrorism is as terrorism does, or so one would think. Dictionary definitions reflect a consensus in meaning at a point in time. But definitions become the prerogative of those in power when it is in their interest to impose parameters on words that impact policy direction. To the victor belongs meaning and historical perspective. Thus it is with the words 'terrorism', 'terrorist' and 'terrorize'. To terrorize, according to the dictionary, means, "to dominate or coerce by intimidation." A 'terrorist' is one who attempts to dominate and coerce by intimidation, and 'terrorism' is "a method of resisting a government."

These definitions incriminate Osama bin Laden and the undeclared leaders of Hamas, Islamic Jihad, and Hezbollah, but they also incriminate the ultra-right Zionists in Israel, and, one could argue, the hard-right Evangelical Zionists in America. More tellingly, and this is the point of this article, they incriminate the United States under Bush, and Israel under Sharon. Obviously, our government cannot allow the consensus meaning to reflect the actuality. Therefore, the United States defines terrorism (18 USC 2331) as "violent acts or acts dangerous to human life that... appear to be intended (i) to intimidate or coerce a civilian population; (ii) to influence the policy of a government by intimidation or coercion; (iii) to affect the conduct of a government by assassination or kidnapping."

Although the dictionary definition is open-ended, allowing for the possibility of governments to be active in terrorist activities, the USC definition does not. The most recent Encarta encyclopedia article describing terrorism is quite specific on this point: "These violent acts are committed by nongovernmental groups or individuals—that is, by those who are neither part of or officially serving in the military forces..." This description precedes the historical evolution of the word that marks its origin during the French Revolution (1789-1799), the *regime de la terreur* (Reign of Terror), a quite specific reference to a government!

In his most recent book, *The Lessons of Terrorism* (2003), Caleb Carr defines terrorism as "simply the contemporary name given to, and the modern permutation of, warfare deliberately waged against civilians with the purpose of destroying their will to support either leaders or policies that the agents of such violence find objectionable." Interestingly, Carr does not excuse armed forces or units of a nation from the definition. Indeed, Carr includes in his understanding of terrorist the likes of Thomas "Stonewall" Jackson, William Tecumseh Sherman, Richard Nixon, and Henry Kissinger, to name a few. Each of these individuals supported deliberate and premeditated attacks against civilians. Carr's historical survey of terrorism, written in response to current world wide terrorist activity, is decidedly more inclusive than the government definition.

Why be concerned with the definition of a word? The answer is simple. By excluding governments and nation-states from the definition, the ruling powers can inflict corrosive and pejorative terms on those opposing them; thereby justifying any actions they use to subdue their enemy.

Hatred, revenge, greed, and insecurity propel terrorists to act; all four motivations characterize the behavior of nation-states as well as individuals and groups. To exclude nation-states from the definition is to accept terrorist behavior against civilians and ultimately to justify it. That is the case with the Bush administration's acquiescence to the Sharon government's terrorism against the Palestinians. It also allows Bush to lie to the American people to incite them to invading another nation that is of no threat to them—and to intentionally inflict harm, including death, on innocent civilians.

Exclusion of nation-states allows for simplistic judgments on those who oppose government action by labeling dissenters as "anti-government," as in "anti-Semitic" or "anti-American" or "unpatriotic," thus avoiding analysis of the government's actions by blanket condemnation. Indeed, the power of the respective governments, that of Sharon and Bush, to silence criticism and marginalize vocal dissenters is well-documented and only points to the need to keep the issue alive.

For the past six months, criticism of Israeli IDF actions against civilians in Gaza and the West Bank has increased exponentially as reported in British, French, and Greek newspapers, and in *Ha'aretz*. *Ha'aretz* has condemned this reaction as "rising anti-Semitism." The nature of the criticism, however, is not against the Jewish people, but against the kinds of actions taken by the Sharon forces against civilians. These actions can only be labeled as "terrorist" acts.

Consider the recent actions taken by Sharon against the Palestinian people. These deliberate, provocative acts have predetermined consequences designed to intimidate and coerce the people to relinquish their rights to their homeland and livelihood. They are acts that force another government to accept the perpetrator's intended goal; that other government is the United States and the goal is the erosion of the "roadmap" and the acquisition of additional land, belonging to the Palestinians, to the state of Israel. The *Jerusalem Post* reported on April 8:

> The construction of over a dozen Jewish enclaves in predominantly Arab neighborhoods in East Jerusalem is aimed at blocking any possibility of dividing Jerusalem in the future."

Edward Sheehan reports in the *New York Review* on June 5:

> Israeli settlements in eastern suburbs effectively detach the Palestinian West Bank from Jerusalem. The final result of this strategy "will be the transformation of Arab Jerusalem into a ghetto and slum."

Earlier this spring, *Tikkun* magazine provided its readers with an inventory of terrorist behaviors by the Sharon government. There are too many to list here but they include: awakening residents in the town of Beit Lahiya in the middle of the night, over two hundred, "including small children and women who had given birth two days earlier were forced to huddle together for hours in the cold winter night until the army let them return to their homes"; "preventing the residents of entire cities from leaving their houses for weeks on end (no exceptions—not for chemo, dialysis, childbirth, buying food, attending school, or visiting your sick mother)"; damaging ambulances; assassinating "people without the niceties of trial and due process; killing children including infants and toddlers, etc."

These kinds of behaviors brought condemnation on Sharon's government by Bishop Tutu; he likened Israel's treatment of Palestinians to the oppression of blacks by the white apartheid government in South Africa. He added, "I can't believe the United States really believes in its impotence" to halt Israel's military reprisals.

Sheehan's recent report details Israeli actions and their consequences to the people. "I visited the town of Beit Hanoun... the army... destroyed twenty-five water wells and the sewage system, which resulted in drinking water being mixed with raw sewage." "Paved roads were broken up by Israeli bulldozers;

great tracks of farmland—citrus groves, olive trees, greenhouses as well—were uprooted to create no man's lands around the Israeli settlements of Alai Sinai, Nevets Sala, and Nissanit." Such actions force civilians to move from their homes either because they have been destroyed or because their source of livelihood has been destroyed.

These are terrorist acts.

Sharon's savagery against the Palestinian people has given rise to reactions in France, Germany, and Greece, especially Greece, and to the anticipated condemnation of these reactions as anti-Semitic. The European Union's Greek presidency "condemned the Israeli raid on Tulkarem and Ein Shams refugee camp last week, where at least 1000 Palestinians were detained and prevented from going back to their homes..." *Ha'aretz* condemned the Greek papers for reporting Sharon's actions as comparable to those of the Nazis against the Jews, the image of Israel as a "Nazi country..." that attacks "...defenseless Palestinians."

The article in *Ha'aretz* does not attempt a comparison that might suggest to the Greeks and others how similar the actions of the Sharon government are to those of Nazi Germany. This past March, at an international conference on human evil, held in Prague, Professor Karen Doerr compared the terminology used by the Germans to that used by Sharon and the Zionist forces in Israel. The Germans "evacuated" and "resettled" the Jews; the Israelis "transfer" and "resettle" the Palestinians. The Nazis used the term "selection" to choose a concentration inmate for murder; Sharon uses "extrajudicial execution." The Germans detained Jews in "work camps"; Sharon uses Palestinian "territories" and only recently added, "occupied" territories. The Nazis had a "final solution" to their problem with the Jews; Sharon adopted "terrorists" following 9/11, a term used generally about the Palestinian people since they are guilty of harboring terrorists, to signify those he had to eliminate.

Language always suffers from those who wish to camouflage the reality of their actions. Israeli forces make "incursions," never invasions, into Palestinian territories; they assault to "flush out" top fugitives, they do not assassinate; helicopter gun ships "exchange fire" with Palestinian gunmen, they don't attack with overwhelming force; Arafat is "confined" to his compound, not imprisoned; he could be "expelled" from

Palestine, never deported or forcefully removed from office by an occupying power; tanks "roll" into the territories, they do not crush and destroy homes and vineyards. Such is the abuse of language.

Is it not possible, then, to understand the reaction of people sitting outside Israel, witnessing the actions of the Sharon government and his IOF as they devastate a defenseless population? Are not these actions comparable to those used by the Nazis? Is not the walling in of the Palestinians with the cement fence and electrified wires, the destruction of water wells and diversion of others to Israeli use, the rounding up of Palestinian civilians in the night, the assassination without trial of leaders of those oppressed, the humiliation and dehumanization of the people, the forceful taking of their means of livelihood, the intentional intimidation of civilians, are not these actions comparable to those of the Nazis against the innocent Jews in Germany? If the ultimate purpose of Sharon's government is the eradication of the Palestinian people, not by use of gas chambers, but by forced removal, euphemistically called "transferal" from their land through intimidation including incremental killings, then the comparison, like that made by Bishop Tutu to the apartheid regime in South Africa, is apt.

This is not condemnation of the Jewish people but of their government that acts in their name. For Americans, who must live with the Bush administration's acquiescence of Sharon's slaughter paid for by their tax dollars, the dilemma is the same: dissent and be damned as un-American, or stay silent and be the means of support for terrorism.

Ran HaCohen writes of the "Hebron terrorists," the fanatical Jewish settlers who "ransack Palestinian shops, cut electricity lines and water pipes, wreck cars, and attack schoolchildren," that they are a "criminal gang actively nurtured by the State," a group of 450 protected by 4000 Israeli troops. This is terrorism defended and accepted by the state.

How effective is this terrorism? "So far, the junta's policy has proven quite effective," according to HaCohen. "Driven away by economic strangulation and fear of settlers' violence, the population of 12,000 Palestinians who inhabited Hebron's Old City has dwindled to 5,000 souls since the division of the city in 1997." That is premeditated intimidation and coercion of

civilians, the very definition of terrorism, done by the state of
Israel supported by the Bush administration.

Hamas has been condemned by the Bush and Sharon administrations for using bombs strapped around the body as terrorism against innocent civilians, and indeed they are. Yet these
same men find the use of "flechette" bullets that scatter pellets
of death into multiple civilians, legitimate weapons to use
against Palestinians. They find no problems using missiles fired
into crowded city streets or the use of cluster bombs in Iraq as
legitimate weapons of war. Both accept as legitimate weapons
for use in civilian areas high altitude bombing whether from
F-16s or Apache helicopters. Yet such use anticipates civilian
deaths and is, therefore, deliberate slaughter and cannot even be
placed in the category of "collateral damage." The day Sharon
left Washington, having conferred his blessings on Bush, Israeli
tanks again fired into a crowded Gaza neighborhood in Rafah
and killed six civilians, including children. This is terrorism.

Even as the Israeli military moved out of Beit Hanoun on July 1,
2003 to begin the process that would bring into existence the
"roadmap," they "leveled dozens of homes and factories, tore
up roads and uprooted trees," according to the *Guardian*. Why?
For "security" reasons. That's why they destroyed 1,000 acres
of citrus trees!

"Security" says it all; it is the cover word for terrorist actions.
Bush uses the same word to detain hundreds of men who have
never been charged with a crime and never had access to a
lawyer. These are the actions of a terrorist state.

Why is it that these two men can act like terrorists and not be
condemned for it? Because a definition has been designed that
excludes them as heads of state and terrorism cannot be applied
to states. Therein lies the power of words. But the world has not
been fooled. Consider the UN resolutions condemning Israel for
such acts: 252 (1968) calling on Israel to rescind measures that
change the legal status of Jerusalem, including the expropriation
of land and properties; 446 (1979) calling upon Israel to abide
by the Geneva Convention regarding the responsibilities of
occupying powers, especially "not to transport parts of its civilian population into occupied Arab territories"; 465 (1980) calling on Israel to cease construction of settlements in Arab
territories; 471 (1981) calling on Israel to prosecute those

involved in assassination attempts of West Bank leaders; 799 (1992) calling upon Israel "to reaffirm the Fourth Geneva Convention in all occupied territories since 1967, including Jerusalem, and affirms that deportation of civilians constitutes a contravention of its obligations under the convention"; 1405 (2002) calling on Israel to allow UN inspectors to "investigate civilian deaths during an Israeli assault on the Jenin refugee camp"; 1435 (2002) calling on Israel to withdraw to positions of September 2000 and end its military activities in and around Ramallah, including the destruction of security and civilian infrastructure; and these are only a few. These resolutions describe terrorist activities, activities supported by the Bush administration, including vetoing such resolutions.

Given the severity of the actions challenged by the UN, one would think Bush would rush to the UN demanding that Israel be brought before it for defying its resolutions, something he used as a "gimmick" to take his "war" to Iraq. But deception and hypocrisy are the *modus operandi* of this administration, not openness, honesty, and reason.

Clearly, Bush's demands to the EU ministers in Washington to declare Hamas a terrorist organization fell on deaf ears because they have been involved in the development of the resolutions listed above. They know the terrorism perpetrated by Sharon and Bush and would find condemning Hamas, a complicated organization that provides humanitarian relief to Palestinians as well as militant activity against the occupying forces of Israel, a gesture in the wind. The beginning of the end of terrorism starts with regime change in Israel and Washington.

16

The Scourge of Hopelessness: Life in a Bifurcated World

[June 21, 2003]

"But modern industrial warfare may well be leading us, with each technological advance, a step closer to our own annihilation."

—Chris Hedges, *War Is a Force that Gives Us Meaning*

Each day the newspapers carry stories from Israel and Iraq describing another IDF or US soldier shot; each day another story about the failed roadmap for peace and the failed promise for Iraqi freedom. Each day we witness America becoming mired in the tar baby that has been the day-to-day experience of Israel for fifty years. Each day the strong arm of vengeance sticks in the tar baby's gut, accomplishing nothing but proximity to more pain and suffering.

Brother Remus told that tar baby story to the plantation owner's son, a story with a long history in Africa, a story of wiliness and endurance, twin traits that enable the oppressed to survive the bitterness of occupation. Would that the "Man" had heeded the truth embedded in that tale. But the oppressor is addicted to his myths of superiority, to his beliefs in only his righteousness, and to his obligation to bring his freedom and his advanced civilization to the inferior people he oppresses. Such is the blindness that afflicts those who see through the lens of force.

Hedges' observation embodies the developed nation's talisman, the power of its technology to conquer, to impose its will, to subdue a people, to exploit its resources, all to advance its own agenda: the hording of more wealth to its ruling class. But that ruling class is blind, not just to the tar baby, but also to the people it governs who suffer its stupidity.

Nothing is more frightening than to read Woodward's *Bush at War* and realize that no one in charge—not Cheney, not Rumsfeld, not Powell, not Rice, not Wolfowitz, not Tenet, not Black, not Ashcroft, no and not the President—asked the most fundamental question that glared through all the dust and twisted steel that had been the Twin Towers and the Pentagon: "Why would nineteen men incinerate themselves in the most glaringly symbolic structures of wealth and power erected by western civilization?" What is the primary cause of the "evil" we have seen visited upon us?

Perhaps the answer is so simple it could not be asked: "We are the cause, we the vested interests bought by wealth to the positions we hold, cannot afford to recognize or accept the devastation we have wrought on the hopeless and deprived of the world."

Israel blossomed fifty-five years ago, not into a reborn land flowing with milk and honey, but into a modern technological Goliath that mimics its ancient foes as it attempts to subdue the indigenous peoples of Palestine... not with the puny shields and swords of the Philistines, but with the tanks, helicopter warships, fighter jets, missiles, cluster bombs, and the ultimate and illusive weapons of mass destruction that give righteousness its almighty power.

For half a century, Israel used every arsenal of contemporary warfare to advance its goal to acquire the fabled lands of Judea and Samaria promised them by their mythical god 2500 years ago. The original fighters used terror tactics, massacres, and ethnic cleansing to advance their cause. The current government of Ariel Sharon, one of the original terrorists, uses laser guided missiles to annihilate individuals he has determined are terrorists, and any innocents who happen to be present when the technologically advanced instrument of death finds its way to its extrajudicial target. He and his coalition forces now control through illegal occupation 78% of Palestine and continue to defy the United Nations resolutions to return the land to its rightful owners. And they do this with the full approbation of their Godfather, the United States of America.

For the infliction of this oppression, Israel suffers the consequences of righteousness' two sided sword: the wily evil that festers in the soul of the oppressed, and the internal suffering that bleeds in the Jewish souls who find this use of force intolerable.

Yet the minority rule in Israel: the minority parties that coerce Sharon to stay the course or lose his seat of power; the minority cults of Zionist zeal that inhabit the illegal settlements; and the minority ruling class that controls the corporations and industries and hence the legislation that gives them the power to impose their will. It is that last that ultimately controls. The military-industrial complex that infects Israel infected the United States over fifty years ago and continues to infect its principles with the toxic lies of compassionate conservatism and compassionate globalization.

The incestuous relationship that exists between the US and Israel breeds ever larger technological children, bigger tanks, bigger missiles, better conceptualized bombs that eradicate more people and, most important, better protection for their military as they press the buttons of war sending death and destruction to unseen foes who might be, "God forbid," children or mothers or the sick, maimed or elderly, the accidental detritus of modern warfare.

That incestuous relationship provides protection for industries producing these advanced technological wonders, ensuring their continued existence despite the havoc they wreak on Israelis to say nothing of Palestinians. That same incest also breeds, for both Israel and the United States, an ever growing family of terrorists who find purpose in their collective fight against the oppressor, and release from their torment in the fanatical illusion that their God calls them to His cause: the destruction of the infidels. Ironically enough, the oppression imposed by Israel on the Palestinians is justified in the name of that same God's covenant with His people and their perceived illusion that they must defend that God against infidels as well. Illusion becomes the propellant of our technological advancement!

Indeed, the myths propel the addiction to slaughter and justify it! How else explain IDF soldiers "beating medical personnel and using them as human shields, taunting young children to throw rocks at their tanks so they could respond with live ammunition, forcing women with infants to stand for hours in the cold a few metres from their homes, destroying food and water systems, and firing heavy machine guns into residential streets and buildings." ["Our Humanity in the Balance," May 4, 2003, Moiseiwitisch, Murray, and Penland, *Winnipeg Free Press*]

How else explain IDF soldiers "urinating on school computers and defecating on the rugs of homes they have garrisoned for
use; accidentally demolishing the homes of innocent people that
happen to be near the homes deliberately destroyed... preventing the residents of entire cities from leaving their houses for
weeks on end; damaging 27 Palestinian ambulances beyond
repair and wounding 187 medical personnel; and assassinating
people without the niceties of trial and due process, not to mention reckless shootings in which 126 innocent children aged 13
or younger (including 19 toddlers and infants aged 5 or
younger!) have lost lives." [*Tikkun* on line, 3/4/03]

How else explain the behavior of Jewish settlers in Hebron
who "regularly attack Palestinian shops, cut electricity lines and
water pipes, wreck cars, and attack schoolchildren."

Or this:
Plans are underway for the construction of a "safe passage," a settlers' "promenade" that would link the settlement of Kiryat Arba on Hebron's eastern flank to the
Old City like a wedge thrust into the heart of the city,
confiscating 64 parcels of private Palestinian property
and razing at least 15 houses in its wake.

Or this:
Associated Press (20/12/02) and the Israeli daily *Yedioth
Achronot* have recently quoted Palestinians in Hebron
describing how "Israeli border police have forced
detainees to choose whether to have a nose, arm or leg
broken.
            —Ran HaCohen, "Hebron: City of Terror," 2/23/03

These are examples of the silent Sharon policies that allow for
the systematic harassment and killing of Palestinians and the
unseen erosion of their lands as Israel confiscates more and
more of what was the Palestinian state before 1948.

"You are leaving behind you a scorched land, a scorched
country, and you are mainly leaving behind you a scorched
people..." the opposition leader Yossi Sarid yelled as Sharon left
to meet with Bush last October 14. There are those who understand the consequences!

What, one asks in wonder, does adherence to these myths and scorched earth policies accomplish? Certainly and obviously not security for the Jewish people! Rather, it creates the scourge of desperation and hopelessness wrapped around the waist of the suicide bomber that plagues Israel, as decidedly as the locusts ravaged Egypt when the Jews were the enslaved! Why, one asks in wonder, does the oppressed take on the mantle of the oppressor with such vehemence that they become blind to the plight of the afflicted? Where, one asks in wonder, will it all end, or do we move ineluctably step by step closer, as Hedges states, to our own annihilation?

And what now of the United States, the incestuous relation that gives sustenance to Israel's Sharon and feeds his insatiable appetite for vengeance and retaliation? We see its fruition in Iraq as we take on the mantle of the oppressor, discarding the pseudo-garment of the liberator now that the oil and military positioning is in place. We read each day accounts of thousands demanding that the oppressor leave the country; we see the troops, our 20-year-old kids, disgorge from their armored vehicles to wade through angry crowds searching in vain for "terrorists" who, also in vain, attempt to inflict some damage on the oppressor whom they see as the "terrorist"; we read of our soldiers ambushed, wounded or killed; we hear stories, even after three months in occupation, of Americans kidnapping and raping Iraqi women, the beginning perhaps of the occupier's attitude about the inferior status of the oppressed.

We hear our beloved leaders decry the wily behavior of the oppressed who should be welcoming our presence, who proclaim our beneficence to those whom we have just bombed into submission. We watch in disbelief the Iraqi people, whose children are crippled because they picked up our cluster bombs thinking them toys, whose hospitals, museums, and libraries have been destroyed, whose natural resources have become the new-found wealth of the western oil companies, yea, we watch them condemn us as invaders and despoilers, the newest nation to attempt to colonize their country.

We have become the new Israel in the Mid-East and we will suffer the same fate not only in Iraq, but also in all the haunts that we inhabit around the world, and here at home. We have sunk our invader's arms into the tar baby of the Middle East without concern for the primary causes that have festered there for more than fifty years and given birth to so much animosity that Americans must hide from the rest of the world for their own protection. We, like Israel, will build walls around ourselves to ward out those whom we oppress, and wonder why it must be so.

Until and unless our leaders confront the primary causes of the world's anger against the west, no solution to our insecurity will arise. We will continue to pummel the tar baby helplessly despite our "modern industrial warfare" and, perhaps, because of it.

We live in a bifurcated world of the supremely rich and the absolutely deprived, of the aggressor and the oppressed, of those willing and able to exploit both humans and natural resources without compunction and those who suffer such pillage. Until and unless we confront head-on these realities, America's obsession with Pan Americana can only secure America's insecurity. The desperate wiliness of the oppressed and their indomitable will to endure has been the story of human history; there is no reason to believe it will change.

17

Moral Insanity: The Cabal That Corrupts

[August 27, 2003]

The recent interrogation of Paul Wolfowitz by a Senate committee and the recent babbling by Donald Rumsfeld at his press conference gives hope that our representatives and the mainstream media may have awakened to the destruction wrought by the Cabal on the American people. Both Senators Biden and Boxer hung Wolfowitz out to dry, condemning his unwillingness to provide adequate information on the cost of the on-going invasion of Iraq, his flippant responses to serious questions, and his duplicity in stating the case for the Iraq war in the first place.

Rumsfeld attempted to hide his ignorance behind his ever present sneer and his, at least in his own mind, witticisms that convey no information but demonstrate to any intelligent listener that he stands on air: In response to a query, "Are we closer to getting Saddam?" he responds with, "How do I know? We haven't got him, but when we do we'll know we have him," or words to that affect. If the matter were not so serious, one might enjoy his idiocy.

Much has been written about the Cabal that runs our government, the cult of little men who absconded with our Democracy, the tight knit myth-makers who designed a foreign policy that catapults America into a global empire and, then, mobilized about a "mythologized" Bush dynasty to make it a reality. These men, and they are all men, formed what might be called "The Cult of Strauss." They studied under or became disciples of Leo Strauss whose concepts regarding leadership and political domination became a template for their rise to power.

Leo Strauss, a Jewish political philosopher, taught at several American Universities between 1938 and 1973. Strauss specialized in Plato and Aristotle, but conveyed many of his ideas by citing the Weimar Republic that fell to the Nazis and resulted in the Jewish Holocaust. Strauss belittled the weak, liberal Weimar Republic's democratic values, charging that a secular Democracy is inherently weak since it depends on the importance of individualism with rights resident in each citizen.

Since Strauss found that rights were resident in those who were superior and had a right to rule over the weak, he did not condone Democracy as Americans know it. Furthermore, Strauss believed those who rule must realize that no morality exists, that nature alone determines who rules and who follows. Thus, determinism is the only "moral" value. Yet he also believed states needed religions to "glue" their people together in a fervent nationalism. Religion for Strauss is not dissimilar to Marx's "opium of the people," although he found it useful for the ruling class, not something to be abolished.

Jeffersonian Democracy did not sit well with Strauss; individualism, relativism, liberalism and dissent were not values to stress but to be suppressed. Those in power held power by using the glue religions provided by way of obedient supplicants and by deceiving the people they led and even the rulers for whom they worked.

Since societies needed strong rulers, any means to achieve control found acceptance. A secular society should be avoided at all costs; hence support for religion, albeit feigned, assured the rulers of obedient citizens ruled by the strong who would care for them. But to ensure control and to mobilize the people into an allegiance with those in power, rulers needed an enemy, even one that had to be fabricated if no real enemy existed. That is the logic for the war against Iraq and for perpetual war, the war against terrorism.

Cults tend to form about an authoritarian leader, one whose voice speaks for the group and whose ideas bridge no alternatives. Such leaders hearken only to their own muse; they live above the law because they conceive the source of the law to be beneath them. Strauss believed "that he alone had recovered the true, hidden message contained in the 'Great Tradition' of philosophy from Plato to Hobbes and Locke." [Karl Jahn, *Leo Strauss and the Straussians*, 2000]

That message, from the classical thinkers to the Enlightenment sages, revealed that there are no gods and, consequently, morals are a human prejudice without validity. Individuals, particularly those who are insecure, join cults in order to bathe in the reflected light of the leader, a person with ideas they themselves are incapable of conceiving. The Cult I refer to here does not represent what may be termed the "School of Straussianism," composed primarily of academics who espouse or critique Straussian political philosophy. The Wolfowitz group, a collection of men (often called neo-conservatives) who have garbed themselves in the aura of Americanism as the Project for the New American Century and the American Enterprise Institute, have attempted to put into practice what Straussian theory implied, using the secretive processes that are integral to the theory.

Cult concepts project a doomsday scenario most frequently based on an immanent Armageddon, a final battle between good and evil. Strauss projected a variant of the doomsday vision. He saw a brand of determinism controlling human life with some born to lead and the vast majority born to follow. His groupies, the cult of men who worshiped at his determinist altar—Paul Wolfowitz (Deputy Defense Secretary), Richard Perle (former Defense Policy Board Chairman), William Kristol (Chief Editor of the *Weekly Standard*), Gary Schmitt (Chairman and Director of the Project for the New American Century), Stephen Campone (Under-Secretary of Defense for Intelligence under Rumsfeld), Abram Shulsky (friend of Perle and head of Rumsfeld's special intelligence unit sometimes characterized as the "Specious Planning Unit"), Dick Cheney and Donald Rumsfeld who are connected through the PNAC—understood themselves to belong to the leader group and hence had an obligation to take control of America, while it stood at the apex of world power, by whatever means necessary if they were to fulfill their role in life.

These men rose to power in the first Bush regime. They consolidated their analysis of America's position in the world in a document designed and prepared for the second George H. W. Bush term, "The Defense Policy Report," prepared by the then Secretary of Defense, Dick Cheney, with help from the Cabal. When first exposed to the light of scrutiny in 1992, the document was ridiculed as "un-American," anti-Democratic, and fanciful. It deserved all three condemnations. Fortunately for

America, unfortunately for the Cabal, they were out of power when Bush senior lost to Bill Clinton.

But the Straussian Cult bided their time, awaiting the second coming of the Bush dynasty by forming the Project for the New American Century and creating the American Enterprise Institute. Both the Project and the Institute promulgated the foundational ideas expressed in "The Defense Policy Report": American pre-eminence in the world, protection of America's global economy, and a pre-emptive strike policy.

But members of the cult went a step further: they became advisors to Benjamin Netanyahu and the right-wing of Israeli politics. As such they prepared a document titled "A Clean Break: A New Strategy for Securing the Realm," issued 7/8/96, written by Richard Perle, James Colbert, Charles Fairbanks, Jr., Douglas Feith, Robert Lowenberg, David Wurmser, and Meyrav Wurmser. This report, although redesigned to reflect Israeli interests, contains the same concepts as those broached in the Defense Report.

In short, it yokes American and Israeli interests into one package, including pre-emptive strikes when needed, with special emphasis on Syria, the non-recognition of the PLO and Arafat, removal of the Saddam regime, and the use of deceptive ploys like weapons of mass destruction to legitimate military or political subversive action. Many of the Cult now owed allegiance to two masters, America and Israel.

But serving two masters does not undermine Straussian dogma, since Strauss accepted the reality that morals do not exist. There is only one natural right, "the right of the superior to rule over the inferior."[Jim Lobe, *Inter Press Service*, 5/8/03]

A year before 9/11, the Project for the New American Century issued a report titled "Rebuilding America's Defenses: Strategy, Forces and Resources for a New Century." This report, released under the Chairmanship of William Kristol, a major figure in the Straussian Cult, not only questioned but derided two congressionally-mandated defense studies: the "Pentagon's Quadrennial Defense Review" [May 1997] and the "National Defense Panel Report." [December 1997] These men, operating as private, unelected, non-appointed citizens, had the gall to declare themselves authorities on America's position in the world, on the adequacy of reports mandated by the peoples' representatives, on the strategies America should use around the world when dealing with friends and foes—and to determine the resources needed to carry out their designs!

Only a Straussian Cultist would have the arrogance to create a National and International policy on behalf of 300 million people when they represented none of them. Two years later, a year after 9/11, this report became "The National Security Strategy Report of the United States of America," a document that details how America will act, nationally and internationally, during the second Bush regime. Needless to say, few Americans ever saw the details of this report before it became policy—not the average American citizen nor their representatives in Congress nor the Senate. Yet we are the ones who must pay for the plans these men designed, be victims of the world's censure as they carry out their designs, and fall prey to their restrictions on civil liberties imposed by this regime as "security measures."

The recent questioning of the Bush administration's deceptions in fostering an invasion of Iraq raises significant issues but does not highlight the primary issue: did America go to war against a country that had neither the means nor the desire to attack America and had no connection with those who perpetrated the attacks of 9/11? Was the invasion of Iraq predetermined by a few men long before 9/11, and 9/11 used as an excuse to invade?

If that is so, then these men are guilty of subterfuge, deceit, and deception causing America to go to war illegally and contrary to the Charter of the United Nations. It is clear now that Rumsfeld, Wolfowitz, Perle, and Cheney all lied about their reasons for attacking Iraq. These men had the removal of Saddam Hussein as a goal as far back as 1992, with subsequent reiterations of that goal as part of the "Securing the Realm" report prepared for Netanyahu in 1996. They even made reference to WMD as an excuse to launch such a pre-emptive war in that document.

The atrocity of 9/11 gave an immediate impetus to attack Iraq regardless of Iraq's connection to the perpetrators. All they needed was an acceptable reason to bring the American people to their desire. That became, in Wolfowitz's words, WMD, a politically expedient term necessitated not by reality or evidence but by the need to have a buy-in to the Cult's goal of placing a significant American military presence in the middle of the Mid-East.

For more than 19 hours, on September 19-20, the Defense Policy Board, the one chaired by Perle, met to discuss the invasion of Iraq, to make the case against Saddam, to fabricate evidence that linked Saddam to the 9/11 terrorists. That action would assure Israel of military support in the region while requiring no military effort on its part, or the loss of Israeli life.

On the other hand, it assures America of continued and increased terrorism as it invades an Arab country without provocation and establishes an even greater American military presence in the Arab world. It also ensures the ongoing deaths of American soldiers as it gets embroiled in an Israeli/Palestinian type conflict. Terrorism becomes a way of life.

It is instructive to watch how the Cabal anticipates the beliefs of the Zionists in Israel and the evangelicals in America as they grasp at the prophecies in the Old and New Testaments. The need for a "clash of civilizations" between the Muslim and Jewish world plays magnificently into their hands. These fanatical groups become the "glue" that the Straussian can use to unite the people and force allegiance to the government that protects their religious interests. They have made legitimate the taking of Palestinian land by the Jews and denigrated the Palestinians and their leaders, especially Arafat.

These understandings have become Bush policy in the Mid-East. The terrorism of Sharon and his IDF gets shrouded in the rhetoric of "fighting terrorism."

"We want," in the words of the Cultists as they write in support of Bush Mid-East policy, "to commend you for your strong stance in support of the Israeli government as it engages in the present campaign to fight terrorism," these words sent by Kristol, Perle, Schmitt, Woolsey and numerous other Straussian cultists from the Project for the New American Century complimenting Bush for adopting their recommendations against the Palestinian terrorists.

The intrigue and secret plotting of these few men begs for exposure. In both the formulation of their agenda for the takeover of power by subverting the electoral process, and subjecting the American people to policies that are not just contrary to

American ideals, but anathema to the humanistic impulses of the American people, they have carried out this power grab unbeknownst to the representatives of the people. They have injected into strategies for world dominance designed years ago, policies that are insidiously beneficial to the state of Israel yet dangerous for America.

Every American should be concerned with Straussian beliefs, particularly with how they advance American values, morals, and principles of governing in a Democracy. Once understood, we can better judge the Cultists and their designs for the "New American Century."

Needless to say, the Democracy created by the founding fathers for America found its essence in the "inalienable rights" inherent in each individual, rights that enabled the citizen to give their consent to those who governed. The founding fathers were Deists; they did not accept the concept of a theocracy. All religions were to be tolerated; none were to share the governing power with elected officials. The Declaration of Independence, the Bill of Rights, and the Constitution detail the values and principles that give life to this nation, and they express with great fervor the right of peoples to determine their own destiny, not to have one imposed from outside. Nowhere, except in the mythology of the far right wing fanatics, does America have a God-given right to impose its will or its governmental process on another people.

American Democracy does not impose morals on its citizens; it assumes that in a nation of diverse peoples from all over the world, who hold beliefs in many gods, who pay homage to varying customs and traditions, who find delight in different fashions and foods, who speak many languages, who wish to live in a country where all participate in governing and all have an opportunity to learn and grow, that morals are inherent in their nature as humans reacting to their brothers and sisters. That morality does not exist is anathema to American Democracy, as is the determinism that Strauss espouses to replace it.

Yet here we are, Americans all, being led by a fanatical cult that does not believe in the fundamental principles of American Democracy, who do not credit the people they govern with the rights inherently granted them in the Constitution. This cult imposes policies that negate the very rights we accept as citizens and impose them on others, who use religion and religious beliefs as motivational crutches to force compliance with their non-religious goals. They do all this using deception and lies to gain their ends.

The America they envision has enemies all over the world who desire to destroy our society, but the real America is made up of peoples from all over the world who come here to share with us our values and become part of that society. The America they envision must export its capitalistic economy to all, regardless of the desires of other people to seek other ways to share resources; while the real America has millions in poverty, thousands homeless, millions without health care, and a deprived underclass that need a sharing of resources, not an accumulation of wealth in the hands of a few. The America they envision controls by force and state-of-the-art technology all peoples everywhere, to ensure protection of investors and the military/industrial complex—even if that requires deployment of our soldiers in 150 countries around the globe and satellite dominance in space; the real America desires to be friends with the peoples of the world, to share with them the responsibility of protecting the deprived, the destitute, the starving, the homeless, and to reduce the need for a military that devours the resources that could bring relief to all in need.

The America this cult envisions is not America. It is a military power that can control the world to protect the interests of the few at the expense of the many. It is the ultimate bifurcation of power assuring that the Straussian doctrine of determinism rules and the weak obey. It is a piracy of American values that negates the existence of morals executed by a fanatical group that believes they alone have the right to power when, in all truth, they are morally bankrupt. They are an insane Cult inspired by a disillusioned man who believed he alone of all philosophers had unearthed a secret message from the ancients hidden between the lines of their philosophical discourse.

Democracy is an open form of government resting on a firm belief in the integrity of a knowledgeable citizenry. It cannot be led by a cult of arrogant, secretive men who have no faith in its premise and no respect for its people.

18

Eating Humble Pie: Less Secure, Isolated and Dead Broke

[September 9, 2003]

A cynic may be the only person enjoying the current scene... Bush administration officials scurrying frantically around, like so many roaches caught with the light suddenly turned on, to the UNSC, to Germany, France, Congress, and the compliant mainstream media talk shows, diligently explaining the virtues of a broader based coalition of forces for Iraq carrying full UN endorsement. But the cynic also sees the roaches peering out from beneath the stove, hoarding the goodies they've acquired by their invasion in the dark of night. Powell and Rumsfeld, buddies once again we're assured, proclaim how this is an international concern requiring all members of the United Nations to join the coalition by sending troops and money. When asked what's in it for them beyond loss of revenue and body bags, the dynamic duo can only mutter, "It's in your best interest."

Thus the spectacle! Powell crawling out from his hiding place, humble pie smeared over his face, groveling before his erstwhile friends, the ones he coddled, cajoled, and abandoned between February and March five months ago, pleading with them to pass yet another resolution making legitimate the administration's illegal invasion. But Chirac and Schroeder, arm in arm, smiles wide and sure, chuckle at the scene even as they delicately step in and around the scurrying roaches, refrain from saying "I told you so," and await wording that would give them what they wanted five months ago. The entire spectacle is deplorable.

Recently in *Counterpunch*, Alex Cockburn caustically noted that UN officials, most especially the Secretary General Koffi

Annan, confused the UN with the US: the UN is the US to all intents and purposes. Annan received his anointment in much the same manner as Bush received his—through the blessings of those who are the real power, the corporations and lobbyists who own the judges and the politicians; for Bush the court system and party operatives particularly in Florida and DC; for Annan, the controlling administration in the US that pulls the strings on who will serve appropriately US interests as Secretary General.

Well, now is the time for Annan to lead the UN, not pick up the crumbs left by the US as it finds itself exposed and totally vulnerable in Iraq. Why, one wonders, should the UN capitulate to the demands of this administration when it had made clear five months ago that it disagreed entirely with the Bush drive to destruction of a country that was no threat to the US and had no part in the disaster known as 9/11?

Indeed, why should the UN consider a resolution from this administration when it was insulted and made a fool of five months ago when this administration pulled the second Iraq resolution knowing it would fail? That action made the US the UN, making it the determiner of international disorder and sole determiner of how to resolve that danger. Now is the time for the UN to assert its mandate to act on behalf of all member states, not be the lapdog of one. Now is the time for the UN to logically, and perhaps ironically, apply the Bush doctrine that asserts the irrelevancy of the UN unless it forces member states to comply with its resolutions—the argument Bush used to bring world-wide condemnation on Iraq in his speech to the UN in September 2002.

Now is the time for the UN to pass a Resolution, I'd suggest number 1443 following the first and aborted second resolutions drawn up by the US to give it face as it groped its way to the invasion. The resolution would condemn its rogue member state, the United States of America, for disregarding the UN Charter and International Law as it illegally invaded a state on false premises, for undertaking terrorist acts against the citizens of that state, for disregarding the provisions of the Geneva Protocols, for acts against humanity, and for supporting and promoting terrorism in selected nations like Israel, Pakistan, and India—thus destabilizing the world community.

Consider the brazenness of the US in going back to the UN. The administration seeks to have the current debacle in Iraq transferred to UN shoulders. Here's the wording of Powell's resolution: "... transfer the US led military force in Iraq into a UN-authorized multinational force under a unified command." This implicitly transfers acceptance for the invasion to the UN and, thereby, transfers the hatred of those attacking US forces to their new mercenaries. It likewise transfers the cost of the reconstruction, including rebuilding of structures already paid for by the UN and subsequently destroyed by the US, back to the UN. Yet the "unified command" remains under the control of the US generals and its puppet administrator, Mr. Bremer. A deal like this the UN cannot turn down!

Having fallen victim to one of the most insidious military strategies ever devised, one that may be cautiously compared to that devised by the Russians when Napoleon, followed by Hitler, invaded Russia, the US watched incredulously as the armies of Saddam evaporated into the blinding sandstorms that accompanied the tanks on their way to Baghdad. Unhampered by an opposing army, snipped at the heels as the supply trucks lumbered behind, the US forces moved swiftly into the center of Iraq. With 150,000 troops spread across 167,000 square miles (or almost one soldier per square mile), a landmass the size of California, keeping tabs on 23 to 27 million people (or one soldier for every 180 Iraqis), the soldiers became sitting targets for snipers, hidden bombs, and occasional missiles. The ensuing water torture of daily deaths, the light of day realization that the devastation wrought from the skies far exceeded expectations, the hate engendered by US weapons of mass destruction on the innocent, and the infiltration of sympathizers for those under US occupation have finally brought home to our politicians the enormity of the cost of this ill-conceived war in both dollars and lost good will of the world community.

Now, then, is the time for the US Congress and the Senate, on behalf of the American people, to stop this administration from further terrorization of the world, to repudiate the administration's National Security Strategy Report of September 2002, with its doctrines of pre-emptive strikes and imposed global dominance by this country, and to bring the perpetrators before the peoples' court, by impeachment, to atone for their crimes

against America and the world communities. That action
should include all members of the Cabal responsible for this
incredible debacle.

Concurrently with this action by our representatives would
come the UN Resolution 1443 citing the United States for its
unauthorized, illegal actions against the state of Iraq. In keeping
with the spirit of the UN Preamble, the Security Council and the
General Assembly would issue resolutions premised on the
authority vested in that body "to save succeeding generations
from the scourge of war, to reaffirm faith in fundamental human
rights, in the dignity and worth of the human person, in the
equal rights of men and women and of nations large and small,"
and most especially, "to establish conditions under which justice
and respect for the obligations arising from treaties and other
sources of international law can be maintained."

The UN can no longer act in fear and trepidation of the US.
It is and must be the arbiter of justice and peaceful resolution of
conflicts among and between nations. The US has realized now
something that liberal thinkers have been pointing out for two
years: the arrogance of the Neo-Cons and the stupidity of their
stated goals can destroy America, not bring it world dominance.
A nation that spreads itself around the world, in 150 nations,
that spends its wealth on state-of-the-art weapons that can
destroy hundreds and thousands at a shot, and that believes it
alone knows truth—therefore, is the determiner of good and
evil for all peoples on the earth—is a nation that cannot sustain
that breadth of deployment. It is a nation that can be defeated
by stones and handguns and hand-held missiles and determined
human will, a nation that must come to the realization that
truth and righteousness are elusive and varied.

The peoples' representatives finally understand as they watch
in horror the scurrying roaches attempt to salvage their hides,
that a nation can amass enormous power technologically, having spent the peoples' wealth to acquire it through the insatiable
appetite of the military/industrial complex, and find itself less
secure, isolated from the community of nations, and dead
broke!

19

Failing America: Duplicity at Home and Abroad

[October 11-13, 2003]

Have the American people capitulated to the fear fabricated by Bush, Ashcroft and Ridge? Are we the sheep Churchill mocked when he said, "Sheep don't need whipping"? Do we sit passively in front of our television sets listening to lie after lie and do nothing, knowing now that these lies sent American boys abroad as administration aggressors, yea, as unprovoked invaders of a foreign land, as occupiers entrusted with securing the natural resources of that land to be used to pay for the reconstruction caused by the invasion?

Had we known the truth would we have agreed to be the mercenaries of the Cabal, to secure for them the millions they will accrue from contracts paid for by our tax dollars while we suffer the indignity of being labeled across the globe, "foot soldiers of the corporate elite"? Has the "dumbing down" of America, that has turned our Democracy into a "Corpocrisy," turned us as well into corporate robots to be used at will by those who buy our politicians?

Tyranny in any guise, the medal bedecked uniform of the military dictator or the meticulously pressed pin striped suit, steals the unalienable rights of the citizen, and we have been robbed! This administration assumed power; it did not receive the consent of the governed. Its actions have not secured the rights of life, liberty and pursuit of happiness. Rather, its actions have fostered insecurity, restricted freedom, and cobbled the pursuit of happiness. A review of this administration's abuses of power tells the tale, and we need only reflect on a few of these abusive actions to prove the case.

The peoples' freedom to authorize their government to go to war in their name cannot be exercised correctly or legally if the arguments presented by the administration have been fabricated to delude the people. Yet that is exactly what this administration has done. It raised the specter of WMD because it would "sell" to the public; it lied brazenly to the people about the existence of nuclear weapons; and, perhaps the most insidious lie of all, it gave the people reason to believe that Iraq participated in the terror that brought death to 3000 Americans on 9/11. None of these purported facts is true.

Nothing a government does has more lasting impact on its citizens than war. To rouse a nation to pre-emptively invade another without provocation forces on its citizens an implicit moral responsibility grounded in the belief that the action is justified. Such justification did not exist; it was manufactured by a group of men for their ulterior motives unknown to the American people. The consequences have been devastating: American soldiers die daily, the cost of the invasion mounts beyond comprehension, more than 7000 innocent Iraqi civilians have died, unrecorded thousands have been maimed and injured, an estimated 30,000 conscripted Iraqi soldiers, many young boys, have been killed, the cultural heritage decimated by bombs and looting, streets, homes, hospitals, schools, water and energy plants destroyed, horrendous unemployment, crime everywhere, and a people distrustful of the Americans with many determined to throw out the occupiers at any cost.

The moral responsibility can no longer be couched in justifiable terms; it becomes now a moral responsibility of restitution due the Iraqi people. Yet, no one in this administration will take responsibility for this turn of events; no one will pay the cost, only the American soldier, only the soldier's family, only the taxpayer.

What protection of American life has this pre-emptive invasion secured for our people? Prior to the invasion, no American woke in fear that an Iraqi would cause them harm. Prior to the invasion, Iraq did not provide sanctuary to terrorists. Prior to the invasion, Americans enjoyed the approbation and sympathy of people throughout the world. Prior to the invasion, Americans united in compassion and charity for those who had suffered the atrocity of 9/11. Now 135,000 soldiers wake to the imminence of death; now terrorists flock to Iraq to foster the fanaticism that fuels terror; now Americans have become the pariah of the world, the cause of the terrorism that we set out to eradicate. Now Americans stand divided, as they contend with the deception fostered by this administration. Rather than protecting American life, the administration imperils American life around the globe.

That reality becomes the more frightening when we remember that the "war" against Iraq became a threat just before the 2002 fall elections, announced in September before the UN, the best time to "sell" a new product following the August vacation break. The selling of Saddam's demise coincided not only with the fall elections but also with the UN report on the inhumane catastrophic conditions in Palestine and the second invasion of the Palestinian refugee camp at Jenin.

Iraq, as the administration knew all too well, would dominate the news, relieving the administration of responsibility to intervene in the Israeli invasion just as it released Sharon from any fetters Washington might impose on his savagery. The deception held until Bush declared the aggression over in Iraq. In the interim, Bush took his case to the UN.

The Arab world sat in disbelief as Bush went to the Security Council to demand that Iraq comply with UN resolutions, condemning its inaction against a nation that defies its resolutions while citing its irrelevance if it does nothing. The duplicity of the administration's behavior was lost on America but not on the rest of the world, for they knew the continued Israeli occupation of Palestinian land and frightening power Israel wielded against its powerless foe, had full American support. Still, Bush went to the UN condemning Iraq. Iraq, Bush claimed, defied 16 UNSC resolutions; he did not mention that Israel continues to defy 69. Iraq, he bellowed with fingers crossed behind his back, has WMD, including nuclear, biological and chemical—a clear threat to peaceful nations. He did not mention that Israel has nuclear, chemical and biological weapons and has threatened to use them.

Iraq, he cried, has invaded its neighbor, Kuwait; he did not mention that Israel has occupied all but 22% of Palestinian land since 1967 and refuses to return that land despite numerous UN resolutions demanding that it do so. He pointed out that the UN has cited Saddam for human rights violations; he did not mention that the UN has cited Israel for such violations over and over since its founding in 1948.

But Bush duplicity does not end there. He condemns Arafat for support of terrorist acts; he doesn't condemn Sharon for hurling $300,000 missiles into crowded streets ostensibly to kill a person judged and condemned to death on Sharon's say-so without recourse to any legal process, while 17 die and many others are wounded—actions that even Israeli pilots have condemned. He praises Israel as a democratic nation, the only one in the Mid-East; but he refuses to recognize the duly elected President of the PLO who garnered more support from his people than the "elected" Prime Minister of Israel, Ariel Sharon, did from his.

He demands that Iraq draw up a constitution before it receives full independence, yet Israel has had 50 years to draw up a constitution and has not done so, but continues to be proclaimed a Democracy. He won't allow Iraq to have general elections, fearing the Shiite majority might win and design a theocratic form of government yet he says nothing about Israel and its Jewish citizenry that denies equal citizenship to non-Jews.

While the world, through its UN representatives, drew up a resolution condemning the Israeli government's statements that it would force Arafat out of Palestine or assassinate him, actions decidedly opposed to democratic principles, Bush chided the UN for one-sidedness. Bush calls upon the EU to freeze the assets of Hamas and condemn that organization as a terrorist front, but he did not ask the EU to recognize as terrorist supporters the right-wing Evangelical Zionist churches for providing millions of dollars to the terrorist settlers in occupied Palestine. This duplicity rouses anger, indeed, hatred against America, not only in the Arab world, but also in Europe and Asia.

Some in America took heart when the administration appeared to balk at the continued construction of the Israeli security "fence" that ostensibly protects Israeli citizens even as it secures the future inclusion of Zionist settlements that exist illegally in Palestine territory. Perhaps this concretion of duplicity would even wake the sleeping American public. But the fence continues, a fence constructed of slabs of cement garnished with barbed wire and electric currents, the kind of impediment used to corral cattle and wild animals in zoos.

And how does the administration demonstrate its anger at thwarting the Commander's orders? By withholding millions in the supplementary Israeli aid package, monies earmarked for years down the road, ensuring that nothing will impede the building of the wall. Avraham Burg put it succinctly: "The Zionist revolution has always rested on two pillars: a just path and an ethical leadership. Neither of those is operative any longer... It turns out that the 2000-year struggle for Jewish survival comes down to a state of settlements, run by an amoral clique of corrupt lawbreakers who are deaf both to their citizens and to their enemies." [*The Observer*, 9/14/03]

Last March I spent time in Prague visiting the Jewish ghetto. Walls surround much of that ghetto even today, walls constructed by the authorities when the Catholic Church through an edict of the Third Lateran Council decided in 1179 that Catholics should not come in contact with Jews who had resided in Prague since the 10th century. This is something like the situation in Palestine where the indigenous population (say Palestinians), lived since the 4th century CE. That edict resulted in the "ghettoizing" of the district, forcing 7,000 Jews to be packed into a network of putrid, squalid alleys where personal indignity rotted beneath the wall that separated those in power from those imprisoned.

Now we have a government that acts in our name, like the Lateran Council deciding for Medieval Catholics whom they shall meet with and whom they shall spurn, as it allows and provides the money to a sordid regime in Israel to wall-in a population in their own land even as that regime defies the world community by refusing to give back the land to the indigenous people to whom it rightfully belongs. America's absolute support for the Sharon government, despite the terrorism it levels at the Palestinians, and its obvious belittlement of the PLO, mocks the roadmap it proffers as a solution to the crisis. How can a people so treated construct an "Israeli wall of humiliation"? How can an American support a President who acquiesces to such degradation of a people?

Condoleezza Rice called the creation of a democratic government in Iraq "the moral mission of our time." Yet she speaks as an advisor to a government that manufactures policy out of politics, fabricates evidence from lies, conjures reason from duplicitous acts, extols freedom of speech as it maligns dissenters, lauds Democracy as it illegally occupies a sovereign state, decries terrorism as it supports the most savage terrorist regime in the world; and she has the gall to overlook the need to create a democratic government in America! This regime, this Bush regime, has failed the American people. It is time we give our consent to those who govern us. Sitting passively is no longer an option.

20

Ministers of War:
Criminals of the Cloth

[October 27, 2003]

Perhaps we have not paid enough attention to *Exodus* and have lost, therefore, the import of General "Jerry" Boykin's words to the evangelical Christians as reported in the *Los Angeles Times* on the October 16, "We in the army of God, in the house of God, kingdom of God have been raised for such a time as this." *Exodus* states it clearly enough: "The Lord is a man of war." [15:3]

Lt. Gen. Boykin, the new deputy undersecretary of Defense for intelligence [sic], no doubt speaks for Bush and Rumsfeld's forces in the field as he takes up his position as fourth in command under Lord General God. It is comforting to know we are under the command of the Head Man in Heaven as we enter the lists against the infidels led by their god, a mere pagan "idol." Boykin, who has probably met "face to face" with that other general, places the US squarely in God's "house," indeed, in His "Kingdom" as we "take up the cross" to fulfill His divine commands, our army having been "raised for such a time as this."

One wonders if all the other ministers of war sat enthroned behind the General as he expounded on God's words: Pat Robertson, Franklin Graham, Jerry Falwell, to name a few. Did they cheer him on? Did any of them suggest, perhaps, that his invocation to the God of War had imbedded in it yet another prayer, the one Mark Twain penned in his caustic satire that turned such fawning gibberish into nonsense—"The War Prayer"?

Let me paraphrase: "Dear God who counseled 'Do unto others as you would have them do unto you,' bless our cause and curse our enemy, destroy their children, leave their mothers' barren and homeless, let the old and infirm weep alone as they await death, devastate their land, burn their fields, and destroy even the memory of their existence, in God's name we pray!"

These evangelical Christians listen in rapture to the general who has become their instrument to effect Armageddon even as they curse those who give the appearance of appeasement against the Islamic hordes, including that former general, Colin Powell who should be "nuked," according to Robertson.

Consider the import of this scene, the general garbed in full combat regalia, spit shined shoes, epaulets ablaze with glistening brass, marching before the attentive congregation declaring that "radical Islamists hated the United States 'because we are a Christian nation, because our foundation and roots are Judeo-Christian...'" And more, "He's [Bush] in the White House because God put him there."

This man, now in charge of "intelligence" in the Defense Department, enlists his Christian warriors to take on "Satan." He becomes the embodiment of the Tele-evangelists' prophecy, those who proclaim "end-time theology," the means by which God will bring about prophecies present in the *Book of Revelation*. This scene contains two important revelations, neither of them resident in the *Book of Revelation*: the ministers of war enlist once again the myths of Revelation to achieve power in the secular realm and the myths that proclaim America's roots as Judeo-Christian rise once again as fact when, in fact, they are anathema to the concept and purpose of Democracy.

The rising chorus of evangelicals decrying Islam as the sole source of terror, the increasing volatility of their wrath, and their visible displays of displeasure and impatience with the policies of government in a Democracy, threaten the very basis of a government based on separation of church and state. Dennis Prager, [October 7, 2003] prophet of the right wing airways, attempts to defend America's need to go it alone against Islamic "terror and tyranny" in this "war of civilizations." He notes that the world is not supportive of the "American mission" to fulfill God's word, and this explains in good measure why they dislike George W. Bush, "the believer in the biblical God and in an American mission."

"We cannot defeat the Islamist threat," he proclaims, "without the same degree of faith fanatical Muslims have." Here he notes Israel and America are one because both nations have fanatical believers who can stand against the infidels. "One civilization believes in liberty and one does not."

Prager fears that Europe and non-believers in America can jeopardize the fulfillment of God's mission. "It is between those who fervently believe in America and in Judeo-Christian revelation and those who fervently believe in neither." Those who do not believe are, in Prager's mind, "the Left, many Democratic Party leaders, pacifists, the cultural elite and academia..." This type of thinking pits religious denominations against the political system because the government must become the instrument to fulfill their interpretation of God's word. Add to Prager's views those of Pat Robertson who beseeches God on public television to intercede to change the make-up of the Supreme Court and declares that only devout Christians and Jews are fit to hold public office and the casting of America as a theocracy takes form.

According to Philip Lindsey ("Are the Neo-Cons Conning Us?"):

> All the major figures of the Christian right have joined the new crusade to defend the Israeli state and spread Jewish settlements around Jerusalem and in the Occupied Territories. The Reverend James Hutchins, president of Christians for Israel/US, proclaimed this support was in order to fulfill a "divine calling to assist the Jewish people in their return and restoration of the land of Israel." A quarter of a million US Christians have sent over $60 million to Israel while Hutchins' organization has financed the immigration of 65,000 Jews. For both the Christian and Jewish right, Islam is the new "evil empire" and Yasser Arafat is Israel's "bin Laden."

With the three prominent Tele-evangelists urging their flocks to reject the rights of Palestinians to a homeland because the Jews have a covenant with God, with their active and visible intervention in political affairs directly affecting this nation, with the financial support they provide to terrorists in the settlements, with their politically motivated sermons directing their congregations to vote for born again Christians and Zionist Jews, with their loud condemnation of non-Christians and Christians not supportive of the Zionist right wing, they have created a fissure of intolerance in America. This crusade threatens not only the pillar of separation of church and state, but the rationale that undergirds this nation's tolerance of all religions in favor of the fanatics that demand obeisance to the ministers of war who interpret God's word for him in the *Book of Revelation.*

The actions of the Christian Zionists are arguably anti-American in their attempts to gain control of the democratic system, anti-American in their efforts to impose a right-wing Christian theocracy upon all Americans, illegal in their incitement to ethnic cleansing of Palestinians, who have done nothing to Americans, through their support of Jewish settlements that terrorize Palestinians, and illegal in their active promotion of right wing factions in Israel that oppose American foreign policy that calls for the creation of a Palestinian state. These militant actions of the Christian Zionists stem from their belief that the on-going crisis in the Mid-East is prophesied in the *Book of Revelation.*

Belief in Revelation compels them to incite their congregations to destroy the infidels. Ironically, this is not the first use of the *Book of Revelation* on this continent by militant ministers of the Almighty that has resulted in the slaughter of innocents. In 1500, as Columbus ravaged the "new world" with the help of the Franciscans who were set to build "the Kingdom of God on earth," a similar intolerance of other religions took hold.

> There had always been a millenarian cast to the followers of Saint Francis... many believed that their founding saint was the angel of the apocalypse who had unlocked the seal of the sixth age of revelation; the gospel would now be preached throughout the new world and then would come the Anti-Christ. Was not Charles V the prophesied world emperor? And had not Mexico fallen to Catholicism just as northern Europe fell to the Lutheran heretics? Were these not signs that the hosts of good and evil were assembling for Armageddon? On New Year's Day, 1525, the friars drove the Mexican priests from their temples and began the "first battle against the devil."

—Ronald Wright, *The Stolen Continent* (1992)

The Franciscans, driven by their fanatical zeal and bound in allegiance to the Spanish Conquistadors to affect the fulfillment of their prophecies, lost sight of the humans they killed in the name of their God. They were the Christian Zionists of their day!

If this was the first abuse of *Revelation* on this continent, it followed 20 others in Europe dating from 1186 to 1492, and yet others in preceding centuries. Not all resulted in slaughter of innocents, but many did, including the crusades initiated by Urban II who used other myths to enlist peasants and knights to the slaughter of the Jews and Muslims in attempts to reclaim Jerusalem for the Church. Does not the shear number of pseudo-prophets who have proclaimed the imminence of Armageddon require us to declare our current crop benighted idiots?

Have we learned nothing from history? Does superstition guide civilized people in the year 2003? Must we fall prey to denizens of myths who find power in prophecy and ego enhancement in incitement to riot? Must we repeat what we have seen in our own past, that fanatics maliciously use their positions of respect to drive their believers to actions diametrically opposed to the teachings of their supposed leader, Jesus Christ?

Are not these religious zealots criminals, exhorting their legions to engage in illegal behavior when they call on them to give millions of dollars to settlements damned as illegal by the UN and the worlds' communities of nations in numerous resolutions? Are not their rabble-rousing harangues designed to justify acquiescence and complicity to the terrorism inflicted by Ariel Sharon on innocent civilians in Palestine in the name of the God of Revelation?

Yet these ministers of war know no more of that God than all the previous prophets of doom that preceded them. But they should; they hold doctorate degrees in theology; they have the scientific evidence that tracks the biblical writings of *Revelation* to an unknown source on Patmos; they know no one knows the authors of the New Testament; they know they cannot speak for God any more than the pseudo-prophets of the dark ages... yet they prophecy, they prophecy for profit and power, the true ends of their proselytizing!

With what absolution then do they preach death and destruction? Shouldn't this administration find these false prophets enemies of the people? Do they not incite to riot and enlist their minions to support illegal activities that are detrimental to the peace of America? Have they not brought America more insecurity by confirming in the minds of those fearful of a clash of civilizations that indeed America is on a crusade to destroy Islam? Have they not given aid and comfort to Osama and his hordes by demonstrating the truth of what he says: the Christians are out to defeat Allah?

Consider the power these men wield over American policy. Not only does the "General of Intelligence" preach before the evangelical hordes, but also Tom DeLay, the anointed leader of the Republican majority in the House and a rabid Christian Zionist, addressed the Israeli Knesset on July 30 urging Israel "to ignore the truce and go on killing Palestinian activists."

Benny Elon, Sharon's Minister of Tourism, appeared with DeLay at the Washington convention of the Christian Coalition where he called for the expulsion of the Palestinians from their homeland, claiming that land for Israel since it was guaranteed them in the Bible. The ethnic cleansing is authorized in that same Bible according to Elon, and confirmed by no less an authority than Richard Armey who called for removal of the Palestinians, despite the presence of an indigenous population of Arabs in Palestine for the last 1900 years!

Even now, this month, 500 evangelicals visited Israel in support of Sharon's divisive actions against Palestinians. The yoking of the Christian Zionists, the right-wing Jewish Zionists and the pro-Israeli Neo-Cons has undermined the foundational concepts that guarantee American freedom of conscience and religious tolerance. Perhaps Melchior Grimm had it right when he declared in the mid 18th century: "It has taken centuries to subdue the human race to the tyrannical yoke of the priests; it will take centuries and a series of efforts and successes to secure its freedom."

We need only pay heed to Thomas Jefferson's words to Dr. Benjamin Rush in his letter of April 21, 1803: "It behooves every man who values liberty of conscience for himself, to resist invasions of it in the case of others; or their case may... become his own."

Freedom of conscience cannot exist in a climate of fear or in a nation that dictates truth. For the Christian right to impose its beliefs on this nation by controlling the ballot box to ensure the election of radical "end time" believers, to impose their religious beliefs through legislation that all must accept, or align themselves with groups like the Neo-Cons who desire a similar goal and would willingly subvert the rights of the people as stated in the Declaration of Independence, the Constitution, and the Bill of Rights to attain it, can and will result in the erosion of the principles that ensure our freedom.

In that same letter to Rush, Jefferson noted the corruption of Jesus' teachings as "doctrinized" by denominations, extolling instead Christ's undiluted teachings: he taught *"universal philanthropy, not only to kindred and friends, to neighbors and countrymen, but to all mankind, gathering into one family, under the bonds of love, charity, peace, common wants and common aids."* [Italics mine] How different in concept this understanding of Christ's teachings that provides tolerance of all as members of one family from the teachings of the Christian Zionists and right-wing Jewish Zionists who would purge a people from their homeland by superstitiously interpreting words that allow them to determine the fate of millions.

How brilliant does the wording of the Declaration seem now, "endowed by their creator with unalienable rights of life, liberty, and the pursuit of happiness," a prescription guaranteed in the Bill of Rights that indelibly marks each and every human with the same rights to live in a free society unencumbered by the dominance of another's infallible thoughts!

Jefferson understood that religions are not tolerant or democratic; indeed, they are inherently neither, since ministers serve as intermediaries to the divine and become the conduit of doctrines and dogma that determine thought for the believer. It followed logically for Jefferson that church and state must be separate if all religions were to exist in the new country. America does not rest on Christian principles; it exists, as all democracies must, in tolerance of Christian beliefs, as it exists in tolerance of all religious beliefs precisely because it was not founded on beliefs expounded by one religion.

Thomas Jefferson, Benjamin Franklin, and Thomas Paine, the principal exponents of the foundational concepts upon which this country rests, were Deists who accepted the genuine precepts of Jesus, not those that have evolved in the various denominations over the course of centuries. Love, charity, and compassion define Christ's precepts; love for all, charity toward all, compassion for all, that all may live in peace. But true Christian love is anathema to General Boykin and the Christian Zionist teachings as they incite their congregations to war!

21

"Shock and Awe!" Failing To Respond To 9/11

[January 3-4, 2004]

Writers and pundits exercise a hallowed tradition in January. They ruminate on the past year's exploits and offer resolutions for the coming year. As we consider the horrific failures done in our name by this administration this past year and contemplate the impending election year, reviews and resolutions become ominous declarations for needed actions based on principles that can "change things and relations," as Henry Thoreau put it.

Thirteen months ago, December 23, 2002, almost three months before Bush introduced the world to "shock and awe," I wrote an article for *Counterpunch*, "US vs. Iraq, the Tale of the Tape: The Road to Basra and Back" [Chapter 7], contrasting the combatants in a vain effort to demonstrate the consequences of the impending slaughter threatened by the Neo-Cons as they deceitfully offered the UNSC a second resolution seeking its blessing on their invasion of a sovereign nation that posed no threat to the US. Let's begin our review at this point.

Cheney, Bush, Powell, Rumsfeld, Rice, Wolfowitz and all the members of the Neo-Con Cabal that rule in this administration sold the American people on the impending threat Iraq posed for the security of the US because it possessed WMD, biological and chemical weapons, and supported the 9/11 terrorists. None of these allegations were true; we knew this to be so then and we know it to be true now. Yet they took America to war. Now, as American soldiers die daily in Iraq, as Iraqi civilians die daily in Iraq, as the number of terrorists increases daily in Iraq and around the globe, we must ask how this administration has made America more secure following the 9/11 attacks. By linking Iraq to 9/11, the Neo-Cons duped Americans into believing that their invasion of that nation continued the administration's "war against terror," thus insuring greater security for the United States. It did the opposite. Even the President has told us that Iraq is the new center of terrorism in the world. He created it.

But the deception that brought us to this state blanketed a reality that the American people knew nothing about—a reality that was well known to this administration. Let me quote a paragraph from Chapter 7:

> Before and during the brief war [the 1991 Gulf War], the US flew more than 116,000 air sorties losing 75 aircraft. Iraq on the other hand lost 36 fixed wing aircraft, 6 helicopters, 87 aircraft lost on the ground, 3,700 tanks, 2,400 assorted armored vehicles, 19 naval ships sunk, 42 divisions made combat-ineffective, and 2,600 artillery pieces destroyed... Since the Iraqi forces consisted, at the time, of 4,280 tanks reduced to 471, and 3,110 artillery pieces reduced to 510, the available hardware for this upcoming war (the present war against Iraq) appears rather thin.... However one looks at it, Iraq has about 10-15% of its former ordinance to hurl against the current US forces, almost 90% of its ordinance having been destroyed.

Add to this accounting the fact that America's sanctions since the Gulf War prevented Iraq from rebuilding its infrastructure that was destroyed as well and it's obvious the second Iraq war was a "turkey shoot" for the American military. For the administration to present Iraq as a threat to the US, given the reality of its devastated military forces and its current population that consists of more than 50% under the age of 15, is more than deception of the American people, it is pure barbaric inhumanity that cost the lives of approximately 9,000 innocent civilians [IBC], three times the number of Americans lost on 9/11. Americans are not a bloodthirsty people; if they had known the hoax perpetrated upon them by the administration and the resulting slaughter and devastation wrought as a consequence, they would be shocked indeed, and, no doubt, stand in awe of the gall that pulses through the veins of those who speak for this administration. What does Bush have to show for his "revenge against the perpetrators of 9/11" but a reverse "turkey shoot" where American boys pop up like targets before the disaffected, the deprived, and the deranged? He created it.

The Bush misadventure in Iraq caused America to lose track of its true purpose following 9/11: what caused that catastrophe and how can further atrocities of like kind be prevented? Consider Bush's sole explanation for the atrocity of 9/11: "They hate our freedoms." Who are the "they"? What "freedoms" do they hate? "Why do they "hate"? We have no answers but the ubiquitous "al Qaeda."

But who are the al Qaeda? Where are they? How many are there? How do we know they caused 9/11? What evidence exists that they are responsible? Did their leader, Osama bin Laden, direct the attack? How do we know? What freedoms do they hate? Freedom of speech? Have they not proven to the world that they can speak their mind whenever they wish? Freedom of movement? Have they not freely moved throughout the world? Freedom of assembly? Do they not meet when and where they desire, in whatever country they desire? Freedom of religion? Have they not practiced their religion wherever they assemble, in whatever country they live? How then do they hate our freedoms? Is the answer so simple that they desire to prevent Americans from having the freedoms they enjoy so readily? What does that accomplish but to prevent them from freely moving within the United States as they become victims of their own ends?

Consider further the actual events of 9/11. Nineteen men, according to the FBI, hijacked four commercial airliners, crashed two of them into the North and South towers of the Twin Trade Center in NYC, one into the Pentagon, and a fourth, destined for an unknown target, was destroyed in a field in Pennsylvania. Why did these nineteen men undertake such a suicidal mission? What mentality would allow a person to guide an airliner, including innocent passengers, into a tower, knowing full well the ineluctable carnage that would ensue?

Did they anticipate the collapse of the towers? Did they know that thousands would perish or did they expect that only a couple hundred would die on the floors hit by the plane? Were they connected to the five Israelis who filmed the planes striking the towers as they danced on top of a van in a Jersey parking lot? Can they be traced directly to Osama bin Laden and hence to the Royal family in Saudi Arabia? If so, why were the family members allowed to leave the US the day after 9/11 on the only aircraft permitted to fly through US air space?

Why, if fifteen of the nineteen came from Saudi Arabia, did the US attack Afghanistan before it determined any connections to 9/11 of the Saudi state? So many unanswered questions; so much havoc and devastation as answers to the unknown.

Now consider what the man accused of these atrocities has actually offered as reasons for attacking America. In his letter to America, November 24, 2002, Osama provided three categories of concerns that propel people to "hate" America: 50 years of oppression in Palestine, US support of Arab and non-Arab countries that bow before American power, thereby suppressing and humiliating their own people and/or capitulating to American interests that exploit their people and their natural resources, and the need for Americans to submit to his understanding of the Qur'an since he "cannot fail." Now ask if this administration ever considered addressing these issues.

Indeed, instead of addressing 50 years of oppression in Palestine, this administration initially disengaged itself from the conflict there (although it continued its monetary and military support to Israel) until Sharon's savagery became so blatant the world community forced it to reconsider. Reconsideration amounted to mimicking Sharon's condemnation of Arafat as irrelevant, an action bound to ingratiate America to the Arab world!

The administration followed that action by acquiescing to Sharon's increased building of the settlements, illegal assassination of individuals without arrest or trial, continued terrorist attacks of innocent civilians from F-16s and helicopters in overcrowded ghettos, destruction of homes without provision for the people so displaced, murder of international dissidents like Rachel Corrie, and construction of a "Berlin" wall around the indigenous population the better to ensure an almost total theft of Palestinian land. This cynical reaction to just demands made by Palestinians and Arabs over decades against the occupying forces of Israel guarantees the continuation of terrorism against America and its interests at home and around the world. Bush's shame-faced cow-towing to Sharon's demands, including his willingness to invade Iraq on behalf of Israel and his obsequious

acceptance of Sharon's commands that he curtail US engagement with Syria, only infuriates those snubbed and degraded.
His more than cynical demand to the UN that it force Iraq to
abide by resolutions directed against it by the Security Council
when no mention is made of resolutions directed at Israel over
50 years, all defied by that state, mocks the very demand being
made even as it makes obvious the administration's bias against
an Arab state.

Add to Osama's condemnation of Palestinians by Jews (with
America's 3 billion per year fiscal support) the invasion by the
US of Iraq and its continued occupation of that country, and it
is graphically clear to all in the Arab world that the US intends
to control all of the Mid-East and its natural resources.
Consider as well the US military's use of Israeli forces as consultants [Julian Borger, *The Guardian*, 12/9/03] to fight the
indigenous population in Iraq—the surrounding of towns with
barbed wire, the check points and ID cards, the searches, breaking in of homes with dogs, and assassination of individuals
"suspected" of acts against the US—and the hatred grows
deeper as America is seen as an Israeli-type occupier, with no
concern for Iraqis as individuals, but as "terrorists" that must
be hunted down like dogs.

Israel becomes a US puppet regime operating in the area
secured by American military might controlled by a predominantly Jewish Neo-Con Cabal that has a decided conflict of interest in its policies toward the Mid-East. Nothing could be more
corrosive to America's security than this Cabal's desire to yoke
America's Mid-East policy to that of the Sharon regime. This failure to address the primary causes of the 9/11 attacks ensures the
continuation of terrorist acts against the US. To use an appropriate Bush analogy, strike one against the administration.

Now consider Osama's second issue, America's control of
other nation states, especially Arab nations like Saudi Arabia
and Egypt, and its infliction of Capitalism across the globe as a
minority of wealthy industrialists exploit and humiliate populations in the under-developed nations. What has this administration done to address this issue? Nothing! Indeed, once again, the
administration has supported the oppressing powers—the trans-
nationals that impose their bottom-line efficiency on exploited
people in Mexico, the Caribbean Islands, Malaysia, Indonesia,

Vietnam, Cambodia, Bangladesh, and China, the corporate agreements that steal local control from the people like NAFTA, GATT, the IMF and WTO—demonstrating no awareness of the consequences of the disparity of income, the joblessness, the hazardous working conditions, the poverty wages, the unsanitary conditions, the overcrowded housing, the debt burden on the populations.

Add to this, America's control of the oil in Iraq, its control of gas pipe lines in Afghanistan, its desire to rehabilitate the oil lines through Iraq and Jordan to Israel, its control of the government in Saudi Arabia through its control of the House of Saud, its control of Jordan, Egypt, Bahrain, Qatar through its infusion of wealth to those who serve its interests, and one can understand how Osama gathers to his cause the disaffected and deprived.

Roger Altman put it succinctly when he cited the dichotomy that exists between the "haves" and the "have nots": "...half of the world's population is increasingly threatened with economic oblivion... that is dangerous for world stability, and we should not resign ourselves to it." What happens if the West does not address a redistribution of wealth and the utilization of the world's resources? "The Fourth World, the least developed parts of Africa and Asia, will become even more fertile territory for brutality, state sponsored terrorism and mass tragedy." Strike two for the administration!

Now we turn to Osama's last concern, the need for America to accept his interpretation of the Qur'an. No one would suggest that Bush should accept his interpretation, but to ignore the implications of this demand is to court doom. We have seen its demented spirit as the Twin Towers slid into oblivion. Yet no one in this administration has addressed this issue; no one has called together the principal religious figures of the various faiths to condemn the fanatical interpretations that propel these movements, the Islamic Jihadists, the Christian Zionists, the Jewish Zionists, any and all who abuse religious teachings, the purpose of which is to bring people together, not to slaughter them. And, yes, it must be the fanatics of the Christian and Jewish right as well as the fanatics of the Islamic faith. All are guilty of inciting to riot, support of terrorism and manipulation and control of beliefs that foster devastation.

For Tele-Evangelists to harangue their congregations by condemning Osama and his cohorts for believing that Allah has demanded obedience to Him and destruction of those opposed to His teaching is no different from the Christian right exhorting their masses to heed the word of the only true God, Jesus Christ, who commands allegiance in the *Book of Revelation* and condemns to Hell all who oppose His inevitable rule following Armageddon. The Christian right's support of the Jewish settlements to the tune of millions of dollars screams to the Islamic world the truth of the Islamic fanatics that they are at war with enemies who would destroy Islam.

This administration must condemn the Christian Zionists and break allegiance with the Likud Party and the right-wing Israeli Zionist parties that support it. It must bring together religious leaders from across the globe, seeking from them their active commitment to stem the influence of these fanatical sects as a primary responsibility of their positions, and declare their serious support for separation of church and state with tolerance of all religions as a fundamental right. Only then will the preaching of the fanatics be quelled and the lie given to those who claim the martyr rises before the Almighty's throne, bringing him immediate gratification in eternal life even as he receives the adulation of those in his congregation as one committed to god's revelations.

Unless and until this administration addresses this issue and makes moot the belief that certain clerics can read the "word of god," the havoc of 9/11, the firing of terrorist missiles into masses of civilians by a state driven by fanatics, and the "Christianizing" of the Mid-East, will ensure continued decades of terrorism against America and its capitalistic interests at home and around the world. By doing nothing, this administration has struck out!

What resolution can be offered in light of this review of our administration's failures to address the primary issues that caused 9/11? Only one: remove it from power, by impeachment preferably, by ballot if required. One can only hope that a year from now, when reflecting on what our government has done in our name, the review will be of a different administration, one concerned with America's role within the community of nations—not concerned, as this administration is, with ruling the world community.

22

Democracy vs. Militarism: Rule by the Capricious and Corrupt
[January 23, 2004]

More than 725 American military bases (are) spread around the world... Many garrisons are in foreign countries to defend oil leases from competitors or to provide police protection to oil pipelines, although they invariably claim to be doing something completely unrelated — fighting the "war on terrorism" or the "war on drugs," or training foreign soldiers, *or engaging in some form of "humanitarian" intervention.* [emphasis mine]
—Chalmers Johnson, *The Sorrows of Empire*

How many Americans understand the implications of Johnson's observation? Bush's "State of the Union" address, with its repetitive mantra declaring America's gift of "freedom" to the world and its on-going fight against "terrorists" (used 20 times) obscures the reality of America's deployment of "over half a million soldiers, spies, technicians, teachers, dependents and civilian contractors in other nations" (Johnson) for purposes of protecting private investors. These investors use American forces to protect their private interests, not those of American citizens. Indeed, it is arguable that our invasion of Iraq and our toppling of the Taliban, a government the US put in place, happened because we needed Iraq's oil reserves; the Taliban refused to cooperate with the deployment of oil and gas lines through their territory. Bush's idealistic rhetoric follows a stream of recent efforts to present this administration's imperialistic and militaristic agenda as economic freedom for the world and security at home.

He was particularly active in November when he spoke to the National Endowment for Democracy, when the administration supported the international business deal cobbled together by the corporate representatives at the Free Trade Area of Americas, and when he addressed the Brits and defended his invasion of Iraq. All these efforts hinge on an abuse of the word 'freedom'. Bush lassos freedom to economics, as in 'economic freedom', implying that the management of income or resources has equal rights with the citizen—that by some occult metamorphosis an economic system has been reborn as a person. The FTAA business deal in Miami managed to avoid any reference to humanitarian concerns or laborers' rights, although Venezuela pressed for such consideration, as they made possible "freedom" for trade. Brazen omission of the citizens from consideration did not cause them to blink as they, too, conferred on "trade," rights that are reserved for people.

Peggy Noonan, Ronald Reagan's speechwriter, told Chris Mathews recently that President Bush's speech to the National Endowment for Democracy was a "masterpiece." In that talk at the beginning of November, Bush used Reagan's speech at Westminster Palace in 1982 as the reference point for his own remarks. Perhaps Peggy penned Ronnie's words? Why else label Bush's derivative remarks a "masterpiece"? Well, there is another reason: it is a "masterpiece" of deception, but, then, so too was Ronnie's. Both speeches embody the manipulative duplicity of the ruling elite as they mouth "Democracy" and "freedom" when they mean in their guts "Corpocrisy" and "indentured servitude." ('Corpocrisy' is the apparent rule by the people through a voting process, but they actually rule by corporate hegemony.)

What Jefferson feared at the inception of this nation has become the reality of our Democracy: a land governed by "pseudo-aristoi," as Jefferson sardonically labeled them— "extremely wealthy individuals and overly powerful corporations." This was the third of the "agencies" Jefferson feared as threats that could destroy a Democracy. The remaining two were other forms of governments like monarchies and organized religions. [Thom Hartmann, *Unequal Protection*, p. 200] Those "overly powerful corporations" now act as individuals claiming rights under the 14th amendment, would you believe, despite the reality that the Supreme Court has never stipulated as "law of the land" that corporations can legitimately claim that right. [Hartmann, p. 107]

For those who would argue that the Court has accepted that status based on precedent, remember that same Court upheld the "Institution of Slavery" on the same grounds! Precedent is often the imprisonment of the people on the cross of coddled consistency.

What Bush describes as the passing of tyranny before the march of freedom masks the reality of these past twenty years of "globalization," the insidious take-over of the rights of nation-states by trans-nationals, at the expense of "universalism"; the caring spread of individual rights of life, liberty and the pursuit of happiness to peoples throughout the world. Perhaps that was what Bush meant when he noted "observers on both sides of the Atlantic pronounced (Reagan's) speech simplistic, naïve and even dangerous."

Perhaps Bush realizes that "observers" sense the truth behind the duplicity. Those observers, particularly sophisticated Europeans, the kind Bush mocks in his talk, understand that Reagan's simplistic truth, freedom for all, masks the reality: the "momentum of freedom" opens the door of exploitation for investors who can hire Chinese laborers at thirty-three cents per hour to replace American workers at the Huffy bicycle plant who earned eleven dollars per hour. Those Chinese laborers also work far more than 8 hours per day, receive no health benefits, are protected by no OSHA regulations, and have no retirement plan. [Example taken from remarks made by Sen. Dorgan, ND at hearings held in Washington in November] Perhaps these same observers understood the naiveté of Reagan's remarks that assumes the world desires the American way, or to be more specific, the American consumer way that requires two incomes to support the American way.

Perhaps "dangerous" is the most explosive of those observations. It cuts to the chase: the imposition, by force if necessary as Iraq makes clear, of America's will on nation-states to ensure ever greater markets for the goods the trans-nationals produce cheaply by exploiting workers throughout the "undeveloped" world even as it ensures control of necessary natural resources owned by those nation-states.

But Bush's duplicity reflects nothing more than a continuation of the abuse of the language that characterizes the American voices that have controlled our government since its inception. What Bush proposes here is nothing new; it simply pushes American economic practice off shore, onto other countries, since our markets are now inadequate to satisfy the insatiable greed of the corporate class. As far back as 1975, Professor Takaki in *Iron Cages* shed light on America's Capitalistic underbelly. He tracked Richard Dana's two years before the mast as it revealed the reality of Capitalistic enterprise and its incessant need to create new markets and exploit labor to produce more goods at the cheapest possible cost.

"The American emphasis on productivity and profits, moreover, had a stifling effect on the quality of human life in the work situation," Takaki notes. But quality of life is not an issue in accounting's bottom line. Dana had left Boston in 1852 on board a trade ship carrying cotton goods around South America to Mexico City and San Francisco. The cotton goods were produced in New England mills on looms driven by Irish girls, indentured servants, slaves to the mill owners and investors. The cotton came from slave plantations that offered the cheapest possible labor. But the cotton was grown on land taken from the Natives who had been "ethnically cleansed" or killed, the land illegally obtained. When Dana arrived in San Francisco, the cotton was loaded on trains that ran on rails over the bodies of Chinese coolies, more indentured servants working for slave wages. The whole capitalistic process thrived on the backs of workers exploited for the purpose.

But now the corporations need cheaper labor because they must pay decent (read "too high") wages in America and that cripples profits. The world now becomes the playground for this most recent "Industrial Revolution." Never mind that we learned about exploitation of workers—unsafe working conditions, no health coverage, no child labor laws, no retirement benefits, no job protection, and no labor rights—two centuries ago during our previous industrial revolutions here and in England. Laborers in China, Malaysia, Vietnam, Mexico, and any other country that can be controlled and exploited must endure what English and American workers endured before the laws caught up with the corporations... and that took a hundred

years! This is the freedom Bush promises: freedom for exploitation, freedom for investors, freedom to profit at the expense of
people unable to protect themselves.

Consider the benefits of "free markets": "US workers lost
879,280 jobs as a result of NAFTA in the past 10 years... with
all fifty states and the District of Columbia losing jobs to
NAFTA between 1993-2002" according to Robert Scott. [the
Economic Policy Institute] If we can do this poorly with two
nations involved, imagine the number of jobs yet to be lost
when we migrate our jobs to 34 nations upon implementation
of FTAA! But lest one think that the Mexican citizen benefited
from America's loss of jobs, think again. "The cost to the
Mexican consumer has risen by 257%" since the inception of
NAFTA and the "earnings of Mexican growers of corn, wheat
and rice, along with beans, have plummeted." [*Los Angeles
Times*, Nov. 20, 2003]

Who, then, benefits from such agreements? Need you ask?
"Free trade eliminates tariffs, giving the economic advantage...
to those industries blessed with governments capable of deliver-
ing massive subsidies. In other words, to the already industrialized and wealthy nations." [*Los Angles Times*] Note how free
trade slips from the legislation when it is detrimental to corporate America.

The Medicare bill recently passed scurried through our representatives in the dead of night and attempted to eliminate "free"
choice purchasing of medicine from Canada even as it ensured
profits of 139 billion to pharmaceutical companies over the
next five years. Free is free only for the "pseudo-aristoi"! Add
to this bill the Fast Track bill that passed the House and the
Senate. "The bill has language that forbids enforcement of
workers' rights and environmental protection" that should
be enforced in agreements like that moving through the FTAA.
Indeed, the bill strips out a clause that would protect women
against discrimination." ["Stop the Free Trade Area of the
Americas,"*www.organicconsumers.org/corp/FTAAResources.
cfm*] Our government guarantees "freedom" to a "paper person"
as it denies it to one of flesh and blood.

If the consequence of free trade in these "undeveloped countries" siphons workers from the countryside, thus depleting
native food sources; stuffs them into overcrowded ghettoes

creating thereby unsanitary conditions; shackles the laborer to
the production line at pitiably low wages and forces them to suffer without benefits of any kind—health care, safe working conditions, unemployment compensation, or retirement—then the
United States, that subsidizes and protects these corporations,
cripples peoples' freedom and denies them the rights it claims to
provide. Worst of all, it indicts the American citizen as complicit
in this exploitation of other people.

Ted C. Fishman made this observation in *Harpers*: "The free-
ing up of the world's markets may have nothing to do with the
declining fortunes of many of its citizens, but the capitalist
impulse can just as powerfully prolong poverty as end it."
[August 2002] To illustrate his point, Fishman notes, "Over the
twenty years ending in 1980, gross domestic product in Latin
America and the Caribbean grew by 75 percent per person, but
over the next twenty years—the period of great market liberal-
ization and international investment—GDP rose only 6 percent." The duplicity inherent in Bush selling Democracy as
"economic freedom" and "free trade" when its real product is
exploitation of the worker and enhanced profits for the investor,
is at best cynical and at worst insidious.

While Bush expounded on the virtues of America's presence
across the world, noting the US had "made military and moral
commitments in Europe and Asia which protected free nations
from aggression and created the conditions in which new democracies could flourish," he failed to mention that "expanding US
military presence worldwide only serves to reinforce the economic
hegemony" that guarantees survival of the corporations that
exploit the citizens of the undeveloped nation-states as they take
control of that nation's natural resources. ["Free Trade May Not
Be Fair Trade," Roger Hollander, *Los Angeles Times*, Nov. 2003]

Bush continues his exhortation of American largesse: "We
also provided inspiration for oppressed peoples." Indeed! How
were the Palestinians inspired? Did our worship of Sharon's savagery inspire? Did our overwhelming financial support for his
indomitable military force inspire? Did the Bush administration's incarceration of over 1,000 in Guantanamo without due
process—no criminal charges, no consultation with lawyers,
and no rights whatsoever—inspire? Did the occupation of Iraq
preceded by an internationally illegal invasion inspire?

But there's more! Bush, energized by the applause from the National Endowment personnel, declaimed, "...militarism and rule by the capricious and corrupt are the relics of a passing era." Really? What is our rule in Iraq? What is more "capricious" than the unilateral invasion of a nation that has done nothing to America but to threaten a new-born Christian Zionist's belief in his mythological mission as portrayed in the *Book of Revelation*? What is more corrupt than support for the war lords of Afghanistan who throttle the poor population of that country while raking millions from the American people through their tax donations? What is more corrupting than support for the terrorists who live in Israeli settlements and thrive on the destruction they can inflict on Palestinians? What duplicity is this?

But there's still more! "China has discovered that economic freedom leads to national wealth... Eventually men and women who are allowed to control their own wealth will insist on controlling their own lives and their own country." How, pray tell, does a person control "their own wealth" when the industry moguls threaten to fire the employee if they object to the working conditions or attempt to unionize, to obtain the benefits and job protection that belongs to them by right—a strategy used to offset unionization in the US as well as in "undeveloped" countries? ["Stop the Free Trade Area of the Americas"]

How does one control their wealth when they make 33 cents per hour and live in squalid conditions with no benefits? When I spoke with the business faculty at Yantai University in China in the mid-90s, they understood then that the new industrialization did not provide for workers' health care or retirement. They saw the pollution that spread like a brown blanket over Beijing. They spoke of streams that had been turned into cesspools. But they also knew the trans-nationals would not enter China if the government imposed regulations that forced the industry to spend on safety, health care, or workers' rights.

"In reality," as Roger Hollander states in the *Los Angeles Times*, "for historical and geopolitical reasons, what Third World countries are 'best at' is having their natural resources extracted and exported to the industrialized nations (which in turn sell back manufactured products at a high cost) and having their populations exploited for cheap labor." If this is the historical reality of Bush's "economic freedom" and "free trade," why does he lie to the American people and convert rapaciousness into rights that will accrue to the citizen? What duplicity is this?

But the duplicity here has a source, the "National Security Strategy of the United States of America," issued in September 2002 as a guide to this administration's foreign policy. There, George enunciated that "free enterprise" made the third leg of "a single sustainable model for national success." He continued, "In the twenty-first century, only those that share a commitment to protecting basic human rights and guaranteeing political and economic freedom will be able to unleash the potential of their people and assure prosperity." How, given the statistical evidence that graphically illustrates the degradation of human rights described above, could the potential of people be unleashed? What has been unleashed and what will be unleashed is the potential for further corporate exploitation of people and resources and the continuing erosion of personal rights. This administration is committed to the empirical dominance of the corporate powers it represents, protected by an unparalleled military that it sustains—all in the facetious name of "protecting American interests" even as they impose their will on all the countries of the world.

One can only resort to cynicism: corporations are rogue nation-states that wander the world like whores seeking to bed with whoever will offer the most breaks for the bang. This is not freedom for the people; it is freedom for the "overly powerful corporation."

23

Faith-Based Fanatics: The Other Intelligence Failure

[February 14, 2004]

"Man is the only animal that has the true religion—several of them."

—Mark Twain

As even the conservative talk show hosts scramble to unravel truth from fiction emanating from the White House, another intelligence failure goes unmentioned and uninvestigated. Which of the monotheistic faiths has the ear of God? Who among the various exponents of truth—ministers, rabbis, or mullahs—gather the "real" intelligence from the purported "sacred" texts that provide God's directions to His creatures?

Who bears responsibility for this "Intelligence" community as it makes its case for eternal war? Should the President create yet another selective investigating committee, composed of trusted friends of truth like Henry Kissinger, Tom Delay, Richard Perle, or Trent Lott (there are no "Muslims" resident in this administration), to search out fact from fiction in the "other" rationale that brought America to invade Iraq: God's directive that guides America to bring His gift of freedom to the Iraqi people—while insuring that Israel regains its right to the covenant land given by G-d to them in perpetuity?

As we watch Pat Robertson's version of the news on the 700 Club, and listen to him "forgive" George his sins of omission in not telling the American people that he was manufacturing the truth about Iraq's WMD and connections to Osama; as we hear him extol God's purpose in placing George in the President's throne at this moment in time, the better to ensure that God's prophecies be fulfilled... we have an unsettling realization that this man, and others of like cloth—Franklin Graham, Jerry Falwell,

Benny Hinn, Hal Lindsey, Pastor Hagee—influence thousands
upon thousands who wallow in their righteousness and leave
the Cornerstone Church secure in belief that God speaks to
these men just as He talks to Pat, assuring him that George will
be reelected by a huge majority.

Must these men bear no responsibility for the meaningless
deaths of more than 535 American soldiers, the pain and suffering of thousands mutilated in missile and bomb attacks, the
continuing agony of those sick unto death with DU poisoning—
not to mention the wanton destruction of innocent Iraqi civilians, estimated now in excess of 10,000? What intelligence did
they omit when they exhorted their followers to rush to war
against the infidels? What fabrications of truth did they extract
from their Bibles, assuring the faithful that they had "received"
the word of God in dreams? That He called upon them to fulfill His prophecies as recorded in the Book of Revelation? That
He cursed the Islamic faith and charged that it be wiped from
the face of the earth? What resident inmates of our nation's
mental hospitals also hear God speaking to them but have neither the gift-of-gab nor the wealth to air their views before the
world?

What understanding of the Creator do we receive from these
self-proclaimed "Ministers of the one true God"? Let's listen to
Osama bin Laden, the alleged "mastermind" of the chaos
inflicted on America and the roaming "evildoer" who haunts
the underworld caverns of the Mid-East, eluding our Texan
cowboy who vows to bring him in "dead or alive."

"We will impose our religion on America... God wills it," he
proclaimed in his "Letter to America," November 24, 2002.
And in the fullness of his vehemence he yells, "Do you fear
them? Allah has more right that you should fear Him if you are
believers. Fight against them so that Allah will punish them by
your hands and disgrace them and give you victory over them
and heal the breasts of believing people."

But that is not all. "It is He Who has sent His Messenger with
guidance and the religion of truth (Islam) to make it victorious
over all other religions even though the Polytheists hate it."
[Quran 61:9]

And, finally, this last bit of chutzpah: "The Islamic Nation...
wishes to remove your evils, and is prepared to fight you. You

are well aware that the Islamic Nation, from the very core of its soul, despises your haughtiness and arrogance."

As an ardent student of Sayyid Qutb, one of the founders of militant Islam, Osama understands that "Islam and the West [are] incompatible, two camps between which coexistence [was] is impossible. There could only be a struggle between believers and non-believers, between Secularism and Capitalism and Islam... and the West with its emphasis on science and technology... obliterate[s] the validity of religion."

Thus we find others of similar mind to Osama, the Muslim Brotherhood, for example, that calls for armed confrontation with Israel [Gregorian, *Islam: a Mosaic Not a Monolith*] or Ayatullah Khomeini who called for a holy war against the "Great Satan," the United States. One turns with some degree of relief from these fanatical fulminations to the expected peace of the other two monotheistic faiths only to find that they too have entered the lists with lances at the ready, swords at their sides, and hate in their eyes.

Consider Sharon's dependence on the National Religious Party headed by Effi Eitan, a self-proclaimed rabid Zionist who brazenly and shamelessly shouts that Palestinians are not ordinary people, but "uncircumcised," "little people," and "evil." The Jews, on the other hand, are "blessed." And they [the Jews] will come with "vengeance against [their] terrible evil" and "make a reckoning with them." [*Los Angeles Times*]

But Effi is not the worst. Gush Emunim rabbis teach that "...Jews who kill Arabs should be free from all punishment... Arabs living in Palestine are thieves because the land was Jewish and belongs to them." [Prof. Israel Shehak] Add to these zealots those who design their own versions of the Talmud citations and preach to their followers hate, vengeance, and annihilation. Their hubris defies understanding: "Whosoever disobeys the rabbis deserves death and will be punished by being boiled in hot excrement in hell"; [Erubin 21b] and: "All gentile children are animals"; [Yebamoth 98a] and: "According to the Talmud, Jesus was executed by a proper rabbinical court for idolatry, inciting other Jews to idolatry, and contempt of rabbinical authority"; [Hoffman and Critchley] and: "Those who read the New Testament will have no portion in the world to come"; [Sanhedrin 90a] and: "Jews must destroy the books of the

Christians." [Shabbath 116a] These and more, more venomous
than those cited, fill the various commentaries that constitute
the on-going words of the living Talmud.

It would appear that Osama finds a sick solace in his God
that will bring havoc to unbelievers and victory to Islam while
the Zionist right-wing Jewish cohort divide G-d's creation into
the blessed and the animals who, as unbelievers, will suffer a
steaming and malodorous sauna in the hereafter. How does one
describe these gods? Having created humans with the capacity
to reason and choose, Allah damns all who disbelieve the militant mullahs while the G-d of the Jews destroys all who disbelieve the right-wing Zionists. If each can be believed, all would
be destroyed and none would ascend to heaven! Indeed, the
Gods they worship are brutish, sadistic, and perverse! But lest
we think the Christian right exhorts its worshipers to "turn the
other cheek" and "do unto others as you would have them do
unto you" and "love thy neighbor as thyself," think again.

For a paltry $25.00, you can purchase three audiotapes from
Pastor John Hagee of the Cornerstone Church in San Antonio,
Texas. These are tapes of sermons that focus on "Allah and
America." Add another $20.00 and you can get the video ver-
sion that permits you to witness the paunchy pastor lift the
Quran high above his head as he cites chapter and verse, in an
ever more excited crescendo, condemning the words of Allah as
interpreted by Pastor Hagee.

It's a marvelous scene; a few thousand of his 17,000 congregation sitting in rapt attention in this hotel-like conference center church, absorbing the truths of the one true God as conveyed
by this minister of war who sees the anti-Christ rising against
God's chosen in the final battle prophesied in the *Book of
Revelation.*

What is the purpose of this exhortation? Is it to bring his congregation to peace and reconciliation with their wayward brothers and sisters? God forbid, "No!" This 21st Century Prophet
rises on his tiered altar steps (he is the altar!) demanding that his
parishioners recognize the grave threat they face as he extracts
passages from the Quran that give credibility to his twisted
interpretation of Mohammad's visions.

What does he see? His evangelical Christian Zionist church is
engaged in a spiritual war for survival and the demonic driven

mullahs of the Islamic faith are waging everlasting war against freedom of religion, against freedom of speech, against the western world! "We are not a sister faith!" he cries over and over again as his congregants lift their arms and eyes to the chandeliers that bathe the hall in celestial light. What must they do to these demented hordes that "want to kill as many Americans as possible," that are developing "long range missiles," that have "suitcase atomic bombs"? They must fight; "Victory must be our only objective!"

"No relationship of any kind exists or can exist between Islam and Christianity," he shouts in stunned and somber tones as he levels his final accusations on this faith of more than a billion people around the world. This false religion serves as Satan's means to present "a false path to Paradise" when Jesus Himself is the "only way to heaven"; He alone is the one true God; "Christ is the only savior on the planet!"

Thus does he echo Osama and Eitam in the absoluteness, no, the infallibility of his belief. "Islam," he cries, "says Christ did not die on the cross... and he is not divine." But, strangely enough, he does not condemn the Jewish faith for similar beliefs. He can't. His need to convince his faithful that Revelation demands the existence of the Israeli state if the rapture is to ensue, requires that he support the Israeli state as God's means of fulfilling His prophecy. Ironically, Hagee does not make public, especially to the Jewish community, that the consequences resulting from the fulfillment of Revelation's prophecies would save only 144,000 Jews—leaving the remaining millions to eternal perdition. With friends like Hagee, who needs enemies?

Monotheism breeds men who wish to bed with God, to bathe themselves in His glory the better to reveal to all how blessed they are in the eyes of the Almighty. Since God communicates with humans only through a chosen few—Moses, Matthew, Mark, Luke, John, and Mohammad— and, conveniently, only in abstruse words and images, these men become the conduits of His meaning. They, like the CIA, must intercept and interpret God's meaning. They, like the CIA, can surreptitiously maneuver political forces to do their will by guaranteeing thousands of votes, thousands of dollars, and allegiance to policies that support their agenda. They, like the CIA, can effect regime change and control governments. Witness Sharon's coalition, the

Iranian Islamic state, and the Bush regime's dependence on the Christian right-wing Zionists. And they, like the CIA, must be investigated!

The havoc currently wrenching the United States, Israel, and Iraq arises as much from faith-based fanatics in all three religions as it does from political drives motivated by acquisition of natural resources and dominance of geographical areas to insure ultimate power. These fanatics resort to documents 1300 to 2500 years old, documents relevant to their time, and use them to manufacture relevance in the 21st century.

The metaphorical narratives of these ancient documents, designed originally to represent the interaction of tribes with the forces of nature, teach how to live in a community with respect to social, economic, and political realities—how to understand the energies that conflict within our beings—become, in the rantings of these madmen, reality today... despite the intrusion of science, reason, technological advances, and hundreds of years of political change. In the process, they must negate the simple yet elegant teachings of those faiths that give promise to the potential of human harmony. Here, in the words of Theodore Parker [in 1841] as he dismantled organized religion that "fetters a man" in favor of the spirit that Christ taught, a spirit equally at home in the Jewish tradition and the Islamic, reside the permanent truths that express the fullness of the human spirit:

> [That spirit] is absolute, pure morality; absolute pure religion—the love of man; the love of God acting without let or hindrance. The only creed it lays down is the great truth which springs up spontaneous in the holy heart—there is a God. Its watchword is, Be perfect as your Father in heaven. The only form it demands is a divine life—doing the best thing in the best way, from the highest motives; perfect obedience to the great law of God. Its sanction is the voice of God in your heart; the perpetual presence of him who made us... Examine the particular duties it enjoins—humility, reverence, sobriety, gentleness, charity, forgiveness, fortitude, resignation, faith, and active love... summed up in the command, "Thou shalt love the Lord thy God with all thy heart,

and with all thy soul, and with all thy mind; thou shalt love thy neighbor as thyself"... The end seems to be to make all men one with God... It allows perfect freedom. It does not demand all men to think alike, but to think uprightly... not all men to live alike, but to live holy..."

Faith-based fanatics offer no humility only arrogance, no reverence only hypocrisy, no gentleness only castigation, no charity only self-indulgence, no forgiveness only condemnation, no faith only fear, and no love only hate. They represent a small minority of the believers who find refuge in these faiths. Of the adult population in the US and Canada, 75% are Christians, and of that number only 35% are born again. Of that number, even a smaller percent are Evangelical Christian Zionists of the Robertson/ Pastor Hagee stripe that exhort our nation to take up arms against the infidels.

Each of these fanatical groups demands exclusivity for their membership, an exclusivity that turns plowshares into swords. By contrast, those who heed the spirit of faith understand in the words of the Psalmist, "Publish His glory among all nations. His marvellous works among all peoples." [96:3]

"Mohammad preached a message that was intensely democratic. He was insisting that in the sight of the Lord all peoples were equal." [Houston Smith, *Islam*] A Creator does not destroy His creation without destroying Himself. No minister, rabbi, or mullah should preach destruction; it is anathema to the purpose of religion.

Hearken to the words of Yonathan Shapira, an Israeli pilot who refuses to fly. He bases his refusal on two of the basic values of the Israeli Defense Forces, only one of which I will cite here:

> Human Dignity: The IDF and its soldiers are obliged to honor human dignity. Each human being should be respected, regardless of his race, creed, nationality, gender, status or his social role.

Nothing taught by Gush Emunim appears in this statement; yet it is Effi Eitam and his like that control Sharon's coalition. Where is the investigation that will expose this reality? The vast majority of Jews hear Yonathan's plea, but it is Sharon's savagery that speaks in their name. "Islam's religious revivalists... often express alienation and anger about the 'ravages' of secularism, perceived amorality, and the loss of 'traditional values' in the modern world." [Gregorian] Osama and his ilk carry out that anger demanding of their followers an uncompromising adherence to a rigid, literal interpretation of the Quran, forgetting there are a multitude of interpretations with that of the Sunnis' dependent on reason, not unquestioned faith. And they represent the majority of Muslims. No unified religions exist; there are 19 major religions in the world with more than 270 large religious groups including 34,000 separate Christian groups.

Such diversity requires separation of church and state. And that is why Jefferson found organized religion a threat to Democracy; religion is not by nature tolerant, especially when more than one claims they have access to the one true God.

Now if these men have incited their congregations to overlook the deception of the Bush administration as it brought America to an unjust war, if they insert their warmongering views in pulpit, TV programs, and politics, have they no responsibility for the consequences of their acts? If they cannot demonstrate the source of their interpretations that served as a base for their allegations demanding Bush and America complete God's prophecy, should they not be brought before the courts for inciting mayhem and levied appropriate damages to pay for the havoc they generated?

And should not Bush demand the same of Sharon and his coalition, since his brutality against the Palestinians is considered the major source of terrorism in the world and has made America a target of that hatred? Perhaps a little intelligence on this matter would bring to light how an administration can be coerced into a foreign policy built on superstition and fear.

24

Israel: America's Albtross
[February 28, 2004]

Ah! Well a day! What evil looks
Had I from old and young!
Instead of the cross, the Albatross
About my neck was hung.
> —Samuel Taylor Coleridge,
> "The Rime of the Ancient Mariner"

Two issues dominate the electoral debate as Kerry battles Edwards, and Bush, abandoning the crisis in Israel, enters the fray: homeland security and job loss caused by exporting jobs "offshore." One issue that encompasses both cannot be mentioned by political commentators and politicians for fear of condemnation as anti-Semitic. Also for fear, among politicians, of loss of their positions: What role does America's support of Israel play relative to homeland security and job loss? Is it the Albatross around America's neck?

Before undertaking this discussion, I need to make this assertion in self-defense: The violence that corrodes the mind and heart of fanatics in Palestine and Israel nourishes seeds of vengeance in children and adults alike, breeding only destruction and death. Vengeance, retaliation, and terrorism—caused by purported freedom fighters or by the state—cannot and must not be tolerated in a world that claims to be civilized. I do not condone suicide bombing any more than I condone the firing of missiles into crowded streets. I do condemn my country's blind support of the government of Ariel Sharon, the principal cause of insecurity in America and the greatest threat to peace in the world today.

"Israel, world's biggest threat to world peace!" blared the headlines in Europe when the "Eurobarometer" poll, undertaken by the European Commission, reported more than 59%

of EU citizens see Israel as a threat to world peace. [Brussels: AFP-Reuter-Agencies, Nov. 2003] The United States, in the company of Iran and North Korea, came in second at 53%. Fifteen countries participated in the poll. Israel voiced outrage at the poll results, claiming it reflected media bias against Israel; this, despite the fact that a terrorist attack against Israeli citizens outpaces Israeli attacks against Palestinians 20 to 1 in media coverage.

This poll follows the Pew Research Center survey of December 2002 that reflected growing discontent with America around the world. Criticism of America is on the rise as 19 of 27 countries disapprove of the actions taken by the Bush administration that reflect an increased movement away from internation engagement to a position of isolationism and unilateralism. "True dislike, if not hatred, of America is concentrated in the Muslim nations of the Middle East and in Central Asia, today's areas of greatest conflict." Less vociferous are America's traditional allies, but they, too, critique harshly "American- style Democracy and business practices."

"Huge majorities (64%, 71%, and 79% respectively) in France, Germany and Russia oppose(d) the use of military force to end the rule of Saddam Hussein." The reason? The war with Iraq will increase the risk of terrorism in Europe, and although Americans seem to believe that terrorism has diminished as a result of the invasion of Iraq, the reality is that we are fast approaching a death rate of American soldiers in Iraq comparable to one-third the number killed in the 9/11 attacks. Are we willing to say that it's OK for Americans to die in the Middle-East as long as they are not being killed on American soil? Similar attitudes about America exist in Indonesia, Senegal, Western Europe, Australia and Canada.

In short, Israel and America are perceived by the vast majority of people around the world as true threats to world peace. What does the world know that we are unwilling to face? In this election year, America's absolute and unswerving support for Israel and its unquestioned spread of corporate-style Democracy (read Globalized Capitalism) remains the unseen elephant in the Oval Office and the campaign rooms of Kerry and Edwards.

Interestingly, John Kerry's Presidential web site mocks Howard Dean for a string of "misstatements" about Israel and

America's unstinting support of that state. What constitutes a "Misstatement"? Disagreement with Kerry's statement that "every candidate who aspires to be president should know that Israel is a Democracy and our closest ally in the region."

What did Dean say? Israel is "a Jewish state, it's not a Democracy." He's right! Israel is NOT a Democracy: it has no constitution after fifty years of existence, yet we demand that Afghanistan, Iraq and Palestine have a constitution; its system of laws is determined by the Torah, a religious document not a secular one; it denies recognition of the Palestinian minority despite UN Resolution 181 calling for such recognition; it defies UN Resolutions requiring it to accept return of the indigenous Palestinians from the refugee camps to their rightful homes taken from them in 1948 or 1967—but allows Jews from Russia and other lands to immigrate and become citizens solely because of their religion, making Israel a de facto theocracy (similar, ironically, to an Islamic Democracy!); and it keeps on the books more than 20 laws that discriminate against the Palestinian minority. [Adalah: Legal Center for Arab Minority Rights in Israel]

John Edwards parrots the same line as Kerry: "John Edwards believes that Israel is one of America's vital allies, and that the US must support Israel to help it fight terror and achieve peace." Such blind support for a state that, in the eyes of the vast majority of the world communities, is seen as instigating terror by its overwhelming military power (the fourth largest military in the world protecting a nation the size of New Jersey and with a smaller population) against an impoverished people that has no meaningful military force to speak of, only desperate people deprived of human dignity and hope, runs counter to reason, to say nothing of human rights.

Ridiculing Dean became a *cause celebre* that all had to join because he refused to lockstep behind the blind leading the blind into the ditch. "He was not ready for the presidency" because he had not joined the chorus directed by AIPAC; an "even handed" approach to the crisis in Israel/Palestine meant criticism of Israel that cannot be tolerated. The Israeli political forces launched a massive attack against Dean, as vicious as any mounted against Arafat, and he folded. Such is the power that controls America's Democracy.

That leaves Kucinich; but nobody pays attention to Kucinich because he, too, contradicts the Neo-Con line that dictates America's allegiance to Israel. Kucinich would not cave to the powers that forced House Resolution 392, expressing solidarity with Israel, into acceptance. This resolution blared to the disenfranchised world America's bias against the Palestinian people even as it solidified in the minds of the terrorists (our term, they see themselves as freedom fighters) America's desire to control the Mid-East through its 51st state, Israel.

Kucinich declared "...we are missing an opportunity to lead people of the Middle East toward a secure and stable future together... The same humanity that requires us to acknowledge with profound concerns the pain and suffering of the people of Israel requires a similar expression for the pain and suffering of the Palestinians."

How simple and how compassionate! Here is recognition that the suffering of both peoples must be our concern, not a wimpish subservience to a powerful elite that controls the current administration and our Congress.

The accepted dogma in the US states that America must support Israel to ensure peace in the Mid-East and to secure America against "terrorism" since Israel, like America, battles and fights the same "terrorists." But how substantive is this argument? If all the states that surround Israel, including the citizens of our puppet states Egypt and Jordan, and fifteen countries in the European Union observe Israel stealing land from the indigenous population of Palestine by defying UNSC resolutions that demand it return land taken in 1948 and 1967; if they see Israel placing illegal settlements in Palestinian territory eating up another 2% of Palestinian land and blatantly defying other UN resolutions; if they see America hypocritically demand that the UN invade Iraq for defying its resolutions while remaining silent about Israel's defiance; if they witness Israel incarcerating the indigenous population behind barbed wire and cement walls, even as they steal more land and isolate the people from relatives, mosques, work, and land, a device resurrected from Medieval days when states walled in the Jews in ghettoes; if they watch helplessly the willful invasion of Palestinian territory by tanks, armored vehicles, thousands of soldiers, and bulldozers that decimate homes—how can we believe that our support of

Israel brings peace when it is so obvious that it is the reason there is no peace?

Bush prides himself on deposing "madmen," "ruthless dictators," "murderers," and "criminals" who kill wantonly, women, children, the old and infirm. In August 1953, a poverty plagued refugee camp suffered an onslaught, supervised by a military commander that resulted in the deaths of 50 civilians as "bombs were thrown through the windows of huts in which the refugees were sleeping." Another village, Qibya, endured a massacre when that same commander reduced the village to rubble killing 69 civilians, two-thirds of them women and children, then buried the victims under their homes as they were blown up over them. In Gaza strip, after the 1967 war, Had'd Street, a narrow alley in a mass of similar alleys that made up a shantytown for refugees, was eradicated and hundreds of homes destroyed by bulldozers to enable tanks and armored vehicles to move unhindered through the camp. This same commander allowed his soldiers to beat the people, leaving them homeless once again. That same commander later destroyed an additional 2,000 homes, uprooting 16,000 people, and assassinated 104 suspected guerrillas without benefit of trial or jury.

In 1982 this same commander directed the bombing of civilian populations and oversaw the massacres of 1,962 people at Sabra and Shatilla refugee camps, all infants, children, women, pregnant women, and the elderly, many mutilated. ["The Crimes of Ariel Sharon," *Counterpunch*, 2/7/04] Was this Saddam? Was he the "little madman" in North Korea? No, quite obviously, he is Bush's mentor in Israel, a "man of peace" according to "W," Ariel Sharon.

Prior to the ascendancy of Ariel Sharon to head the government of Israel, prospects for a peaceful settlement existed. Sharon cripples any and all peace efforts and he does so with the complicity of the US administration and our government. He knowingly caused the current intifada by taking a 1000 IDF entourage to the holy Al Aqsa Mosque, understanding his act as a defilement. America said nothing, but the world looked on and the world objected. He alone of all Israeli leaders has used the full force of the Israeli military machine to subdue a defenseless people who fight against all odds to retain even a sliver of the land they owned before the state of Israel was forced upon them, a military machine bought and paid for by our tax dollars. And the world looks on and the world objects. He instigated the creation of settlements in Palestinian territory, creating in the process, groups of "terrorists" who plague Palestinians on their own land under the protection of the IDF.

These settlements are paid for by our tax dollars, and the world looks on and the world objects. He prevented the introduction of UN Peace keepers as a means to resolve the crisis, and the world observes and objects. He instituted the pernicious practice of "extra judicial executions" that abandons the most rudimentary principles of Western justice, and America adopts that same pernicious practice in Iraq and Yemen; and the world looks on and the world objects.

He cries to the world that he must defend Israelis against "terrorists" by any means, even as he crushes 30 to 40 Palestinian homes per month under the relentless treads of America's paid-for caterpillars, arrests and detains young Palestinians without charge, allows torture of some, accepts in silence the murder of international peace observers, and America says nothing to this man Bush calls a "man of peace"; and the world looks on and the world objects.

But the Arab world sees more than just Sharon and his savage legacy. They see what Benny Morris, author of *Righteous Victims: A History of the Zionist-Arab Conflict 1881-2001*, has revealed recently that confirms a planned genocide against Palestinians by Ben-Gurion and Moshe Carmel as far back as 1948. The massacre at the Dahmash Mosque [July 11, 1948] that resulted in the deaths of 350 worshippers by the 89th Israel Commando Battalion commanded by Moshe Dayan, exemplifies the nature of the genocide and savagery of its execution as Dayan's forces stripped the dead of their valuables and tossed the bodies out of the Mosque into the boiling sun. [Gains, UK] Although the West bought the lies of the Israeli historians and the media covered up the reality of "transference," what we now euphemistically call "ethnic cleansing," and what properly should be called massacre and theft, the release of Ben-Gurion's orders tells the truth and confirms what the Arab world has said all along.

That alone gives reason for the world to see Israel as the cause of instability in the Mid-East, since it gives legitimacy to the cause of the Palestinians to resist Israeli occupation and insist on return of the refugees. Morris reveals, "In the months of April-May 1948, units of Haganah (precursor of IDF) were given operational orders that stated explicitly that they were to uproot the villagers, expel them and destroy the villages themselves." [Ari Shavit, *Ha'aretz*, Sun. 2/15/04]. When asked how many acts of massacre occurred, Morris replied, 24, in Dawayima, Saliha, Deir Yassin, and Abu Shusha. "Ben Gurion silenced the matter. He covered up for the officers who did the massacres."

Should not these revelations force a reconsideration of America's one-sided support of Israel? Doesn't Dean's observation that a more "even-handed" approach seem justified and Kerry and Edwards' blind adherence to an unanalyzed policy to a purported "democratic" Israel and a "peaceful" Israel need reconsideration?

Now let's take a more selfish look at the consequences this parasitic allegiance to Israeli interests causes the American taxpayer. The *Washington Report on Middle East Affairs* summarizes the amount of US tax dollars going to Israel: $134, 791, 507, 200 from 1949 to 1997. Tom Malthaner writes in "US Aid to Israel: What US Taxpayers Should Know" [WRMER 2/16/04]: "When grants, loans, interest and tax deductions are added together for the fiscal year ending in September 30, 1997, our special relationship with Israel cost US taxpayers over $10 billion."

Using that figure, we can increase US aid to Israel by 10 billion from 1997 to 2004 or something close to 200 billion in taxpayer support. Would you believe that this is the conservative figure? David Francis of the *Christian Science Monitor* notes that "Since 1973, Israel has cost the United States about $1.6 trillion. If divided by today's population, that is more than $5,700 per person." [CSM, 12/9/02] This, he points out, is an estimate by Thomas Stauffer, a consulting economist in Washington, who notes that this represents more than twice the cost of the Vietnam War!

Considering that Israel is the 16th wealthiest nation in the world with a per capita income just below that of Britain and France, one has to ask why the American taxpayer spends one-third of its foreign aid budget on Israel, a country with a population only two-thirds the size of New Jersey representing

1/1000 of the world's population, a give-away comparable to Bush's tax relief program for the well-heeled! For every dollar we spent on an African since 1948 (a continent that desperately needs foreign aid), we have donated to each and every Israeli standing on the street corner, cup in hand, $250.65! [Adhaf Soueif, 11/03]

To put it another way: "The per capita US foreign aid to Israel's 5.8 million people (that doesn't include the 20% Arab population living in the Israeli state) during the same period was $10,775.48." [Richard Curtiss, "The Cost of Israel to US Taxpayers"] Turn that into dollars per American taxpayer: the cost to each taxpayer up to 1997 amounts to $23,240 per Israeli. A quarter of Israel's income comes from the taxpayer in America. Perhaps they need it, since they have a higher life expectancy than that of the US!

But what if 10 billion were distributed to individual states? California could use 10 billion and it has more than 34 million people, not a paltry 5.8, and its land area far exceeds that of Israel. Now there's bang for the buck! But Alan Cranston in 1984 created an amendment to the US Foreign Aid bill that compels the US government to provide Israel enough Economic Support Funds to meet its debt burden to the United States, an act of generosity not offered to California, the state he represented! And what have we gotten for our investment?

Putting aside the origins of the state of Israel that by itself could account for a major portion of the hatred of the United States in the Arab world, Israel has given the US taxpayer the following return on their investment:

(1) An absolute unwillingness to return land stolen from the Palestinians during the 1967 war, despite UNSC resolutions demanding that return. This left the indigenous population with about 14% of the land they originally inhabited before 1948, when the Palestinians owned all but 6% of the land in Palestine and constituted 69% of the population. The Jewish population in 1948 was only 806,000. Thus, the result is a defiance guaranteed to bring hatred, not peace.

(2) An absolute defiance of more than a hundred UN resolutions demanding that Israel abide by international law

and the Human Rights guarantees of the Geneva Accords; a defiance guaranteed to bring disdain, not peace.

(3) A sadistic disregard for American friendship and loyalty by its insidious use of spies against America as the Jonathan Pollard case readily demonstrates and David Tenenbaum before him. These actions are guaranteed to undermine the taxpayers' loyalty to Israel, if this Democracy had an uncensored press.

(4) An absolute defiance of expected behavior between allies by executing an act of war against America in its attack on the *US Liberty* in 1967. This crime was covered up by the Johnson administration as it acquiesced to Jewish interests. It is a crime that almost forced the US into another war on behalf of Israel, and cost the American taxpayer untold amounts of dollars even as it demonstrated to the world the extent the Israeli government would go to protect its own interests.

(5) A sadistic strategy of infiltration into US government affairs through the Neo-Con Cabal that worked on behalf of Israeli interests as laid out in their advisory report to the Israeli government, "Securing the Realm," that brought America to war against Iraq, based on lies generated by these men. This is an act guaranteed to bring hatred, not peace to the Mid-East.

(6) An open defiance of the American government's desires regarding the invasion of the Jenin refugee camp, the bulldozing of thousands of Palestinian homes, the murder of international peace observers, and the construction of the Israeli Wall—all defiances that disregard American interests and guarantee hatred of America, not peace.

(7) An insidious desire to encourage Evangelical Zionist Christians to invest millions in Settlements that cause terrorism in Palestinian territory while inciting hatred of Arabs by encouraging their fanatical beliefs in the "Clash of Cultures" that will come with the fulfillment of the prophecies of Revelation. These are actions guaranteed to rouse deeper suspicion and hatred, not peace.

(8) A defiance of the Arms Export Control Act that provides US military hardware to Israel on condition it be used only for defensive purposes by using US-made

cluster bombs in 1982 against civilian targets in Lebanon,
an action guaranteed to cause hatred, not peace.

(9) Finally, and this brings us back to the second issue that
dominates this year's election debate: a maneuvering of
the agreements that provide Israel with taxpayers' dollars, an arrangement that allows Israel to purchase military equipment from Israeli manufacturers even though
they are available here in the US; and an arrangement
that requires that the US purchase with Department of
Defense funds military hardware from Israel. This is an
action that in effect ships American jobs to Israel, jobs
paid for by the taxpayer! Talk about robbing Peter to pay
Paul. And we haven't mentioned here the sale by Israel of
US classified technology to Ethiopia, South Africa, Chile,
Venezuela and China contrary to the agreements made
between the US and Israel. [Shawn Twing, *Washington
Report on Middle East Affairs, 4/96*]

Why does this administration pretend it is in the best interests
of this country to continue to spend an estimated 10 billion a
year on a relatively wealthy people that is protected by the
fourth largest military in the world, one that possesses nuclear
weaponry as well as chemical and biological, for a population
that is slightly larger than the population of the city of Los
Angeles? Wouldn't it be more effective to force that state to
make peace with its neighbors by returning to the ideals that
gave rise to its existence in the first place? These ideals are not
the driven purpose of the Zionists, but the compassionate values of Europe and America when it sought to establish a homeland for Jews who had suffered for centuries, the racism that
eventually resulted in the holocaust of WWII.

How can peace be brought to the Mid-East unless Europe and
America recognize that they bear responsibility for imposing a
population on an existing indigenous people, without their consent, who were innocent of the evil done to the Jews in Europe?
How can peace arise when Palestinians look back at the forcible
eviction of 737,166 of their people in 1948 and, in 1967, an
additional 69,000 from the West Bank, Gaza, and the Golan
Heights, a population that has grown to over a million people
now living in refugee camps and denied both compensation for

their stolen homes and right of return that flaunts international law? Rights denied are sores that infest the soul only to explode in vengeance and retaliation.

But do we have a return for the compassion that the world offered to the Jews? Do we address the consequences of the actions that have given rise to the unrelenting horror of oppression, occupation, and insane reaction that uses humans as bombs? No! We have the erecting of an American taxpayer Wall, an Israeli constructed "Wall of Fear" that creates an Israeli Pogrom to encircle the most deprived in the world, the mirror image of the suffering of the Jews at Terezin. The world sees fear on both sides—fear of imprisonment and deprivation and fear of retaliation for wrongs inflicted.

I empathize with Shlomo Shmelzman when he cries, "I see bombs falling on a city, on innocent civilians—men, women, children and babies. Houses crumbling, dead bodies in the streets. I remember a morning in September 1939, when my mother and I were running to my grandmother's home, through the fire and smoke under a heavy bombardment, finding our way between dead bodies lying in the streets of Warsaw. Too many things in Israel remind me of too many other things from my childhood... Today, as a citizen of Israel, I cannot accept the systematic destruction of cities, towns, and refugee camps. I cannot accept the technocratic cruelty of the bombing, destroying and killing of human beings."

Coleridge's Ancient Mariner carried the Albatross until "A spring of love gushed from my heart/ And I blessed them unaware.../The self same moment I could pray/ And from my neck so free/ The Albatross fell off, and sank? Like lead into the sea."

And so must America bring peace by forging an alliance with the Jews for Peace and their counterparts in Palestine. When love and fairness guide our policy toward both peoples, when love and fairness rise in our hearts "unawares," then will peace come to the Mid-East and America's Albatross sink like lead into the sea.

> He prayeth best who loveth best
> All things both great and small.
> For the dear God who loveth us
> He made and loveth all.

25

What's in a name? Fence, Separation Barrier, Wall

[March 20, 2004]

"Something there is that doesn't love a wall."
—Robert Frost, "Mending Wall"

Funny how Frost's fallen boulders, the size of bread loaves and small balls, when placed back on the other rocks that form a separation line between pine trees and apple trees on a New England farm, a border two or three feet high, becomes a *wall* while another, constructed of cement forms, 25 feet high augmented by chain link fence topped with rolled barbed wire, spiked by electric currents, and secured by Medieval guard towers, becomes, as it snakes its way over 400 miles of sand hills and green valleys, slips through towns and villages, and slithers through the debris left by bulldozed homes and uprooted olive groves—becomes a *"fence,"* a "separation barrier." Remarkable what we do with words! Brutality masked as innocence. What lies we tell each other to hide our fears.

From Jericho to Jenin, walls have played an ironic and paradoxical role in the lives of the Jewish people. Joshua led his people, at the Lord's command, to circle the walls of Jericho, and he said to them: "Shout: for the Lord hath given you the city." And they shouted and the walls came tumbling down. "And they utterly destroyed all that was in the city, both man and woman, young and old, and ox, and sheep, and ass, with the edge of the sword." [6:21] But victory, as complete and devastating as it was, turned to defeat as the spoils of war overcame love of the Lord and "the anger of the Lord was kindled against the children of Israel." [7:1]

What lessons might be learned from this passage from Joshua? First and most graphically, walls do not protect a people!

Determination, the will of a people destroys walls. Secondly, the corrupt appetites that lay hidden in the bowels, especially greed and power, destroy the achievements of a people and corrupt its will. After 2500 years, these lessons have yet to be learned.

Frost taunts his neighbor, "Before I built a wall I'd ask to know/ What I was walling in or walling out,/ And to whom I was like to give offense." I would suggest that Sharon's "Wall of Fear" walls in both the Palestinians and the Jews. It gives offense to those on both sides, and it offends the moral sensibilities of any civilized person anywhere in the world. Sharon prepared for the building of the wall by laying its foundation in the guts of his people—fear of four million terrorists and fear that the future offered no hope for peace.

Having bulldozed the Palestinian Authority out of relevance, he removed the possibility of negotiations, and, by that act, left the Jews without hope for peace. This gave him the freedom to force the erection of the "Wall." But there are Jews who find the Wall odious, Jews who object to the US Congress' Resolution 371 that supports Sharon's walling in of human beings because that resolution shows no regard for human rights' violations resulting from this wall, to say nothing of its illegality as contrary to prohibitions against occupying forces confiscating land.

Jews for Peace in Palestine, peace loving Jews in Israel, the TIKKUN community and others around the world understand that this Wall raises anger against the United States to new heights, thus lowering, ironically, the barriers protecting our security. Why this Wall does not offend our representatives boggles the mind, since it makes graphic how biased this administration is against the Palestinians. It confronts the Arab world with a visible and ugly icon of its racist mentality. The simple answer to Frost's question slithers over the Palestinian landscape, offending in its moral depravity every human that has a soul.

Consider, as Frost suggested, how the Wall walls in the Israeli people: it looms on the horizon a daily reminder that they have failed to achieve their primary goal. That goal is a peaceful assimilation of Jews from around the world into a haven, given to them by a remorseful Europe and America, where all could live in dignity and respect, without rancor or fear of racism, hatred and oppression. The Wall is a daily reminder that they have walled in a poor and deprived people behind barriers that isolate them from the community of nations, from their fields and shops, from relatives and families, not unlike the Pogroms suffered by the Jews in Poland, Austria, Russia, Hungary, and Czechoslovakia. It is a daily and fearful reminder that someday, somewhere, someone will scale or circumnavigate the Wall as people have done from time immemorial—as the Huns did when they mocked the efforts of the Chinese to keep them at bay on their side of the Great Wall, or the Germans when they laughingly skirted the Maginot Line—to make absurd the efforts of one people to subdue the will of another.

The Wall is a daily reminder that their purported Democracy mocks itself as it seals off an entire population in full sight of the world community despite the vocal objection of that community, indeed, in complete and utter disbelief that the Jews, of all peoples, could undertake such a heinous act. It is a daily reminder that they have created a monstrous gray monument to the harm they have inflicted on another people, a monument that in time will have the same effect as the march around Jericho: "And they utterly destroyed all that was in the city, both man and woman, young and old, and ox, and sheep, and ass, with the edge of their sword."

It is a daily reminder that visible or no, each and every name of an incarcerated Palestinian is carved into that cement just as the names of the fallen Jews, victims of Nazi atrocities, are carved into the marble slabs at the Holocaust Memorial in Florida. And, finally, it is a daily reminder that this Wall is but the beginning of a Wall that must stretch north and south along the Jordanian border, farther north along the Syrian line, west along Lebanon's southern coast, and south along the Sinai; thus completing the incarceration of the Jews once again.

Now consider how this Wall entombs the Palestinians: it becomes a daily reminder to the indigenous people that they can no longer hope to return to their land. Indeed, they can't even see their land, and their longing turns inward to wrestle with an absolute despair. It festers in the gut as a concrete reminder of villages lost in the 1948 battles, of the forced relocation of relatives and friends to refugee camps, of the theft of more land in 1967, and the complete defiance by Israel of UN resolutions to return their land.

It is a reminder of the world's indifference to their plight; it looms a constant reminder to their children that they must grow up in the shadow of the Wall and watch the setting sun slide beneath the barbed wire and black silhouetted forms that become for them a stark and unnatural horizon lacking the magnificence of the receding sun and the hope it symbolizes for the coming day. It harbors in its very existence the seeds that grow terrorists even as it makes possible the manufacture of bombs undetected by Israeli forces unless they venture behind the Wall and become sitting targets for the deranged—similar to the situation facing American troops in Iraq—negating thereby the very reason for erecting it. It rises, an eyesore among eyesores, in a barren landscape, a fitting symbol of oppression and occupation that prevents the people from gaining employment, forcing them to leave their homes in desperation, an act much desired by the builder of the Wall.

It stares down on the people like some dumb force that feeds the hatred of the fanatics and supplies them with an endless stream of recruits able and willing to wreak havoc on the innocent in Israel, since Israel has inflicted this insidious presence on them. And, finally, it begs the Palestinians to carve their names on that Wall to remind them they are the victims of an occupying government... a government that has failed to respond to their legitimate rights as expressed in numerous UN resolutions, and that has resorted to barbaric means to assure safety for its people, even as it creates conditions that will result in deprivation and death for those oppressed.

What is this Wall but a fitting monument for Ariel Sharon, the final stone that will be his gravestone etched with the names of all the Palestinians he has ever slaughtered since he was 23 years of age and began his march of destruction into history. This is Sharon's Vietnam Memorial, and, thank God, it is 400 miles long because he has far more than 58,000 names to carve on its hideous surface.

No glowing black marble here; rather a gray, dull cement color appropriate to its purpose as a memorial for the enslaved that must live in its shadow and contemplate how a civilized world could allow the erection of such a tomb. How absolutely sadistic are the actions of this man who decimated the very buildings and infrastructure of the Palestinian Authority and declared their leaders irrelevant even as he demanded they stop the terrorism in their midst. Having made the conditions of peace impossible of achievement, he resorts to the creation of the very symbol that gave credibility to the plight of the Jews in Europe, the walls of Auschwitz-Berkenau, and turns that symbol inside out!

What is this Wall to the American whose government is complicit in its creation? Aside from its feeble entreaties to Sharon to stop construction, and its shameful retreat when he tells our President to shove it, this government does nothing. Its cowardly behavior deserves nothing but our contempt. But it acts in our name and this is what it has done: my tax dollars and yours have paid for the factory that made the molds that have become the Wall. Our tax dollars have paid for the architectural design of the Wall, paid the workers to pour the cement, paid for the bulldozers that were used to clear the land of olive groves and houses, paid the drivers of the bulldozers, hired the men who placed the cement forms in lock step fashion over hill and dale, erected the chain link fence and the barbed wire, constructed the guard towers that stand like pitiful replicas of ancient days when the only recourse to disputes was the destruction of the powerless, not reasoned deliberations based on fairness and justice, accepted the illegal acquisition of Palestinian land by encircling illegal Israeli settlements, accepted as well the theft of water in aquifers beneath Palestinian land, accepted the necessity of continued support of this monstrous insult to humanity that will cost the American taxpayer more and more millions as the years go by, and, finally, and most tellingly, paid the price of insecurity for Americans around the world as the deprived of the world resort to the only retaliation left to them: a hatred of America engendered by our blind support of the state that inflicts such suffering.

"Something there is that doesn't love a wall"; that something abhors what is not natural, and a wall is not natural. It is a humanly made structure, the purpose of which is to exclude some for the alleged benefit of others. But when that purpose denies people freedom of movement, freedom of participation in the affairs of humankind, freedom of discourse with their fellows, freedom of fulfillment of individual initiative, freedom to raise a family, freedom to express opinions contrary to the power elite, freedom of self-expression, and freedom to believe according to their conscience, then the wall is destructive and anathema to human society.

How distant the memory that offered UN Peacekeepers to stand between the Palestinians and the Israelis that they might resort to deliberations, not oppression. Certainly, Sharon's Wall of Fear strangles freedom both for the Palestinian and the Israeli. It erects a barrier to peace; it does not encourage peace. It emblazons fear; it does not elicit hope. It stands a monument to failure, to retaliation and to vengeance. It could be nothing else.

26

The Yassin Assassination: A Monstrous Insanity Blessed by the US

[March 27, 2004]

Madeline Albright, this past Tuesday, offered the 9/11 Commission her recommendations for dealing with terrorism in the coming months and years. She made no mention of Israel and no Commissioner asked her about Israel. Yet the ink still ran on every front page around the world reporting on Sharon's insanity at unleashing American missiles (more than one!) to savagely murder Sheik Ahmed Yassin, an unarmed, deaf, half-blind, crippled, 67-year-old paraplegic being pushed in a wheelchair!

Does it not strike any sane individual, Commissioners included, that this act by our blest "man of peace" does more to raise hatred against America than any failing by our benumbed President who sat immobile in a classroom while New York burned? Sharon, with this monstrous act, declared war on America on behalf of Hamas. Sharon unilaterally burned the "roadmap." Sharon crucified America, sacrificing it for his own political interests.

This last in a series of "extra judicial executions," a euphemistic way of avoiding the true word, "assassination," buries justice beneath the mailed foot of the 21st century Medieval King who reigns by terror and brute force. We've created a new Dark Age! Rage determines behavior; rage becomes its own justification; rage liberates the beast to devour at will. But what is good for the beast is equally good for its intended victim; all kings become targets of fanatical rage justified as "extra judicial executions." After all, one individual's "good" is another's "evil" and we have made acceptable the individual as judge, jury, and executioner.

The world community abhors this state of affairs, yet the world's body, the UN, does nothing about it. Where is the condemnation of Israel for its illegal action? Where is the Security Council resolution citing Israel for flaunting the Geneva Accords and mocking human rights? Where is the United States Congress and Senate condemnation on behalf of its people of such a heinous act by a government that we support to the tune of 10 billion a year? Why do we cower before Sharon's bluster as he unleashes our $300,000 dollar missiles from our F-16 aircraft to kill a helpless man and the innocent that become victims of his vengeance? Why do our leaders not address the most obvious and glaring reason America is targeted by terrorists: the aggressive use of massive force by the state of Israel, using American-supplied ordinance against a defenseless people, while its leader, Ariel Sharon, deifies, mocks, and ridicules the President who is responsible for providing him the means to enforce his invasion and occupation of territory belonging to another people?

The entire world has stated its objection to Israel's intrusive militaristic policies. The entire world has stated that Israel is the principal cause of terrorism in the world. The entire world has marched against Israel's incarceration of these hapless people behind Sharon's "Wall of Fear." Yet this nation stands aside, stuttering mealy-mouthed platitudes that Israel has a right to defend itself against terrorists and, after all, Israel is our only friend in the Mid-East.

If Sharon's action in hunting down a man in a wheelchair and hurling missiles of massive destructive capability at him, missiles larger than the intended victim, knowing that by this act he was sowing seeds of fanatical hatred in the community of the deprived and deranged, than I would suggest that Sharon is the enemy of America, not its friend. How can our lawmakers listen to the chorus of countries that cry to us to stop Israel's intentional rousing of terrorism, intentional unsettling of any moves toward negotiation, intentional belittling of America and the UN when they utter, *submissa voce*, that perhaps the Wall should not be built; and intentional defiance of the UN for over 50 years—and stand like deaf mutes before an oncoming train of destruction?

It takes no genius to understand what Sharon has created by his kingly decision to determine in his own mind that a particular individual is a murderer and terrorist and deserves to die. He has given license to those who see him as evil personified to kill the "elected" leader of the state of Israel, and, by extension, the right to execute the "elected" leader of the state that supports his terrorism, George W. Bush. More than this: Sharon's witch hunt for the terrorist mind embedded in the frail frame of a 75-pound paraplegic who, would you believe, threatened the fourth largest military state in the world, opens the gates of Hell for those religious fanatics who believe right-wing Zionist zealots and American Christian Zionists like Franklin Graham, Pat Robertson, John Hagee, and Jerry Falwell, have blasphemed against the Quran and deserve to die. And Sharon has shown them the avenue to pursue: hunt them down like animals and take them unexpectedly as they emerge from their respective citadels of worship.

Bush and Sharon have co-opted the right to preemptively kill anyone who does not agree with their determination of who is evil, who threatens their respective states, and who poses a potential threat to their capitalistic systems. It's all in Bush's "National Security Strategy Report" of September 2002. This is our new rule of law! This is the advance of civilizations into the 21st century.

Consider what might have been the civilized way to deal with Sheik Yassin. Israel had done this twice before. Arrest him. Why did Sharon not drive a "handicapped" van to the Mosque to pick him up, take him to a detention center, submit allegations of murder, inciting to riot, and unjustified creation of a militant organization, and let an international court sit in judgment to find him guilty or not guilty?

Nothing prevented Israel from taking Yassin at will. Indeed, they have been on a new rampage of invasion of Gaza this very week; bringing Yassin to "justice" in the traditional western way would have been but a diversion. Such action would have forced the world to listen to the allegations and address Israel's righteous outrage against Hamas. Should the allegations prove true, the world would have to accept, perhaps with reluctance, Israel's on-going fight against fanatical terrorists. Such behavior would have created a positive atmosphere about Israel and America, in both the Arab world and around the world, that would go a long way to dissolve the bitterness and hatred that is fueling vengeance and retaliation.

But Sharon knows that America is in the midst of a 9/11 inquisition that fills front pages and TV screens. He knows Europe is
consumed, and rightly so, with the bombings in Spain. He realizes the people of the United States are more concerned with the
rising death toll and continued waves of destruction taking place
in liberated Iraq than with events in Israel. Knowing these realities, he is free to act undisturbed by a beleaguered George Bush.
And Sharon does not want peace or a Palestinian state. He wants
all of Palestine for his Jewish state and he wants the Palestinians
out of Palestine. If this action does not show the Bush administration that Sharon is a liar, nothing will.

Consider this. If Sharon acted unilaterally, without US knowledge, to murder the Sheik knowing he was placing America in
the midst of a religious war, then he is a traitor to the country
that supports him because he has put America in jeopardy. If he
contacted our President before he decided to murder the Sheik
and received no objection, then our President willingly acceded
to an act that would enflame the Mid-East and raise America's
fear of terrorism to a level unforeseen heretofore.

If it is not the responsibility of the 9/11 Commission to investigate why America became a target of fanatical zealots in 2001,
it should be because Sharon's execution of the Sheik endangers
America and begs for a meaningful understanding of why fanatics hate us. Fanatics find fault with America because it supports
a regime that occupies Arab land, a regime that knowingly
defies the United Nations and has done so over a fifty-year span
of time, a regime that refuses to return that land to its indigenous people. These fanatics watch America over the years control puppet governments in Saudi Arabia, Iran, Iraq, Egypt, and
Jordan while we control the natural energy resources of their
states and they remain in poverty.

Fanatics understand that America needs Israel as its military
weight in the Mid-East, a state that condemns their religion and
considers their race inferior. This Commission needs to ask why
Madeline Albright made no mention of Israel. Indeed, they must
ask themselves why they do not raise the specter of Israel as a
possible cause for terrorism against America. Sharon's monstrous insane act demands it.

27

How Far the Apple Fell from the Tree: George I to George II
[April 21, 2004]

To: Jeffrey St.Clair, Co-Editor, *Counterpunch*

Dear Jeffrey,

I came upon this letter while searching through my junk mail file. I have no idea how it got there unless the FBI or CIA was combing files under the Patriot Act and this got misplaced. But it is a curious piece, both because it comes from George the First and because it gives an unusual insight into his revisionist study of world events since he left office. I immediately thought of you and your readers at *Counterpunch* since I know they would be delighted to learn of George I's conversion to liberal thinking.

Peace, William A. Cook

Dear Son,

It's time we had a talk. I'm sitting here at breakfast in the gazebo at Kennibunkport, the sun greeting me as it glides up over the gilded, distant sea, a warm and so sweet breeze coming through the screens on this unusually mild spring day in Maine (notice how eloquent I've gotten in retirement!); you remember days like this when you escaped from the icky, sand-blown lawns of our Texas compound when you were a kid? I never did understand why you liked that place, although I must admit, you were able to meld your ineptness with the English language with the rowdies you trucked around with down there. Unfortunately, you also adopted their brand of "cowboy mentality," a rather New England way of saying "pig-headed," "close-minded," or "obstinate." Yes, George, this is a "father to son" talk of the kind I tried to hold with you from the time you entered your teens; I know they were few and far between because I was gone so much of the time doing government work, something you must now understand, although, again, I am amazed at how much vacation time you take. Who's minding the store may I ask? I hope it isn't Cheney and Rumsfeld; you can't leave them alone, George; they have nothing better to do in life than to amass fortunes and crucify others.

This letter follows two recent events that captured the headlines, your third (!) press conference in prime time in three years and your appearance with Ariel Sharon before the cameras, handing him the knife he used to stab you in the back! Do I sound angry, George? I am, I'm furious. I knew that I should have had these "father to son" talks before, and many of them, but I didn't and nothing has made that more obvious than these two events. Let me put it simply: you, George, like it or not, are head of this nation, let's call it a family because that's what we're supposed to be, so you are head of the family. As such you must set an example for the people, how they should act and behave toward each other, something like the expectation thrust on ballplayers like Sammy Solsa or Bond or that BB player who was traded because he did nothing but curse at fans and fight with other players; I don't remember his name but I'm sure you do. You get my point.

So what got me steamed? Let me tell you. You were asked a question at the press conference, a typical question asked of any person applying for a management job, "Can you describe any mistakes you've made and what you'd do differently if you had the opportunity?" What did you do? You stammered and fuddled around as though you'd been asked to clear up Einstein's theory of relativity or as though you'd never been interviewed for a job (come to think of it, that might have been the problem!), and you could not come up with any mistakes nor could you find any reason to apologize to the American people for the consequences of 9/11. Well, Junior, let me line up the mistakes for you so you can ask yourself if you have reason to apologize to the American people.

What insanity made you capitulate to that ogre, Sharon? Every time he comes here you melt, and Christ, Son, you're bigger than he is, at least you're taller and in better shape. What's he do, write your letters for you? Look what you've done!

(1) Before the Israelis have a chance to vote on the "internment" plan Sharon concocted for the Palestinians, you absconded with their right and made the decision for them.

(2) You unilaterally decided you'd discard international law by determining by yourself what national borders will comprise the state of Israel and the future state of Palestine without consultation with the UN or the parties involved.

(3) You broke the only multi-national agreement left, the "roadmap" (having discarded all the cooperative agreements I pulled together) that included Russia and Europe, by letting Sharon yoke the West Bank settlements into the state of Israel contrary to Resolution 242 of the UNSC and the vote of the UNGA at the creation of the Israeli state. And, Son, you did this without consulting Sergei Lavrov or Javier Solana or Kofi Annan or probably, for God's sake, Colin Powell. Worse than that, you didn't even talk to anyone in Palestine! When did you become dictator of the world?! Indeed, when did the "roadmap" become "your vision"; did you forget that others contributed to its design?

(4) You demand that the Palestinians stop terrorism but say nothing to Sharon about murdering Sheik Yassin or walling in the Palestinians, the two grossest terrorist acts yet perpetrated by Israel, both guaranteed to enrage the Arab world and ensure terrorist acts against America for decades to come.

(5) Now that you are caught in the quicksand of Iraq, you should know there is a difference between an indigenous population fighting for its country against an occupier, and a terrorist who wants only to inflict harm against a perceived enemy for perceived indignities. That realization should make you rethink your support of Sharon because he has turned the population attempting to throw off the occupying IDF into the same category as the terrorist—thus justifying everything he does with your blessing. Wake up, George, you're being used!

(6) You accept without question the right of a Jewish State to exist but will not accept an Islamic State in Iraq, a point not lost on the Arab world.

(7) You state that negotiations between Israel and Palestine will happen in "accordance with Resolutions 242 and 338" but you have closed the door on that possibility by stating in the same paragraph that it is "unrealistic to expect that the outcome of final status negotiations will be a full and complete return to the armistice lines of 1949." George, only Sharon could have written that sentence.

(8) You proclaim for all the world to hear that you are doing God's work. Where did you meet Him, George? At the ranch? Only a Texas mind could conjure up such a thought. You've got to get back to New England, Son, where we've put Puritanism behind us after the Salem witch trials in 1692.

(9) Now, George, I'm going to close this list with just one more item (though I could, in fact, continue if my eggs were not getting cold), the one where you have determined that international law that governs right of return does not apply for the Palestinians. And you believe that you make it so by saying it! My God, George, where is your head? As your father, I've got to intervene.

Now I can't focus on all those items above, but I can concentrate on a couple. I'm going to begin with Sharon; he is "ground zero," not New York's Trade Center and not even Iraq, although you've done mightily to make it so. If you'd spend some time reading, you'd understand that Osama, the people of Jordan, Egypt, Saudi Arabia, Asia, the EU countries, Canada, Australia, North Africa, God damn it, George, everyone in the world, sees Sharon and his government to be the cause of terrorism.

His incarceration of the indigenous population, his slaughter of 545 Palestinian children since he mocked the al-Aqsa Mosque in 2000 (and, George, 266 of these children had not reached their 14th birthday), thus bringing on the plague of suicide bombers, his theft of their land—all with your support and encouragement—outrages the Arab world. Why can't you see that? Have you swallowed the insanity of the Neo-Cons that surround you? They are dead men who never had real experience struggling in life beyond sitting entranced by other dead men, Leo Strauss and Bernard Lewis.

They tried to control me, Son, and I had to fight them off, especially Cheney and Rumsfeld. They wanted me to take out Saddam. But I was the only one who had real experience; they did what you did, they chickened out.

This is what I told them: "Trying to eliminate Saddam would have incurred incalculable human and political costs." Notice that word, Son, 'human', that's one the Neo-Cons never use. "Apprehending him was probably impossible. We would have been forced to occupy Baghdad and, in effect, rule Iraq."

I should underline that sentence, shouldn't I? Even you, George, can understand that Dad was right. "There was no viable exit strategy we could see, violating another of our principles." Perhaps I should have noted that it would also have violated international law. Well, I guess I did do that in a later sentence. "Going in and occupying Iraq, thus unilaterally exceeding the United Nations mandate, would have destroyed the precedent of international response to aggression that we hoped to establish." But you have no use for international agreements, do you? Certainly, Cheney and Rumsfeld don't, and they are more than likely telling you what to do. Here's the final sentence that you should have paid attention to, Junior: "Had we gone the invasion route, the United States could conceivably still be an occupying power in a bitterly hostile land." How's that for prophecy, Son? No God had to tell me that.

Now let's get to that dismissal of "Right of Return." Have you been so bamboozled by that Cabal that you think you can simply change international law by making a proclamation? The EU has already defied you! These are grown men, George, experienced men. They won't accept the dictates of would-be "men behind the throne" like Cheney, Rumsfeld, Wolfowitz, Perle, Feith, Libby, the whole cabal that clusters behind your butt, groveling to get to the top hitched to someone else because real people can see right through them.

Grab hold, Son. The right of return is a blessed right even if you don't have a religion. But go back to your Bible. Remember the Prodigal Son? He took off, abandoned his birthright for heaven's sake. But he returned and his father received him with open arms. Isn't there something in that story that tells you people have a right to return to their home?

The Palestinians were forced from their homes and villages in 1947 and '48; Benny Morris has confirmed that fact, George, and he's an Israeli Historian. They've been living in slums ever since, their homes and land taken from them, even bulldozed down for heaven's sake, whole villages disappeared—Mahlul, Jibta, Huneifis, Tal al-Shuman—and you take it on yourself to tell them, "Too bad, you lost!"

Are you out of your mind? Listen to the voices no one hears, the voices of children born in refugee camps in foreign lands, strangers there, homeless. "Their dream is of a Palestine that was their father's home, that they heard about, and maybe one day they'll go and visit the land he spoke about, all the years they were growing up." [Saida Nusseibeh] Doesn't that make your hair curl, Son? (Which, by the way, I notice you've let grow in, like all guys in your age group that have reached a mid-life crisis. What's with this?).

One final item, George, one that a father must raise and one that perhaps only I can raise: God has not given you a mission, Son; the only missions God has ever given—to Urban II, Innocent III, Martin Luther, St. Francis, Hal Lindsey, Pat Robertson, Oral Roberts, or any of the thousands of others who heard from Him—were given to delusional men needing an excuse for warped behavior! God gave no command that you must bring His gift to all humankind.

Only one thing is more certain than knowing God may not exist, and that is knowing what He knows. Why, George, would God want to destroy 15,000 innocent people in Afghanistan and Iraq to revenge 3000 killed in the Twin Towers and Pentagon? Why would He have you kill thousands of others defending their country and let thousands of them and thousands of our soldiers be maimed for life? Why would He kill and maim His creatures? What kind of a God do you believe in?

Wouldn't He want all of His creatures to share the glory of this morning, as I am here in Kennibunkport, and share the bounty of the earth He provided for all? Isn't that what your church teaches you, at least if you listen to the words of Jesus and not to the minister? "Clothe the naked, feed the hungry, shelter the homeless." And isn't that what the G-d of the Old Testament (after He got over destroying Canaanites and Hittites, et al) demanded of His people? Share your wealth with all less fortunate? And isn't that what Mohammad said God demanded as well? Give of your wealth to those who have nothing? Can't you see that the Cabal uses your religious beliefs to gain their ends? Didn't they tell you that Philip Zelikow, the guy on your transition team and now executive director of the September 11 Commission, would you believe (conflict of interest comes to mind, George; you might reflect on who recommended him for that post) stated it plainly enough: Saddam was no threat to America, "I'll tell you what the real threat (is) and actually has been since 1990—it's the threat against Israel. And this is the threat that dares not speak its name because... the American government doesn't want to lean too hard on it rhetorically because it's not a popular sell." In short, Son, you've been used and so have the American people. The only way you can stop the terrorism is to stop your support of Sharon!

This has been a long talk, Son, and while you may not be happy about it, I am. Age brings wisdom as it should bring respect. Consider what I've said. Don't get huffy the way you used to at Yale. You're no longer a cheerleader, Son, you're a head of state; pompously parading around doesn't cut it anymore. You must read and reflect, weigh options with care in full deliberations with all parties, not for special interests only, but for the good of all. Then, having decided on a course of action beneficial to all, act. But first, Son, you must be willing to admit that you have made mistakes. Growth, strength and wisdom come to those who recognize their talents, know their weaknesses and limitations and willingly and humbly admit their failures even as they move to correct them. You should have answered that question, Son. Never be afraid to admit mistakes and never fail to apologize for them. That's the sign of a man.

28

Tweedledee and Tweedledum, Kerry and Bush Melt into One

[April 24-25, 2004]

It occurred to me after Kerry's performance on *Meet the Press* this weekend that Americans have a choice this coming November between George Walker Bush or George Kerry Bush, the Tweedledumb and Tweedledeedumb proffered to us by the Republicrats Party. How clever: one party with two candidates playing at politics for the amusement of the world. John pretends to have disagreements with George on taxes and outsourcing of jobs while he obsequiously crawls behind the President when asked about Israel, and, in that shadowed place, regurgitates the policies of Bush that have locked the US into a "war" of terror. Lewis might have altered his verse a bit to accommodate these twins:

> Georgie Bush and John Kerry
> Agreed to have a battle,
> For Johnny thought that Georgie
> Did nothing but war and prattle.

> Just then appeared a monstrous terror,
> As evil as a tar-barrel,
> Which evaporated our heroes' valor,
> So they quite forgot their quarrel.

When asked by Russert if he agreed with the President's position on Israel as displayed at the Sharon and Bush entertainment special this past week, Kerry, quicker than a click of the mouse, answered, "Absolutely!" followed by the obligatory line: "Israel has a right to defend itself against terrorists." Now considering that Bush had just unilaterally extinguished the policy of the preceding four US presidents as it applied to the UN's demands that Israel return stolen land to the Palestinians, that he had erased the universally accepted right of dispossessed people to return to land taken from them illegally, that he had, hand cradled in Ariel's, granted license to anyone anywhere, Hamas leaders included, to murder any individual determined by that person to be a terrorist (laws of the land be damned), that he had shoved the "roadmap" up the respective noses of its co-authors without mentioning to them that he was about to rip it up, that he had jumped blindly into bed with the man considered by the vast majority of the people of the world to be the greatest threat to peace in the world (outside of himself) thus shoving his finger you know where at world opinion, [see "Eurobarometer," November 2003] that he had rejected even the semblance of understanding that hatred of America has a source of greater depth than his hollow cry that these fanatics hate our "freedoms" negating by his obsequious fawning before Sharon the statements by bin Laden [see ABC 1998 interview with Miller] and the people of Palestine, Syria, Egypt, Saudi Arabia, Iran, and Jordan that America's blind support of Sharon is the primary cause of unrest and attacks against the US, and, finally, that he had failed once again to distinguish between legitimate fighters against oppression and occupying forces that exist in Palestine and now Iraq, and terrorists that attack western interests around the world because they find fault with western values and impositions on their cultures—you'd think Kerry would have ruminated a bit before answering.

But no such thoughtful moments intervened; he had the answers programmed into his head: "Israel has a right to defend itself against terrorists." Then, as the cannibal said to the civilized man chewing on his nails, "Perhaps you should defend yourself against yourself," for that is the position Israel finds itself in; it is its own enemy isolating itself from the world community as it walls into a ghetto a defenseless population whose land it stole in 1948 and in 1967. The world cannot comprehend this behavior nor can honest Jews around the world, including vast numbers in America who protest at every opportunity Sharon's policies and Bush's capitulation, and now Kerry's, to this shameless victimization of a people that did no harm to the Jews before 1947. Listen to the words of Gerald Kaufman, veteran Labour MP:

> Sharon is a "war criminal" who ordered his troops to use methods of barbarism against the Palestinians... It is time to remind Sharon that the Star of David belongs to all Jews and not to his repulsive government. His actions are staining the Star of David with blood.

Bush's, and hence Kerry's, capitulation to Sharon's new rules continues efforts by Israelis to liquidate the indigenous population of Palestine. Sharon's removal of 7,500 settlers from Gaza is a token gesture to obscure the annexation of more than 150,000 settlers in the West Bank to Israel proper, stealing in the process the land, the groves, and the aquifers that exist there... decreasing the remaining land available to the Palestinians to approximately 10% of the pre-1948 land they had inhabited for more than 1900 years. [Henry Siegman, *New York Review of Books*] And this, Israel claims, demonstrates their commitment to the peace process! Sharon's "Wall of Fear" continues unabated, the largest open air prison ever constructed in the history of humankind, entombing millions in refugee camps and cramped ghettos cemented in by the wall on the west and the Dead Sea on the east (how appropriate an enclosure).

And this, Israel claims, demonstrates their commitment to the peace process! This Wall, that snakes through Palestinian land as it encircles the Sharon-protected settlements that rest illegally on others' land, locks out a few hundred thousand Palestinians from their groves, their villages, their families, their hospitals, their friends and their Mosques... a population Sharon intends to nudge out of their homes and "transfer" to the other side of the wall, thus enlarging Israel's land grab by an untold percent.

And this, Israel claims, demonstrates their commitment to the peace process! All this Sharon does in our name blessed by Bush and Kerry, thus demonstrating our commitment and Israel's to the continued slaughter of our young men in uniform and the agonizing unknown of terrorist attacks on innocent civilians throughout the world for decades to come.

Sharon's actions follow those of his predecessors that had commandeered Palestinian land, then rewrote history to tell the world that they legitimately acquired it. Moshe Dayan, in an address to the Israel Institute of Technology in 1969, stated openly,

> Jewish villages were built in the place of Arab villages. You do not even know the names of these Arab villages, and I do not blame you because geography books no longer exist. Not only do the books not exist, the Arab villages are not there either... There is not one single place built in this country that did not have a former Arab population.

Indeed, 369 Palestinian villages were destroyed and depopulated in the 1948 war, [*All That Remains*, Walid Khalidi] a calculated depopulation and forced "ethnic cleansing" of the indigenous people, constituting 54% of the total Palestinian population in Mandatory Palestine, as Benny Morris the Israeli historian, has confirmed. Lest we overlook the obvious, consider what this Israeli general accomplished with his tanks and bulldozers as he slashed the homes in these villages, burying under the sand and remnants of buildings the identity of the people whose birth records, property deeds, business records, yea, the historical evidence of their very existence, the memories of families, sank beneath the blades of the dozers—even as Rachel Corrie's life was snuffed out a year ago beneath another bulldozer driven by another merchant of death, Ariel Sharon.

This "colonization" of the Palestinian homeland took place in full glare of "civilized" media continuing to this day, and no one cared, nor do they care now—not even our only alternative to the new Pope, now resident in Washington, Bush II, whose "crusade" on behalf of God is now underway. Thus do we demonstrate our commitment to continued slaughter of the innocent, accepting as the crusaders did, that God's ways are unfathomable but surely just.

Having obliterated the villages and massacred or forced out the people, the Israeli leaders moved quickly to control the area designated by the UNGA as Israel's by importing Jews from around the world. In 1948, 806,000 Jews lived in Palestine, approximately 33% of the total population and they owned about 6% of the land; by the time the Israeli military completed its devastation of Arab villages, driving almost 800,000 Palestinians out, the indigenous population had been reduced to a minority. By 1972, the Jewish population had increased to 2,450,000, and by 2003, to more than 5,400,000, the vast majority immigrants. They now live in Arab homes or in new settlements constructed on top of razed Arab villages or in settlements illegally constructed in Palestinian territories while the Israeli government controls 93% of the land with provisions that prevent ownership by Palestinians.

But those who lived in Palestine, children of children of Palestinians who lived on the land since the Roman Empire expelled the Jews in 70 CE, cannot return to their homeland because Bush said so. No power given to the President by our Constitution gives him that authority; no provision in the Charter of the United Nations grants an American President such power; nothing written into the Geneva Accords provides such license. Yet having taken that authority unto himself he has guaranteed that the nations of the world will react negatively to America's arrogance. And the Arab world will understand, and rightly so, that this President has assumed the mantel of the ancient Crusader, a veritable King Richard the Lionhearted, in quest of the extermination of the Infidels, as he announces to the world that he has a mission from God Himself to bring His gifts to all of humankind. And Kerry, Catholic that he is, may find comfort in that mission and in its comparison to the glory days of the Medieval Church.

Both Bush and Kerry, by embracing Sharon, have embraced the continuation of terrorism against America for decades to come. Neither has thought out the causes of the hatred that resides in the world against the west, nor have they distinguished between legitimate freedom fighters struggling to regain stolen homeland, land occupied and controlled by foreign forces, and terrorists that rise in multiple countries around the globe, including our own (witness the Oklahoma bombing)... terrorists who have ideologies that conflict with western ideology and find need to assert their anger in random acts of retaliation for perceived wrongs inflicted by the west—including western control of their leaders and western control of their oil and gas reserves.

Unfortunately, legitimate freedom fighters, deprived of military resources and reduced to stones as weapons, ultimately resort to the last expedient, the suicide bomber, to regain their lost land. This is the case in Israel, which occupies illegally the land of the Palestinians since 1967 and which defies more than 155 UN Resolutions demanding that they cease and desist Human Rights violations and return stolen land.

It is also the case in Iraq because Bush's invasion of that country was as illegal as it was stupid. The Arab world has made it clear that Sharon's subjugation of a defenseless people in Palestine and America's invasion of an Arab state on behalf of Israel are the primary causes of anger in the Arab world. America's support of Israel's oppression and occupation makes it, to use Bush's own logic, an accomplice in the terrorism inflicted by Sharon on the Palestinians. His acceptance of his Neo-Con Cabal's use of American forces in the service of Israel adds fuel to the fire that resides in the soul of the fanatic. America has gone awry, and Kerry remains blind to that reality.

One would think that a man educated at a prestigious university would meditate a moment or two on issues like those above. And, if not on issues that raise righteous indignation because they spotlight moral concerns, then perhaps time might be spent on economics. Considering the current cost to the American taxpayer, a modest 10 billion per year if all costs are calculated including those paid out to Egypt and Jordan to assure that they will continue to recognize Israel, a citizen might expect a candidate for President to wonder if it is worth it. After all, cannot the fourth largest military in the world, defending a population of five million, care for itself against a population that has no army, air force, or navy but only the stones created by the demolition of homes by the IDF?

And should we, after all, pay for the removal of the Gaza settlements as Sharon has requested, after we paid for them to be built in the first place despite whispering to Sharon that he should cease building them? After fifty-seven years of support to the 16th wealthiest nation in the world, couldn't America consider cutting off its payments? Shouldn't some time be given to calculate the cost of our invasion and occupation of Iraq as it was done on behalf of Israel according to the Executive Director of the 9/11 Commission, Phillip Zelikow? I believe the cost has been calculated at roughly a billion a day. Since we demanded that the UN take decisive action against one nation, Iraq, for defying 16 of its Resolutions, should we continue to support a nation that defies 155 of them? Since we demand that all nations discontinue development of nuclear weapons or destroy those they possess, shouldn't we consider demanding the same of Israel that has in excess of 200? Fair is fair after all.

Wouldn't a common ordinary citizen think that a man who studied law might find some problems with the very concept of extra-judicial execution? Doesn't the reality of it make moot the need for law? Shouldn't Kerry understand this? Shouldn't he remember that assassinations are prohibited by Article 23b of the Hague Regulations, 1907? Shouldn't he know that American policy bans political assassinations? Even if credibility were given to Bush's repeal of that order, it would be difficult to claim that Sheik Yassin was a political and not a religious figure.

In short, Yassin's assassination was a symbolic act of destruction against the Palestinian culture. If those who rise to power can determine right from wrong, and have the power to impose their will, what need have they for courts of law? I was under the impression that this reality, that existed in the early Middle Ages and before, when barbarian hoards roamed Europe at will, inflicting their rule by might on all, gave rise to the need for civilized societies to construct a system of laws that would apply to all equally. Yet Bush and Sharon find no need for courts, for lawyers, for juries, for laws drawn up by the people's representatives; they are the law and apparently Kerry agrees. Perhaps the belief that God has appointed Bush as his emissary to the world to fulfill His mission makes Kerry believe he must assume that mantle when he defeats Bush in the November joust.

Watching Kerry surrender his intelligence to the mantra of Israel's demands on our representatives forces the citizen to resort to the UN for resolution of the dilemma facing the American voter. There is no hope of change in the future even if Kerry wins. Therefore, it is up to the UN nations to bring the US to task before the UNGA for indictment of all the international laws that have been decimated by this administration in its illegal invasion of a sovereign nation and in its support of the nation of Israel for its indiscriminate exploitation of Human

Rights violations against the Palestinians, and its defiance of UN Resolutions for over 30 years.

Unless it takes action, Sharon and Bush will have succeeded in returning the purported civilized nations of the world back to barbarian times as they plot their crusade against the Greater Middle East. Riding with them, apparently in full agreement with their arrogance, is John Kerry, the Tweedledee of the duo, chanting his mantra beneath a banner that proclaims his allegiance to the ancient Kings of Israel—"Me Too, Me Too!"

29

The Unconscious Country: Righteous Indignation Nakedly Displayed

[May 11, 2004]

Have we heard from everyone yet? The President blurted out how "disgusted" he was when he saw the photographs. The Secretary of Defense cringed at the "pictures" that had far greater impact than words alone. Senator Warner expressed "shame" that such vivid images of American wrongdoing had been on display for the whole world to see. All of the 24 members of the Armed Services Committee of the Senate offered how displeased, outraged, offended, and nauseated these explicit and un-American photos made them feel. Even John Kerry checked in, noting that the President should take full responsibility for this shameful display that has humiliated America before the entire world.

How courageous to witness this righteous indignation by America's pin-striped warriors as they cringe before the visible, graphic, four-color "pictures" that capture, as words alone cannot because they can be so easily skipped over, the horror of this "war" that they perpetrated on a defenseless people at the instigation of a President committed to the defense of Israel, as Senator Hollings has noted recently, a "just" war wrapped in lies and effectively executed with the latest state-of-the-art (SOA) weapons that suck the living air from the lungs, that pepper a child with pellets tearing the skin in hundreds of places, that cut cars into slices as easily as slicing a loaf of bread, that sear the eyes and the throat with devastating pain as the depleted uranium seeps silently on the wind-blown ash of the bombed-out home.

How courageous these men and women, beating their chests before the whole world, demonstrating like paid mourners their grief at the outrage even as they display the "openness" of the "Democracy" they bring to the infidels through their "precision" war that cleanses the evil from their corrupt regime, leaving only the good to blossom in the "greater Middle East."

Let us put aside the questions that were not asked of the Secretary of War or the Supreme General of our Space Command:

(1) When the Pentagon (the talking building in Virginia—no wonder we pay no attention to words) announced "to the whole world," as "Rummy" informed the Committee, that an investigation was underway concerning allegations of prisoner abuse, did it not occur to the Secretary that the President and the Armed Services Committee must be apprised immediately of the allegations, since the very thought of Americans committing torture could not be contemplated?

(2) Wouldn't the Secretary immediately command one of his trusted assistants to read the entire report and extract from it the most damning items, with recommendations on how to respond and when?

(3) Wouldn't it have occurred to the Secretary, since it has been his "state of the art" approach to military procedures and policy implementation, that private contractors, employed to "outsource" activities formerly undertaken by government personnel, were involved in these allegations and that he should know in what way they were involved?

(4) Wouldn't it have been a matter of concern that such contractors could be Israeli "consultants" like those hired to help American forces employ the tried and true "occupier" strategies employed by the IDF in urban areas, hired here to guide naïve Americans in the sensitive area of prisoner interrogation, the "softening up" process used so effectively against Palestinian detainees—consultants who would be anathema to sensitivities in the Arab world and associate America even more closely to the despised state of Israel?

(5) Would the use of such consultants have been considered initially, precisely because they cannot be held accountable to the Geneva conventions or to Iraqi justice (since it no longer exists when the country is under "occupied" status), thus allowing various methods of torture to be used—sleep deprivation, electric shock techniques, sexual humiliation, forced lewd and lascivious acts, intimidation and fear for wife and children—while protecting American commanders and soldiers from possible prosecution under existing US codes or the Geneva requirements?

It occurred to me as I watched the Committee members interrogate the Secretary, expressing outrage at Americans straddling naked Iraqi men stacked like sacks of grain on a warehouse floor, that their righteousness was misplaced if only because American forces should never have been deployed in Iraq. Where was their righteousness when the President announced in September of 2002 that Iraq had to be invaded, an announcement held until September because you don't sell a product in August? Where was their righteousness when his administration published the National Security Strategy Report that gave America license to invade any nation on earth at the behest of the President, a document imposed on the American people without consultation with their representatives, much less the people themselves?

Where was their righteousness when this same President declared the United Nations irrelevant, when he mocked the people who took to the streets in every major city around the world, when he brazenly and hypocritically presented the UNSC with an ultimatum that they authorize the US to attack Iraq, when he declared "war" on a word—'terror'—a word that at best describes a method of belligerence against a perceived enemy but in its vagueness, its intended vagueness, allows for unending war?

Where was their righteousness when the bombs began to fall on cities that had no air force to defend their residents, when pictures arrived showing fathers cradling in their arms their dying daughters, mothers weeping beside their mutilated children in dingy hospital beds, the graphic horror of little twelve-year-old Ali Abbas, armless and orphaned by a precision missile, the air pressing down over his skinless body? How righteous can a Senator be if they are responsible for placing our soldiers in an illegal war, a war conceived in secrecy by a band of self-serving ideologues, souls sold to Charon, bound in servitude to the state of Israel? A war reveled in by the Zionist evangelical hordes that grovel before ancient myths that make them "Chosen" in the eyes of their imagined God... a war declared and owned by the industrial-military complex that feeds itself on the oil and gas reserves of nation states that it buys and controls with American tax dollars, indeed, a war that keeps the Senators in power through the paid contributions to their re-election chests by these same corporations. How righteous to demand that someone beyond a private or sergeant be chastised for demeaning America before the world!

It occurred to me as I watched the Committee members interrogate the Secretary, as they sat in splendor in the paneled chambers of the Senate office building, a palace as resplendent as that used now by Consul Bremer, a palace built by Saddam himself for himself—that this Democracy no longer belonged to the people of America, but rather to a fragment of the one percent who own America. It occurred to me that our President had been appointed to his post by five members of a Supreme Court, self-declared cardinals anointed by the Almighty to elect their infallible Pope.

It occurred to me that we now have an opportunity to choose one of two to rule us for the next four years, elevated by virtue of their exalted bank accounts, two who mirror each other in all significant ways: unbridled acceptance of the need to invade Iraq despite world opinion and international law, obsequious adoration of the state of Israel caused, no doubt, by fear of retribution by AIPAC and their donors... committing America to war on behalf of another nation regardless of its impact on the American people, and blind acceptance of extra-judicial execution of opposition leaders... knowing full well the consequences of such action in the world community, most especially in the Arab world, and its devastating destruction of rules of law and basic democratic principles. Kerry and Bush, exalted members of the chosen few allowed to enter the inner sanctum of the Skull and Bones, scions of the patrician class that have bought our Democracy.

But what can one expect from those who rise out of the Tomb? What is there about an organization whose members take an oath to absolute silence about fellow members, regardless of the actions perpetrated by their fellows? What unlimited power does this permit? What is there about an organization whose nascent members must prostrate themselves before their superiors as they confess their most lascivious desires and acts... recognizing the absolute humiliation of their position as they recoil naked before these mocking eyes? What unbridled mentality does this unleash before those less fortunate?

What is there about an organization whose members understand their exalted status as scions of the chosen few, who from time immemorial have had license to lord it over the hordes that roam the earth, the privileged who have inherent rights to rule, recognizing their superior status in the world?

What unshackled power rises in the soul that has accepted its unquestioned right to rule? How curious that our compassionate conservatives have understood what took place in Abu Ghraib as little more than, in the words of the Lord of Conservativism, Rush Limbaugh, "fraternity initiation rights, pranks only." How appropriate that the Skull and Bones sanctuary is called the Tomb. There in its innards resides an exclusive population of maggots that coil about each other in an ugly love ritual of huddling and clinging while feeding on others' deprivation, releasing from time to time one of its membership to rise to the pinnacles of power the better to control the masses and ensure the continuation of their resplendent Tomb in that citadel of idyllic learning walled off from the slums of New Haven.

I would that our Senators represent the people, the people corralled by the military recruiters who place an estimated 70% of their recruiting offices in poverty neighborhoods where our minorities reside. I would that they represent the average wage earner who is strapped each month to a pile of bills too great to pay, forcing them into greater and greater debt day after day.

I would that they represent the laborer who receives from our corporations the pittance of a wage that keeps them floundering below the poverty line. I would that they recognize that America is not an island in the world, able to navigate alone and use others to its benefit alone, avoiding the shoals and currents that make all residents of the earth neighbors in a community dependent on each other.

I would that they responsibly act against an administration that has lied and deceived the people they represent, that has brought humiliation on America equal in depth and kind to that inflicted on the prisoners in Abu Ghraib, that has destroyed the fabric of American oneness by creating a fissure within our population that decries dissent as unpatriotic, and that has brought shame to the very concept of Democracy.

These are the Senators who scream so loudly when pictures are displayed of flag-draped coffins bearing the dead soldiers that they had sent off to die. What insensitivity to show such pictures to Americans! These are the Senators who allow this administration to prevent photographers from meeting the planes at Dover air base, to photograph the wounded and maimed in Germany, to let the journalists and their cameramen photograph where the missile lands, that prevent Americans from soiling their eyes with graphic pictures of dead and rotting corpses lying in the streets, or scenes of innocent civilians murdered in their cars at check points, or hit by sniper fire as they helped put a wounded person in an ambulance.

These are the Senators who accept without question, extra-judicial execution done in our name by CIA operatives, a practice taught us by Sharon as he directed the murder of the paraplegic Sheik Yassin with missiles fired into a crowded street "accidentally" killing innocent bystanders. Why wake Americans to the reality of their complicity in this carnage, the war they, the Senators and Congressmen, have created in our name? Perhaps it is time we heard from America.

30

Violence Disemboweled of Law: Manufacturers of Fear and Loathing in Radfah

[June 1, 2004]

Violence, less and less restricted by a system of laws built up over centuries, strides naked and victorious over the earth, caring not one jot that its sterility has been demonstrated and proved many times before in history. It is not just coarse violence itself that is triumphant, but also its shrieks of self-justification. The world is overrun by the brazen conviction that force can do everything.
—Alexander Solzhenitsyn, Nobel Speech, 1970

The ravaging of Rafah continues to this day, a month-long siege of unbelievable violence, despite the UN resolutions condemning Israel's complete disregard for human rights, an open defiance of both the UN and international law. Does anyone deny, in the deepest recesses of their heart, the barbaric behavior of Sharon's hordes as they devastate the defenseless inhabitants of the Rafah refugee camp?

Are we all blind and mute, silent witnesses to murder and mayhem, cowed by fear of the inevitable Israeli stamp—Anti-Semitic—should we condemn Sharon's atrocities? What have we to fear but the realization that we are complicit in the slaughter should we do nothing to halt it and suffer that acid to fester in our soul?

Silence is a two-edged sword: it cuts out the moral guts of the citizen even as it gives license to those who inflict this shame on the defenseless in our name. No, we need a deafening, earsplitting call to moral arms that condemns without equivocation the near genocidal eradication of the Palestinian people from the last vestiges of their homeland. Enough is enough! Condemn Sharon as an Anti-Semite; he has destroyed the values that sustain and nourish the Jews, not those who condemn Sharon's savagery.

We need to join the 150,000 Jews who marched in Rabin Square against Sharon, making clear that fear has not muffled all in Israel. We must extol the moral courage of Gideon Levy and Uri Avnery who keep alive the true values of the Jewish people despite the overpowering forces that control their country. We must support the Jews for Peace in Palestine and the TIKKUN Community as they rouse the ire of the American Jew to condemn the brutality of Sharon who brought such worldwide shame on Israel.

Uri Avnery calls it "The Rape of Rafah," a fitting analogy since it is being waged by the three old goats that guide Israel's bloody rampage in the prison that is Gaza: Ariel Sharon, the architect of the massacre of Sabra and Chatila; Shaul Mofaz, his Defense Minister; and Moshe Ya'alon, the IOF Chief of Staff. These three carrions of death and slaughter must "bear responsibility," in the words of Gideon Levy, "for... the virtual imprisonment of the Palestinian people, the prevention of medical care, the mass arrests, the assassinations, the needless killing, the bombing of residential neighborhoods."

Some 56 years have passed, Meron Benvenisti writes in *Ha'aretz,* since Moshe Dayan and his crew drove the Palestinians from 418 towns and villages so they could be demolished and replaced with Israeli settlements. Now "the sights of Rafah are too difficult to bear—trails of refugees alongside carts laden with bedding and the meager contents of their homes; children dragging suitcases larger than themselves; women draped in black kneeling in mourning on piles of rubble. And in the memories of some of us... arise similar scenes that have been a part of our lives, as a sort of refrain that stabs at the heart and gnaws at the conscience... the procession of refugees from Lod to Ramallah in the heat of July 1948."

The ethnic cleansing continues, decade after decade, month after month, day after day, a forced colonization of the Palestinian homeland by an immigrant population done in broad daylight in this modern age of communication and electronic media.

What do our world leaders do? They pass yet another resolution condemning Israel! Count them if you can, 157 or 158, or do we count only those not vetoed by the US? What difference does it make? Will the UN enforce any one of them? Will George W. Bush appear before the UNSC arrayed in full indignation at the reprehensible behavior of this rogue state that defies the UN turning its deliberations into irrelevant gibberish? Will he demand that this latest resolution be obeyed, number 1544 (passed by the UNSC 20 days after this massacre began!), that Israel "respect its obligations under International Humanitarian Law... not to undertake further home demolitions (191 homes in Gaza alone by May 20)," not to continue the slaughter of innocent children (28 killed by the time the UN passed its resolution), and not to shamelessly ignore the hapless plight of the 2500 made homeless by this wanton destruction?

Will George W. Bush accept responsibility for using American citizens' money to pay for this massacre? Will he recognize his responsibility for aligning America behind a sadistic regime ruled by a demonic madman who takes advantage of the world's preoccupation with the crimes perpetrated by American forces at the Abu Ghraib prison to rampage through the squalid and cramped quarters of Rafah? Does he understand that Sharon perpetrated this massacre to remove from the front pages further news of his illegal laundering of money and his loss in the polls of his "Gaza initiative," an act of political retaliation that has cost the lives of more than 125 Palestinians and hundreds wounded? Does he unquestioningly accept Sharon's lies that this massive invasion has been done for "security reasons" when Gaza is responsible for only 12 of the 116 attacks perpetrated on the Jews since September 2000? What heinous and heartless immorality do we support!

How does one convey the unjustifiable vileness of this ravaging of Rafah, this "military incursion" euphemistically cloaked as "operation rainbow" that covers, no doubt, Israel's "pot of gold"—the land that Rafah and Gaza occupy; it need only be cleansed of its rabble! Should operation rainbow have been inflicted on my hometown atop the San Bernardino Mountains where 8700 residents live, every resident would now be homeless and that number would represent only half of those homeless in Gaza! Mercifully, the residents of Crestline have

homes scattered over miles of treed hills and valleys. They are
not crammed into concrete and wooden structures erected 50
years ago when they were first driven from their villages by the
advancing Israeli forces. This is their second "ethnic cleansing"
that has left a mile-long "swath of broken concrete, splintered
wood and twisted metal," the ignominious detritus left in the
wake of American Caterpillars. Certainly they deserve their
fate. After all, Israel only targets "terrorists and the structures
they use." One might hope this mile-long swath has destroyed
all terrorists and the buildings they use. Israeli intelligence must
be as accurate as our CIA information stream to identify 17,594
terrorists, all conveniently located in this section of Rafah and
now all homeless, thank God.

But let's drop the facetiousness and address the reality. Let's
move all of Crestline's residents downtown, clustered in bunga-
lows jammed wall to wall. Now, awaken them at 2AM as the
Caterpillars rumble into the streets, crushing the first home on
the block, shoving it into the next. Mothers and fathers with
children in their arms rush screaming from the houses lest they
be buried beneath the twisted wood and stone. Floodlights scatter the early morning darkness, casting eerie green-black shad-
ows across the streets as masses of people crowd into the alleys;
the whirl of helicopter blades vibrate overhead as tank turrets
point threateningly down the streets; a clash of sounds erupts on
every side, the thunder of tank treads, the piercing cry of splitting steel, the shrill screech of wind twisting through alleys, and
the wail of weeping children that falls from shattered walls.
Suddenly, from the belly of the copter, flashes of lightening
appear as missiles scream through the air exploding into walls
and the crowds scatter, leaving behind on the rubble the bodies
of the dead. Fear explodes in the streets bursting from the
body's pores like sweat, and loathing for the tormenters swells
in the heart as hot as bread that rises in the oven. This is the
rainbow that rises above the blackened remains of Rafah portending the prophecy the Jews know well: "God gave Noah the
rainbow sign, no more water, the fire next time."

That conflagration burns now beneath the loathing and the
hate fueled by the inequity so visibly evident in the massive military Israel thrusts against a helpless population. It drives the insanity that finds recourse in suicide and the fantasy of martyrdom; it

is the mythical seed that finds ultimate justice in an unknown, unseen, all just God. It alone dispels the depression that comes with the isolation and abandonment, the complete absence of sympathy from the people of the world.

Nothing changes. For fifty years they have waited for the world to respond to their plight. For fifty years they have witnessed the impotence of the UN to enforce any of its resolutions that demand Israel's compliance with its rules and international law. Two years ago they listened as the UNSC Resolution 1435 reaffirmed resolutions 242 (1967), 338 (1973), 1397 (2002), 1402 (2002), and 1403 (2003) reiterating its "grave concern for recent tragic and violent events carried out by Israel and the continuing deterioration of the situation in Palestine..." specifically, the bombing of a Palestinian school at Hebron, the bombing of Palestinian civilians on September 18-19, 2002, the reoccupation of Palestinian cities and towns by Israeli troops, imposing restrictions on the freedom of movement of citizens and goods, the need to respect International Humanitarian Law including the 4th schedule of the Geneva Convention for the protection of civilians in time of war, and the destruction of Palestinian civilian infrastructures, to name a few.

They listened May 20, 2004 as the UNSC issued Resolution 1539 concerning the responsibility for the safety of children where violence and armed conflict takes place. These resolutions, including 1544, require that Israel respect its humanitarian obligations, immediately implement its obligations under the roadmap, and withdraw from ALL Palestinian territory beyond the 1967 border line. These documents are signed by all 15 members of the UNSC, including the US (George Gains, Swindon, UK). They listened and they wait.

They wait in Rafah, all 120,000, the poorest of all Palestinian cities, and they wait in the Shaboura district, the poorest section of Rafah where whole families "live together in one-room shacks made of corrugated iron with dirt floors and sheet metal, cardboard and tarpaulin roofs... Nowhere in Palestine will one find conditions as miserable and destitute as they are in Rafah, approximately 80% of whose citizens are refugees sometimes two and three times over." [Jennifer Loewenstein, *Counterpunch* 1/04] Who will listen to their plea for justice? Who will offer them the freedom promised to the Iraqis? Who will plead before the United Nations that their resolutions must be attended to, all 156 of them, that peace might at last reign over the Hell that is Palestine?

Embedded in Solzhenitsyn's cautionary observation, violence disemboweled of laws is sterile, is the truth it foretold, not only about the implosion of the Soviet Union, but the inevitable erosion of the values inherent in Judaism and the destruction of America's Democracy as it seeks dominance of the world by force. As Sharon and Bush isolate Israel and America from the community of nations, as they instill fear in the hearts of their people, made real by the arrival of unspecified threats against unspecified targets at unspecified locations; as they undertake an ever more obvious crusade against Muslim peoples using lies upon lies to justify their actions against Palestine, Iraq, Syria, and Iran, the Israeli and American people witness the intrusion of their respective regimes into their daily lives. They witness the erosion of their freedoms as they are forced into bunkers built of fear.

Two forces propel these administrations, both fueled by the realization that fear obliterates sense and commands allegiance to those who promise security for all: the Zionist zealots in Israel and those in the Evangelical Christian ranks and the Neo-Con Likud sympathizers who yoke Israel's interests to those of America. Fear destroys reason, leaving the individual's conscience in the hands of those who instill the fear. The Christian right deploys Satan (read fear) against God's believers while the Neo-Cons raise the specter of "terrorists" that threaten free men everywhere. Thus does violence and force ride naked over the earth.

31

The Legacy of Deceit: If Dante Knew of Bush and the Neo-Cons

[July 6, 2004]

> "...the hypocrite's outward appearance shines brightly and passes for holiness, but under that show lies the terrible weight of his deceit which the soul must bear through all eternity."
>
> —From John Ciardi's notes, Canto XXIII, *The Inferno*, by Dante

Dante approached the injustice and corruption of his day by creating a concrete and graphic image of the Medieval visualization of Hell in *The Inferno*. He then populated its sundry levels of excruciating punishment with the politicians, clerics, militarists and businessmen who caused that injustice and corruption. It occurred to me that Florence in 1300 mirrors in microcosm the injustice and corruption of Washington, D.C in 2000.

As I watch the President, the Vice President, other administration officials and FOX news anchors, in direct contradiction to the findings of the 9/11 Commission, regurgitate the lies they told to send 850 American soldiers to their deaths, to cripple and maim more than 4000 others, and to murder an as yet undetermined number estimated at about 10,000 Iraqi civilians, I could not help but reflect on the legacy these men must leave to future generations. With that in mind I attempted to find the appropriate circle of Hell in which to place these leaders of the "free" world. Given the religious intensity of this administration, proclaimed by the President repeating without end his known truism "...it's not our gift that we bring to the nations of the world but God's gift of freedom that belongs to every man and woman on the earth," the Medieval mentality that permeates Dante's vision of Hell seemed an appropriate place to begin.

But in which circle of Hell do they belong? The Opportunists, those souls that lived without regard for good or evil but only for themselves, certainly described the reality of Cheney, Rumsfeld, Perle, Feith, Wolfowitz, Libby and the whole crew at the American Enterprise Institute and the Project for the New American Century. But they were housed in *The Inferno* in the Vestibule experiencing only the sting of wasps and hornets as they run round and round through the dirt infested air, their bodies flowing with the putrid smell of pus and blood feasted upon by worms and maggots—hardly, I confess, an adequate retribution for their crimes. After all, Dante understood the wasps and hornets to image a guilty conscience, but these men have no guilty conscience. Indeed they have no conscience at all. I decided to withhold judgment.

Circle two and three offered promise at first sight, circles devoted to those who in life gave themselves to carnal desires and gluttony. But this administration is composed of many "born-again" believers, like Bush and Ashcroft, who have foresworn the sensual life for bigger and more fulfilling sins. Hoarders occupy circle four, those who destroyed God's light within their souls by thinking of nothing but money. That seemed most appropriate for Cheney and the merchants of death who make money from war profiteering: the Halliburton, Bechtel, Titan, CACI corporations and their ilk that sit on the edge of the ravaged plains like carrion birds awaiting the appropriate time to fly in for their meal.

But certainly they deserve more punishment then hurling great weights at each other, the retribution Dante conceived for Hoarders, especially since hoarding money represents only a fraction of their sins. Circle seven promised more. Here reside murderers and war makers, tyrants and dictators, those violent against their neighbors. Perhaps no place is more appropriate than to have Bush and Rumsfeld reside side by side with Saddam and Sharon! What a fitting place where the inhabitants wallow in boiling blood forever, a constant reminder of the butchery they inflicted on the innocent in life.

Dante did not provide for a soul to spend time in one circle before moving on to another, a decided flaw in his conception when one has sinners of the like we have in DC. Consider the value of moving Bush, Rumsfeld, Rove, and Cheney, after an appropriate number of centuries in the boiling blood of circle seven, to circle eight where the fraudulent and malicious are driven in an endless walk by horned demons, a punishment that mirrors their crime: in life they prodded others to serve their fraudulent and illegal ends, so now they in turn are goaded in an endless walk in the eighth ditch.

Crammed into that same ditch, perhaps with an opportunity from time to time to wiggle their feet at each other, belong the tele-evangelists Franklin Graham, Jerry Falwell, Pat Robertson, and Pastor John Hagee among others, who are placed there because they sold ecclesiastical favors and offices for personal gain. These are the corruptors of God stuffed upside down in tube-like holes, feet jutting out, a veritable mockery of the baptismal font, the source of the water they used as their instrument of fear to push their congregants to their will. This ditch, packed wall to wall with their ilk from Moses to the present day, provides an oily fire that licks at their feet, a just retribution for their crimes against their respective Gods, Yahweh and Jesus. Dante understood that the greatest disaster to afflict the church came as a result of its corrupt quest for wealth; things have not changed.

Only two circles remain, but they are the most graphic in representing the Eternal retributions due our leaders. Hypocrites tread the forlorn track of the bolgia that is their home for all eternity in circle eight. Robed in leaden monk's habits, glowing in gilded splendor, the outward show of holiness, they carry the terrible weight of deceit beneath these garments, "so heavy that we, their weary fulcrums, creak and groan." Here is an appropriate circle for our band of hypocrites: politicians, military fawners and churchmen. But they are more than hypocrites; they are thieves as well, having stolen the citizens' wealth for decades to come. Fortunately, thieves, too, reside in circle eight wrapped in pits of monstrous reptiles that twist and curl about their loins. What an apt retribution since they borrowed Nietzsche's corrosive philosophy, used ironically by the Nazis against the Jews, to gain power by blindly following Strauss' negation of morality: use religion—Zionism and Christianity—to manipulate millions by invoking fear on one side and prophecy on the other—instinct and superstition—as motivating drives to empire. Perhaps Dante would allow them to experience the retribution of both sins since, as followers of Strauss, they are bound by no morals whatsoever, only power.

Now there will be those who would draw a distinction between Bush as Puppet and his handlers, the evil counselors that use his dim wit to their advantage. Should we accept that distinction, we must separate Rove, Cheney, Rumsfeld, Wolfowitz and the cabal of neo-cons from their shadow boss as they enter the ditch set aside for evil counselors where they will move about endlessly, hidden inside enormous flames. Hidden forever, consumed by flames that represent the destruction of the gifts given to them by God, the perversion of their intellects from seeking what is good to manipulate others by wiles and stratagems, they sinned by glibness of tongue and so are consumed by tongues of flames. Conscious deceit corrupts both the deceiver and the deceived: the deceiver decays into demonic decadence, the deceived into an unreasoning pawn inflicting the deceivers' will on the innocent.

Circle eight, however, does not end with tongues of flame. Below that ditch circles a group of hideous and mutilated souls, the sowers of discord. Certainly, the whole army of this administration must join this parade of deceivers. They tore asunder the very threads of unity that God had created to bind all peoples into one so they, for all eternity, must be hacked apart by the bloody sword wielded by demons. Day after day they drag their torn bodies through the pit as their wounds heal, only to be hacked again and again by the demons, a continuing circuit of constant torment and mutilation. What an awful band they are! Sowers of Religious Discord, Sowers of Political Discord, Sowers of Discord between Kinsmen, the reapers of the whirlwind.

Here reside all the clerics of the evangelical right, sowers of prophetic discord, liars who deceive by proclaiming communication with God Almighty as they interpret the *Book of Revelation* and drive their respective congregations to invest in terrorism in Israel. Here beside them crawl the Zionist right-wing members of Sharon's brigade of fanatics who deceive the Jews even to accepting the deadly Christians for political expedient reasons. Here Karl Rove worms his way hacked by demons, the very face of deception and discord. Here stumble beneath the blows all who used their kinsmen, their fellow Americans, as fodder for their wars, the lowest of all in Hell, an incestuous legion driven to fratricide to attain their ends. And here, no doubt, we will see George W. Bush cry out, as Mosca dei Lamberti did to Dante from this deepest abyss:

> Remember me; see what a sentence has been passed upon me, and search all Hell for one to equal this!...I set son against father, father against son... and since I parted those who should be one in duty and in love, I bear my brain divided from its source within this trunk; and walk here where my evil turns to pain.

And so he walks for all eternity holding his severed head by the hair before him like a lantern as it weeps in its despair.

All of these await entrance into the final ditch in circle eight, a ditch reserved for the falsifiers. Since they corrupted society through their falsifications, they exist in darkness, filth, disease, din, and stench, the sum of the corruptions they inflicted on humankind.

But there is one final ditch, the ninth, a bolgia designed for those treacherous to country, an apt accommodation for our crew of sinners. Here they remain locked in ice, in close proximity to their lord, Satan, only half their faces above the ice, where even tears freeze in the sockets, making impossible the relief that comes with tears of remorse.

Our righteous indignation might revel in the potential Dante provides in *The Inferno* for our criminals, but my cynicism doesn't allow for it. No, I'm afraid that "W" will retire from office to Crawford where the next Presidential Library will be built, albeit the smallest of all since he does not read or write and most, if not all, Presidential papers will either be classified or non-existent. The only point of comparability between this library and others will be its silence. Perhaps cynicism is a cry of despair? After all, there is a legacy created by this administration, a legacy of deceit that hovers like a dark shadow above all America.

The good Prayer Book (5:6) observes "the Lord will abhor both the bloodthirsty and deceitful men," perhaps as comfort for those who have had to live through their vileness. But I do not believe they will suffer their due rewards. We will and our children will. Consider the real and painful legacy these men have bequeathed to all Americans. The most insidious legacy and most corrosive for a Democracy is the dissembling of trust in our fellow men, those we must select as our leaders. Erode trust and the very pillars that support consent by the governed crumbles. This administration has eroded trust.

But there's more, there is erosion of belief in the perceived values that are the bedrock of America's uniqueness in the world...honesty, fairness, and equality for all. Act illegally, attack with overwhelming power, and impose beliefs where they are unwanted and the substance of the American experiment evaporates. This administration has corrupted America's values.

But there's more, there is questioning now of the ideology that gives America its primary position among the nations of the world—a belief that rights reside inherently in the nature of the individual, a belief that embraces the sacredness of all and grants respect to all. Force nations to heel to America's will and the very concept of individual rights vanishes. This administration has destroyed the American character and its promise.

Consider also these legacies of national distrust: distrust in the Supreme Court that steals the vote from the people to fulfill its political obligation to the Republican Party; distrust in the political system that has been co-opted by corporate money; distrust in the Congress that can impeach one President for a personal failure and let another lie to the people in order to wage his personal war using our soldiers' lives to achieve his end; distrust among the people as they watch a band of Neo-Cons abscond with their government and impose their ideology on the world's communities in their name; distrust among the people as they witness a small group of religious zealots attempt to force their superstitious beliefs on the country, subverting thereby the separation of church from state; distrust of the media that has been acquiescent in the corruption that has plagued this administration; distrust of the government departments created to uphold and secure our safety because the administration has refused to cooperate in the proper investigation of the terrorist acts that resulted in 9/11; distrust of those in our society that represent privilege, power, and wealth as above the law while the deprived, impotent, and poor fill our prisons; and, finally, distrust in a system that promised individual control and consent betrayed by those who took control and mocked consent.

Consider also these legacies of international concern: perception of America as a nation that will subvert and undermine the Geneva Conventions regarding human rights and prisoner rights, a perception that destroys the very premise of America's declaration of individual rights; cynicism regarding America's stated motives to bring "freedom and Democracy" to all when the worlds' communities witness this administration impose its will by force or coercion on weaker nations; an understanding that America is willing to lie to its people and to the people of the world to gain its ends, making impossible trust in American policies; questioning of the logic and sense of Democracy if it allows for such stupidity to gain control of the most powerful nation on the planet by a few ideologues who have no belief in the system they have subverted; awareness that this government will inflict its retaliation on those who do not agree with it negating thereby honest and sincere dissent; recognition that corporate power determines the actions of America and its foreign policy and determines the use of the world's natural resources by control of America's might; realization that America has locked itself irrevocably to Israel regardless of the consequences of that allegiance to international security and peace in the Mid-East, recognizing in its support of Sharon a nation that wants instability in order to ensure Israeli theft of Palestinian land and eventual hegemony in the "greater Middle East"; an appreciation that America under this administration will deny any responsibility for creating conditions that breed terrorism because it denies responsibility for ravaging the world's resources—causing endless harm to the environment and great disparity in health and wealth around the world.

And, finally, recognition and fear that this administration has created a new foreign policy that has opened the door to chaos and destruction by claiming its right to pre-emptive strikes against other nations, disengaging unilaterally from international treaties and agreements, negating the concept and function of international law, accepting the use of civilians as fodder for war to invoke shock and awe, mocking the value of the

United Nations as a collective body for international peace, and most viciously, destroying the principle that gives meaning to government by law, acceptance of extra-judicial execution— thereby giving license to all to kill at will, negating both individual rights and belief in human equality. This legacy of understanding by the international community becomes our legacy as we travel the world.

Some would argue that I have omitted the most significant legacy, the economic debt thrust on the American people and their children. Let me recognize that legacy as a just retribution imposed on a people (imposed unfairly on those who fought against this administration) that let this administration stay in power by not speaking out against the representatives that coddled to its power, that allowed its media to become but sounding brass for corporate voices and administration lies, that enabled Ashcroft to cripple our freedoms with his right-wing religious prejudices and his shackling of our rights with his Patriot Acts, and that listened to the pseudo-prophets of the National Church of Television as they excused Bush's lies that has resulted in close to 900 dead American soldiers and 10,000 Iraqi civilians, countless wounded and maimed, all in the name of the peaceful Jesus they purportedly worship.

Unfortunately, that debt may become the anchor that sinks America in time. While the Neo-Cons extol America's world dominance both militarily and economically, reality suggests that another power has arisen that could undermine that dominance. With the rise of the European Union and its currency, the Euro, America's dollar has competition. As America's debt builds, as its losses in the military theater become more and more obvious, as its acceptance as an international partner continues to erode, as more nations see it and its parasite in the Mid-East, Israel, as terrorist states and the greatest threat to peace on the planet, confidence in the dollar will fall and the Euro will become more and more attractive. That could be disastrous for America, resulting in the worst tangible legacy of all: an economic depression of incalculable consequences.

Perhaps we must return to the Prayer Book (43:1), "Oh God...defend my cause against the ungodly people: O deliver me from the deceitful and wicked man."

32

The Rape of Philomela: Silencing the Voice of the People

[August 10, 2004]

Dissent disrupts democracies, yet without it there is no democratic discourse. That point struck home as I watched the Democratic National Convention unfold and realized the voices of the delegates, the representatives of the common people, had been muffled by the preordained celebrants of the Kerry command. With rare exception, notably Jimmy Carter and Rev. Sharpton, no voice spoke against the appointed incumbent; no voice raised the rabble about the lies that led to slaughter; no voice questioned the silencing of the people behind the curtain of the Patriot Act; no voice damned the administration that dared to impose on Americans the impious "pre-emptive strike" policy that destroys the very concept of Democracy; no voice asked why America does nothing to respond to the silent genocide taking place in our name in Rafah and the refugee camps crammed together in Gaza; no voice lamented the incarceration of the Palestinians by the illegal wall made of hatred and racism erected by the notorious terrorist, Ariel Sharon; no voice blasted the erasure of western law by the acceptance of extra-judicial executions; no voices, not a sound.

Why?

Recently I happened upon an apocryphal story told about the Nuremberg trials [sic]. Day after day an old man made his way to the front of the courtroom, slid quietly into his seat, and listened attentively to the proceedings. During the Adolf Eichmann hearings, he seemed engrossed in the man. His eyes never left Eichmann, as though he of all the prisoners might reveal some hidden truth that would give understanding to the horror of their acts.

One day, with Eichmann on the stand, the old man uttered a strange, muffled cry and fell to the floor in a dead faint. Once roused back to consciousness, he was asked what caused him to faint. He said he had expected to see in Eichmann some visible monstrous flaw that would explain how the Nazis could inflict such pain and suffering on a defenseless people. He saw none. He saw only a common ordinary man like himself, like all in the courtroom.

Curiously enough, what this old man realized captures the reality of all human existence, "Custom is the principal magistrate of men's life," as Bacon put it. Eichmann went home after work, took off his uniform, ate dinner with his family, talked with the neighbors and played with the children. He performed what he was told to perform assuming, as do we all, that our customary behavior as dictated by our society is correct.

When that society controls the communication media, directs the employment opportunities, provides the resources for society's infrastructure and provides the arguments that give motivation to its people, what is customary becomes the correct and acceptable order for living. A principled conscience does not exist in a void; it is framed by the narratives that shape a society. How else explain what is good for one is evil for another?

A Democracy must allow for the expression of multiple voices; it is the one form of government that can prevent the absolute control Eichmann represents in that story. That is what makes the muffling of voices at the DNC so abhorrent.

But the question persists: what is gained by not raising the issues that divide the country? The answer resides, perhaps, in the hoped for possibility that a positive campaign will win voters' hearts, that a "smiling liberal" will beat a "compassionate conservative." Or the answer resides in the reality that Kerry and Edwards supported Bush's "invasion" and they would be contradicting themselves if they now ran against it. So the best they can do is waffle and claim it was badly planned. Indeed, they can't even raise the specter of lies because they either stupidly accepted what this administration said or they failed to research the details and failed to listen to the world's communities that argued against it. Or the answer resides in fear of retribution by the forces that control our media, the forces that capitalize on the billions that Bush is expending to prosecute his war, and the forces that support our ties to Sharon for whom we undertook the war as Phillip Zelikow, Director of the 9/11 Commission, has stated.

But muffling voices blunts exposure of truth. Varying perspectives become shrouded in ambiguous statements; conflicting views go unaddressed; the ordinary citizen hears nothing that demands serious response unless they encountered by happenstance the remarks of Carter or Sharpton. They heard nothing that discloses the corruption resident in this administration as it conducts illicit business practices in Iraq using our tax dollars; nothing that exposes the fabricated news produced by FOX as it pretends to present fair and balanced reporting; nothing that decries the lies that seeped into American thought through the controlled media and brought this nation to invade another without provocation; nothing that questions the absolute control of American politics by corporate powers, allowing starched collars to buy their way out of prison as the blue collars sit out their lives imprisoned for a felony; nothing that raises the alarm against the religious right that clamors for war while it damns the Islamic community for wanting it; and nothing that warns against the Neo-Con Cabal, infected with conflict of interest, for absconding with our Democracy by instituting illegal actions as policy in the National Strategic Security Report that upends the principles of our land by sanctifying behavior reserved heretofore for Dictators.

What a missed opportunity for the dissenting voice to be heard throughout the land! What a missed opportunity for the world to hear what the other half of the American people think! The sin of omission lies heavy on this opposition party. Ignorance of the issues can be condemned if the people refuse to reflect on evidence presented, but ignorance resulting from imposed silence concerning the issues cannot; rather, the condemnation must be addressed to those who disallowed discussion, open debate, and freedom of speech.

The ancients understood the power of truth not told, of lies fabricated intentionally to deceive, to hide the true motive for actions, and they clothed this understanding in stories as dreadful as the perversity of those engaged in the deceit.

Ovid's tale of Philomela captures the consequence of personal desire fulfilled at the expense of another followed by the silencing of truth as it is masked by deceit. Tereus, Philomela's sister's husband, rapes her and rips out her tongue when she threatens to tell the world of his crime. That action he believes will silence her as he prepares for her sister a tale of lies about her death. But Philomela weaves the story of her shame on a tapestry depicting Tereus in his shameful act. That tapestry is brought to her sister, Procne, who reads the story of her husband's lechery and his lies in her sister's sorry tale of incest.

What we learn from this story is simple enough: truth in time dissembles the most determined of liars, "Ye Gods! What thick involving darkness blinds/The stupid faculties of mortal minds!"

Nothing can withstand the power of truth to surface: "My mournful voice the pitying rocks shall move,/ Hear me, O Heaven! And, if a God be there,/ Let him regard me, and accept my prayer," cries Philomela in the agony of her despair and deceit.

Consider the metaphorical reality couched in this ancient tale: those engaged and responsible for an insidious act of defilement silence all dissent that questions the truth of their hideous act. They fabricate a story that masks their rape of a people with a tale that places blame for the defilement on the people, or on the weakness of the people to prevent the defilement. They present themselves as innocent bystanders suffering the consequence of the retaliation of the victim of the rape. They turn the victim into the perpetrator of the crime and the true perpetrator into the victim. So long as they can control the voice of the victim, so long can they deceive those who have not witnessed the crime. The DNC cut out the tongue of the dissenter. They silenced those who would contest the status quo, who would create a tapestry of truth that all might see.

33

The Day of the Lemming: From Boston to NYC; Two Weeks of Distraction

[September 7, 2004]

As the Little Men disappear, more and more economic power comes to be wielded by fewer and fewer people... We are far indeed from Jefferson's ideal of a genuinely free society composed of a hierarchy of self-governing units—"the elementary republics of the wards, the county republics, the State republics and the Republic of the Union, forming a gradation of authorities."...Never have so many been manipulated so much by so few.
—Aldous Huxley, *Brave New World Revisited*

The Republicrats have now met, the unwashed in Boston manipulated by the managers of the Kerry command that allowed no dissent from the predetermined platform, a platform that supported the war (although an estimated 90% of the delegates attending decried the war according to Joe Scarborough's unquestioned authority on *Hardball* 8/31) and supported Bush's total acquiescence to Sharon's shattering of the "Road Map" (an acceptance that guarantees the continuation of terrorist acts against America), and the pin-stripers in New York controlled by a well-oiled machine driven by Karl Rove who allowed "moderates" like Guiliani, McCain, and Cheney (an oxymoron in any language) to speak about the inclusiveness of the Republican Party even as it forced all to rally around a preset platform that denied access to thousands upon thousands of Americans. "Never have so many been manipulated so much by so few," as Huxley notes, and he spoke in 1958!

These are not the first days when the few manipulated the many in America. Those in charge before our Revolution and those in charge after it manipulated the majority by using fear of economic chaos and congressional gerrymandering to allow the continuation of slavery until the people took control and ended it with a bloody civil war. John Greenleaf Whittier, a mild and gentle American poet, understood that America could not be free until it accepted its guilt and consciously confessed: "That all his fathers taught is vain—/That Freedom's emblem is the chain." For his efforts he was beaten, chased, derided; his books and papers burned. Today we remember Whittier for this aphorism: "...of all the words of tongue or pen, / The saddest are these: it might have been." How appropriate! It might have been that George W. Bush admitted his guilt and consciously confessed his lying to the American people!

But that wasn't the end of the manipulation of the slave population; another 100 years had to pass before a semblance of equality penetrated our society, and that only after a second "civil war" uprooted the status quo and forced our representatives to acknowledge what our Bill of Rights claimed was due all the people. Three massive issues drove the people to the streets during this period, issues they literally forced their representatives to not only acknowledge but correct: civil rights (more properly called human rights), feminism (more properly called human rights), and the Vietnam protests (more properly called "taking back America from the oligarchs"). Then the people forced their representatives to admit their guilt and consciously confess their obstruction of citizen rights. Would that George W. Bush admit his guilt and consciously confess his lying to the American people.

During those years I served the people of a small Massachusetts town as Moderator. I wrote these words in 1967 in a talk to the Whittier Society:

> Today there exists another band (the Abolitionists were the first) who publish and demonstrate and march in yet a second massive attempt to rouse the conscience of this nation, not against an institution, but against the insidious fact of actual slavery—economic, political, and social. Both groups have had their share of righteous

indignation... In "Stanzas for the Times," Whittier proposed the ironic possibility that this nation founded on freedom for all should harbor and protect those who wielded the slaves' whips. He asked ironically if each American should not bend his pliant knee "and speak but as our masters please."

Whittier states in effect that America's claim to freedom, equality, and justice is a sham. We worship God, we invoke his name, we ask his blessing, we sing his praises, and we enslave his children. We turn to the Pilgrims' spirit, to Plymouth Rock, to Bunker Hill to affirm our claim to freedom, yet we justify and protect the Master that fetters his slave. We say there is freedom of speech, but any thoughts that disrupt the status quo will not be tolerated: to say there is enslavement will cause hatred and resentment, and to do something about it will cause disruption and chaos. Therefore, it is best to do nothing. (Shades of Ashcroft!) Don't disrupt the status quo. Whittier responded: "Shall tongue be mute, when deeds are wrought/which well might shame extremist Hell?/ Shall freemen lock the indignant thought?/...Shall pen, and press, and soul be dumb?" And the people disobeyed and both groups prevailed momentarily against the manipulators.

Yet Whittier's idealism and his dream of an awakened America was but an illusion. Melvin B. Tolson wrote "Dark" in 1944: "They tell us to forget/ Democracy is spurned,/ They tell us to forget/ The Bill of Rights is burned./ Three hundred years we slaved,/ We slave and suffer yet:/ Though flesh and bone rebel,/ They tell us to forget!"

These are the statistics for a hundred years of freedom: in Los Angeles proper, there are 7.5 people per acre, in Watts, there are 27.9; if a black man loses his life in Vietnam, his widow gets $10,000.00 but she can't live in any neighborhood she wants to. Dick Gregory said, "If my daddy had been killed in WW II, the German that killed him could move to this country today and buy a house in a neighborhood where my Daddy's son would be excluded." The Federal Trade Commission has reported that prices in ghetto area stores are 265% higher than in suburban areas. Blacks today are one-half American: one-half of all Blacks live in sub-standard housing; Blacks have one-half the income of whites; twice as many Blacks are unemployed as whites; twice as many Black infants die as whites; twice as many Black soldiers die in Vietnam in proportion to their numbers in the population. Black elementary schools are three years behind the white and receive less federal support. One-twentieth as many Blacks as whites attend college; 75% of employed Blacks hold menial jobs. These are the statistics of 100 years of freedom.

It took the National Advisory Commission on Civil Disorders to admit that the cause of these conditions resulted from "white racism." That caused the laws that allowed these conditions to exist. How abominable that the American people had to endure the atrocities inflicted on the civil rights movement to correct these abuses. How horrendous that our representatives, driven by special interests, created the legislation that allowed these abuses to exist and continue for a hundred years. How ironic that it took us a hundred years to grapple with the reality that Whittier understood when he wrote: "Let him go where the cold blood that creeps in his veins/ Shall stiffen the slaves whip, and rust on his chains:/ Where the black slave shall laugh in his bonds, to behold/ The white slave beside him, self-fettered and sold!"

James Baldwin, a Black writer of great perception, interprets at this time an American conscience that is tragic and pitiful. He writes that "the Negro has been formed by this nation, for better or for worse, and does not belong to any other..." He places the responsibility for the Negro problem where it belongs, on each of us as Americans. We can toss the problem back to our forefathers, we can shift the blame to the South, we can attempt to escape responsibility by half-baked allegiance to some time-worn principle, we can refuse to admit of equality, we can blame the extremists—but no matter what means we take to avoid the fact, the problem exists because we Americans have made it a problem. It exists in our minds because we will not expunge it from our minds. It exists in our hearts because we fear, perhaps subliminally, either the potential overthrow of our dominance or the inevitability of it. The problem in turn exists in the Negro, but only because it first existed in the white. We have not only made the problem, we have fostered its existence and its acceptance on the object of that problem. The roots of the problem lie deep in the puritanical background of this nation. While being raised in the charity of a personal God, while being imbued with the equality of all men, we have existed in the past with an institution diametrically opposed to these principles and we perpetuate today the inequalities of that institution while claiming that we have obliterated it.

Those puritanical roots have not rotted over time. They exist today as this administration pursues its racist superior agenda against the peoples of the Arab world, and that pursuit will result in exactly the same enslavement for the American people that the institution of slavery created for over three hundred years.

But as Baldwin states, "the sloppy and fatuous nature of American good will can never be relied upon to deal with hard problems... freedom is hard to bear. We can talk of freedom, we can mouth the word, but the Negro is the key figure in this country and the American future is precisely as bright or dark as his." Freedom is more than cutting chains, the conscience too must be unshackled.

The Civil Rights movement forced America to confront its conscience by taking to the streets and forcing each representative to confront his conscience. Americans went to the streets, suffered the punishment of police club, beatings, mockery, even jail because they knew that principle trumps power, that America had been hijacked by special interests, and that America's future depended on returning its control to its rightful source, the people themselves, or it would cease to exist except as a hideous sham dressed in hypocritical platitudes and fatuous phrases.

As I watched the Democratic Convention, meeting in Boston where I taught years ago, in the state of Massachusetts where I lived for many years, I saw Democracy mangled before my very eyes. Here in a state that retains, as John Kerry knows all too well, the only remaining vestige of true Democracy, the Town Meeting, where ordinary citizens can congregate, create laws, propose and argue them before their peers, and vote on them, here he and his henchmen muffled free speech in favor of the special interests that find war profiteering and imperial ambitions the diet to feed America.

As if that were not enough, the Republican Convention of obsequious and pious sycophants, arms raised in holy supplication to their resident saviors, made Democracy a joke. Pastor George W. Bush, like Pastor John Hagee of the Cornerstone Church in San Antonio Texas, encircled by his worshiping penitents, proclaimed God's word as he is mandated to fulfill them, and like Pastor Hagee he found no sister religion in the Islamic world but only the completion of God's wrath as He threatened the ultimate annihilation of his chosen enemies.

But I tell you this, those who know how I should be governed without asking my opinion are not virtuous, though they may be well bought. I will not throw away for lack of corporate support my responsibility as a citizen to give voice to those who will serve me in my government though they control what voting machines I can use and what vote electors will make in my name. If Democracy does not exist in the convention hall then let it exist in the streets!

In 1973, a different time with a different cast of manipulators, I wrote this as Town Moderator in protest to the prevailing powers:

> No time in our history dramatizes the virtues of the town meeting form of government as well as this. Our current administration, though elected by a vast mandate, rules the nation without consent of the governed, without, indeed, even lip service to the representatives of the governed. Silence and political coercion compel the few in Congress and the Senate to acquiesce to the dictates of a

President who has no concern for the uninvolved citizen and a callous disregard for their opinion.

The town meeting forces those governed to confront the governed. Here they are held accountable. Here they must provide reasons for their acts. Would that were so at the federal level. I do not elect another man's conscience when I vote on election day. I will not be subjected to the inhuman, insensitive, and barbaric behavior of that man simply because he holds office. If the elected official cannot face the people he governs, if the people have no recourse to alter the actions of their elected officials, then why go through the farce of an election?

People deserve that form of government which they allow to exist. America has been the haven of the poor and afflicted, but only because the people of America have cared for those in want and offered succor to those in pain, not because the government was a haven and a shelter. It is the people of the country that constitute its virtues, not the government that acts in their name. But note what happens when the institution becomes more sacred than the people that compose it. An aura of infallibility surrounds the office, a quality of royalty cloaks the incumbent, a sense of righteousness shrouds the acts of the civil servant. The opinion of the individual citizen, so necessary before the election, is no longer sought, his concerns no longer heeded, his expectations no longer fulfilled, his citizenship, indeed, is buried beneath a monument of scented semantics, platitudes, and patriotic clichés.

A government that does not face the people does not have to account to the people. Under this sinister reality lies interred individual rights. We have become victims of our own propaganda. We apply to our individual lives and our rights as individuals theories that are advantageous to our economic base, Capitalism. Streamlined efficiency, hard-headed decisions, practical reality, these are the virtues that guide our day to day behavior. To thrust their effectiveness on our governmental structure is to erase the principles upon which it was built. For the individual to have a say in how he will be governed is a most time consuming, controversial, and inexpedient process. To respond to the needs of the governed, as diverse as that population must be, is most impractical, most cumbersome, yet very Christian and very Democratic.

A government that operates on the basis of business principles is not and cannot be a government of the people or a government for the people. It is and must be a government of the few, accepting as a matter of course profit and loss, both in matters of money and in lives. A humanitarian government cannot be operated efficiently nor can it confront practical reality only.

We cannot have it both ways. Either our government serves us or we become the servants of the government. Every election day should be a day of revolution. No office holder should be secure in his seat. He only will respond who must beg for our vote again. We insure our rights by keeping the office holder tottering on a wall of uncertainty. The town meeting is followed by the election of town officials; woe to him who would mock my voice or disregard my opinion. Democracy dies when we elevate our leaders to seats made precious by divine right. I will know the reasons for my acts even when they are perpetrated by my elected representatives.

We have in the complexity of our lives and in the numbers of our people foregone the simple rights we first professed two hundred years ago. We have surrendered our money, our principles, our consciences to our legislators. We assume erroneously that having stated our beliefs at the outset of the nation, they are secured forever. It is not so.

Our government no longer walks the streets; it comes to us in the form of papers, cards, questionnaires, legal documents, and tax forms; it speaks through a ghostly 'White House' voice, an anonymous person close to the President, a mumbling spokesman for the War Department, an innocuous press secretary—voices with no blood, no emotion, no love or hate, no compassion or sympathy, no human vital signs at all.

Our government is no longer people; it is a functioning thing; it operates within the construct of its own system. We keep it alive with our memory of what it used to be; we breathe life into it by asserting its morality; we pump the blood of principles into it believing in our hearts that it is good. But we live a dream. The principles carved above the portals of our government buildings no longer penetrate within. The voice of the people is silenced by the strident bombast of the military; the cry of the poor is drowned in the cant of the Capitalist; the lame, the afflicted, the aged, the child in Appalachia, the migrant in the field, the stranded in the ghetto, that whole chorus of need is not heard. Priority goes to military honor, to political face-saving. Our leaders will have honor even if it is mutilated; it will stand like a statue in some park, medals pinned to its chest, though it reeks of maggots that rummage within its soul.

Democracy is a feeble form of government. It is afflicted by apathy; it becomes ill with ignorance; it succumbs to silence. Constant vigilance, tempered with conscience, keeps Democracy alive. Comfort, leisure, dependencies, procurement, acquisitions, affiliations, programmed learning, acceptance of platitudes, allegiance to institutions, chauvinistic loyalty, blind trust in leaders, unquestioned acquiescence to authority, these are the symptoms of a decaying Democracy.

Where are our representatives? Where have they been for the past eight years (substitute four now)? Special interests, obligations, party loyalty take their toll of the free man's conscience. When the legislator's security depends on his vote, he is no longer a free man. When the people have no means of confronting their elected officials, they are no longer free... Any attempt to remove the people from their government is an act of betrayal. We have had almost two hundred years of erosion now; let us stem its steady way. If we find it difficult to spend time at governing ourselves, then we deserve to be governed by those who will. Our voice, which speaks for our rights, is our only weapon against oppression. Let us keep that last vestige of our Democracy...

I firmly believe there is a silent majority in this country, but it is neither pro-Nixon Administration nor pro-withdrawal from Vietnam. It is pro-nothing and it is con-nothing. It is a silent majority, an apathetic, uninformed, non-committed "mass of men who live lives of quiet desperation." It is unhealthy to have in a Democracy a mass of citizens who know nothing and care nothing about the government of their lives.

Those citizens who affirm the government and those who challenge it, those who commit themselves to work for the government, and those who test it and debate it and dissent against it with reason and feeling, these are the citizens of a Democracy.

What need to draw parallels between Nixon's secretive administration, the one Arnie found a "breath of fresh air," and the Neo-Con administration that believes the people must be led like sheep, and so use the Christian symbol of the protective Shepherd watching over his flock keeping them safe from terrorists. Why mention at this convention or the Democratic one that our leaders lied to the people, asked them to sacrifice their children in battle for an unjust cause, nay, more than an unjust cause, a fabricated cause shrouded in the sacred garments of God's word fulfilling not the words of God but those of Aldous Huxley, "...behavior is determined, not by knowledge and reason, but by feelings and unconscious drives... The driving force which has brought about the most tremendous revolutions on this earth has never been a body of scientific teaching which has gained power over the masses, but always a devotion which has inspired them, and often a kind of hysteria which has urged them into action." Does that quote not describe the Republican Convention?

Zell Miller, the yet to be cleansed racist crossdresser from the former land of Dixiecrats, Dick Cheney whose very words curl like venom out of his snarling mouth, and the compassionate conservative with the Texas walk who mouths the words given to him by his alter ego, Karl Rove, did Hitler proud as they systematically exploited the "secret fears and hopes, the cravings, anxieties and frustrations of the German (Republican) masses... It is by manipulating 'hidden forces'... that Hitler induced the German masses to buy themselves a Fuehrer, an insane philosophy and the Second World War." (Huxley).

Watching this triumvirate manipulate the mass of delegates so that they wept in adulation before their king, buying in their turn yet another war, another insane philosophy of pre-emptive killing to ensure world dominance, and another Fuehrer, I could only weep at the demise of Democracy. Huxley quotes Hitler: "All effective propaganda must be confined to a few bare necessities and then must be expressed in a few stereotyped formulas...only constant repetition will finally succeed in imprinting an idea upon the memory of the crowd." How effective has been the Bush machine that has lied and continues to lie regardless of the truth using fear to motivate its forces and to maintain control.

What drives these people to deliver their conscience to the manipulator? Why would purported religious people forego the promise of knowledge and salvation, achievable only in the individual mind, to cast their lot with demigods and charlatans?

Dostoevsky in a passage from The Brothers Karamozov, "The Grand Inquisitor," suggests that the freedom offered by Jesus required each person to think for herself, to judge for herself, and to act in concert with that judgment. That responsibility Dostoevesky concluded was too hard for the masses to bear. Those in power, the Power Elite, understand this reality and capitalize on it. It is, in Huxley's words, "the subhuman mindlessness to which the demagogue makes his appeal, the moral imbecility on which he relies when he goads his victims into action...(these) are characteristic not of men and women as individuals, but of men and women in masses." These masses, like the lemmings, move irresistibly, irrationally, ineluctably to the cliff, driven by devotional distraction perpetrated by politicians and prophets to their intellectual death, destroying in the process their right to a Democracy. "Never have so many been manipulated so much by so few."

34

Agony of Colin Powell: A Dramatic Monologue in One Act

[October 9/10, 2004]

This one-act play is a work of fiction. The Protagonist and characters he presents on screen are fictional characters as well, even though they are named after living persons currently holding positions in the government of the United States. No attempt has been made to accurately penetrate the inner thoughts or feelings of the living man, Colin Powell. Indeed, Colin Powell may not be able to do that, although he is in a much better position than I, to attempt such a feat.

The Colin Powell in this play is a representative character, not unlike Everyman, who must face his inner self, having lived a life contrary to the values, principles, and morals that had governed his behavior before his ascent to the pinnacles of power. The Colin Powell in the Bush administration has appeared at times to openly confront the decisions that drive this administration, yet has always backed down, accepted the necessity of the acts, or remained silent in acquiescence of them. That behavior gave rise to the intent of the play as it seemed to eloquently represent an individual in crisis—duty versus self. The play is a fictitious portrayal of a person in spiritual and emotional agony confronting his dark night of the soul.

The Agony of Colin Powell
A Dramatic Monologue in One Act

Scene: A five star hotel suite close to the UN building in NYC. The room opens from the main double doors at the rear of the stage. The entrance offers a crescent table to the right of the entrance and a door to the bedroom on the left. A few steps from the door there is a step into the main room. It offers a large 'L'-shaped couch set, end tables with elegant lamps, a credenza with appropriate liquor bottle and glasses and a lounge chair. There is a desk of some size to the left, with a desk chair, computer, phone, etc. A huge TV screen is visible on the sidewall. A full length mirror hangs next to the entrance doors facing the audience. Faint elevator music can be heard riding quietly over the set.

As the curtain parts, a shuffling of feet and muffled voices can be heard outside the door. The door opens with a flourish as Powell comes into view. He's dressed in formal overcoat and scarf; he carries an attaché case. As he enters the room, he appears to dismiss someone with a rapid gesture of his free arm. He grabs the doorknob as he moves through the opening and slams the door fiercely, muttering as he enters, visibly upset. As he utters the words below, he has moved toward the desk on which he hurls his attaché case, throws his coat over the chair, and moves to the lounge chair pulling at his scarf as he goes. He's dressed in full business suit, but tears at his tie and collar as though he's ridding himself of a prison uniform or slave's rags.

POWELL:

GOD damn! God DAMN! Won't this ever end?
What madness am I mired in? What slough is this?
What lures me to this swamp, this pit of despond?
Where I drown in hopeless depression?
Alone! Oh, so alone!
   Would that I could
Slough off this role that smothers me,
Hides me from me, for God's sake,
And I become a buffoon, a comic player
Mouthing the words of idiots, fools,
That mock those they claim to serve.

[He rises from the chair, shirt now open to the waist, and prances in imitation of Bush's strutting as he mocks his Pretend

Texas drawl exaggerating Bush's sense of superiority as he plays
the "common man."]

"Now, you know what the man wants, Powell,
I mean, you know what he wants ta he'ar.
He wants you to tell him it's OK to kidnap...
Well, maybe not kidnap, maybe, help Aristide
Get safely out a Haiti, to save his life,
You know, 'cause we're the good guys!
We need you there, Colin, 'cause you's
The black guy that knows what's good for them.
And if you say it's OK, then it's OK!"

[He returns to his own voice, and in fury speaks the following
lines.]

Mouthing the words of idiots; the fool
That plays his part, then departs to play
The fool again to the plaudits of the powers
That pull the strings that make me twitch.

[He suddenly grabs at his chest as a real pain hits. He stops talking and lets the moment pass. Then he speaks the following lines
in a subdued meditative reflection.]

Where have I buried everything I longed to be?
What road led me to this barren place?
Why do I do what I do when I can see
That it has blackened my soul and whitened my face?
Have I succumbed to such hypocrisy
That I can no longer trace
The roots that hungered to be free,
That gave purpose to my being and to my race?

[He grabs the remote and turns on the TV to find the evening
news. He watches in silence as the anchorman turns to the UN
story of the flight of Aristide out of Haiti. No one seems to
know where he has gone or why, just a desperate flight to safety
done with American aid. The cameraman turns to his interview
with Powell, the administration's spokesman on the issue. He

explains how Aristide's life and those of his family were in danger and the US offered him a flight out of the country. He explains that Aristide had signed a letter of resignation and the US was acting in a true humanitarian spirit to help the beleaguered President. He shuts off the TV and tosses the remote on the couch]

[Mocking himself.]

That is the most influential "Oreo" in the Nation!
Colin, "Oreo" Powell! Black
On the inside, white on the outside,
The inside-out cookie, baked in a white oven!

[He reverts to dialect as he responds to his own image on the screen.]

'Who is dat man? How come he look like me?
He sound like me, but he not be me!'
Oh, how I wish that were so,
That I might rest in the black night
Knowing I had deserved the sleep
That crowns those who fought the good fight.

But sleep eludes me, escapes my grasp
As though it were a convict on the loose,
And I the Pink Panther's stumbling fool
That follows the rule to its inevitable end,
An ironic ridicule of reason and civility.
The face before the camera, quiet, assured,
The very cadence of civilized man
Explaining the unexplainable in measured
Tones that none would dare to question
Lest they appear the fool!

[He moves to the desk, opens the attaché case and rummages inside, pulling papers and disks from its innards. He appears to be searching for a specific disk. He locates it, turns to the computer and inserts the disk. The images come on the big screen.

He lands in the desk chair. It has wheels so he can move around
on the upper floor and he enjoys this mobility.]

Ah! Got it!
    Fools caught in the act!

[He gleefully points the remote at the screen. Cheney's face
appears.]

Here, here's the Iago with infernal sneer,
Tilted head, and varnished voice;
The asp in the ear of the mannequin,
That slips its hateful venom
Into that vapid space, unknown
To a mind grown dull in time,
Doltish from drugs and drink.

What demonic demands does
He inject into that dummy?
What mind possesses such scorn
For the common man called to slaughter?
What evil ego glows so deep
In the cauldron of his soul
That he can send the innocent
To their death without remorse
Even as he slides guiltlessly
Beyond the killing fields he creates?

This! This face must I face
Each day, feign joy
In its presence, bestow my obsequiousness
Like some sheepish lapdog
On this grotesquerie that leers
At the world from behind its
Sadistic mind, sick with desire
To control, aye control—not
Just a man, but the Goddamn world!

To this I bow, the house nigger
That ties his fortune to white power

'Cause he knows the whip's sting
Awaits should he turn against
Those who gave him entrance
To the hollowed halls that control all!

How high do I rise!
Ah, so far, the cries of those in chains
So long ago are but whispers now,
No longer the lingering lamentations
Of kindred souls searching for one
To right the wrongs they endured.

That was me when I was young,
Full of vinegar pulsing through my veins,
Afraid of none, hero to all!
I lived the Goddamned dream!
Naïve perhaps? No! No! Ignorant!
Stupidly believing it was there for me;
A dream for whitey only,
Dressed in lies, wearing a black face,
Mocking my every step as I crept
Up the ladder, rung by agonizing
Rung, and lost my soul!

[He lurches for the remote and desperately points to the screen
for another picture. Cheney disappears and the screen goes
blank.]

Enough of this gargoyle
Whose slimy thoughts drip
Over his protruding tongue
And fall like acid drops below.
Another, I'll have another
To sooth my smoldering anger.

But first, I need an elixir
To drown this gnawing pain
That strains at my gut
Like some knife of shame,
A two-edged blade bloodied

By deeds done in silence
And lies told to hide the truth.
It twists inside cutting honor
As deeply as it does my heart.

[He lifts himself from the rolling chair, and as he does so he
instinctively grabs his gut as if in pain, and makes his way to the
decanter where he pours a tall glass into which he tosses a couple of ice cubes. He takes a long drink letting the liquor slide
smoothly down his throat. He moves silently and dejectedly to
the 'L'-shaped couch and points the remote.]

Now! Now there's a face!

[Wolfowitz' face comes on the screen. He leans forward looking
intensely at the face.]

Conceited, conniving, coarse,
No! More! Warped, obsessed;
Ah, yes, obsessed and diabolical,
The Rasputin of our noble court!
Out of his pen pours prejudice
Garbed in learned jargon,
Absolute in its oblique assertions
That turns the simple mind
That rules this misguided nation.

That, too, must I bow before,
Lest I offend the ass to which
His nose is hooked, browned
By years of cowering subservience
To hold the pants of those in power!
If I grovel, how much more does he?
But I know it; he cares not
For he has no morals, nothing
But the void beneath that face.

What evil has he perpetrated
And forced on a beguiled nation!
What deceit lives behind those eyes,

A veritable nest of maggots
That lives on lies,
    Yet he greets
The world in fawning smiles,
The very image of the candy man
Who brings hope to all,
When in fact, he is the Iceman!

God, what a bloody crew
Of blind men leads this country
Down the path to the ditch of doom.

I grow morose and cynical;
There must be laughter
To quell these doldrums
Or I go mad!

[He gets more and more animated as the following lines are spo-
ken and rises from the chair moving around the room.]

    What fool
Can I beckon to my cause?
Whose image presents itself?
I feel like Faust
In the fulness of his power
As he summoned Mephistopheles
To raise the radiant Helen
Before his eyes.
    Here, here is my
Demon on call, a plastic remote
That summons the radiance of, Rumsfeld!

Now, there is grace, comeliness, charm!
A smile to bedevil the gods,
Eyes squinting in the glare,
Of his own brilliance that shines
Forth from his eloquent mouth
In phrases picked from the Tree of Knowledge
Before the gates of heaven slammed shut.
Or so he believes in his gut.

So sad how an ego can pluck
Sense from the mind of men.

How he beguiles the press,
Who prance before his podium
Like homeless waifs in old England,
Awaiting the proffered pence
From the hands of the blessed chosen.

He regales them with known knowns,
Known unknowns, and unknown unknowns
And they scribble these pearls of wisdom
Onto their notepads like obedient children,
Ignorant of their sense while he
Loses the horror of war and terror
In jazzy riffs of obfuscation,
And they, befuddled by his merriment,
Forget the death and destruction
He came to announce to the nation.

Oh, how many talking fools bob
Before the multitudes on fluid screens,
Chortling with glee this clown's
Distortions of truth,
      Fed things
That haven't happened, could not
Have happened had they sense.
They have mesmerized the people,
Who sit in silent acceptance
Of fallacies only an O'Reilly or Rush
Could conjure as certitude,
Minds made infallible by ignorance
And ego.

      To think I knew them,
Knew them all before, yet yielded
To their feigned entreaties to join
The team to make "America great."
And, "Yes!" "Yes," I would have
Total control of State, free

To assert a direction and design;
The fulfillment of a dream deferred,
The mark of the oppressed visible
To all at last as I guided the ship of State.
What a joke! What ignorance propelled me?
What made me think power
Would be handed to a nigger?
Did I think the true thought
Evaporated when the word was expunged?
Have I joined the Hollow men:
Heartless, cruel, vengeful, cursed?
Shall I ride this frightful hearse
To its ineluctable end,
Or shall I pluck myself free,
And pray I can salvage eternity?

If there is one face that epitomizes
This ship of fools, it is this!

[He points the remote and Rumsfeld disappears. In a moment,
Karl Rove's face covers the screen. He moves close to the screen
drinking in the features of this man. Now subdued by some hidden force, grasping his temples as if in pain, he turns toward the
audience and mutters the following.]

This, this is not a face of flesh.
There is no person here, no form
That grew in time from the mewling child;
Rather this is the face of heaven cursed
To wander the earth forever;
Lucifer incarnate in our shape,
Vengeance made palpable,
Searching the destruction of God's creation;
The Mariner damned to repeat his crime
Day after day, to live its horror
Before all mankind, alone and barren,
Bereft of human kindness and love,
A pitiless wandering form without substance
Without conscience, without compassion, without remorse.

Power and control propel this monster;
Oblivious to pain and suffering
Since he cannot die again;
His life is everlasting death.
Damned to wander through the world's
Byways witness to the weeping
Mothers and children who cling
To each other despite the devastation;
He sees the love that binds, a love
He cannot share though he knows
It alone is life's fulfillment.

Such is the power that plays with **this** putty!

[He points the remote to the screen and blanks out Rove; in his place appears Bush. As he continues his litany of fools, he changes the picture of Bush to depict the points he's making. Bush in uniform, Bush in a Ranger baseball jacket, Bush with a hard hat, Bush leering, Bush sneering, Bush walking the Texas walk, i.e., like someone walking through a field of corn stalks.]

Here is true *comedia dell'arte*,
The mask presented to the people,
And the voice that speaks through the mask,
Personified evil in the form of Rove.
America hears the self-mocking fool
And loves his bumbling manner;
But neither the fool nor the people
Know the source of his mindless banter.

This Lucifer ties two threads of fate
With magnificent dexterity:
The Neo-Cons' sugar-coated hate
And God's gift to humanity,
As sold by the righteous marketers
Who coat the hearts and minds
Of their idolaters with fear and prophecy.

Oh, I should raise the specters
Of all his evil horde this night,

To haunt my dreams and drive my despair
As I grope in blindness to confront
What comfort I have conferred on this crew,
That does the bidding of Beelzebub,
Casting the naïve and innocent to their doom.

I can't let them escape this catalogue of hate
That spreads their images before my mind,
As they spread their lies and deceit before
The people they vowed to protect,
Images of hypocrisy garbed in the gowns
Of God's chosen;
    Prophets as real
As the storied Patriarchs that predicted God's
Reign of wrath threatening his creatures
With the sword of fire to destroy those
He came to save!
    Their names
Must be emblazoned on the forehead of time,
A monument to their everlasting crime:
Falwell, Graham, Robertson, and Hagee,
The Dominionists, End-timers, and Lindsey,
All who presumed to know the word of God,
Using fear, not love, to drive their ambitions!

These deceivers drove the frightened
And afflicted to give aid and comfort
To terrorists who plagued the poor Palestinians,
Finding justice in the horror of God's
Armageddon that gave right to might
As it blessed the lies of these dissemblers.

I saw them come and go,
And met them in their temples of gold,
But said not a word of dissent;
What stubborn will kept me silent?
Why could I not speak, why not cry
To the very heavens how they betray
The compassionate Christ they claim to love?
Where have I buried my sinful soul?

[He turns to point to Bush's image on the screen, flicks to one
that shows him humbly bowed in prayer, in church, eyes closed.
He turns toward the audience as though to continue his medita-
tion but shows in a grimace the pain inside. After a moment, he
begins.]

There bows the born again Christian,
Self-righteous in his indignation of those
Who question his declaration of who is evil,
And who is blessed by God to lead his mission
Of salvation against the infidels that threaten
His dominion throughout the world!
In his humble hands lies the fate
Of humankind. Does he believe these myths?
Is he an imposter, a fraud, blind, or delusional?
Does the deception reside in Rove's artifice
Or do I serve a man of infinite deceit?

Certainly I am to blame for this.

[He uses the remote to bring up a picture of Bush in his guard
uniform.]

I chose to serve the chicken hawks,
The very image of those I once decried,
Cowards who send the young and poor
To serve in their staid, whole bodies
Used as organs to salvage the rich!

What images come to mind
Of Cheney's snarl, face to face
With the sergeants' call to pushups!
Wolfowitz and Perle bedecked in ribbons
That flow over their protruding guts,
While Junior wades through fields of mud
On his way to the local pub!
What visions of security they portray!
Perhaps it's better they not serve,
But rather salute real men in battle array.

Yet to him and to them I pay homage,
To Hollow men come to life;
No longer the forgotten images
Of Eliot's barren waste, but
Bones fleshed in cynicism and hate.

[He shuts off the remote, and in quiet dejection moves across
the room to the full-length mirror. His face reflects the pain that
flares up from time to time throughout the monologue. He turns
to look at himself in the mirror, back now to the audience,
though they can see his front in the reflection. He begins to
speak in a quiet but deeply meditative manner.]

Eyes I would not dare to meet
In death's dream kingdom,
I greet in full obeisance,
Like some Mas'sr of old,
With shifting feet and eyes to the ground,
The invisible man shuffling around
Lest I be flung from these citadels
That I breached these many years ago.

Oh, God, what years I have devoted
To duty and dedication that it should
Come to this night of reparation,
Where I confront myself, defeated
And alone, like some aged penitent
That shambles toward the confessional,
Trembling and terrified that absolution
Will be denied and death will not come;
But morning will, and every store window
Will tell of deeds done in silence
Truths not told, defiance put on hold.

I stand here before the only face
That must confront the faces it has met,
That must judge itself, not them,
For they are but ghosts of my own decisions
Or indecisions that have wrought the chaos
That plagues me this night.

Now must I play priest and penitent,
Conjure up points in time that
Pricked my soul as I capitulated
To those who held my future
By a tether, like Edward's spider over the flame,
Ready to drop me into the perdition
Of lost opportunity and advancement,
To breach the walls of whitey's fortress,
After four hundred years of sweat,
Of humiliation and defeat, to subvert
From within the very system that controlled
The oppressed and determined their fate.
That was the dream that turned to nightmare.

[He wanders before the mirror, weaving back and forth as he
unfurls these lines, stopping to look at himself, sometimes with
an expression of deep depression, sometimes pain, physical pain
that finds visibility in his breast or temples. It is as though he is
mirroring his emotional state in the deterioration of his body.]

I know the day and hour of my defeat!
It was a sin of omission, of known
Horror untold, of cold bodies
Buried beneath the clay of My Lai.
I knew and said nothing, and learned
That silence has its own rewards
For those in power, who control others
By controlling what they know.
That omission earned me stars,
And forged the first link in my chain
That grew like Morley's day by day
Until I was fettered as solidly as any
Of my forebears who served as chattel
For that civil society that shackled the slave.

[He stands before the mirror and buttons up his shirt, straight-
ens his collar. He stands at attention, shirt tucked in, belly
pulled in, looking at himself and imagining his early years in
uniform.]

I cut a pretty picture then,
A useful tint to present to the public,
Carefully manicured in my ribbons and stars,
The perfect image for the Party of the people.

Used, used as only Patricians use the slave:
I dressed out their dining hall,
I stood, impassive and pressed, beside
Their elegantly dressed wives bedecked
With pearls and diamonds... and gleaming smiles.
I knew my place and kept it well,
Adding, day by day, a new link
To the chain that choked my conscience,
Shutting out the air of reason and right,
As I crawled home each night
To seek solace in darkness,
Ah, yes, to crawl out of the light!

[He slumps down on his knees, head bowed like the penitent.]

How corrupt have I become?
Do I act now without regard
For right or wrong?
    Do I
Instill my desires on my own kin?
Do I link them to my chain, prisoners
Of my foibles, victims of "duty's" excuse
That releases me from judgment to acquiesce
To those who pull my chain?

Oh, I am not Prince Hamlet, in deed,
A pun as corpulent as my dejected mood;
I'm not even Lord Procrastinator,
Who has at least the prospect of becoming;
I have forgone all, lost the chance to act.
I have become the victim of Cheney's venom,
Just another mannequin to be placed
In his window, dressed to do his bidding,

[He rises from his knees and goes for another drink. As he stands at the credenza, his hand begins to shake and the liquor spills. He grabs at his breast. Puts the glass down hurriedly, and stumbles to the couch edge. A little time passes and then he begins the following gaining momentum as he speaks.]

Why, if I am content to be his lackey,
Do I suffer so?
    I tried, I tried to stop
The first slaughter that ended
In the Highway of Death, that graveyard
Of bleached skulls and seared skin,
Our everlasting memorial
To that glorious little war,
That made me a household name.

But once started, I did nothing to stop it.
No, that's not true, I did do something;
I supported it, lying to myself
That duty required I obey;
The pitiful lie all must use
Who follow the bloody trail
Their master takes.
    That lie
They knew I would tell myself,
And so I became both Master and slave!
What irony rules a life
That turns the whip upon itself.
That blackness in evil seals my fate!
Shackled to duty I abhor,
Champion of slaughters demanded
By those I hate, the loathsome horde
That guides this benumbed state!

That time passed, and I pushed
My guilt deep inside that I might hide
It from myself.
    But it festered there;
It haunts me now; it grows a cancer
In my breast and taunts my being.

It metastasises, for God's sake,
Because it multiplies each day I
Live in this den of vipers who
Entwine their lies like serpents in a nest,
Strangling my will, my desires, my soul.

[He is circling the stage at this point as though tracked by some
unseen fury. He grasps his temples at times, desperate to flee the
torment he is recalling.]

How I gagged when Rumsfeld shoved
Those sheets of deception before me;
Page upon page of distortion and invention,
Equivocation and evasion, presented as truth
To beguile the world by this Charlatan,
Who coquettishly delivered the Judas kiss
To those he admired, the very diplomats
That cried out against the Machiavellian
Antics of this Satanic crew!

Then, too, I objected when I threw
Those sheets against the wall,
Demanding they give me evidence,
Not concoctions hatched by sick minds,
That, once delivered, makes me their Pharisee.
Yet Pharisee I became,
Presenting their law before
The world's court, mouthing their lies
As truth, while my innards burned!

Had I then stood against their will,
The very heavens would have given thanks!
And the chains, the chains that bind
Even now would have fallen
From my heart and sunk like lead
Into the swollen sea.
    And, blessed God,
I would be free!

But now I walk the world a clown,

Bush's buffoon, believed by none!
Pushed around the globe to justify
Neo-Con hypocrisy, a roving dummy
Doomed to drive an agenda of destruction.

Ah, what self-hate sits like ice in my breast,
Freezing my heart against the pain
I witnessed in Jenin, as Sharon's siege
Laid waste the destitute and helpless;
People oppressed, damned by indifference
And deceit to suffer in the sun's glare
The cruel savagery of these fiends.
I, I live their pain, captive of these same
Demons, and I suffer with my brother.

Yet I did a dastardly thing
When I circled their plight,
Taking unnecessary flight to Egypt,
That Sharon have time to ravage their homes,
And massacre the mothers and children
Who could not flee the terror of his wrath.
The whole world cried in despair
As I crawled slowly to the carnage
That I let happen for their sake,
Adding still more dead to the links
That I drag weeping into eternity.

Why can I not act?
What makes me cow to those I loathe?
What force drives this shame?
For force it is that compels me to live
In a cauldron of self-hate, yet go forth
Each day to build another crime
More hideous than the last,
To approve the wall that stands
A monument to racist hate, encircling
Those held captive by murderers and thieves;
To cry foul when the world court
Condemns the ethnic imprisonment of people
Unable to defend themselves against oppression;

To proclaim as justified the stealing
Of Palestinian land negating by my act
The declared will of nations united in voice
Against this insidious betrayal.

Good God, what reparations must I make?
To whom do I make them now?
Have I a soul to save?
I have lived this dark night
In fear and dread having cast
My lot this day with tragic irony
As I stood alone, the bumbling Patsy
For this pathetic crew, escorting
Democracy out of Haiti!
    Kidnaping it
In the dead of night, a tragicomic Knight,
Destined to be mocked and derided,
A figure of infinite ridicule and scorn!

How fitting this end to this ignoble career.
What message does it send?
Am I at least an example that can teach
The folly of impregnable duty,
Of deeds done in silence that corrupt,
Of deceit made truth that corrodes
The decency we've been taught,
Of dreams deferred and lost?

When pride rides its phantasm steed,
Seeking the golden apple of greed
And gain, and power, believing it
The elixir of life, time intrudes
To erase the mirage, leaving only
A residue of lost hope and desire.
Oh, God, I would I were dead!

[He collapses on the lounge chair, arms spread, head on chest as
the curtain closes.]

35

Turning Myths into Truths: Fodder for the Mindless

[October 14, 2004]

The lies used by the Bush administration to rally support for its illegal actions in Iraq and Palestine have moved with glacial slowness before the public. The reason, we have learned, exists in the main stream media that controls news fed to the public. Alison Weir, Executive Director of "If Americans Knew," established, for example, that 150% of Israeli children's deaths (more than one story on some) were the subject of front page articles and photos in the *San Francisco Chronicle*, although only 5% of Palestinian children's deaths made it to the front page. Fairness and Accuracy in Reporting noted that NPR reported on 89% of Israeli children's deaths and only 20% of Palestinian children's deaths. These studies mirror the reality for most American, corporate controlled media.

Recently, an Ariel Sharon advisor, Dov Weisglass, revealed to *Ha'aretz* that the "ulterior motive behind Sharon's unilateral decision to withdraw from the Gaza strip" was not to further the peace process but to "freeze it" in order to prevent "the establishment of a Palestinian state." Where did you read about this in America's mainstream media? In another news article last month, *Ha'aretz* editorialized that Israel is responsible for the terror that exists in Palestine! That confession also went unnoticed in the US. The sin of intentional omission more often than not creates the perceptions we hold on issues of great significance. The elite powers that control the message, control what we think is true. Let me offer three examples of intentional deception that fabricate a myth that becomes truth.

Ha'aretz, the Israeli newspaper not controlled by the right-wing Zionists of Sharon's racist administration, editorialized a couple of weeks ago on a matter of paramount concern to America, the cause of terrorism in Israel and the Mid-East—a matter not mentioned at either of our national conventions, and unreported in the main stream press:

> The underlying basis of (this) terrorism lies in the territo-ries. Nowhere else. The main motivation for the war against us is the aspiration to shake off the cruel yoke of the occupation. The checkpoints, the humiliations, the suppression and the mass imprisonment are the true infra-structure of terrorism.

This editorial exposes the truth about terrorism in Israel and elsewhere in the Mid-East and gives lie to the myth that it is the Palestinians that have caused the terrorism that afflicts that state. It denudes the fiction that Sharon perpetrates and uses as a collar around Bush's neck in order to lead him to accept the state terrorism that he imposes on the Palestinians.

This editorial decries the blatant and unfounded accusations made by the Chief of Staff, Moshe Ya'alon and the military that blames Syria for the terrorism in Israel. "The attempt to cast responsibility on Damascus is intended to avoid having to cope with the true causes of terrorism," *Ha'aretz* argues. "Colonial regimes have always accused external sources of intervening in the liberation struggles waged against them, in order to under-mine the justice of the struggles," a point that America has to face in Iraq as it imposes its will on a people that has no desire to be suppressed. The *Ha'aretz* editorial blows open the whole charade that Israel and its American apologizers (not friends) like AIPAC use to defend its occupation and oppression, that has praised Sharon's atrocities in the US as defensive acts against terrorists, not as the cause of the terrorism:

> Palestinian terrorism was not engendered in any external command post. It had its birth among the rubble in the territories, in the hearts of the children who saw their parents humiliated and their lives trampled underfoot. Anyone who truly wants to put an end to terrorism must fight the occupation. Any other war is pointless.

This point makes a mockery of AIPAC's and Wolfowitz' and Sharon's push to "change regimes" in Iran and Syria even as it bares the insidious intent of their efforts. Deception destroys discernment of truth, and omission of any reference to this argument, made by a major newspaper in Israel, can be nothing more than intentional deception.

Consider now a second myth that has prominence in America, one defended by Israel's most renowned apologist, Alan Dershowitz, in his most recent book *The Case for Israel*. According to Dershowitz, "Jews were a substantial majority in those areas of Palestine partitioned by the United Nations for a Jewish state." The official UN estimate of the population of mandatory Palestine allocated to the Jewish state, according to Dershowitz, although he provides no source for his numbers, only the claim that they are authoritative, are 538,000 Jews and 397,000 Arabs. Interestingly, he does not question the accuracy of the population numbers provided by this writer in a Counterpunch article that appeared 4/6/03 (figures Dershowitz questions); he simply changes the base of the argument and thus allows himself to offer numbers that fit his argument.

What he does not provide, what he omits to record, are numbers based on historical and archeological data collected in a huge tome that identifies the populations of every village within the pre-1967 borders of Israel, titled appropriately, *All That Remains*, a work edited by Walid Khalidi, a distinguished historian and one time Senior Fellow at Harvard's Center for Middle Eastern Studies. In this work, Khalidi accounts for 418 towns and villages that were systematically razed by the Jewish military, citing exact population statistics for each location, statistics that appear as they did in the Mandate Government's *1945 Village Statistics*. Each of these 418 towns and villages had been in recorded existence since the 16th century inhabited by an overwhelming Arab population.

The statistics tell the story. In 1948, over 390,000 inhabitants of these towns and villages were forced to move, and an estimated 254,000 inhabitants of cities in the same areas and 70,000 to 100,000 Beduins, a mobile population, were driven out by the Jewish forces. Another 13,000 were killed in the battles that took place in these areas. The total amounted to an estimated 54% of the population in the areas that constituted the UN proposed land to be given to the Jewish state. Khalidi's accounted for population of approximately 727,000 Arabs gives the lie to Dershowitz' figures even if one accepts his argument that the population of the proposed Jewish state only should be the basis of determining that the creation of it was justified.

But statistics do not tell the human side of this catastrophic movement of people. These major urban areas—Acre, Beersheba, Baysan, Lydda, Majdal, Nazareth, al-Rama—were emptied of their Palestinian residents:

> Their immovable assets—commercial centers, residential quarters, schools, banks, hospitals, clinics, mosques, churches, and other public buildings, parks and utilities, all passed en bloc into the possession of the nascent State of Israel. Also appropriated intact by Israelis were the personal moveable assets: furniture, silver, pictures, carpets, libraries, and heirlooms—all the accoutrements of middle-class life of the erstwhile Palestinian residents.

In *All That Remains*, Khalidi provides two maps, divided by areas that constitute the proposed Jewish state, with graphics that demonstrate the population comparison between Palestinian and Jew. There are 8 areas that make up the proposed state: Safad, Tiberiae, Baysan, Haifa, a large section of Tulkarm, Jaffa, a sizeable section of Al Ramla, and Beersheba; a separate area designation is provided for Jerusalem. Only in Jaffa did the Jewish population outnumber the Arab, including Jerusalem which had an Arab population of 62% versus 38% Jewish. One might note that Dershowitz mentions only that western Jerusalem had a majority of Jews; how deceptive. He also notes that Hebron, not designated as part of the proposed state, had a Jewish population for thousands of years, a fact somewhat at odds with the population statistics in 1946 when less than 1% Jews were in the area.

Hidden within the myth that Jews were the larger population in the proposed Jewish state, thus making legitimate their right to the land, is another myth more insidious than the first: Palestinians left that area of their own accord or upon the demands of the Palestinian authorities. This myth opens the door for innocent Israelis to claim the deserted land for themselves. But according to Henry Siegman, in a rebuttal letter in the *New York Review of Books* to Benny Morris, the Israeli historian who had questioned a Siegman article:

> The issue I addressed in my article is whether the mass exodus of 700,000 Palestinian Arabs from the areas in Palestine assigned to the Jews was the consequence of the chaos of war or whether it was "planned"—the result of a deliberate decision by Jewish leaders to expel Palestinian Arabs from these areas... I noted in my article that in the revised edition of Morris's book, he writes that he had conclusive evidence that there was indeed a deliberate decision by Ben Gurion to expel—the term 'cleanse' is used extensively—700,000 Palestinian Arabs. Their flight was therefore not the unintended collateral damage of a war started by the Arabs but the result of decisions and actions taken by the Yishuv's top political and military planners.

Siegman goes on to point out that Morris does not object to the decision to "expel" Palestinians from their land because he understands that a Jewish state could not exist in an area where the Arab population outnumbered the Jews: "Without the uprooting of the Palestinians, a Jewish state would not have arisen here." The title of Siegman's article suggests the consequences of the lies that give feigned legitimacy to illegal actions: "Israel: the Threat from Within."

My third myth, presented as truth universally, may best be presented by Elsa Walsh from her article for the *New Yorker* (3/24/03), titled "The Prince." The article is something of a brief biography of Prince Bandar of Saudi Arabia and his political manipulations in our nation's Capitol. Walsh writes:

> But when Dennis Ross showed Bandar the President's (Clinton) talking papers Bandar recognized that in its newest iteration the peace plan was a remarkable development. It gave Arafat almost everything he wanted, including the return of about ninety-seven per cent of the land of the occupied territories; all of Jerusalem except the Jewish and Armenian quarters, with Jews preserving the right to worship at the Temple Mount; and a thirty-billion-dollar compensation fund.

Arafat, as Walsh notes, agreed to accept the proposals as offered by Clinton, but only as the basis for new talks. The world heard that Arafat had refused the proposals and offered no explanation or alternatives.

Did Clinton's papers offer Arafat "everything he wanted" as Bandar claims? In 1993, Arafat sent a letter to Prime Minister Yitzhak Rabin, September 9, stating most pertinently these points: The PLO recognizes the right of the state of Israel to exist in peace and security; the PLO accepts United Nations Security Council Resolutions 242 and 338, the 1948 and 1967 borders and right of return; the PLO commits itself to the peace process... all outstanding issues... will be resolved through negotiations.

Did Clinton offer Arafat all of the land captured by the Israelis in 1948? Did he offer a return to the borders as delineated by the UN in 1967? Or did he offer Arafat 97% of the West Bank and Gaza? Did Clinton provide a set process for the refugees, a right to return to their homes whether in the remaining Palestinian land or in Israel? Did Clinton's plan provide for recognition of a Palestinian state's right to exist, a right recognized by Israel?

It's clear that Clinton did not offer Arafat everything he wanted. Arafat had no option but to refuse Clinton's proposal or accept it only as a basis for new negotiations; and that he did. It's instructive to note that the one-sidedness of Clinton's offer was so blatant that Yossi Beilin, an Israeli architect of the Oslo Accords, and former Palestinian minister Yasser Abed Rabbo, worked for two and a half years to create the Geneva Accords to right the wrongs of the original proposals.

The GA, while not official, stipulates the immediate recognition of a Palestinian state by the state of Israel. It addresses forthrightly the issue of refugee right of return and compensation for their suffering and loss of homes in accordance with UN Resolutions 194 of 1948 and the principles of International Law. And it notes that the relations between Israel and Palestine shall be based upon the provisions of the Charter of the United Nations. Furthermore, it makes the borders that compose the state of Palestine those of June 1967 in accordance with Resolutions 242 and 338. Most of the settlements are to be disbanded and territorial integrity to be respected by both parties. Palestine will be a non-militarized state protected in part by the creation of a multinational force established and deployed in Palestine. Finally, a joint committee will monitor the crossing borders, an item originally in the Oslo agreement but later cancelled by Israel. This document addresses the issues Arafat had to contend with, without which he could not commit his people. Curiously enough, the GA offers a resolution to the dilemma addressed by *Ha'aretz* in its editorial, a just resolution to the conflict that rages in Palestine.

There you have it, three myths presented as truth to a world benumbed, especially in the US. All three exist because our press and our talking heads, especially those that snarl on FOX or obsequiously fawn disbelief on CNN or MSNBC, intentionally omit the requisite investigation of the truth or coddle to the power of corporate America and to the belief, in itself a myth, that we must not question our one true friend in the Middle East, the "Democratic" [sic] state of Israel. But, then, myths are the staple of those who want to know without engaging the mind or the senses. Besides, a little blather about issues of no consequence coddles the public mind and doesn't really disturb their contentment.

36

The Destructive Power of
Faith: Killing for Christ
[October 22/24, 2004]

A pall hangs over this election, a shroud of darkness that oppresses the heart because its outcome guarantees no change, only the certainty of continued chaos if Bush should win and the unknown direction a Kerry victory might take—a direction that could continue the chaos America is mired in—a darkness, then, to appall. I read each day the crippling accounts of soldiers caught in a maelstrom of unseen death lurking on roof tops, in narrow alleys, behind cement walls and black windows, beneath tires littering the streets. I see pictures of burned out buses, sidewalks and curbs bathed with blood, faces twisted in pain, bits and pieces of flesh scattered about like fallen leaves, blown helter-skelter by the wind. Faces, I see suffering on so many faces, mothers weeping over their dying children, old women and men huddled in the debris left of their bulldozed home, medics carrying the lifeless body of a man whose hand rests beside his face held there by the torn shred of his sleeve, his arm gone, his body black with grime.

This is a world gone mad, a madness on all sides, the madness of greed that sees in oil the riches of Sultans and Kings, the madness of arrogant pseudo-philosophers who conjure beliefs of personal superiority that gives them license to conquer and enslave, the madness of ancient minds that dreamt of power and glory in covenants with gods, the madness of fanatics that fabricate fantasy out of indecipherable images lodged in pages of metaphors, the madness of little minds that grab onto faith as the golden ring that will bring them salvation, the madness of those born again to the child's world of impossible dreams forgoing in their new world the reality of this.

Today I read of depleted uranium, 1000 metric tons made from the deadly U238 isotope dropped on America's killing

fields, that wafts on the wind like aerosol spray, a toxic death that
sticks in human lungs, bringing a slow and painful death. I saw
pictures of new born children bloated and bruised by scars, eyes
missing, a nose of scar tissue and nostrils, no lips, the detritus of
our advanced civilization scattered on hospital beds in Baghdad.
I read of soldiers twisted in mind and spirit by no visible symptom except the phantom of our cursed nuclear waste that encircles them in their tank and haunts them the remainder of their
lives. Our young return from this nightmare of devastation devastated themselves, courtesy of our Commander-in-Chief.

And I read today that 24,010 Americans have been evacuated
with wounds and injuries from our "war" zones, that 37,000
innocent men, women, and children in Afghanistan and Iraq
have died and more than 500,000 have suffered wounds. And I
hear the silence, the deafening silence of indifference that our
compassionate conservative leader offers to those who suffer the
consequence of his acts, and feel with them the utter helplessness
of their plight. And I wait for a word from Kerry that he, too,
hears their pain, that he will stop the slaughter in Afghanistan
and Iraq and Palestine... and I wait in vain; there is no condemnation, no plan to end the conflicts, no recognition that states
terrorize, no acceptance of the right of people to fight the oppressor, no confession of wrong waged against the innocent that had
not the intention or the means to threaten America.

I have heard these men, both Bush and Kerry, attest to their
deep rooted religious principles, the depth of their faith in the
teachings of Jesus, comforting the citizenry that they are fit for
the White House because they believe. But I see nothing of Jesus
in their behavior, nothing of the compassion that attended his
ministry, nothing of the inclusiveness of his teachings, nothing
of the love he proffered as the binding source of peace throughout the world.

I look in vain for this Christ in the Christianity practiced by
the right wing, fanatical sects that preach the Book of
Revelation, reveling in the glory they perceive to be their reward
if they destroy the enemies they identify as the enemies of God.
I wonder where in this acclaimed Christian land of TV
Evangelists and literalist ministers is there a man who acts as
Christ would act? I see none. I see only a God forsaken Tele-
Evangelist land of vitriol and bigotry where none could say

I "love the Lord my God with my whole heart and mind and soul, and my neighbor as myself." They have buried the teachings of Jesus in the quagmire of a malevolent and malicious God of the Old Testament, a God that would order one Semitic tribe to exterminate another. We have not moved beyond the racist hatred that blotted the landscape 2500 years ago.

I would have thought the founding fathers' voices would have turned us against such barbarity, for they knew that such religions were anathema to the rights of the people and to the fledgling Democracy they desired to create. They expunged such organized zealots of religion from civil discourse precisely because they knew its inherent destructive nature. But, no, we have the airwaves turned into streams of venom that flow from the mouths of the heralded self-worshipers whose mantra is hatred for their fellow man, the likes of Pat Robertson, Pastor John Hagee, Franklin Graham, Hal Lindsey, and, now, even our blessed generals who defile the houses of worship not with coins but with cursed bigotry in the person of General Boykin.

I wonder how any person can stand against the tribes that follow these accursed men? What voice can reach the soul of men, if soul they still have after their life of crime, that has been lodged deep in their bloody wallets made fat with their racist hatred for their fellows whose only sin is their belief in a God different from their own? They mount their campaigns on fear, fear lodged in a word that defies definition because it slips and slides, nay, it slithers through meaning like molten lava over rock burying it beneath layers of hot and passionate rhetoric, a word without substance or sense, a word seething with diffidence, anxiety, suspicion, even horror, the word is faith. No word evokes more fear and mistrust; no word has caused more chaos and wanton destruction, as the Crusades and the Conquistadors, rampaging through Central America, attest; no word can put people in such a state of doubt that they acquiesce to prophets of doom century after century; no word has been and continues to be more destructive in the mouths of fanatics. That is the destructive power of blind faith!

Fanatics have a way, whether they be the Imams guiding Hamas or the robed ministers of Robertson's TV Club or the ultra right Zionists in Israel, with those who abdicate responsibility to think for themselves, those who hand over their minds and conscience to them as they thunder their prophetic curses in dramatic tirades, bathing their flocks in fear and loathing. These fanatics in America, who exist through the courtesy of a democratic secular system that tolerates their presence if not their message, fetter the minds of their laity with absolute truths generated out of myths, negating thereby the very semblance of democratic thought that is premised on individual responsibility; and the lambs they lead to slaughter do not know it. These fanatics defy the laws of the secular state by determining for their congregations what political party they must support, what candidates they must vote for, and what policies they must accept. And for this defiance they pay no taxes!

But it's worse than that. These same fanatics literally compel their congregants, on fear of eternal damnation in Hell's fire, to strap themselves in the swaddling clothes of death and bring that gift to all around them, to support terrorists in the occupied territories of Palestine, to proclaim an enemy identified in the Book of Revelation, an Arab enemy who worships in the Islamic faith. And for this incitement to murder they pay no taxes and suffer no incarceration. What else do we call it but killing for Christ, killing for Allah, killing for Yahweh!

This is our dilemma. We Americans pay the bill; they act in our name. How can we, who speak with the conviction of our conscience, hope to remove the hatred a Hagee or a Robertson breeds against God's creatures? The pictures I saw today of dead and dying children in Iraq, pictures too horrific to be put in mainstream newspapers or shown on TV, pictures that cry to the human soul that the pain and suffering must stop, also cry out to every true Christian that Jesus' teachings never allowed for such wanton slaughter. Yet these are the innocent victims of our fanatical dependence on the preaching of these men who sit safely ensconced on their splendid chairs amidst tall vases of flowers, smiling beatifically for the cameras.

How can we witness Bush's acceptance, indeed his encouragement, of Ariel Sharon's savagery and not condemn his acts as anathema to the teachings of the Christ he proclaims as his God? How can we suffer in silence the ferociousness of Sharon as he spreads his hatred and nihilism over the bloodied landscape of the unholy lands of ancient Palestine? Our indifference, our silence blessed the rape of Rafah in May, God's month of renewal; our indifference and our silence blessed a summer of slaughter in the season of God's increase; and today, our indifference and our silence acquiesce to a season of harvest that gathers in the dead and maimed in Gaza.

Where is the voice of America that should cry against these killing fields, these American supported killing fields, these murderous rampages that defile the love Jesus begged we have for our neighbor, a love equal to that we have for ourselves?

Where are the Priests, the Rabbis, the Imams, the quiet Buddha monks, all who claim to love humankind? Why does silence reign? Whose voice are we afraid of? Where are the voices of our leaders, where is Kerry, where is Dean, where is Edwards? Why do we hear words of condemnation when we witness the wanton slaughter in Beslan of children in school yet hear not a word when the IDF slaughters the children in the kindergarten in Jabaliya or our missiles miss their intended target and destroy the lives of innocent people? Does one mother's weeping reach our ear and another goes unheard? I would that every mother's cry would reach our ears as it rents the sky that we might know what Christ meant when he said, "Love the Lord thy God with thy whole heart and mind and soul, and thy neighbor as thyself."

37

Bush, Osama and Israel: Concealing Causes and Consequences, Reflections of Times Past

[January 10, 2005]

As we approach the crowning of our Emperor for another four years, a short two months to the day when he launched the United States into its imperialist policy of pre-emptive invasions of foreign states, we might pause to reflect on how deeply this administration analyzed the causes that gave rise to the atrocity of 9/11, the ostensible basis for our attacking a nation that had done nothing to the US to warrant its destruction and occupation. Consideration might be given, for example, to the two antagonists who entered the lists recently, appearing almost simultaneously before the American public, Osama bin Laden via a recent tape aired by al Jazeera and Mr. Anonymous, Michael Scheuer, author of the recent CIA approved *Imperial Hubris: Why the West is Losing the War on Terror*. Interestingly, while they carry lances from opposing Lords, bin Laden's lifted on behalf of Allah and Scheuer's questioning our Lord of Misrule, George W., both proffered the same perspective, the causes that gave rise to the atrocity of 9/11 have never been addressed.

Osama stated it this way in his address to the American people:

> ...thinking people, when disaster strikes, make it their priority to look for causes, in order to prevent it happening again. But I am Amazed at you. Even though we are

in the fourth year after the events of September 11th, Bush is still engaged in distortion, deception and hiding from you the real causes. And thus, the reasons are still there for a repeat of what occurred.

Scheuer made this observation: "(Osama's) genius lies in his ability to isolate a few American policies that are widely hated across the Muslim world. And that growing hatred is going to yield growing violence." Scheuer goes on to say that Osama "...is remarkably eager for Americans to know why he doesn't like us, what he intends to do about it, and then following up and doing something about it in terms of military actions." Yet our President continues to claim that the al Quaeda terrorists hate us because of our freedoms while the real causes for their actions go unaddressed.

As I contemplate the horrendous consequences of this election and the solidifying of Bush's neo-con crew and right-wing evangelical Zionist supporters into positions of power, I am forced to reflect on 9/11 once again, the catalyst that propelled America into Bush's unending war against the forces of evil. America awoke that morning to an atrocity incomprehensible to contemplate, an act that defied common sense, a wanton act of inane dimensions that inflicted catastrophic destruction on innocent people, an act we could not grasp because we had never experienced anything like it before, an act that galvanized our people in brotherhood, in anger, and in fear.

I was driving my stepdaughter to her high school that morning and stopped at a convenience store. As we entered, we saw two proprietors, Mid-Eastern by descent, transfixed before the TV screen, horror struck at the burning towers, transfixed by images that seemed at the time to come from some Hollywood action film. There before us, she in her teens, I having lived sixty years in the last century, lay the ruins of America's might symbolically destroyed in the World Trade Towers, the first instance of such destruction on American soil by a foreign force.

How incomprehensible those images to a teenager, the unfathomable realization that humans could inflict such suffering on another human; indeed, how incomprehensible to a man who lived while the firestorms of Dresden raged, while the US firebombed 64 Japanese cities before the dropping of the atom

bombs on Hiroshima and Nagasaki, while Nixon lit up the skies
with the Christmas bombing of Cambodia and Hanoi, and
while I witnessed in a hotel room in Prague the shock and awe
destruction of Baghdad less than two years ago.

Though I had lived five decades longer than she, I had not, as
is true of all Americans who have lived between our far flung
shores, ever heard the drone of Super fortresses far overhead,
the screech of bombs hurtling toward earth, the wrenching split
of buildings bursting beneath the explosive power of tons of
TNT, the intense heat generated by thousands of phosphorus
bombs that roll in waves of fire over cars, down streets, into
buildings turning everything into an inferno of searing heat that
melts human flesh, sucks the breath of life from the lungs, and
leaves the landscape a barren waste, miles and miles of debris,
the shattered remnants of human toil.

These reflections struck home with a vengeance, when I
received an email in response to an article I wrote for
Counterpunch, October 22, titled "Killing for Christ." That
article described pictures of death in Iraq, death wrought in part
by Christians goaded to war by fanatical ministers. "Not until
the US lies in ruin—the same carnage I witnessed as a child in
post-war Europe—will Americans be forced to face the kind of
evil they have unleashed upon the world," Sandy wrote,
"...These wars are not about religion, or even oil—they're about
ignorance. Ignorant people who have never watched their cities
burned, have never dug through the rubble of their bombed out
home for the dismembered remains of their children, have never
shuddered to hear the tanks and planes coming to destroy their
homeland."

The thought contained in that letter, ignorance and hence
indifference resulting from America's isolation from aerial devastation, surfaced again in Osama bin Laden's "talk to the
American people" printed in *al Jazeera,* October 24. As Osama
describes the events that brought him to imagine the destruction
of the Twin Towers, events resulting from "...the oppression
and tyranny of the American/Israeli coalition against our people
in Palestine and Lebanon," he recounts unforgettable scenes of
carnage, "...blood and severed limbs, women and children
sprawled everywhere. Houses destroyed along with their occu-
pants and high rises demolished over their residents, rockets

raining on our home without mercy... And as I looked at those demolished towers in Lebanon, it entered my mind that we should punish the oppressor in kind and that we should destroy towers in America in order that they taste some of what we tasted and so that they be deterred from killing our women and children."

How terrible the thought, ignorance of what we Americans have wrought on others believing in our hearts that what our leaders did in our name was done to ensure peace, to ensure our freedom, to bring Democracy to the rest of the world. But that is not the thought present in Osama's head. He reacted to the Israeli invasion of Lebanon as it hurled American bombs from American supplied planes in a totally different and personal way. "And that day, it was confirmed to me that oppression and the intentional killing of innocent women and children is a deliberate American policy. Destruction is freedom and democracy, while resistance is terrorism and intolerance."

Michael Scheuer confirms what bin Laden says according to the CBS *60 Minutes* interview: "Right or wrong, he (Scheuer) says Muslims are beginning to view the United States as a colonial power with Israel its surrogate, and with a military presence in three of the holiest places in Islam: the Arabian peninsula, Iraq, and Jerusalem. And he says it is time to review and debate American policy in the region, even our relationship with Israel."

But there is no discussion of this as a cause in the United States; indeed, as Scheuer notes, "But the idea that anything in the United States is too sensitive to discuss or too dangerous to discuss is really, I think, absurd," a comment directed specifically at the Congress, the administration, and the mainstream media to open discussion about the impact of our Israeli policies as it can be a cause of the terror that confronts America.

"No one wants to abandon the Israelis," Scheuer comments, "but I think the perception is, and I think it's probably an accurate perception, that the tail is leading the dog—that we are giving the Israelis carte blanche ability to exercise whatever they want to do in their area." In short, Bush policy, essentially that designed by his Neo-Con controllers, has put the United States in danger, made it an accomplice in Sharon's oppression and occupation of the Palestinian land and his savagery against its people. Not the least of which is the stridently visible manifestation of it in the illegal and inhumane Wall of Fear he's erected around their homes and villages, and, for the past year and a half, the occupation and devastation of Iraq by America, seen as a joint venture by the United States with Israel.

From Osama's perspective, the United States has moved to take control of Arab land and resources using Israel as its accomplice in the area. That perception of US policy nourishes the hate, a hate that flows from two sources: the hard right Israeli Zionists and the mentality that guides Osama's fanatical brethren who drink from the same well, the mythological stories that prophesy an inevitable war of destruction between Jews and Arabs, the religious war of Armageddon. America's support for Zionist goals is, therefore, a direct attack on Allah and can only be repelled by counteractions that will result in destruction of America. That is the kernel of Osama's talk to America. Address the cause or suffer the consequences. That means, as Scheuer notes, open debate on America's policies in support of Israel or we continue our steady march to the ditch of doom.

Open debate, however, means more than an investigation into the Neo-Cons' paper trail from 1991 to March of 2003 calling for and carrying through the invasion of Iraq; it means as well an opening of America's soul to a catharsis caused by an acute and painful examination of the chaos and havoc it has wrought throughout the world. Osama's glib yet understandable comment that Sweden was not attacked, points the finger at America as an instigator of actions that have raised the hatred of people in nations throughout the world. Witness our emperor's recent reception in Chile.

But Americans, for the most part, know little or nothing of the actions taken in their name that have given birth to the visceral hatred, evident throughout the world, that plagues their every step. What graphic pictures have we seen of our devastation of the holy city of Fallujah? What pictures show the bodies buried beneath the rubble of bombed homes? What images of humans mangled and eaten by roaming dogs have we seen in our press or on TV? What pictures show the terrorism of Israeli forces and their indiscriminate murder of innocent civilians? What graphics depict the horror of the wall that incarcerates women and children, steals farms and orchards depriving families of their livelihood? What graphs show the American taxpayer how their money is being used, not just to surround and decimate a people but to implicate America in the carnage caused by Sharon and his government? How terrible the thought: the ignorance and indifference of the perpetrators of the devastation, that allows for its continuation, becomes the source of hatred for those who see themselves the victims of the government Americans elect to lead them.

The Twin Tower atrocity allowed for a moment of reflection, a chance for Americans to look inward, to see the world as those beyond our borders see us, victims of a horror too incredible to contemplate, the intentional detonation of civilian structures with the explicit and calculated knowledge that innocent lives would be cremated beyond recognition. And, indeed, the reaction was visceral in the heart of every American! How instantaneous the response to the crumbling towers, not only by my teenager 3000 miles away from the carnage, but on the part of all Americans. How galvanized the response across America, with an outpouring of money for the fallen firefighters and police, the mourning for the relatives of the victims, and the flooding of the blood banks. All felt the impact, shared the loss, and suffered the anguish of those who fled in terror the flaming debris, the falling stone, the blowing ash. Americans knew firsthand the horror of war at home.

That awareness drove them to follow without question their leader's plea to go to war against the evil forces that wanted to destroy America's "freedoms." That war, first in Afghanistan, then in Iraq, sent wave upon wave of bombers to unleash untold tons of explosives on untold numbers of civilians who suffered the revenge of America's determination to destroy its unknown enemy. But as I reflect on this galvanizing of America's desire to eradicate its enemy, I begin to understand that we have not merged our feelings with the feelings of those who have suffered at our hands in Europe, in Asia, and in the Mid-East. What we experienced on 9/11, a deplorable atrocity that took the lives of 3000 people, that brought havoc and chaos to our people for weeks on end, that destroyed a collection of buildings on approximately four acres of land in the middle of a city, could not compare to the totality of devastation wrought by American bombing on Fallujah, or Baghdad, or Lebanon, or Hanoi, or Tokyo, or Hiroshima, or Dresden. That these acts were seen as acts of war by most Americans does not erase the impact of the slaughter they brought to thousands of innocent people caught in the accepted euphemism that allows the innocent to be sacrificed on the altar of collateral damage.

To bring the American mind to a point of recognition that allows for comparison of the suffering we have inflicted against others as a possible rationale for the hatred that has been leveled at America is a task beyond our powers. But something has driven millions around the world to look at America as a fearsome power willing and able to devastate smaller states to achieve its goals and to protect its purported interests. Why? Why this attitude about America?

As I reflect on times in my own life when America unleashed its mighty power on those incapable of defending themselves, I need only consider the firebombing of Dresden. "On the evening of February 13, 1945, an orgy of genocide and barbarism began against a defenseless German city, one of the great cultural centers of northern Europe. Within less than 14 hours, not only was it reduced to flaming ruins, but an estimated one third of its inhabitants, possibly as many as half a million, had perished in what was the worst single event massacre of all time." ("The WWII Dresden Holocaust") Dresden had no military installations, no aircraft to defend it, no munitions factories, only factories that produced cigarettes and china, and a hospital filled to overflowing.

Winston Churchill and Roosevelt needed a "trump card" over Stalin for the upcoming Yalta meeting, "a devastating 'thunderclap of Anglo-American annihilation' with which to impress him," in effect, an act of unimaginable terror. That thunderclap took the lives of half a million people. It took the form of a firestorm where huge masses of "air are sucked in to feed the inferno, causing an artificial tornado. Those persons unlucky enough to be caught in the rush of wind are hurled down entire streets into the flames. Those who seek refuge underground often suffocate as oxygen is pulled from the air to feed the blaze, or they perish in a blast of white heat, heat intense enough to melt human flesh." 700,000 phosphorus bombs dropped on 1.2 million people, 1 for every 2 people, where the heat reached 1600 degrees centigrade, in a bombing raid that lasted over 14 hours. Those who lived through this Hell on earth had to pile the bodies on huge pyres for cremation, 260,000 bodies counted; the remaining dead, indistinguishable, melted into the cement or charred beyond recognition. "In just over an hour, four square miles of the city—equivalent to all of lower Manhattan from Madison Square Garden to Battery Park—was a roaring inferno." (Murray Sayle, "Did the Bomb End the War?") We Americans gasped at the horror of four acres of destruction and 3000 dead; we could now, should we but reflect on time past, understand how others felt when they endured a slaughter of far greater proportions.

This horrendous description of our might has been repeated over and over again since WWII and during it. Tokyo and 63 other Japanese cities felt the brunt of America's air power. "334 Super fortresses flew at altitudes ranging from 4,900 feet to 9,200 feet above their target (Tokyo)...For three hours waves of B-29s unleashed their cargo upon the dense city below... the water in the rivers reached the boiling point... 83,793 killed and 40,918 injured, a total of 265,171 buildings were destroyed and 15.8 square miles of the city burned to ashes."(Christian Lew, "The Strategic Bombing of Japan") Then came Hiroshima. "...the bomb instantly vaporized, at a temperature of several million degrees centigrade, creating a fireball and radiating immense amounts of heat... Heat radiated by the bomb exposed skin more than two miles from the hypocenter... between seventy thousand and eighty thousand people are estimated to have died on August 6, with more deaths from radiation sickness spread over the ensuing days, months, and years." (Murray Sayle, "Did the Bomb End the War"?) Why did we drop the bomb? Without going into detail, suffice it to say, "Some scholars... have found it hard to believe that the act that launched the world into nuclear war could have come about so thoughtlessly, by default."

Consider these statistics: the Germans "dropped 80,000 tons of bombs on Britain in more than five years"; America dropped over 100,000 tons *in a month* on Indochina, and between Lyndon Johnson and Nixon, America delivered "7 million tons of bombs on Vietnam, Cambodia and Laos," far more than we, and the British, unleashed on Germany and Japan in all of WWII. Nixon found reason for this devastation in his anger that North Vietnam had broken off peace talks in Paris.

That brings us to our illegal invasion of Iraq, an invasion we now know was engineered years in advance of 9/11 and for reasons that had nothing to do with the purported "war on terror." We also know that we did it to aid Israel in its desire to destroy one of their enemies, a nemesis that supported "freedom fighters" against Israeli occupation of the land of Palestine. And today we have a second letter from Osama bin Laden, delivered via video, that proclaimed for a second time that Israel's subjugation of the indigenous population in Palestine and its continued "cleansing" to rid the land of them, is a reason for the destruction caused by 9/11. Now, 100,000 civilian deaths later, more than 1300 American soldiers dead, cities in ruins, and the people in revolution against the American oppressor, we, as a nation, have chosen to continue our unilateral aggression making America more of a pariah nation and even less likely to share the grief of millions who have suffered at our hands.

And that returns me to that horrific morning of 9/11 when I attempted to share with a teenager the inhumane nature of humans. How to demonstrate the enormity of that act, yet put it in relationship to time past that we might share the torment of those who have felt the oppressor's boot and the wanton slaughter of innocents? In reflection days after 9/11, I had a vision of Hiroshima's ashen landscape stretching for miles as far as the eye could see, an image indelibly marked on my mind as a young child. But in that barren waste rose the Twin Towers, silhouetted against the distant hills and sky, a reference point for reflection just before the planes struck, turning them into candles to light the darkness that shrouds the fields of death that once stood as the city of Hiroshima. Perhaps in the light of those candles we might see, what we have not wanted to see in our ignorance, that we have spread pestilence and death throughout the world and now we are reaping the whirlwind.

38

A Mock Epic Fertility Rite: The Bush Inauguration

[January 20, 2005]

As we enter this New Year, we are, like Tantalus, trapped between extremes: unable to reach the fruit that hangs just beyond our reach and unable to quench our thirst by drinking from the water that laps at our chin. Hope hung before us during the election season, hope for any change that might arrest the Cabal that has taken control of our government, gone now into the ephemeral mist of paperless ballots and absent voting booths. And that river of change we thought we floated in, the ever-changing river that would nourish us in the coming years with its clear waters and purifying powers, now only a dream of what might have been. But we are here nonetheless, caught in the flotsam of the past four years that turned this country into a cesspool of lies and deceit, overflowing now with even greater arrogance and vengeance, determined to spread its toxic waste throughout the world.

This month America inaugurates a newly elected President, a ceremony that traditionally celebrates the promise of our Democracy, recognition of the people's right to consent to be governed by a person they selected and fulfillment of the promise of the Constitution and the Bill of Rights. How ironic, then, this immanent inauguration of the Lord of Misrule, this comic fool who struts his hour on the stage, full of sound and fury, signifying nothing!

What pray tell is there to celebrate? Why spend forty million dollars to recognize a man whose efforts to date have been to undermine our democracy, not to strengthen the pillars on which it rests; to carve the nation into the haves and the have nots, not to build bridges of support to aid all our citizens; to

sever alliances with the nations of the world, not to forge agreements that bind us as one to better conditions for all; to make
America a pariah among nations, not loved for its rational policies but feared for its erratic, unpredictable actions that threaten
stability in the world; and, perhaps worst of all, to turn America
from a nation revered by many because of its compassion for
others and its perceived desire to bring the significance of individual rights to all, to one that supports oppression and occupation, torture, and disdain for human rights?

What has this administration brought us but disrespect, dishonor and despair? Disrespect for our democracy as it has
become the lackey of corporate powers and religious zealots;
dishonor as a people, seen now as manikins manipulated by
money and ministers before all the nations of the earth; and
despair resulting from our inability as individuals to prevent the
wanton slaughter wrought by our weapons of mass destruction
on all the helpless in the Mid-East? What, then, is this inauguration but a mock-epic fittingly tuned to the roots from which it
sprang: a fertility rite conducted by a druid priest ceremoniously
inducting Bush into office ensuring that the few will reap a rich
harvest from the many who bow obsequiously before his altar.

I'm afraid I do not hear rising above the processional lofty
anthems signaling the ascendancy of a worthy man with compassionate ideals to the position of "most powerful man on
earth." I hear instead the marching drums and shrill patter of
the fife leading the congregation of believers in "Onward
Christian Soldiers" as they assemble for the final battle Christ
has promised them if they are to attain everlasting glory.

But I hear as well the distant wail of children blinded and
burned by our depleted uranium, and those crushed beneath the
rubble of our precision bombing, and those caught in the savagery of "green parrots," tantalizing toys created by our
weapons merchants to dismember and maim innocent children,
and those caught by chance in the crowds as Israel hurls missiles
at men it has judged worthy of death but not worthy of a trial,
a decidedly democratic way of celebrating the rite that brings
Bush to the presidency of a purportedly Christian nation.

"All those who take the sword will perish by the sword,"
(Matt. 26: 52) appears to be a forgotten admonition, as forgotten as the words of the Psalmist by the Jews: "O Lord, if I have

done this, if there is injustice on my hands, if I have rendered evil to him who was at peace with me, or, without cause, have plundered him who was no enemy, let the enemy pursue and overtake my soul; let him trample my life to the ground and lay my honor in the dust." (Psalm 7: 3-5)

No, I'm afraid this inauguration is not a celebration for me or for half the nation that voted against this Cabal, whose ruthless and un-Christian actions hurl America backward in time and morality to barbarous days when might made right and life was reserved only for those willing and capable of killing. No, I'm afraid the righteous must do the celebrating even as they attend his coronation as Emperor of Fools. Let them celebrate his morality that proclaims salvation for the yet to be born while he mutilates children in kindergartens with misplaced missiles; decries terrorist acts of wanton slaughter even as he and Sharon, his puppeteer, terrorizes innocent civilians with crippling and deadly missiles hurled into crowded streets and apartment buildings; feigns outrage at suicide bombers but demands his minions torture and kill prisoners, then, shamelessly denies that he is responsible; admonishes the nations of the world for per- mitting the UN to be ridiculed by rogue nations that defy their resolutions while he supports, nay encourages, Israel to terror- ize the indigenous population of the land they have stolen despite having mocked the UN by defying more than 155 Resolutions; brazenly condescends to Israeli demolition of homes, thousands of them, in full violation of human rights and international law; lures the compliant citizenry of the US into a devastating, illegal and immoral invasion of another state by lying to the people, time and time again, compounded by his lying that he had not lied; and, most ironically, ridicules the evangelical Christian community, those most devoted to his cause, by hypocritically declaring he is a messenger of God, indeed, on a mission from God since he receives messages from Him, when, in fact, he is but a deluded fool responsive to myths believed as reality. Zealots, unfortunately, succumb to imposed literalism as a salve to suppress ignorance, and that in turn allows the most insidious evil to escape scrutiny.

These pseudo-Christians, these end-timers, dominionists, Zionist evangelicals raise their collective hands in swaying unison proclaiming passionately their belief in Jesus, damning disbelievers who threaten their institution of marriage with civil unions and their pro-life commandment with a woman's right to choose, believing erroneously that Jesus preached these truths. He did not. "Be merciful, even as your Father is merciful," (Luke 6:36) that is what He said; "As you wish that men would do to you, do you to them," (Luke 6:31) that is what He said; "So also my heavenly Father will do to you if you do not forgive your brother from your heart," (Matt: 18:35) that is what He said; "Judge not, that you be not judged," (Matt: 7:1) that is what He said; "This I command to you to love one another," (John 15: 16-17) that is what He said; "You have heard that it was said, 'You shall love your neighbor and hate your enemy.' But I say to you, love your enemies and pray for those who persecute you, so that you may be sons of your father who is in heaven," (Matt: 5: 43-45) that is what He said; "A new commandment I give to you, that you love one another, even as I have loved you. By this all men will know that you are My disciples, if you have love for one another," (John 13:33-35) that is what He said. These are the words of the Christ, not "Kill, Kill!" Where is the NEW Testament in the rants of the ministers of war? Why do they resort to the wrathful, malicious, judgmental G-d of the OLD Testament? Let that G-d judge His chosen people; let Jesus open salvation to all in mercy and forgiveness. Enough of vengeance and retaliation; bring back the sun of Christ's spirit.

These ministers mock the democracy they claim to support by denying the unalienable rights guaranteed in the Declaration of Independence since they crush freedom of thought under the monolith of prescribed dogma and doctrine; they turn religion into tyranny over the mind, forcing their faithful to negate thought in favor of "belief" in them, regardless of reason's questioning the literalism of their teachings or the probability that Robertson or Bush talks to God, a convenient ruse that allows them to accept "faith" without question but denies that route to God to those of other faiths; and, most deceptively and insidiously, they convert Christianity into cruelty in the name of the most peaceful man to tread the earth as they raise their collective swords against the infidels in the Mid-East. Their religion is a religion of hate, of oppression, of fanatical singleness of belief, of divisiveness, of arrogance, of exclusivity that denies the ideal of the brotherhood and sisterhood of humankind, of mercy and charity, of love and forgiveness, the sun of Christ's spirit.

Ironically, the Neo-Cons who wrote the sacred books of this administration—the Patriot Act, Powell's WMD presentation before the UN, the National Security Strategy Report—deny the validity of Christianity even as they delight in the blindness of the faithful as a tool to be used to solidify their intent to control the world. These modern, Machiavellian manipulators salivate at the millions who accept on faith that God has chosen Bush to fulfill His mission to bring about the Rapture and usher in the 1000 years of peace. Equally ironic one could argue is the laughable parallel between this inauguration and that held when Cromwell took power in England in the mid 1600s, another time when mis-guided clergy predicted the coming of Armageddon as that state moved toward a theocracy. How many times must Armageddon come before we realize Revelations is a work of metaphors, not a history text or the word of God?

The last time a king was crowned believing in his heart that God Himself had anointed him, he found himself in due time brought before the court of the people's representatives, would you believe on January 20, 1648 in the Great Hall of Westminster, where he was charged with "High Treason" because he had broken his oath of office by seeking "unlimited and tyrannical power, attempted to overthrow the peoples liberties," and "traitorously and maliciously" made war against the people. Charles I went defiantly to his death insisting that no earthly power could dissemble what God had foreordained. But this was the time of the Levellers, those who, long before our Founding Fathers extolled the idea, held that "all power is originally and essentially in the whole body of the people."

Now this country is faced, somewhat incredibly, with a bunch of men who believe they are the chosen, either by Straussian determinist beliefs as fitting to rule or by God's recognition of them as of the elect. They come to celebrate the crowning of George W. Bush, the self-proclaimed disciple of the only true Lord, sent on His mission to bring His gift to all humankind, a veritable "divinely anointed Emperor" of the world, a return to days of yore when people accepted what their ministers preached, that God blesses those leaders they, on His behalf, anoint, and negate, thereby, the unalienable rights that reside in the body politic, each and every citizen of this nation.

How quaint, indeed, that this bastion of the 21st century should resort to concepts long dead as the means to effect the dreams of the Cabal that has stolen the American Dream, the belief that the people rule the country, substituting in its place rule by fear that they, like ancient conquerors of old, might impose their imperialistic designs on powerless nations in order to ensure their ultimate control. How fitting, then, that we witness this cabalistic inauguration orchestrated by our own Cabal, not dissimilar to that which surrounded Charles II, progeny of the doomed King Charles I (another irony I might add), an inauguration filled with intrigue and ritual, a mock rite sanctified by self- proclaimed interpreters of God's word.

39

The Lost Ur-Version: Bush's Second Inaugural Address

[January 26, 2005]

[*Note on text*: While roaming the Internet, looking for a map that would guide me around Washington D.C. during the Inaugural festivities, I came upon a blog that had the following version of the President's Inaugural Address, a version prepared apparently for delivery to the Skull and Bones Society and invited guests who were major donors to the Bush campaign. Delivery took place after the January 20 Inauguration where a shorter revised version was presented to the American people. A careful reading of this document will attest to its faithfulness to the version delivered before the cameras on Inaugural day, but reveals as well, some disturbing variations.]

On this day, prescribed by law, as is true of the oath of office that I took the liberty to change, and marked by ceremony costing 40 million dollars provided by corporations that seek access to the President beyond that provided to ordinary citizens, we celebrate the durable wisdom of our Constitution, and recall the deep commitments that unite our country, providing we forget the 79 years of slavery and 181 years of segregation that seemed divisive at the time. I am grateful for the honor of this hour, mindful of the consequential times in which we live, and determined to fulfill the oath that I have sworn and you have witnessed, an oath that requires that I uphold the principles upon which this nation was founded, principles that unfortunately embraced a secular state providing only a tolerance of religions and not, as I espouse, a Christian theocracy, principles that respect the rights of individuals to determine their own beliefs and governments not ones imposed by this nation, a decided flaw in the thinking of our founders, and principles that provide for freedom of speech and assembly among others, all of which pose a threat to a government that must control these freedoms if we are to control those who think differently from us.

At this second gathering, our duties are defined not by the words I use, words that have been made fun of by my enemies thus casting aspersions on the Presidency itself, but by the history we have seen together which, as all of you now know, will mean more lies and deception, more illegal wars, more amoral destruction of innocent human life, and more corruption fostered in league with corporations that are profiting from our war efforts and computer companies that provide us with voting machines. For a half century, America defended our own freedom by standing watch on distant borders, including the Mexican border in 1846 when we fabricated a Mexican attack on our nation in order to expand "freedom and democracy" to the land we stole from Mexico, or when we falsely accused Spain of blowing up the *Maine* giving us an excuse to create Guantanamo which, you've noticed, is still in use ensuring freedom and democracy, or when we lied about the attack in the Gulf of Tonkin to prevent our enemies from gaining control over the oil in that region while safeguarding freedom and democracy for those who supported our efforts there, or, for that matter, when I lied about Iraq having WMD and a connection to 9/11 as a means to bring freedom and democracy to the Mid-East in the same fashion as Israel has brought freedom and democracy to the Palestinians. After the shipwreck of communism came years of relative quiet when we had no visible enemy to keep the coffers of our military industrial complex humming, years of repose, years of sabbatical that required, obviously, the creation of an enemy to give purpose to our government and a false reason for our citizens to rally around the President—and then there came a day of fire which provided the excuse for the creation of an unending war, a war with no visible enemy, no specific state or nation, a ghost-like mirage, a war against an illusion that threatened America, a war against "Terror" without addressing causes for that terror, only filling our people with constant fear the better to ensure their freedom and democracy.

We have seen our vulnerability and we have done our best to hide it through our lies and deception by ignoring the causes for unrest against the United States—and we have seen its deepest source, which we will never admit, the extravagant abuse of natural resources and exploitation of peoples around the world by this nation's corporations allowing our 5% of the world's population to wantonly waste the limited resources that should be shared by all nations. For as long as whole regions of the world simmer in resentment because we use 40% to 60% of the world's resources and do nothing to alter that reality, thus allowing the US to create cooperative dictators who tyrannize their people on our behalf—tyrants prone to ideologies that feed hatred and excuse murder like those we support in Saudi Arabia and Israel—violence will gather, and multiply in destructive power, and cross the most defended borders, and raise a mortal threat to our corporate interests that keep politicians like me in power. There is only one force of history that can break the reign of hatred and resentment, and expose the pretensions of tyrants, and reward the hopes of the decent and tolerant, and that is the force of human freedom asserted by the people as they move toward revolution against our corporate government and replace it with a people's government, a threat we obviously cannot tolerate.

We are led, by events and common sense, to one conclusion: The survival of our corporate liberty in this land increasingly depends on our success in planting more and more US affiliated dictators of our brand of liberty in other lands. The best hope for peace in our corporate world is the expansion of Capitalistic freedom, meaning privatization of all state resources in all countries so that they can become the property of a few of us controlled through the IMF and the WBO, as we've done through the exertions of Paul Bremer in Iraq, and hope to achieve in Iran, North Korea, and Syria in the next four years.

America's vital interests, the continued expansion of our corporate power and the continued belief by the people that outsourcing of their jobs is in their best interests, are now one. From the day of our Founding, we have proclaimed that every man and woman on this earth has rights, and dignity, and matchless value, because they bear the image of the Maker of Heaven and earth, and we have successfully imposed that illusion on them with the unrelenting support of the myth makers on TV and those in the pulpits of all the Zionist evangelical churches who predict the coming of Armageddon. Across the generations we have proclaimed the imperative of self-government while denying it to women for 135 years, and we have declared that no one is fit to be a master, and no one deserves to be a slave as we proved by fighting each other in a savage civil war in a vain effort to keep that institution in place in Texas and throughout the red neck states, and they still believe they govern themselves. Advancing these ideals is the mission that created our Nation and allowed us to ethnically cleanse the native Americans from their lands, steal northern Mexico from its rightful owners, and provide us with precedent for invading Iraq and occupying its land in the name of freedom and democracy. It is the honorable achievement of our fathers, an achievement I intend to expand upon in the coming years. Now it is the urgent requirement of our corporations' security to have our people believe that the poverty stricken nation of Iraq was a threat to us even though they had nothing to do with 9/11, had no weapons of mass destruction, and posed no threat to the US, thus providing an opportunity for America to safeguard Israel and control the energy sources in Iraq and its neighbors for our own purposes; it is the calling of our time.

So it is the policy of the United States to seek and support the growth of global Capitalism and institutions sympathetic to our interests in every nation and culture, with the ultimate goal of ending true democracy to ensure that corporate beneficence and wisdom controls the world.

This is not primarily the task of arms, though we will defend our corporate investments and our friends by force of arms when necessary. Capitalistic freedom, by its nature, must be chosen, and defended by citizens molded to the purpose, and sustained by the rule of law, which we write and legislate, pretending that all are protected including minorities, indeed, all peoples of color. And when the soul of a nation finally speaks, the institutions that arise may reflect customs and traditions very different from our own, and this we must guard against lest the founding principles of this nation be reasserted and turn the people against us who rule. America will not impose its own style of government on the unwilling, but we in corporate America must impose our will on all nations. Our goal then is to mold the voices of the people to express our voice, to attain our understanding of freedom, and make them believe they have it their way.

The great objective of ending tyranny is the concentrated work of generations that creates an illusion that it is opposed to it when in fact it creates the means for tyranny to exist. The difficulty of the task is no excuse for avoiding it. America's influence is not unlimited, but fortunately for the oppressed, America's influence is considerable, and we will abuse it confidently in Capitalistic freedom's cause.

My most solemn duty is to protect the corporations that control this nation and their people against further attacks and emerging threats. Some have unwisely chosen to test my resolve, and have found it firm in supporting those who support me and my administration.

We will persistently clarify the choice before every ruler and every nation: The moral choice between oppression, which is always wrong, unless done by this administration, and freedom, which is eternally right, but hazardous to Capitalistic enterprise, and, therefore, must be suppressed. America will not pretend that jailed dissidents prefer their chains, recognizing how difficult this is when we have unpatriotic Americans releasing photos of Abu Ghraib and Guantanamo, or that women welcome humiliation and servitude, when Human Rights organizations show what our corporations allow in the sweat shops of Mexico, Indonesia, Cambodia, Vietnam, Malaysia, and China, or that any human being aspires to live at the mercy of bullies, knowing that we cannot keep the lid on our atrocities in places like Fallujah.

We will encourage reform in other governments by making clear that success in our relations will require absolute control of their people so that our investments can be stabilized and protected. America's belief in human dignity will guide our policies on paper and through our talking heads on TV regardless of how we behave in reality, yet rights must be more than the grudging concessions of dictators, they must be fabricated so that they are believable; they are secured by apparent dissent and the participation of the governed. In the long run, there is no justice without freedom as we and our Israeli allies demonstrate in our extrajudicial killings, and there can be no belief in human rights without a controlled press to make it so.

Some, I know, have questioned the global appeal of liberty, especially the kind that we offer to the world—though this time in history, four decades defined by the swiftest advance of Capitalistic freedom ever seen, is an odd time for doubt, at least if we overlook the exploitation of the poor, the failure of our privately owned health systems, and the infliction of the worst civilian death toll in the history of the planet. Americans, of all people, should never be surprised by the power of our ideals. Eventually, the call of freedom comes to every mind and every soul. We do not accept the existence of permanent tyranny because we do not accept the possibility of permanent slavery. Liberty will come to those who love it, and this, my friends, is our only true threat in the near future.

Today, America speaks anew to the peoples of the world: All who live in tyranny and hopelessness can know: the United States will not ignore your oppression, or excuse your oppressors, we will take their place or put those who cooperate with us in place as we have done in Iraq and Palestine. When you stand for our liberty, we will stand with you.

Capitalistic reformers facing repression, prison, or exile can know, America sees you for who you are: the future leaders of your free country under the military protection of the US.

The rulers of outlaw regimes can know that we still believe as Abraham Lincoln did: "Those who deny freedom to others deserve it not for themselves; and, under the rule of a just God, cannot long retain it." It's comforting to know that Abe was talking about slavery in America, not about the kind of economic slavery we impose around the world. And since we are on a mission from God, His justice allows us to impose this kind of slavery as part of His prophecy.

The leaders of governments with long habits of control need to know as we do: to serve your people you must learn to mold them. Start on this journey of progress and justice, and America will walk at your side.

And all the corporate allies of the United States can know: we honor your friendship, we rely on your counsel, and we depend on your help. Division among free Capitalistic nations is a primary goal of freedom's enemies. The concerted effort of free nations to promote democracy is a prelude to our corporate defeat.

Today, I also speak anew to my fellow citizens:

From all of you, I have asked patience in the hard task of securing America, which you have granted in good measure.

Our country has accepted obligations that are difficult to fulfill, and would be dishonorable to abandon and detrimental to our corporate goals. Yet because we have acted in the great liberating tradition of this nation, tens of millions have achieved their freedom because we have said it's so, as witness the free Afghans, Iraqis, and Palestinians. And as hope kindles hope, millions more will find it. By our efforts, we have lit a fire as well—a fire in the minds of men. It warms those of us who feel its power, it burns those who fight its progress, and one day this controlled fire of Capitalistic freedom will reach the darkest corners of our world.

A few Americans have accepted the hardest duties in this cause—in the secret work of intelligence and diplomacy... the amoral work of helping raise up free governments... the dangerous and necessary work of fighting our enemies. Some have shown their devotion to our country in deaths that honored their whole lives—and we will always honor their names and their sacrifice.

All Americans have witnessed this idealism, and some for the first time. I ask our youngest citizens to believe the evidence not of your eyes, that told you the Iraqis would welcome your efforts with flowers strewn in the streets when in fact they want you out of their land, but to believe in the words of your President that you are liberators making safe the path of Capitalism that will provide the bread of Heaven in this life. You have seen duty and allegiance in the determined faces of our soldiers. You have seen that life is fragile, and evil is real, and evil, not courage, triumphs. Make the choice to serve in a cause larger than your wants, larger than yourself—and in your days you will add not just to the wealth of our country, certainly not to your own wealth as soldiers fighting on behalf of our corporations, but to its consumer based character.

America has need of idealism and courage, because we have need of unthinking robots to bear our weapons—the unfinished work of American free enterprise. In a world moving toward Capitalistic liberty, we are determined to show the meaning and promise of selfishness and consumer pride.

In America's ideal of freedom, citizens find dignity and security in economic credit dependence, instead of laboring on the edge of subsistence as a quarter of our population does this very day.

This is not the broader definition of liberty that motivated the Homestead Act, the Social Security Act, and the G.I. Bill of Rights. It is new and now we will extend this vision by reforming great institutions to serve the needs of our time. To give every American a stake in the promise and future of our country, we will bring the highest standards to our schools forcing the poorest out, and build an ownership society for the few at the expense of the many. We will widen the ownership of homes and businesses, retirement savings and health insurance—preparing our people for the challenges of life in a free society where greedy financial planners can hold out the promise of great wealth while they steal the meager savings of the uninitiated. By making every citizen an agent of his or her own destiny, we will make our fellow Americans victims of predators that will cheat them of economic freedom leaving them in want and fear, while making the "haves" more prosperous and just and equal.

In America's ideal of freedom, the public interest depends on private character—on integrity, and tolerance toward others, and the rule of conscience in our own lives. Self-government relies, in the end, on the governing of the self. That can be detrimental to our ends. That edifice of character is built in families (which we have effectively destroyed by forcing both parents to work in order to survive), supported by communities with standards (which we have effectively destroyed by creating divided communities), and sustained in our national life by the truths of Sinai (which we exploit in the products we produce that lure our people into sin), the Sermon on the Mount (which we have downgraded since it encourages socialistic programs), the words of the Koran (which we do not believe), and the varied faiths of our people (which we do not tolerate). Americans move forward in every generation by reaffirming all that is good and true that came before, blind to the reality that created a holocaust of Native Americans, the enslavement of one-fifth of our population, discrimination against women, acceptance of poverty, and, worse yet, acceptance of civilian death as a "product" of war—ideals of justice and conduct that are the same yesterday, today, and forever as we continue to feast on these idealistic, yet totally illusion based beliefs.

In America's ideal of freedom, the exercise of rights is ennobled by service, and mercy, and a heart for the weak. Liberty for all does not mean independence from one another. Our nation relies on men and women who look after a neighbor and surround the lost with love. Americans, at our best, value the life we see in one another, and must always remember that even the unwanted have worth. And our country must abandon all the habits of racism, because we cannot carry the message of freedom and the baggage of bigotry at the same time. We must encourage these ideals so that it appears that we want to help, but discourage the belief that it is government's responsibility to cure them. Belief in the individual, belief in an ownership society means "take care of yourself," don't be a burden on others. If we are to be strong, the weak must be weeded out.

From the perspective of a single day, including this day of dedication, the issues and questions before our country are many. From the viewpoint of centuries, the questions that come to us are narrowed and few. Did our generation advance the cause of freedom? And did our character bring credit to that cause? We need only look at our "democratically" imposed dictator in Afghanistan, our puppet in Iraq, our newly elected (with the help of Israeli controlled checkpoints and walls) obsequious servant to Sharon, the duly elected Palestinian replacement for Arafat, our cooperative leaders in Jordan and Egypt, to know that we have controlled the "advance of freedom," our kind of freedom with the type of characters that will ensure the spread of free markets to better the condition of all peoples to answer that question positively.

These questions that judge us also unite us, because Americans of every party and background, Americans by choice and by birth, are bound to one another in the cause of freedom as we let them define it. We have known divisions, which must be healed to move forward in great purposes—and I will strive in good faith to heal them which will require your support in money and control of the media. Yet those divisions do not define America. We felt the unity and fellowship of our nation when freedom came under attack, and our response came like a single hand over a single heart. We, the chosen few, must determine how that heart beats, and we must determine what unity and pride means in America—what is good and what is evil— and who are the victims to be given hope, and who will encounter our extrajudicial justice, and who will be set free.

We go forward with complete confidence in the eventual triumph of Capitalistic freedom. Not because history runs on the wheels of inevitability; it is human choices that move events. Not because we consider ourselves a chosen nation but because we are the chosen that moves and chooses. We have confidence because our freedom is the permanent hope of mankind, the hunger in dark places, the longing of the soul. When our Founders declared a new order of the ages; when soldiers died in wave upon wave for a union based on liberty; when citizens marched in peaceful outrage under the banner "Freedom Now"—they were acting on an ancient hope that is meant to be fulfilled. We can't let that hope rise again or it will threaten our cause and all we have worked for. History has an ebb and flow of justice, but history also has a visible direction, set by liberty and the Author of Liberty, and that is fine as long as we determine what that liberty is and who that Author is.

When the Declaration of Independence was first read in public and the Liberty Bell was sounded in celebration, a witness said, "It rang as if it meant something." In our time it means something still. We on behalf of America, in this young century, proclaim Capitalistic liberty throughout all the world, and to all the inhabitants thereof. Renewed in our strength—tested, but not weary—we are ready for the greatest achievements in the history of freedom.

May God bless you, and may He watch over our United States of America.

40

Imperial Zealotry: Righteous Racism Running Rampant
[February 22, 2005]

We on the right side of freedom's divide have an obligation to help those unlucky enough to be born on the wrong side.
—Condoleezza Rice, 2/9/05

David Stannard, in his thoroughly documented work on genocides, *American Holocaust* (1992), introduces his 5th Chapter with a passage from Toni Morrison's *Beloved*: "White folks were still on the loose... While whole towns wiped clean of Negroes; eighty seven lynchings in one year alone in Kentucky; four colored schools burned to the ground; grown men whipped like children; children whipped like adults; black women raped by the crew; property taken, necks broken... (and as Stamp Paid, a black man, came to his flat-bottomed boat he saw) a red ribbon knotted around a curl of wet wooly hair, clinging still to its bit of scalp." He pulled the ribbon loose and let the scalp sink in the river as he asked to no one in particular and the world in general, "What are these people? You tell me, Jesus. What are they?"

What fuels slavery, ethnic cleansing, land theft, and genocide? What enables a mind to justify imprisoning another without cause, without trial, without rights of due process and assumption of innocence until proven guilty? What enables a soul to accept dominance over another, to degrade and humiliate other humans, to participate in or acquiesce to genocide?

Let me mutter a response to Stamp Paid's question to Jesus since He seems silent on the subject. I'll posit two trends of thought, two of many perhaps, that seem to reside at the root of

Western culture, trends that swirl like infected eddies beneath the surface of our ideals allowing for slavery, ethnic erasure of populations, land theft and genocide. The first blossoms when men, driven by a commitment to an ideology they accept as absolute, as those who zealously and fanatically proclaim they alone know God's word, rise to power and force their beliefs on others, knowing in their hearts that they are chosen to lead because of their innate superiority, men like Ferdinand, the King of Spain, Columbus and the Pope who guide their legions of friars and conquistadors to impose their divinely ordained right on others. The second follows from the first, when men, who accept unquestioningly their superiority over others deemed by them to be sub-human or inferior in intellect or will, move to positions of power not driven by an ideology, but willingly use those so possessed, to impose their covetous desire to acquire land, natural resources, or labor regardless of the consequences.

Elie Wiesel said of the Nazi perpetrators of the holocaust: "All the killers were Christians... The Nazi system was the consequence of a movement of ideas and followed a strict logic; it did not arise in a void but had its roots deep in a tradition that prophesied it, prepared for it, and brought it to maturity. That tradition was inseparable from the past of Christian, civilized Europe." Wiesel's observation implies that the Nazi holocaust utilized the belief structures in the church and the faithful's acceptance of them as articulated by their leaders to carry forward the devastation of the Jews. Both trends were in operation as the Nazi leadership imposed its will on the German citizenry while enunciating the innate superiority of the German nation.

Condoleezza Rice noted in her Paris speech "...history does not just happen, it is made. History is made by men and women of conviction, of commitment and of courage, who will not let their dreams be denied." Once again the past of Christian, civilized Europe is on the march; its dreams of God's mission to bring His gift of "freedom" to all the peoples of the world will be executed whether or not they are the dreams of all the peoples who will accept them or die. What mind decides, "We are on the right side of freedom's divide"? What mind declares it will impose its righteousness on all the peoples of the earth? What soul will succumb to the will of its leaders to slay the infidels who deny the "right" as determined by an elite group of fanatics driven by a self-determined superiority and a zeal to impose their beliefs on all? Let us note that the Secretary of State did not say history is made by those seeking oil to ensure its military dominance, nor did she say that history is made by the nation that supports America's and Israel's interests in the Mid-East; she said, most emphatically, what the Zionists of the Christian right claim to be "right," that God gave this land to a Christian nation, to be a "City on a Hill," a beacon to all the world that they might see what God expected His creatures to do on His behalf, and in that covenant, the responsibility to bring that gift to all the world.

Imbedded in that belief resides the spirit of superiority of God's chosen, an awareness that they alone possess the truth, and, consequently, are the most civilized creatures on the planet. Indeed, refusal by a people to accept conversion to Christianity became a mark of irrationality and subhuman status. Now, this most Christian of nations brings God's gift to the nations of the world judging them fit to join the "advanced, civilized, and developed" nations of the West if they adopt willingly or by force America's form of Democracy, a form dominated by Corporate power and control, where "advanced and developed" means in reality new markets for Capitalism and new resources to fuel its continued growth. Strange how the "bread of heaven" has metamorphosed into a euphemistic "freedom" for all if they become cooperative consumers for extended Christian Capitalism. Both trends that give rise to genocide swirl beneath the rhetoric of "freedom and liberty," a virtual whirlpool of Zionist Christian fanaticism and neo-con covetousness for land and resources, and will erupt in a tsunami of devastation for those who oppose the will of this administration.

But even more insidious is the unquestioned acceptance of their right to impose their dreams on all, by force if necessary, since they, like their Christian ancestors, accept Augustine's view, "Any violation of God's laws... could be seen as an injustice warranting unlimited violent punishment. Further, the guilt... of the enemy merited punishment of the enemy population without regard to the distinction between soldiers and civilians. Motivated by righteous wrath, the just warriors could kill with impunity, even those who were morally innocent." (Frederick H. Russell, *American Holocaust*.)

The "dreams" of the Spanish priests who came with the Crown's forces, the Conquistadors (who had their own dreams), believed, as do our current crop of TV evangelists and right wing Baptists, that God was about to fulfill the prophecies of the *Book of Revelation*. Columbus had calculated the end time as 150 years away, roughly 1650, and the Franciscans understood their founder to be an angel of Revelation, Charles V to be the Anti-Christ, and the Reformation wars of northern Europe the catastrophes predicted in that book. Since they were obviously born on the right side of the divide, they had a responsibility to bring God's word to the infidels. This they did with a vengeance, including the Miranda Law of the day, the *requerimiento,* that forced the natives to abandon their beliefs and tribes and accept the authority of the Papacy and the Crown. Should they refuse, perhaps because it was read to them in Spanish, they were tortured and killed.

Sounds familiar, doesn't it. We need only turn on our television set to the indomitable Hal Lindsey to hear the most recent predictions of God's ultimate twisting of events to force the prophecies of Revelation into reality. When do we bring this man and all his ilk—Hagee, Dobson, Hinn, Robertson, Falwell, to name a few—, to court to stand trial for inciting to riot and crimes against humanity? What right do they have, whatever side of the great divide they claim to be on, to intimidate the faithful with eternal damnation if they do not press forward with their war against the Muslims?

Genocides and holocausts arise out of unchecked zeal, unquestioned duty, and silent acquiescence. They are fueled by blind belief, personal fear, and a sense of superiority that gives license to slaughter. Both the United States under Bush and its clone under Sharon exemplify the presence of racism resulting in genocidal devastation as they impose their respective wills on Iraqis and Palestinians. The facts alone demonstrate the rampant racism running unchecked as Israel shackles the Palestinian people in chains as grotesque as any imposed by America's plantation owners on their property in the old south; and the United States, not to be outdone, occupies and oppresses the Iraqi people in methods learned from their Israeli tutors who teach them how to subdue, intimidate, humiliate, torture, and eradicate a people considered inferior to their oppressors.

Let Lt. Gen. James Mattis "tell it like it is" as he instructs our soldiers in the grace of war: "It's a lot of fun to fight. You know, it's a hell of a hoot... You go into Afghanistan, you got guys who slap women around for five years because they didn't wear a veil. You know, guys like that don't got no manhood left anyway. So it's a hell of a lot of fun to shoot them." Imbedded in that statement resides America's superiority over the Afghanistan people: a superiority in moral values based on the wearing of a veil, a veil not unlike those used in years past by Catholic nuns to show their modesty before God and their awareness of the frailty of men who "lust in their hearts," to borrow a phrase from a former President of the United States, caring not to be the source of that lust; a superiority in judgment since this general can determine that his indictment justifies killing every male that has reached the age of marriage; and a superiority in legal rights because he can, as we learned from our Israeli brethren, predetermine who is guilty of breaking our laws, and, without leveling a charge, without representation by jury, without trial before peers, execute all of the male gender in Afghanistan. That is genocidal thinking, base, irrational, and savage.

Perhaps we think the General's thinking is that of only one man. Here is MKB1957, a soldier commenting on criticism of the General's remarks on *forums.military.com:* "The general spoke forthrightly, but CORRECTLY. Our way of thinking, the American way of thinking, does not accept a religion OR a society that mistreats women or treats them as property. He was speaking for many, many people who are forward thinking, and not in the dark ages." How different is this thinking from that of the Conquistadors who came with their enlightened faith to the new world, pulled children from their mothers' breasts, flung them in the air, and cut them in two with their swords? What, pray tell, is the American way of thinking: the male behavior of women espoused by the Southern Baptist Convention or the righteous hypocrisy of Bill O'Reilly and the Reverend Jimmy Swaggert or the flourishing industry of pornography? How can this society determine the correct behavior of another regarding women when it relishes its own variety of abuses and desires to thrust them upon all the nations of the world?

How does this thinking translate on the ground as our forces follow the training offered by Lt. Gen. James Mattis? Dahr Jamail recounts this painful account of a conversation he had with a doctor about the rape of Fallujah. (Dahr Jamail is an independent reporter in Iraq serving many news organizations because he's one of a few who move through the streets and byways of Iraq unhindered by military escort. You can read his reports at *http://dahrjamailiraq.com.*) "One of my colleagues, Dr. Saleh Alsawi, he was speaking so angrily about them (American soldiers). He was in the main hospital when they raided it at the beginning of the siege. They entered the theater room when they were working on a patient... he was there because he's an anesthesiologist. They entered with their boots on, beat the doctors and took them out, leaving the patient on the table to die."

Jamail offers a second story, one recorded by the doctor on video tape, "'... a young girl who is 16 years old... stayed for three days with the bodies of her family who were killed in their home. When soldiers entered she was in the home with her father, mother, 12-year-old brother and two sisters. She watched the soldiers enter and shoot her mother and father directly, without saying anything.' The girl managed to hide behind a refrigerator with her brother and witnessed the war crimes first hand. 'They beat her two sisters, then shot them in the head,' he said. After this her brother was enraged and ran at the soldiers while shouting at them, so they shot him. 'She continued hiding after the soldiers left and stayed with her sisters because they were bleeding, but still alive.'"

Add to these pictures the bodies left in the streets and in the rubble of Fallujah, bodies eaten by roaming dogs, bodies caught in the debris of fallen buildings and left to die; consider the military's take over of the medical facilities and prevention of medical supplies from entering the city, acts in direct contravention of the Geneva conventions; consider as well the determination that anyone left in the city should be considered enemy, a city of over 250,000 people left homeless so that we could level it in retaliation for their "insurrection" against our occupation, and you have a picture of absolute self-determined superiority over another population that can be treated like vermin as we cleanse the city by destroying it. Yet we continue to proclaim that we are the liberators of this people as we slaughter more than 100,000 of them, devastate their cities, destroy their homes, and leave our most lethal calling card for later generations to enjoy, our gift of depleted uranium, God's gift, perhaps, to this nation that we invaded on behalf of a lying President bent on bringing his born-again religion to the people of the Mid-East while gaining control of the oil that will fuel his military machine for years to come. That is genocidal thinking, base, irrational, and savage.

But we are not alone in the Mid-East; indeed, we are there in good measure because our clone, Israel, is there and has prepared the way for us in its treatment of the indigenous population that lived in Palestine for two thousand years. Nothing is more grotesque than to witness the United States mimic, adopt for God's sake, the racist actions of Israel as it attempts to subdue the Iraqis: create checkpoints to control freedom of movement of the citizens, impose curfews and erect barbed-wire barriers to ensure control of freedom of assembly, give reconstruction contracts to American firms to make sure the Iraqis have little or nothing to achieve freedom from want, shoot at medical vehicles lest they be manned by terrorists to prevent the right to life and health, inflict indiscriminate killing, the extrajudicial method designed by the Israelis to stop terrorism even as it ensures the abandonment of law, a freedom we were meant to bring to the Iraqi people, and humiliate the people by torture techniques accepted by our elected and appointed leaders, offered to us by Israeli consultants who use these methods to control the minds and actions of the Palestinians. This is racism, base, irrational, and savage.

Many in this administration have been consultants and advisors to Israel. They are the creators of our foreign policy, a policy designed as long ago as 1991 when they were first in the daddy Bush administration. Our pre-emptive drive into the Mid-East accomplished for these men what they saw as essential for Israel, the removal of Saddam, a major threat to Israeli dominance in the Mid-East, and the establishment of a puppet regime favorable to the west. By gaining control of this Bush junior administration, they have turned America from a nation seeking peace in the Mid-East to one that savors the removal of Palestinians from Jewish land, the dream of the Zionists, a dream Condoleezza Rice obviously understands. How absurd to

consider as serious Bush's mouthing of a Palestinian state sitting
side by side in peace with a free Israeli state when he has removed
the need for Israel to return the land it stole from Palestinians
leaving them two patches of land, separated from each other by
Israeli controlled territory, representing approximately 14% of
the land they lived on for almost two thousand years.

How have they accomplished this theft? By turning
Palestinians, those able and willing to fight their occupation and
all who support them, meaning the whole of the Palestinian
people, into terrorists. That becomes their justification for ethnic erasure, a practice they have copied from America's past,
only they have put this eradication on a fast track. Phyllis
Bennis noted, "From its origins in the 19th century, Zionism
centered on the idea of creating a specifically Jewish state in
which Jews would be protected and privileged over non-Jews."
(Posted at *globalresearch.ca* 29 August 2001).

Understood in the context of racism, this dream of a Jewish
homeland on another's land compares to the dream of the
Puritans to establish their religious state on land inhabited by
others, land they, too, believed was ordained for them by a
covenant with God. And the Puritans, like the Israelis, enslaved
and murdered the indigenous people, thanking their God in the
process for giving them the privilege of destroying His enemy.
"Over 80% of the land within Israel that was once owned by
Palestinians has been confiscated," according to Bennis, and
that was in 2000 before Sharon decided to construct a Wall to
imprison that population on a reservation surrounded by Israeli
military forces, a Wall that moves like a sidewinder confiscating
ever more land as it moves over the hills and valleys of the little
land left the Palestinians.

Compare, if you will, the rationale as enunciated by the leaders of Israel and the leaders of early America: "There is no such
thing as a Palestinian people," Golda Meir; "There is no other
way than to transfer the Arabs from here to neighboring countries.. All of them; not one village, not one tribe, should be left,"
Joseph Weitz, 1967; "The only good Arab is a dead Arab. When
we have settled the land, all the Arabs will be able to do about
it will be to scurry around liked drugged cockroaches," Rafael
Eitan; "It is forbidden to be merciful to them... Evil ones,
damnable ones. May the Holy Name visit retribution on the

Arabs' heads, and cause their seed to be lost, and annihilate them...," Rabbi Ovadia Yosef, Shas, 2001.

Now a word from our illustrious leaders. The land, William Bradford said, was a "hideous and desolate wilderness... full of wild beasts and wild men." Thomas Jefferson wrote that the government was obliged "now to pursue them (Indians) to extermination, or drive them to new seats beyond our reach." George Washington mused that the natives deserved nothing from the whites but "total ruin." Our revered Reverend Cotton Mather remarked in his Christian way, "Once you have but got the Track of those ravenous Wolves, then pursue them vigorously; Turn not back till they are consumed... Beat them small as the Dust before the Wind."

David Stannard writes of these commentaries, "For two hundred years to come Washington, Jefferson, Jackson, and other leaders, representing the wishes of virtually the entire white nation, followed their ministers' genocidal instructions with great care. It was their Christian duty as well as their destiny." Compare Bennis' observation about the Jews to Stannard's about our forefathers, "The majority of Israeli Jews are willing to accept the killing of Palestinians and collective punishment of the Palestinian population as justified state policy." This is racism, base, irrational, and savage.

Bush has yoked America to the vicious racism of Sharon giving him license to steal 86% of the land originally owned by Palestinians; he has given him license to wantonly kill innocent civilians as he undertakes his extrajudicial murders of Palestinian leaders; he has permitted him to construct the most racist icon visible in the world today, the hideous Wall of Fear that Sharon has used to incarcerate the people Bush says will have their own state. With hypocrisy of this kind manifest before the world, how can the United States proclaim itself a nation that dreams of democracy for all the peoples of the earth?

Silence in America and silence in Israel allows this racism to continue. Gideon Levy stated recently, "For more than four years Israel has been doing anything it wanted in the occupied areas, practically without any domestic criticism. It killed and demolished, uprooted and brutalized, and practically nobody protested. The world saw what was going on and shouted about it. But not us. When Israel desperately needed an alternative view, a clear sound of protest, practically nothing was heard, not a peep, except from a few small and brave organizations." (Good Morning to the Israeli Left). Where in the American press do we see words of this kind? Where are the voices that will condemn Sharon's demolition of Palestinian homes in Gaza and Rafah? Who condemns the IDF for firing indiscriminately large caliber machine guns and tanks at civilian areas in Khan Yunis? What TV journalist condemns the use of private homes by snipers of the IDF forcing residents to remain inside as shields? Where is the commentator who provides an accurate number of civilian dead, the 393 killed in Rafah between September 29, 2000 and August 31, 2004, including 98 children under the age of 18? Nowhere! We condone these acts with our silence. And the world listens. This is racism, base, irrational, and savage.

How strange to have America's Secretary of State, who comes from a race once enslaved in the country she represents, extolling actions by her administration that parallel the behavior of the slave owners who by sheer force and the complicity of the dominant population controlled all aspects of their lives including the religion that gave them promise of freedom but did nothing to free them until a civil war erupted and released them from bondage. How strange to have Israel represented by children of holocaust victims who have forgotten the racism inflicted on their parents where identity badges proclaimed their inferior and subjugated status, where their religion was a means of condemning them to ghettos, where walls were constructed, ironically in some cases by Jews themselves, as is pictured at the Holocaust Memorial Museum at Vad Yeshem, Jerusalem, to prevent them from participating in the affairs of the city, where gates became checkpoints to control their lives making them totally subservient to their masters, and where deprivation caused the illness and disease that decimated their people. How strange that these two nations, self-proclaimed democracies, have become but the most recent forces for racism in the world because, as Condoleezza Rice has said, "We are on the right side of freedom's divide..." Now we have an answer to Stamp Paid's question of Jesus, "What are these people?" They are men driven by their fanatical will to achieve their desires regardless of the havoc they have caused in the lives of others.

41

Cheerleading War and Slaughter: Resurrecting the Neo-Con Failures

[March 16, 2005]

A Conservative Government is an organized hypocrisy.
—Benjamin Disraeli

As we commemorate the now annual date of America's March of Madness into Iraq, where the Neo-Con forces of liberation became the forces of occupation, we witness these very same Pharisees lifting their respective heads above the roiling waters of the river Styx into which they sank this country, tentatively waving their cheerleaders' pom-poms in celebration of their ultimate triumph, the democratization of the Mid-East. This March 19, America's "Day of Infamy," the day we launched Bush's illegal pre-emptive invasion of another country, a day that should be celebrated in this good Christian land with a Mass of the Dead accompanied by the anguished cry of Mozart's *Requiem*, we have instead an advertising campaign from the board rooms of the American Enterprise Institute, the Project for the New American Century, AIPAC, the Pentagon, and the White House extolling the success of Bush's "Shock and Awe" as it elevated the Arab states from their "Age of Darkness" to the "Enlightenment" of civilized Capitalistic society.

No voice speaks more loudly the anthem of this Cabal than one of its founding fathers, Charles Krauthammer, whose two page advertising spread in *Time* this month, "Three Cheers for the Bush Doctrine," rouses the troops in glowing accolades to celebrate Bush's determination and resolve to carry forward, despite world opinion, to bring freedom and liberty to the people of the Arab world. "It took this marriage of power, will and principle to produce the astonishing developments in the Middle East today," Krauthammer stammers in ecstatic admiration of the "Bush Doctrine" that states apparently, "the will to freedom is indeed universal" and that "America's intentions are sincere." "Contrary to the cynics," he notes, "Arab and European and American, the US did not go into Iraq for oil or hegemony, after all, but for liberation—a truth that on Jan. 31 even al-Jazeera had to televise."

Milton observed in *Paradise Lost*, "For neither man nor angel can discern/Hypocrisy, the only evil that walks/Invisible, except to God alone." No doubt Krauthammer and his minions understand this truth believing they can manipulate the public to believe whatever lies they wish to perpetrate. And why shouldn't they, since the whole debacle of the Bush Doctrine, so-called, began in lies, continues in lies, and will, with Krauthammer and his ilk as historians, convert lies to truth as the victors write the texts for the defeated. These Bush apologists take the onion of Bush's doctrine, discard without comment each lying skin, then rediscover its core in euphuistic generalities that ignore the facts and turn fiction into truth.

Consider this prevarication: "That America, using power harnessed to democratic ideals, could begin a transformation of the Arab world from endless tyranny and intolerance to decent governance and democratization." What democratic ideal calls upon one people to determine for another that they will assume the principles of democracy or they will be imposed on them by force? The fundamental premise of democracy is self-determination, not imposed or coerced determination. America's power in Bush's doctrine, if such there be, is not harnessed to any democratic ideal; rather, it is harnessed to an illegal policy of pre-emptive force and Zionist Christian mythology that negates the rights of nation states, dissembles the unifying fabric of the United Nations, casts America back to the dark ages of lawlessness, and turns these United States into a pariah nation understood by the vast majority of nations on the planet as a terrorist state.

Lest he give all the credit for this remarkable "spring" of new found civil discourse in the Mid-East to Bush alone, Krauthammer promotes his own narcissistic image as the architect of this beneficence by asserting, "I argued (two years ago)... that force-fully deposing Saddam Hussein was, more than anything, about America 'coming ashore' to effect a 'pan-Arab reformation'—a dangerous, 'risky and, yes, arrogant' but necessary attempt to change the very culture of the Middle East, to open its doors to democracy and modernity." How refreshing that the Arab world and its culture should be "corrected" by a man of such intellect who had, without question, only their best interests at heart. None of this, certainly, had to do with what Krauthammer, dur-ing the fall campaign, described as Kerry's trump card should he win the Presidency, "sacrificing Israel" to appease the Europeans and the Arabs. "America's power harnessed to democratic ideals" certainly had nothing to do with Israel's interests in the Mid-East any more than it had to do with oil or hegemony. Certainly, America's interests were purely altruistic, and misread-ing "coming ashore" to mean that America would arrive at the shore where Israel exists as a military presence, is perversion of the truth. Perhaps we should be satisfied that he admits the arro-gance of the statement, knowing as we do that arrogance walks blindly through its path of destruction led by its white cane of egoism, tipped by the red blood of its superiority and racism.

Blind arrogance can see no fault, assume no responsibility, nor bear any guilt. It omits all that disturbs the comfort of its proclaimed truth. Hence, Krauthammer's "Elections in Afghanistan, a historic first. Elections in Iraq, a historic first. Free Palestinian elections producing a moderate leadership, two historic firsts. Municipal elections in Saudi Arabia, men only, but still a first. In Egypt, demonstrations for democracy— unheard of in decades—prompting the dictator to announce free contested presidential elections, a historic first," omits the facts in favor of the platitude. That American power controlled the election process and the candidates in Afghanistan, that the pre-determined winner, America's CIA gift to the country, President Karzai controls only a small section of the country, that warlords are paid by America to keep the lid on uprisings need not be mentioned. That Iraqis did not know the names of the candidates, that a major percent of the population did not vote, that Americans controlled access to the voting areas and the counting of the ballots, that the Kurdish 27% of guaranteed seats is a political payoff, that the outcome will be a Shiite state not a democracy need not be mentioned. That the Palestinians had elected a UN monitored President of the PLO prior to this election, a President made inoperative by Israel and the US, thus negating the purpose of a democratic election, that America and Israel made it clear that there would be no financial support or political support for a Palestinian state unless they elected Mahmoud Abbas, the man both Bush and Sharon accepted because he would cow-tow to Sharon's demands, that the Palestinians did not have free access to the polling places because they had to go through Israeli checkpoints, need not be mentioned. That Saudi Arabia's Saud family and Egypt's Mubarak have been puppets of American power for decades when it was in our interests to have them in total control of their populations, need not be mentioned. Sins of omission corrupt democracies as readily as righteous arrogance makes impossible their creation.

The last time America oversaw an election comparable to the one Krauthammer sees in Iraq was in Vietnam when 83% of the population voted; that vote no more reflected the feelings of the South Vietnamese than the Iraqi vote which, if it portends anything about the Iraqi people, tells us what they tell the Pollsters, they voted to get the US out of Iraq. Fraudulence comes in many packages as Krauthammer demonstrates when he waxes poetic "... the most romantic flowering of the spirit America went into the region to foster: the Cedar Revolution in Lebanon, in which unarmed civilians, Christian and Muslim alike, brought down the puppet government installed by Syria." What he does not mention, of course, is the fractious nature of the ethnic and religious groups that constitute Lebanon and the potential chaos that could ensue from a destabilized government. Nor does he mention that the demonstrations were orchestrated and made possible by the coercion imposed on Syria by the US, not the impulsive reaction of people seeking to assert their new-found rights. Nor does he mention that the forces that took the streets in favor of Syrian support, estimated in excess of 500,000, far outnumbered the young, flag-waving crowd brought to the square by our minions. This demonstration belongs in the same category as Saddam's capture and the pulling down of his statue, the Hollywood fiction made fact.

"Three cheers for Bush's doctrine" celebrates a spring of hope and promise in Iraq and the Mid-East caused by America's invasion of that country and its aftershock in the region; it is a justification for Bush's war. It assumes on its face that America has the right to force Bush's beliefs on the world and that those beliefs are founded on the principles of our democracy and reflect the beliefs of all Americans. These assumptions are wrong. Acceptance of Krauthammer's assumptions gives license to any demagogue to assert the same. Indeed, it justifies Adolf Hitler's abuse of power. The assumption that one nation has the right to forcefully change the culture of another negates the concept of "principle" based on morality. It is on its face anarchy.

But the board members directing this campaign have no regard for democratic principles, only the abuse of the words to manipulate the public. It does not matter that Bush's Cabal determined to invade Iraq as far back as 1991, a policy totally familiar to Mr. Krauthammer; it does not matter that Iraq had nothing to do with 9/11, a lie that Bush used to cajole Americans to accept his invasion; it does not matter that Bush lied about WMD or chemical weapons, reasons added to the list when needed to ensure the peoples' support; it does not matter that the vast majority of the nations in the world objected to his invasion since he had determined it was justified. Neither reason nor morality determines behavior here, power and will do.

Perhaps the most glaring arrogance present in Krauthammer's advertisement crawls out from between the lines, the voices not heard because he takes on the prerogative of speaking on behalf of all Arabs. Oh, he quotes a few toadies, those untouched by America's beneficent power, but he fails to interview the people in the streets, or mention the polls that give a contrary opinion. None of the Iraqi 100,000 dead have a voice to cheer Bush's Doctrine; none of their family members have been asked about its benefits; no one concerned about the ensuing years' invisible companion, depleted uranium, has a voice; none of the maimed—the blind, the limbless, the sick and dying—have a voice; no one has been asked about America's 14 military bases being a permanent part of the Iraqi landscape; no one has been asked about America determining that Iraqi resources should be sold to the most favored private bidder, primarily non-Iraqi; none of the prisoners subjugated to torture at Abu Ghraib has been asked about America's virtues and its democratic ways; and none of the reporters killed in the line of duty or those not allowed to report openly what has gone on in that country have a voice.

As these apologists for Bush's largesse hype the changes going on in the Mid-East and elsewhere around the globe, changes that auger a new age of democracy and freedom, they disparage the past as though America had no hand in its creation: "The region has long been a card catalog of repressive, hereditary kleptocracies, held in place by exported oil and internal security forces, and, since September 11, a source of violent enmity toward the US." So speaks Michael Duffy in *Time's* editorial, an adjacent piece of advertising from Time Warner on behalf of our Emperor. Without blinking, Duffy omits any reference to America's 60 years of support for the family in Saudi Arabia that has caused the repression in that country, nor does he suggest that a healthy portion of the Bush clans' wealth can be directly attributed to that same family, nor does he mention that the resulting poverty of the masses in that country have not been on America's list of the most needy. Perhaps the admission of hypocrisy sticks in the throat. Why tell the truth when you can create your own.

Then there's this observation by Duffy that the "sudden upheaval in Lebanon, set in motion last month by the assassination of former Prime Minister Rafiq Hariri, in itself might have been enough to permit the Bush team to issue a whispered 'I told you so' to critics who thought the President's optimism was naïve." But Duffy makes no mention of the on-going investigations that implicate both Israel and the US in the extrajudicial execution of Hariri, a reality that, if true, might explain the President's optimism, nor does he mention the 500,000 Hezbolah sympathizers that flooded the square where the 25,000 anti-Syrian demonstrators, that he does mention, appeared. Perhaps the admission of hypocrisy sticks in the throat. Why tell the truth when you can create your own.

"Criticism of Hosni Mubarak is still dangerous in Egypt," Duffy notes but fails to explain why America continues to pour billions into that country since it acquiesced to US demands to recognize Israel, if their leader is not sympathetic to democratic values. Perhaps the admission of hypocrisy sticks in the throat. Why not add "The US labored for years to hold elections in Haiti, only to see the country dissolve in chaos," but fail to note, as the Center for the Study of Human Rights detailed in its report, "top officials (in Haiti), including the Minister of Justice, worked for US government projects that undermined their elected predecessors"? Perhaps the admission of hypocrisy sticks in the throat. Why tell the truth when you can create your own.

Let's have three cheers for Krauthammer's doctrine! It, too, rests on a principle, one dear to advertisers and charlatans: accomplish your goal by obfuscation and deceit. The role of government must be asserted through hypocrisy, it must claim its opposite: if it acts by force, if it acts illegally, if it subjugates other nations, if it destroys other people through torture, imprisonment or rape, if it walls people in ghettoes, bulldozes their land and fruit trees, if it terrorizes with overwhelming force, if it murders without trial by jury or access to lawyers, if it curries friendly dictators in Pakistan, Turkmenistan, and Kazakhstan, if it covertly undermines democracies in Chile, Iran, or Haiti while establishing its own dictators in those countries, it must declare itself the savior of the people so subjugated and devastated, claim it has brought democracy to their land and freedom to their people while requesting from them the gratitude the oppressor so rightfully deserves.

We must empathize with Mr. Krauthammer and his peers in the Neo-Con club who have to endure long hours of contemplation away from the crowds, sitting in their frosty air-conditioned offices, beads of sweat glistening on their foreheads as they peer intently at their computer screens, conjuring up the concepts that must be proffered to our government officials if the world is to be corrected to fit their desires. How many of us after all have the opportunity to change cultures, to redirect whole countries to adjust to the Capitalistic forces that define modernity, to send a nation to war by fabricating reasons to pit the greatest military force the world has ever known against an enfeebled nation subjugated to 12 years of sanctions, bereft of needed medical and food supplies to keep its population alive, indeed, even to care for the half million children that succumbed to this deprivation? How many of us have the gall to believe we have the right to convince our fellow citizens that they must go to war against Iraq because that country is a threat to America, that it possesses WMD and chemical weapons, that it took part in the 9/11 attacks, knowing all these things to be a lie?

How many of us would dare to look at ourselves in the mirror if we had brought this government to war against Iraq knowing the devastation that would ensue for America, thousands physically maimed and thousands mentally destroyed, the 1600 soldiers killed to date for their ideas, the phony ideas of liberation, removal of a terrible dictator, freedom and liberty and the democratic way, knowing in their hearts that it was Israeli security and oil that drove them? How many of us could sit down to our family dinner knowing we were responsible for more than 100,000 dead Iraqi civilians, tens of thousands wounded by our WMD, for the bombs that scatter death and pain indiscriminately across the land, the depleted uranium that singes the skin and sears the innards in slow agonizing suffering? How many of us live in a mind that elevates itself to a plane of superiority knowing it has by genetic code the right to lead all and use all to further its preconceived ideals of the civilized and modern world, able to accept the inferiority of the masses, especially those who obstruct their need to possess the resources of others' land to carry forward their designs, to live in full knowledge that thousands upon thousands must die to accomplish their ends and that this is not only necessary but justified because they are the chosen? How many of us would let our neighbor take up the burden of war as long as we can stay behind and direct the slaughter from our plush recliners, having spent the morning laboring on our computers?

Perhaps we must reword Disraeli's observation quoted at the beginning of this chapter, to fit the times: "A Neo-Con Conservative Government is an organized hypocrisy."

42

Glossing over Israel's Human Rights Abuses: The Janus Face of the Department of State

[April 9/10, 2005]

The World is not bound by borders ultimately, it is bound by a moral order. If we do not lead by moral force, we are by acquiescence the followers of those who fail to act and subjects of those who impose their will.
—from *A Time to Know,* by William A. Cook

Two recent reports issued by the US Department of State, "Country Reports on Human Rights Practices" and the "Report on Global Anti-Semitism," deserve attention in light of the Department's professed declaration that "a central goal of US foreign policy has been the promotion of respect for human rights, as embodied in the "Universal Declaration of Human Rights" promulgated by the United Nations and asserted by the Department as it "seeks to (a) hold governments accountable to their obligations under universal human rights norms and international human rights instruments; (b) promote greater respect for human rights, including freedom from torture, freedom of expression, press freedom, women's rights, children's rights, and the protection of minorities; and (c) promote the rule of law, seek accountability, and change cultures of impunity." (*www.state.gov*). The "Universal Declaration of Human Rights applies equally to all humans wherever they live or, as expressed by Martin Luther King, Jr.: "Injustice anywhere is a threat to justice everywhere."

Should we apply this moral stance to the Department's two reports, we Americans face a conundrum... In the words of Shamai Leibowitz, an Israeli human rights attorney from Tel Aviv and a reserve sergeant in the Israeli tank corps: "For years, American taxpayers' money has funded the occupation—the torture chambers, the military apparatus, the bulldozers used in house demolitions, the building of settlements and now the construction of the West Bank wall, declared illegal by the International Court of Justice (ICJ). Americans should be held accountable for where their money is going." (*The Nation*: 3/16/2005) Our Department of State, despite its more than fifty years of monetary support to Israel, more than that given to any other nation on the planet, does not hold the state of Israel "accountable to their obligations under universal human rights norms and international human rights instruments," nor does it "promote respect for human rights" in Israel, or "freedom from torture," nor does it "promote the rule of law" regarding Israel's wall, and these are only the allegations as noted in Leibowitz's article. A more thorough review of these reports reveals the Janus face of the Department of State.

The "Report on Global Anti-Semitism," released by the Bureau of Democracy, Human Rights, and Labor on January 5, 2005 notes: "The increasing frequency and severity of anti-Semitic incidents since the start of the 21st century, particularly in Europe, has compelled the international community to focus on anti-Semitism with renewed vigor." No analysis is offered to explain why these incidents erupted since 2000. No mention of the Intifada and Israel's occupation of Palestine, no mention of the million bullets fired by the IDF in the opening days of the Intifada, a bullet for every Palestinian child according to Noam Chomsky ("Anti-Semitism, Zionism, and the Palestinians," *http://www.scottishpsc.org/uk/Events/events_chomsky2.html*— 3/22/05), no mention of the military crackdown in the West Bank or Gaza, the destruction of homes, the torture chambers, the wanton killings of civilians, the checkpoints and humiliation of the indigenous population, or the illegal continued construction of settlements, to mention a few items identified interestingly enough in the "Country Report," though buried in an appendix. No mention of the Bush administration's rise to power in that year and its acquiescence to Sharon's dictates

concerning his invasions into Jenin or Rafah, or his adding to
the settlements or to the continued construction of the Wall, all
items at deviance with the "Road Map" designed by the US and
its three accomplices. No mention of how the US protects
Israel's outrages in the UN Security Council, the vetoes it uses
to deflect world opinion as it wishes to assert that Israel return
to the demands of Resolution 242 and to remove the illegal
wall. In short, while the report reflects a renewed anger and
frustration against the Israeli state beginning in 2000, it does
not address what may have caused this rise in what it terms
anti-Semitism; it merely lists the incidents and denies the possibility that people across the globe, including member states of
the EU, which it condemns outright, could have as much reason
to express resentment and outrage at the government of Israel
as they do about the government of George W. Bush.

What is anti-Semitism as defined by the Department of State?
"For the purposes of this report, anti-Semitism is considered to
be hatred toward Jews—individually and as a group—that can
be attributed to the Jewish religion and/or ethnicity. An important issue is the distinction between legitimate criticism of policies and practices of the State of Israel, and commentary that
assumes an anti-Semitic character. The demonization of Israel,
or vilification of Israeli leaders, sometimes through comparison
with Nazi leaders, and through the use of Nazi symbols to car-
icature them, indicates an anti-Semitic bias rather than a valid
criticism of policy concerning a controversial issue." The
Department's definition of anti-Semitism resides in the first sentence, "hatred toward Jews... attributed to the Jewish religion
and/or ethnicity." The remaining two sentences attempt to draw
a distinction between "legitimate criticism of policies and practices of the State of Israel and "veiled" hatred that demonizes
Israeli leaders especially as they are compared in their behavior
to leaders in Nazi Germany.

How legitimate is the distinction? If anti-Semitism is hatred
expressed against the Jew as a person or against their religion or
ethnicity, how does criticism of Israeli political and foreign policy, determined by its elected or appointed leaders, fit that definition? When I criticize George W. Bush and various members
of his administration for their policies, domestic or foreign, I do
not criticize individual Americans for being American nor do

I criticize their religions or their ethnicity. If I place Bush's National Strategic Security Report objectives, its expressed empirical goals, in context with those of former leaders with visions of empire, including Hitler, I do not criticize an American for being American or convey a veiled hatred for Americans because they voted Bush into office. I criticize, rather, policies that are anathema to democratic principles and America's expressed values and morals as a nation. The distinction is at root subterfuge; it forces legitimate criticism of a state's political and human rights actions into a category that stops the criticism in its tracks, thus, in effect, legitimizing the undemocratic, illegal, and abusive state actions should they exist.

Having made that point, let me extend the analysis even further to explore the rationale behind the use of the term "anti-Semitism." Joseph Massad, Professor of modern Arab politics and intellectual history at Columbia University, published an article on this very term in *Al-Ahram Weekly On-Line*, (2004/720/op63.htm) wherein he presented the evolution of the term and its various misunderstandings in different countries of the world. He marks the philological basis of the term, the "positing of modern European Jews as direct descendants of the ancient Hebrews," the identifying of Jews as Semites because their ancestors spoke Hebrew, a Semitic language (a mistaken fact, since they spoke Aramaic, the language of the Talmud), the subsequent transformation of the Jews into a racial category based on this understanding (as noted in the State Department's definition), and the resulting hatred of European anti-Semitism as directed against European Jews. As Massad notes, "The claims made by many that any manifestations of hatred against Jews in any geographic location on Earth and in any historical period is 'anti-Semitism' smacks of a gross misunderstanding of the European history of anti-Semitism." Yet this is precisely what the State Department definition does; it applies one understanding of anti-Semitism to all peoples everywhere, judging their actions as derived from the same context.

Noam Chomsky questions even the need for such a document in the United States directed at anti-Semitism, "You find occasional instances of anti-Semitism, but they are marginal. There's plenty of racism, but it's directed against Blacks, Latinos, and

Arabs that are targets of enormous racism. Those problems are real, but anti-Semitism is no longer a problem, fortunately... It's raised (by privileged people) because... they want to make sure there's no critical look at the policies the US supports in the Middle East."

Given that context, consider the very fact that the State Department has singled out only maligned and discriminated Jews for its report when the world is filled with people who have endured hatred and discrimination worldwide: in Rwanda, Darfur, Bosnia, Iraq, India, East Timor, the United States, and Palestine to name a few, and all since 2000. Should the State Department publish a report identifying hatred and discrimination against the Jews? Yes. Should it also publish a report that identifies such abuse against all others who suffer such animosity, such disrespect, such indignity, such humiliation, such dehumanization, such suffering and death? Yes. Indeed, this is the point. Our State Department declares it has responsibility to uphold the "Universal Declaration of Human Rights," thus stamping its actions as pluralistic, objective, and sincere. And although the Department issues the "Country Reports on Human Rights," it does not extract from those reports the human rights abuses as they are directed against individuals or groups because of hatred of that group whether perpetrated by leaders of the state or hate groups within the state. Unless our State Department demonstrates its impartiality across the world, it presents to the people of the world a Janus face that claims equality of treatment even as it looks away from those in torment. Dr. Massad closes his piece with these observations:

> Today we live in a world where anti-Arab and anti-Muslim hatred, derived from anti-Semitism, is everywhere in evidence. It is not Jews who are being murdered by the thousands by Arab anti-Semitism, but rather Arabs and Muslims who are being murdered by the tens of thousands by Euro-American Christian anti-Semitism and by Israeli Jewish anti-Semitism... Anti-Semitism is alive and well today worldwide and its major victims are Arabs and Muslims and no longer Jews. The fight should indeed be against all anti-Semitism no matter who the object of its oppression is, Arab or Jew.

How just have been the efforts of our Department of State as reflected in these documents? Here's the wording that characterizes Israel's practices regarding human rights as described in the "Country Report":

> The Government generally respected the human rights of its citizens; however, there were some problems in some areas. Some members of the security forces abused Palestinian detainees... The Government detained on security grounds but without charge thousands of persons in Israel... The Government did little to reduce institutional, legal, and societal discrimination against the country's Arab citizens. The Government did not recognize marriages performed by non-Orthodox rabbis, compelling many citizens to travel abroad to marry. The Government interfered with individual privacy in some instances. Discrimination and societal violence against women persisted... Trafficking in and abuse of women and foreign workers continued to be problems.

This constitutes the summary paragraph on human rights abuse in Israel. The body of the report identifies the areas of concern that constitute "Respect for Human Rights." For example, section 1, "Respect for the Integrity of the Person, Including Freedom from (a) Arbitrary or Unlawful Deprivation of Life." "There were no reports," according to the report on Israel, "of politically motivated killings by the Government or its agents during the year." And, indeed, there are no listings of politically motivated killings in section (a) of the report. However, if one turns to the "Appendix" at the back of the report where Human Rights abuses are reported in the occupied territories, areas ostensibly under Palestinian Authority control (though since 2000, the report indicates, Israeli forces have resumed authority in the greater part of the occupied areas), we find on page 27, under section (g) "Excessive Force," the extrajudicial assassinations of Sheikh Ahmad Yassin and Abd al-Azziz al-Rantisi, high ranking political figures of the Islamic Resistance Movement, Hamas, and this does not include the 33 innocent bystanders killed as these two political figures were eliminated by missiles and explosives. An oversight? Deception? No other listing in (g) refers to political figures of this sort. There's reference to the 800 Palestinians killed during the course of Israeli military operations during the year, including 452 innocent Palestinians and another 4,000 wounded. There's notation that Israeli forces used tank shells, heavy machine gun rounds, and rockets from aircraft at targets in residential and business neighborhoods. There's mention of the Israeli invasion of Rafah and the Human Rights Watch condemnation of Israel's destruction of 50% of Rafah's roads, water, sewage, and electrical systems. There's a litany of dates and deaths, mostly of children: on May 18, two 16-year-old kids, on July 6, a university professor, on September 7, a girl sitting in school shot in the head, on September 19, an 11-year-old shot and killed while standing in a doorway, on September 28, Human Rights groups listed as many as 130 Palestinians killed and 430 wounded including 26 under the age of 18, on October 5, a 13-year-old girl shot and, then, repeatedly shot at close range as she lay in the dust, and on and on through the rest of October, November and into the following year.

Here, in an appendix devoted to the only two remaining areas of Palestine left to the indigenous population, buried at the back of the report, not included in the section devoted to the Israeli Government, we find horrendous acts of Human Rights abuse committed by the Government of Israel, some deceptively misplaced, scattered among Palestinian abuses executed by Hamas or the PA. And I would note that the above paragraph is only a sampling of this deception. In each section of item 1, "Respect for Human Rights,"—(a) Arbitrary or Unlawful Deprivation of Life; (b) Disappearance; (c) Torture and Other Cruel Punishment; (d) Arbitrary Arrest or Detention; (e) Denial of Fair Public Trial; (f) Arbitrary Interference with Privacy; (g) Excessive Force—the Israeli Government's acceptance of Human Rights abuses is itemized, by the US Department of State, page after page: Israeli settlers' murder of Palestinians; Physicians for Human Rights in Israel reporting on torture, "techniques prohibited by law," used against Palestinian detainees; 8,300 Palestinians held as security prisoners; the admission that "Israeli military courts rarely acquitted Palestinians of security offenses"; recognition that virtually no resolution to any allegation of wrongdoing by an Israeli, whether

military or settler, has occurred during the year of the report;
admission that the Israeli Government has destroyed over 6,900
acres of Palestinian land to construct the illegal wall; and 15,000
Palestinians have been made homeless by demolition. Each and
every one of these abuses cries out for action by the Department
of State, based on its own declaration, that it will "hold accountable governments to their obligations under universal human
rights and international human rights instruments."

But there is no action by those who act in our name. I would
revert back to Shamai Leibowitz's admonition, "Americans should
be held accountable for where their money is going." But he does
not stop there; he offers us a legitimate means of curtailing these
abuses to human rights endorsed by our Government:

> According to the Foreign Assistance Act of 1961 (22
> USC &2304), "No security assistance may be provided
> to any country the government of which engages in a
> consistent pattern of gross violations of internationally
> recognized human rights.

The State Department can act, it can stop all sale of arms and
military equipment to Israel. It can act in our name; it can turn
its shameful face from the mirror of deception and confront the
American people openly, forthrightly, and honestly.

The moral foundation that supports individual action does
not reside in the laws of a state. Such laws can be discrimina-
tory and hence unjust; an individual's conscience determines
obedience to the state dependent on a conscious understanding
that all are equal before the law and receive due recognition,
respect and dignity as individuals. Neither states, groups nor
individuals has a right to impose their beliefs on others to
achieve their respective ends if those ends incarcerate others,
express open hatred of others, wantonly destroy the property of
others, physically abuse others even unto death, enslave others,
exploit others, or indoctrinate others. Abduction of children
into youth armies, indoctrination of youth to be suicide
bombers, intentional indoctrination of civilians, exploitation of
girls into prostitution, sanctioning torture, all belong in this category. States that employ weapons of wanton destruction resulting in the deaths of innocent civilians belong in this category.

Morality abides no borders drawn by man; it recognizes the singleness of the soul that gives rights to every human anywhere. The oppressor never willingly withdraws; freedom to live with dignity and respect must be demanded by those opposed to oppression. Our State Department, speaking and acting in our name, must oppose oppression, not condone it, not stand silently in its presence, and not become the oppressor. Our responsibility is to ensure that it acts in accordance with true morality, a morality that applies justice equally to all. Recognition of that reality and acceptance of it requires that we deplore the inhumane acts of savagery used by the fanatical elements in Palestine as well as the fanatical elements in Israel. Our support for justice must engage the Muslim faithful to constructively confront the fringe groups to cease and desist acts contrary to Islamic teaching, and to bring together the powerful moderating voices of the Christian and Jewish faiths to stand against the Zionist zealots in both religions to halt the savagery they inflict on God's children.

"If we do not lead by moral force, we are by acquiescence the followers of those who fail to act and subjects of those who impose their will."

43

The Destructive Power of Myth: Implications for 9/11

[October 11, 2001 –
Crossings, vol. 5/6, 2002-3]

Never before have the people of the world, watching with trepidation, even with fear, witnessed a leader of a powerful nation stand before his assembled nobility to address both them and the populace about measures he would take to retaliate against the forces of evil that had devastated the nation by incinerating 3000 of its people. Never before had the peoples of the earth been congregated together in the Cathedral of Television to hear a sermon from a consecrated man who had publicly vowed to eradicate the world of the forces of evil. Never before have we as a people had to consider the power of ritual, pageantry, and rhetoric as motivating forces to carry out the will of one power against another.

The above scene, however, has its analogies in history, though on a far less dramatic scale. On January 8, 1198, Innocent III ascended to the Papacy of the Roman Catholic Church. Consider the scene. We enter the great church of consecration where the Cardinals, Bishops, Monsignors, monks of the many monastic orders, priests and seminarians are gathered in the crossing of the nave and in the choir, with the peasants and the parishioners massed in the nave and aisles. Above float banners declaring the fealty of the noble houses throughout the land, gleaming brilliantly in the ethereal light that seeps through the stained glass and clerestory windows. The organ resonates lightly above the hubbub of noise when suddenly the great doors open and the yet to be anointed Pope's Celebrant announces to the assemblage the presence of God's chosen.

The organ swells forth with thunderous sound as the entire congregation rises in splendor as the Cardinals in scarlet robes, the Bishops in glistening white capes, the Monsignors in cassocks trimmed in purple, the monks in tan and black cloaks and cowls, the seminarians in red vestments, the variegated colors of the parishioners greet the entrance of the appointed by God whose coronation they are about to witness.

The Pope to be, head adorned with miter, crosier in left hand, right hand raised in blessing, dressed in brocaded vestments with cape flowing behind, moves majestically, with pomp and dignity down the central aisle. As he enters the transept and steps through the choir, the Cardinals bow in salute, some reach out to touch his cloak, and he nods his approval before reaching the altar that overflows with flowers and candles. He genuflects before the tabernacle, then turns, under the direction of his Celebrant, to stand before the Chair of St. Peter. There, at the podium and in front of the chair that symbolizes his direct descent from the great disciple, he will speak to the people where he will declare that "...He is indeed the vicar of Jesus Christ, the successor of Peter, the Lord's anointed... set in the midst between God and man... less than a God but greater than man, judge of all men and judged by none."

Now convert the above scene to the great Hall of Congress as the President of the United States makes his entry: his Celebrant, brandishing his symbol of office, announces "The President of the United States." The position is announced, not the man who holds it. Dress the congressmen in tan and black cloaks, the Senators in white robes, the Cabinet members in purple trimmed garments, the Supreme Court members in scarlet, turn the applause into the resonance of the organs' swells, the lights into heavenly hues that bathe those present, and watch the President move with dignity and splendor down the aisle to his anointed place, where, before he turns to address the assembled, he nods to the Speaker of the House and to the flag. Now we have the pageantry and ritual that is the hallmark of myth.

Consider now President Bush's address to the nation on September 20. That address included an ultimatum to the Taliban rulers of Afghanistan to turn over Osama bin Laden, the alleged mastermind of the terrorist attacks against America that took place on September 11. Almost immediately, the

Talibans rejected the ultimatum. That is invariably the fate of any ultimatum. But issuance of an ultimatum to those who have nothing to lose but the mythology that gives them an identity and a purpose, is an empty gesture, doomed to failure before its very conception. The President's speech did not address the primary cause of the atrocities that were visited upon America on September 11, and his proposed actions will not bring an end to terrorist attacks even if bin Laden and other terrorist leaders are captured, tried, proven guilty, and put to death.

Both bin Laden and the Talibans are driven people, but they are only a fraction of those infected with a rabid hatred of the United States and Western Capitalism who have multiplied since World War II. For it is since that war that western culture, particularly its insidious necessity to find new markets for its ever expanding need to consume goods to fuel its investors' drive for greater and greater profits, has made its way inexorably across the globe. And while that spread of Capitalism first took form in the manufacture of products in distant places like Japan, China, Korea, and Indonesia, it has in more recent decades been more obvious in the spread of American television programming with its ever-present commercials that provide its support and, indeed, reflect western values. The consequence of this transportation of western society's economic power has had a twofold impact: a dramatic recognition that the world's resources benefit a small percentage of the world's population, a self-absorbed population suffused with comforts unknown and unavailable to the vast majority of peoples around the world; and a determined belief by a minority of those deprived, that they will rise against their oppressors, and, with the power of their God behind them, bring down the infidels that threaten the existence of their governments and the values that govern their way of life.

Statistics can help us understand the reality that gives credibility to the disenchanted and deprived. The UN Human Development Report of 1997, for example, noted, "The world's 225 richest individuals have a combined wealth equal to the annual income of the world's poorest 2.5 billion people." That same report showed Americans spending $8 billion a year on cosmetics and Americans and Europeans spending $17 billion a year on pet food, $4 billion more than needed to supply basic health and nutrition for everyone in the world. And, as reported in *Time* magazine November 9, 1998, the US government provides $125 billion in corporate welfare every year, an amount equivalent to all the income tax paid by 60 million individuals and families.

The Fellowship of Reconciliation has made graphic the inequity of the world's distribution of resources by noting that 40,000 homeless could be adequately housed for the cost of one Trident Submarine, a submarine capable of multiplying by 10 the number of deaths of the Holocaust. And, finally, the columnist David Smith has written, "The richest fifth of the world's population receives 86% of global income. Some 1.2 billion, nearly a quarter of the earth's population, live on the equivalent of less than a dollar a day—an annual income of 250 English pounds (or less)—and are the poorest of the poor."

One of the most glaringly obvious meeting places of the "haves" and the "have-nots" occurs at Khan Younis in the Gaza strip. Chris Hedges writes in the October 2001 *Harpers* that the Israelis have constructed 32 wells there and a pipeline in 1994 that carries the water into Israel. About 1000 Israelis live in the settlement and consume about one-third of the water supply, though about 160,000 people live in Khan Younis. The Israelis have in effect issued an ultimatum to the Palestinians that they will take the water from the aquifers in this deprived area, regardless of the inequity of its distribution. The consequence of such blatant disregard for those living in the city is the hatred that infests the population, especially the young who have grown up with the omnipresent TV images of the western wealth that supports Israel.

As Hedges makes clear, there is a prevailing attitude on the part of the Israeli soldiers who guard the crossings into Gaza, that the Palestinians are scum and they treat them that way. They entice the young Palestinian children to the dunes by cursing at them, making their futile attempts at retaliation a right of passage into manhood. Hedges provides the figures: Of over 1200 youth killed in the past year, over half are below the age of 18 and many nine to twelve years of age. When these children return home, they enter overcrowded rooms where the stench of sewage permeates the air. Tires and cinder block hold down the tarpaper roofs. They live in squalor. Their misery is palpable, making conscious the deprivation that festers in the soul, breed-ing vengeance and retaliation.

Their parents have to go through checkpoints to get to work, sitting for hours awaiting the hand movement that allows pas-sage. Unemployment hovers at 40%, making the trek even more vital, although the checkpoint is often closed altogether. Drivers keep the window down and their hand on the door handle, despite the heat, because they may have to dive from the car should bullets fly. They watch the Israeli settlers, who have free passage, drive past the bumper-to-bumper traffic in which they are locked. The consequence of such conditions breeds hatred both of those at the guard points who inflict the injury and those who support them, the United States in particular. These children grow up without dignity, respect, or the expectation that things will improve. Indeed, generations have now been raised in these abysmal conditions. The Israelis who were pro-vided a homeland as a gesture to compensate for the horrors of the Nazi atrocities, now oversee a deplorable ghetto teeming with people who have no homeland since they do not own it, no sense of dignity since they depend on the largesse of their oppressors for the meager sustenance they have, and no hope for the future, since it has been denied to them so many times in the past. Is it any wonder that numbers of these people find sol-ace in beliefs that they can attain a glorious state of everlasting reward by sacrificing themselves for their people and for their God?

It must be pointed out that Hedges' article is a rare glimpse into the conditions that prevail in Gaza. The American public has no understanding of these realities. US television, newspa-pers, and magazines do not show images or run articles about these conditions. Only non-mainstream publications have the freedom to publish these insights. The mainstream press shows only the resulting carnage of the suicide bomber's detonation with accompanying stories about his fanatical beliefs as expla-nation for his insane act. Controlled ignorance by the corporate powers that support the government's policies toward Israel and the oil producing nations that fuel our economy, becomes the controlled knowledge of the electorate. That in turn gives rationalization for further support and greater restriction of those identified as terrorist sympathizers or collaborators.

Corporate control of communications has done much to limit an American's perception of the conditions that exist in the Mid-East, and even less concerning our understanding of the peoples or their cultures. Since eight dominant corporations (General Electric, AT&T/Liberty Media, Disney, Times Warner, Sony, News Corporation, Viacom and Seagram, and Bertelsmann) control worldwide communications, the interests of those corporations color virtually all information coming to the western nations. They are also the dominant source of contributions to political candidates in western nations, thus ensuring that policy and legislation address their interests.

The dearth of information regarding the beliefs that motivate the terrorist bombers is a case in point. The press invariably presents such information in the form of ridicule as Michael Ramirez' political cartoons in the *Los Angeles Times* demonstrates. No comparison to Judaeo-Christian beliefs has been discussed, even though zealots with perverted views of those faiths continue to gather believers around them as the Rev. Jones made all too obvious. Sacrifice for one's faith, duty to the one and only God, elimination of the unbeliever, and resurrection to eternal life have been tenets held by members of the Jewish faith and of Christian denominations for centuries. Indeed, reflection on events from the past where these beliefs were prevalent, could help us understand the actions of those who sacrificed themselves to a cause.

The Old Testament is filled with God's commands to His people to destroy the infidels who could obstruct their passage to the Promised Land. From the book of Exodus to Joshua and the fall of Jericho, we witness a ruthless God demanding total obedience even to the slaughter or elimination of whole tribes of people. This God shall have no other gods before Him [Deuteronomy 6:14] and His people will "cast out all thine enemies from before thee." [Deuteronomy 6: 19] And if the Testament is to be believed, they did just that. Were these people fanatics or believers of a true faith? How would we view their adherence to their religion today? Are the myths that gave them identity and purpose acceptable today?

If there were a world court at the time of these atrocities, would belief in a "jealous" God justify the slaughter of the Canaanites, the Hittites, or the citizens of Jericho? Does belief in a God who discriminates against other peoples, who finds them so unclean that His people are not to marry them but can use them as concubines or slaves, justify the derogatory insults of the soldiers at the cross-points, and the Ultra-Orthodox perception, expressed publicly, that Palestinians are "animals" and "inhuman"? Or should adherents of this faith today, recognizing the untenable beliefs that have been part of its tradition, repudiate them, understanding that a new time requires new myths that are more in harmony with the needs of the world community?

The President inadvertently commented on the need for a "crusade" against the terrorists and then apologized for the use of the word. And he had reason to make the apology. Members of the Islamic faith have suffered at the hands of "crusaders" before, victims of Christians during the Medieval Period who willingly sacrificed their lives to recover the Holy Land from the infidels. These same Christians just as willingly slaughtered the Jews because they had killed their God, Jesus Christ. The office of the Pope, speaking as God's representative, justified these incursions into the Holy Land. Those participating would be guaranteed everlasting life for sacrificing their time and/or their life for the one true faith. Can we look back at this effort and condone it because it was done in a prior day and cannot be judged by our standards? Or do we look back at it and say that no belief based on a set of stories purported to be the word of God could justify such actions? Do we learn from this history that humans are quite capable of fabricating myths that will justify their goals for control of populations and accumulation of wealth and power, and use whatever means feasible to attain those ends?

These questions beg for a deeper understanding of the causes that would entice one people to join an effort to exterminate another people with whom they have had little or no contact, and willingly accept the probability that they might sacrifice their own lives in that cause. An examination of the events during the Albigensian Crusade instigated by Pope Innocent the III against the Cathar sect reveals multiple causes—economic, social, political, and religious— culminating, however, in beliefs that formed the basis of motivation driving Christians to slaughter of the innocent and to self-immolation.

Thirteenth century France submitted to the domination of four kings; France, as we now know it, was, in fact, a gift of Pope Innocent III to the Kings of France. At the beginning of the 13th century, Philip Augustus held sway in northern France and was the smallest and least rich of the kingdoms. By contrast, the King of Aragon, Peter II, controlled land far beyond the Pyrenees as far as the Ebro for which lands he paid homage to the King of France, although in practice this meant little. Indeed, the Counts of these areas, of Bearn, Aragnac, Bigorre, Cominges, Foix and Roussillon, lived under Aragon's protection, as did the viscounts of Narbonne, Carcassone, and Beziers. Both the Lord of Montpellier and the Count of Toulouse depended on Aragon's protection despite the relative independence Toulouse maintained. The entire area known as Provencal, developed its own language and discarded the Flemish French of the North and created a unique and beautiful culture crowned by the lyrics of the troubadours. Generally these people can be considered the most cultured and educated of the time.

This, too, was a time of great inquiry into the teachings of the Roman Catholic Church, not just by the fathers of that church who were reaching beyond the writings of Augustine—men like John Scotus Erigena, Abelard, and Aquinas—but by others in Bulgaria and Italy as well as Provencal. These teachers included Pop Bogomil in Bulgaria, John I. Tzimisces in Philippopolis, and Papa Nicetas in Constantinople. Various sects, motivated in good measure by the corruption in the Church, preached to a population desirous of understanding the truth.

The Cathars were one of many sects, variously identified as Waldensians, Bogomils, and Humiliati, that believed in some form of dualism understood in varying ways by practitioners, but basically taking the form of two ruling principles, one good, one evil, spirit and matter, God and the Devil, doctrines originally known as Manichaeanism. The Cathars of Languedoc, the name applied to the region surrounding Toulouse, denied the incarnation of Christ because matter was corrupt and the evil it housed must be shunned. Christ could not have entered the world in a human body. They likewise denied the doctrine of Atonement, believing instead that salvation was reached through a series of progressive reincarnations. These beliefs grew out of their interpretation of the book of Genesis, the

Bible's story of the flood, God's covenant with Abraham, and the destruction of Sodom and Gomorrah. These events were caused by the Devil, called God in the Old Testament. The intricacies of their teachings cannot be recounted here; however, it is clear that the Cathar beliefs are as complex and derivative as those of the Catholic Church and, in point of fact, amount to a different religion. Both rely on the stories from the Old Testament that tell of the Creation and Fall, and God's intervention in the affairs of humankind. They differ in how they interpret those stories.

Catharists found favor with the common people and their lords because their ministers, called Perfects, lived rigorous and ascetic lives by contrast with the Priests and Monks of the Church, who were seen as self-serving profligates. Cathars did not use churches, preferring to speak to the people in their homes or in small community gathering places. The contrast of the Cathars' asceticism with the Catholic Church's land holdings, its rich raiments, rituals, and the splendor of its houses of worship appealed to many, and Catharism became a primary threat to Catholicism's control over the people.

This contrast is pertinent to our concerns here. Where power, induced by fear, is exercised through an elite, who are determiners of what people must believe if they are to attain salvation or retain favor, the maintenance of that power depends upon the controls that can be enforced on the masses. Fear compels obedience: mortal fear through torture and threat of death; spiritual fear through excommunication and threat of damnation.

The Cathars had no such power: they had no Pope, no central place of authority, no churches, no synods, no accouterments of power, and no commitment to their God that they must bring all people to their truth, that unless accepted, would cast the unbeliever into perdition. They did have friends and a committed flock who walked into the flames prepared for them unless they denounced their beliefs. Commitment to beliefs is no evil until and unless others are forced to the commitment. That is the difference in the interpretation of the myths between the two faiths.

The 12th and 13th century Catholic Church proclaimed its authority throughout the land, in civil matters as well as religious; it demanded allegiance and it enforced allegiance through the establishment of Papal Inquisitors, Synods, Legates, and armies that took up the cross against its enemies whether heretic or infidel. It accepted its authority as direct from God, that God speaks through it, that the coming of God was immanent and that all were to be converted to the one true faith. It marshaled its power through its legions of priests, bishops, monks, and cardinals, all under the authority of the Pope, and it used the power of mystery to control its faithful. God is the Creator of all things and is, therefore, omnipotent, omniscient, omnipresent, and immutable, attributes that contain by their very definition the reason we cannot understand. Jesus, His Son, sacrificed Himself to save humankind from damnation, and gave to Peter, and through him to each of his successors, the keys to the kingdom of heaven. Only through the Church could salvation be attained. This required belief in, among other mysteries, the Trinity, the Atonement, the Immaculate Conception, and the Resurrection, teachings derived from interpretations of the myths resident in the Old and New Testaments

The reality of Papal authority, both religious and civil, found confirmation in the actions of Innocent III who ascended to the Papacy on January 8, 1198, and, curiously, was ordained on the 21 of February and made a Bishop the following day. Innocent believed that he, "as vicar of God," was the only universal power, he alone was answerable for the souls of kings and he alone had responsibility before God and all Christians. These are his words preached at his consecration: "Only St. Peter was invested with the plenitude of power. See then what manner of servant this is, appointed over the household; he is indeed the vicar of Jesus Christ, the successor of Peter, the Lord's anointed... set in the midst between God and man... less than a God but greater than man, judge of all men and judged by none." No question here whose authority held sway; no question here where truth resided. He was anointed by Jesus Christ Himself to carry out the dictates of the Church, and carry them out he did.

Prior to his ascendancy, throughout Provencal (roughly what is now southern France), northern Italy, and Bulgaria, particularly Bosnia, there existed the many different religious sects noted above, offering varying interpretations of the teachings of Jesus. The Cathars' influence spread widely throughout this region in good measure because of the corruption present in the Catholic Church. Preceding Popes had not forcefully moved against these sectaries, but Innocent did. Simonde de Sismondi, the chronicler of French History, writes of Innocent III, "... he menaced by turns the kings of Spain, of France, and of England;... he affected the tone of a master with the kings of Bohemia, of Hungary, of Bulgaria, of Norway, and of Armenia;... as if he had no other occupation, watched over, attacked, and punished, all opinions different from those of the Roman church, all independence of mind, every exercise of the faculty of thinking in the affairs of religion."

Innocent believed that if he did not eradicate the heresies and put all Christendom in fear, the kingdom of God on earth would be threatened. Innocent did not turn to conversion of the unfaithful, he "charged his ministers to burn the leaders, to disperse the flocks, and to confiscate the property of every one who would not think as he did." He excommunicated or laid under anathema the lay leaders, the Counts, the viscounts, the Barons, who harbored these heretics, and placed their lands under an interdict. In the first year of his reign, Innocent appointed two monks of Citeaux, Brother Guy and Brother Regnier, to search out and pursue the Cathar heresy invested with his full authority.

Regnier fell ill shortly after his appointment and Peter of Castelnau was sent to join him. They were Papal legates to the provinces of Embrun, Aix, Arles, and Narbonne. These legates, together with their followers, traversed the provinces identifying heretics, confiscating property, and sending people to the stake. Peter, in 1207, excommunicated Raymond VI, Count of Toulouse, a friend of the Cathars because he refused to allow an army to march through his lands looking for heretics. Innocent reacted angrily, publishing a Bull declaring "the Devil" had instigated Raymond to refuse the Papal legates' desire to subdue the heretics.

That same year, in November, Innocent exhorted Philip Augustus to "declare war against the heretics," the enemies of God and the Church by taking up the cross. He proffered Philip the same route to salvation given to those in the Crusades against the infidels in the Holy Land, indulgences for sins, as well as confiscation of all goods resulting from their actions. But Philip did not take up the offer, and, consequently leadership of the crusade fell to Simon de Montfort, a brave, ambitious, and ruthless man, a baron from the Ile-de-France. He had much to gain in title, power, and land in addition to the indulgences.

The power of the indulgences cannot be overestimated; the Barons believed firmly that fighting in the Holy Land guaranteed them a place in Paradise. Fighting on behalf of the Church in Provencal now awarded that same guarantee. Thus began what we now call the Albigensian Crusade, an army of over 50,000 according to the estimate of the Abbot of Vaux Cernay. Ultimately, the only power Innocent possessed to compel both noble and peasant to the cause, was belief in the teachings of the Church as expressed by him, God's representative on earth.

In 1209, the crusaders marched on Beziers—peasants, knights, and lords—the masses, mantled now in the mysteries of God's omnipotent power, radiant in the armor of the righteous, marching to the will of God's almighty ministers, committed to the extermination of the infidels who were pitted by the Devil against the forces of truth. Entering the city, they massacred the entire population estimated at 15,000 to 30,000 souls depending on your source, 7000 of whom had sought sanctuary in the Church of Magdalin to no avail. That church still stands as it did then in the heart of the city, a massive granite edifice dedicated to the sinner saint, now a tombstone for the martyrs and a monument to Innocent's reign of terror. When the Pope's legate, Arnold Amalric, abbot of Citeaux, was asked how the crusaders should determine heretic from Catholic, he replied, "Kill them all; the Lord will know well those who are his." "Not a house remained standing, not one human being alive." And this was just the beginning; the extermination of the Cathars continued into the 14th century.

At issue here is the primacy of the myths as they played a major role in determining the fate of the Cathars. If the Catholic Church of the 12th to 14th centuries had not held that it alone had ultimate authority over the souls of all humans relative to their salvation, and the supreme authority in civil matters to effect it, both positions based on their interpretations of the stories of the Old and New Testaments, the Church would have had no reason or license to exterminate a people. But the Church did act through the powers inherent in their leaders, the elite ministers who controlled the machinery of the denominations and the civil government, who offered to their laity, an exclusive body of adherents distinct from the heretics and the infidels because chosen by God, the reward of salvation through indulgences. Therein lies the destructive power of the Medieval interpretation of myth.

But let's bring the analysis a little closer to home. This is a story about America's forebears, the Puritans who sought refuge from persecution in England: a stalwart, upright, courageous people who dared to enter an uninhabited wilderness and create there a new Zion, God's "City on a Hill" as a testament to all the world. They, too, were a Christian sect, one decidedly different from the Roman Church. However, the tenacity with which they exercised their faith allowed for slaughter of the innocent.

"On May 1, 1637, the Connecticut Court, meeting at Hartford, declared war on the Pequot Indians, a Mohegan tribe living on the shore of Long Island Sound from Rhode Island west to the Thames (then called the Pequot) and Connecticut rivers." Before the month was out, on May 26, a force of over 400 led by Captain John Mason and Captain John Underhill consisting of Sachem Uncas, Narragansetts, and Puritan regulars crept into the area near the mouth of the Mystic where the Pequots had their encampment. They surrounded the fenced village of the tribe and at daybreak, while the Pequots were asleep, forced their way into the village, torched the dwellings, and, from their encirclement, "...proceeded to pick off those who sought to escape. More than four hundred (by some estimates 600-700) men, women, and children were killed," according to Larzar Ziff.

A month after this slaughter Ziff records, Captain Israel Staughton with 120 Massachusetts men set out to pursue the remnants of the tribe and wipe them out as a warning to others. Mason tracked the main body to a swamp in Fairfield, Connecticut and killed or captured all but 60, who escaped. "An entire tribe was eliminated."

What drove the Puritans to exterminate this tribe, to torch women and children, old and young alike? Alden T. Vaughn commenting on this slaughter noted "it resulted in the extermination of the most powerful tribe in New England, it witnessed one of the most sanguinary battles of all Indian wars—when some 500 Pequot men, women, and children were burned to death... and it opened southern New England to rapid English colonization."

But Vaughn sees the land acquisition at best as only a partial answer. The Puritans were prodded into righteous action by the Pequot hordes, Satan's legions, and by the Puritans' frustration with Pequot retaliation attacks resulting from an earlier (General John) Endecott expedition against them. Concerning this expedition, Vaughn states "...the Endecott expedition may well have represented something even more fundamental at stake here—the struggle between Puritans and Pequots for ultimate jurisdiction over the region both inhabited. The Puritans, determined to prevent Indian actions that might in any way threaten the New World Zion, had assumed throughout their government's responsibility for maintaining law and order among all inhabitants, Indian and whites."

According to John Winthrop, Endecott had a "...commission to put to death the men of Block Island, but to spare the women and children, and to bring them away, and to take possession of the island; and from thence to go to the Pequods to demand the murderers of Capt. Stone and other English, and one thousand fathom of wampom for damages, etc., and some of their children as hostages, which if they should refuse, they were to obtain it by force."

Francis Jennings' comprehensive and scholarly account of the Pequot slaughter notes that the expedition was intended to be "highly profitable." The "soldiers" under Endecott's command were volunteers who were to "nourish themselves on plunder."

Gary Nash in his work, the *Red, White & Black* [1992] claims that all the factors that motivated treatment of Native Americans in the southern colonies such as Virginia, were operative in New England: English land hunger, a negative view of native culture, and intertribal Indian hostility. But he adds that the Puritan sense of mission, the "... anxiety that they might fail in what they saw as the last chance to save corrupt Western Protestantism..." could be stalled by the Indian who stood as a "direct challenge to the 'errand into the wilderness.' The Puritans' mission was to tame and civilize their new environment and to build in it a pious commonwealth that would 'shine like a beacon' back to decadent England."

If Vaughn and Nash synthesize the viewpoints of the scholars who have reviewed this period, one could conclude that the Puritans' extermination of the Pequots had many causes. The

Pequots were living embodiments of Satan's demons placed there to prevent the establishment of God's "City on a Hill"; the Pequots represented, therefore, a hindrance to the "Mission" God had given to the Puritans; the Pequots had terrorized the locals with retaliatory attacks following Endecott's expedition against them; the Pequots prevented the expansion of English settlements in southern New England; and, finally, the Pequots posed a problem politically for the Puritans, since they controlled a significant land area which the Puritans believed should be under their (i.e., God's) control.

I would propose that there is a more fundamental cause that wrought the slaughter of the Pequots, one that is the root cause of all the above "causes." It is a primary cause if you will, that gives credibility to actions that would, at a distance, be seen as barbaric. I would suggest that all of the above causes find their roots in the Medieval Era's interpretation of the myths that gave credence to the peculiar tenets of Puritan doctrine. In the power of these myths resides the destruction of the Pequots.

The "principall Ende" of the Massachusetts' plantation, according to its charter (Records of Massachusetts, 1, 17) was "to wynn and incite the Natives of [the] Country, to the Knowledg and Obedience of the onlie true God and Savior of Mankinde, and the Christian Fayth." Or, as the Reverend Increase Mather put it in his Brief History of the War (King Philip's War of 1675), and recounted by Jennings:

> The "Lord God of our Fathers hath given us for a rightful Possession" the land of "the Heathen People amongst whom we live" and that said heathens had unaccountably acquired—but without having been injured—some "jealousies." That they had remained quiet so long "must be ascribed to the wonderful Providence of God, who did (as with Jacob of old, and after that with the children of Israel) lay the fear of the English and the dread of them upon all Indians. The terror of God was upon them round about." There could be no clearer equation: the dread of the English was the terror of God.

Jennings also cites the Puritans' frequent reference to Psalms 2:8 and Romans 13:2 as justification of God's gift to His chosen.

This is the "Mission" given to the Puritans by their "covenant" with God: possession of the land he had provided for them and the responsibility to bring the heathen to the true God. To the extent that the Pequots represented Satan's hordes and they possessed land rightfully belonging to God's chosen, they had to be disposed of by the "armed band of the Lord," as Larzer Ziff puts it. It is instructive to note, and perhaps ironic, that the Puritans did nothing before 1643, if the evidence is to be believed, to "wynn and incite" the natives to the "onlie true God," years after the extermination of the Pequots.

What circumstances existed that allowed the Puritans to exercise their will on those who came as part of the Puritan cult and on the populations that lived on the land before they arrived? A variety of scholars have addressed the demographic background of New England as well as the nature of Indian culture prior to the arrival of the Puritans. Suffice it to say here that their numbers had been drastically reduced by disease brought by Europeans, a reduction of about 2/3rds just prior to the Puritan settlement. And, perhaps more tellingly, they had little inclination to adopt Christianity.

If their depleted numbers and the internecine tribal wars prevented the natives from mounting any significant resistance to the newcomers, the fact that they occupied the land did not; they were used and abused as the Puritans pursued their errand for God. This was made possible in part by the reality of circumstances; according to Thomas Wertenbaker, in his work, *The Puritan Oligarchy*:

> In the Bay Colony the Puritan leadership had a free hand in building their Zion exactly after the blue print which they were confident God had made for them... For a full half century they were permitted to shape their government as they chose, they could legislate against heresy and Sabbath breaking, they could force attendance at worship, they could control the press, they could make education serve the ends of religion.

Wertenbaker points out that "... It is more accurate to call it (the government in Massachusetts) an oligarchy, since it was a government of the many by the few."

This is an important point, as we shall see, since it is the elite (those who control and are a minority) who determine the myths for the many. Myths derive, as Joseph Campbell says, not from the masses but from the elite. The few create the stories that become the guideposts for the many. The elite perform the rituals that become the means by which the many experience the myth and make it part of their lives. Campbell believed it necessary to liberate religion from "tribal lien," or the religions of the world would remain—as in the Middle East and Northern Ireland today—the source of disdain and aggression.

Puritan theologians, the elite group that masterminded the "new Canaan," what they termed "doing God's errand," would concede that the physical universe is the work of God, but it did not follow that the visible universe was God Himself. They knew this distinction had to be maintained; they thought, after all, as the Medieval mind had thought for 1500 years, that the transcendence of God could not be called into question; neither mysticism nor pantheism could be tolerated. "The Puritans carried to New England the historic convictions of Christian orthodoxy," states Perry Miller, "and in America found an added incentive for maintaining them intact. Puritanism was not merely a religious creed and a theology, it was also a program for society."

If individuals had the right to seek understanding independent of the ministers, then the solidity of that civil and ecclesiastical order would be threatened. This was a society of laws but laws established under the guidance, indeed the rule, of Scripture. Puritanism sought an ideal of social conformity either through obedience, or mandatory compliance. This, then, was a society determined by those in authority and defined by them as, in Winthrop's words, "good, just and honest."

It is important to recognize that the Puritans maintained this Medieval perspective because they, too, would not tolerate heresy in their midst. They understood the need for authority to intervene, as the Catholic Church's Inquisition had intervened and as Henry VIII had intervened to cause the burning of 30 heretics, to control errant thinking. But intervention also meant force, if warranted, against those not "elected" to be saved, those destined to the torments of hell. This was Calvinism; "...based on a division of the elect and the damned that ran throughout mankind." This theology grew out of Augustine's

reasoning that some men are born "concupiscent rational animals" and some are "grace-endowed rational animals," one or
the other. They also understood the battle between the forces of
good and evil, the presence in the world of Satan's power
attempting to undermine God's will; and they made evident that
belief in the extermination of the heathens called the Pequots.

"The Indians were Satan's helpers," as David Stannard says,
"they were lascivious and murderous wild men of the forest,
they were bears, they were wolves, they were vermin. Allegedly
having shown themselves to be beyond conversion to Christian
or to civil life—and with little British or American need for them
as slaves...straight forward mass killing of the Indians was
deemed the only thing to do."

Two issues are of immense importance here: from whence did
this authority emanate and what were its consequences? I cannot
in this chapter present the arguments that rationalize the evolution of Christian thought, though W. T. Jones' work *The
Medieval Mind* provides a good path to that end—except to note
that as the Roman Empire crumbled, the Catholic Church, with
its doctrine of the Divinely inspired word of God as its authoritative base, took control over both the civil and spiritual lives of
the people. This was in stark contrast to the first three centuries
of Christian development when that sect was considered by the
general population as nothing more than a small Jewish cult.

The times, however, called for a supreme authority and for
belief in a life with purpose even if that life were to be in the hereafter. Jesus' teachings, according to Jones, required "conformity
to God's will" resulting in God's approval. That required understanding of Jesus' teachings and interpretation of them. This was
the role undertaken by the Roman Catholic Church and succes-
sively by various Christian denominations, including the Puritans.

Much of what Christianity teaches grew out of the epistles
and writings of St. Paul, the leader of the Gentile mission. "It
may be said," according to Jones, "that he more than any other
individual, was responsible for the development of Christianity,
as a distinct religion..." Of particular importance to the authoritative base of Christianity is the interpretation Paul provided.
Here is how Jones presents it:

> It will be seen that Paul first made the historical Jesus
> into a savior god and then built up a mythical setting for

this god out of the Jewish legends and stories that he and Jesus, as Jews, knew in common. How, for instance, did we come to sin and so to require the services of Christ the Savior? For answer Paul fell back on the old Jewish myth of the creation. God created Adam, the first man, free from sin. But Adam disobeyed his Maker, and we, his descendants, have inherited his sins. Just as the sin of one man (Adam) brought death and all our woe into the world, so the virtue of one man (Jesus) saves us; and just as Adam's sin was disobedience, so the virtue by which Jesus redeems the many is obedience.

This became the teaching of the Roman Church and continues to this day as the teaching of Christianity. The church as an organization undertook responsibility to determine who would be and who could not be a member. It also prescribed the doctrines and dogma that would bring its members to obedience in Jesus. Since Paul had in his letter to the Romans written that God had "marked out" and "predestined" some for salvation, adherence to the true faith was necessary for salvation. The Puritans subscribed to this belief.

Indeed, orthodoxy required adherence to Puritan doctrine; tolerance of differences was not allowed. "Persons who accept the 'right' beliefs," as Jones says, "are saved; persons who mistakenly accept the 'wrong' beliefs are damned." Those who accept "wrong" beliefs were labeled heretics and subject to punishment, banishment, slavery or death. "...New England had early taken the lead and throughout the colonial period held more Indians in slavery than any other colonies except South Carolina..."

The Puritans carried out this understanding of their God-given authority by linking the civil government to the church. Wertenbaker makes this observation:

In ardent sermons they warned the people that God had chosen His own from the mass of those predestined to damnation... that the one sure guide for the state as well as for the individual was the Bible, that the civil government, while separate from the church, shall be in the hands of godly men who would give religion their hearty support and suppress error.

Obviously, the understanding of the Bible was to be in the hands of the ministry. Malcolm Lambert states, in referencing actions taken against heretics in the Medieval Era, "Scripture was to be mediated... to the faithful through authorized preachers; the base text was not to be put into the hands of anyone who might misuse and misunderstand." That, too, was the position of the Puritan Divines.

But what, then, of those who had never heard of the Bible or its teachings? Can they suffer damnation regardless of guilt? "Yes, the Puritan preacher says," and Ziff recounts, "because they are men and as men in justice they deserve damnation; salvation is theirs only through divine mercy, and mercy has not been extended to them. 'They who never heard the Gospel, shall never answer for not believing in it as revealed or offered,' the preacher admits, because it was not so made known to them, but yet they shall answer for that habitual infidelity whereby they would have resisted it, and whereby they are opposite unto it."

What consequences resulted from this adherence to a set of beliefs that placed the authority of God's word, indeed the determination of what was God's word, in the hands of an elite few? Of necessity, we focus here on the Puritan determination to exterminate a people, the Pequots. First, according to Stannard,

> ...there is little doubt that the dominant sixteenth-and-seventeenth century ecclesiastical, literary, and popular opinion in Spain and Britain and Europe's American colonies regarding the native peoples of North and South America was that they were a racially degraded and inferior lot—borderline humans as far as most whites were concerned.

Second, the establishment of the "new Zion" in the "New World" offered an opportunity to link the civil government with the church's teachings where the word of God should supersede the word of men. "We came hither because we would have our posterity settled under the pure and full dispensation of the gospel, defended by rulers that should be ourselves," wrote Cotton Mather. Those who came with the Puritan divines were but subjects of them, obedient servants to the Lord God made manifest through them. What they came to understand was not only the inferior status of the natives, what we would now understand as racism, but the inherent right of their company to possess the land held by them. This was understood before they left England as Wertenbaker notes:

> John Winthrop encouraged his counterparts to leave England because "God had given the whole earth to mankind "...why then should we stand striving here for places of habitation, etc., many men spending as much labor and cost to recover or keep sometimes an acre or two of land as would procure them many hundreds as good or better in another country..."

This was the economic reason behind the migration according to Wertenbaker. That reference to God giving the land to His people comes from the Old Testament and was understood by the Puritans in exactly the same way. "For the covenant the congregations claimed direct authority from the Bible and direct precedent in the history of Israel. 'The covenant of grace is the very same now that it was under the Mosaical dispensation,'" stated William Brattle. They saw themselves, Mather himself has said, as the chosen of God, that He had made Himself manifest to them, and that He had directed them to the new world. But it went further than this:

> The Lord hath planted a vine, having cast out the heathen, prepared room for it and caused it to take deep root...We must ascribe all these things, as unto a grace and abundant goodness of the Lord our God, so to His owning a religious design and interest.

These teachings allowed for the slaughter of the Pequots. It is clear that the myths gave credibility to the Puritan behavior against the Pequots. Campbell remarked about this myth of the "Chosen" and its allowance for slaughter in his interview with Moyers:

> ...the Ten Commandments say, "Thou shall not kill." Then the next chapter says, "Go into Canaan and kill everybody in it." That is a bounded field. The myths of

participation and love pertain only to the in-group, and the out-group is totally other. This is the sense of the word 'gentile'—the person is not of the same order.

Stannard quotes the Puritan Captain Mason upon witnessing the plight of the Pequots:

> God was above them, who laughed his Enemies and the Enemies of his People to Scorn, making them as a fiery Oven: Thus were the Stout Hearted spoiled, having slept their last Sleep, and none of their Men could find their Hands: Thus did the Lord judge among the Heathen, filling the place with dead Bodies.

And William Bradford added this commentary:

> It was a fearful sight to see them thus frying and the streams of blood quenching the same, and horrible was the stink and scent thereof; but the victory seemed a sweet sacrifice, and they gave the praise thereof to God, who had wrought so wonderfully for them, thus to enclose their enemies in their hands and give them so speedy a victory over so proud and insulting an enemy.

Cotton Mather noted that the extermination was the "just judgment of God" who had allowed five or six hundred "who had burdened" the earth to be "dismissed" from it. These represent God's interpreters on earth. These basic Christian myths, the foundations of Puritan thought and hence behavior, grew out of the understood relationship of God to His creatures: humans are conceived in guilt, live amidst evil, and must find their way back to the Creator. As Campbell says, "But when nature is thought of as evil, you don't put yourself in accord with it, or try to, and hence the tension, the anxiety, the cutting down of forests, the annihilation of native people."

To put this in the words of a contemporary, William Bradford in 1617:

> The place they had thoughts on (in coming to the new world) was some of those vast and unpeopled countries

of America, which are fruitfull and fitt for habitation, being devoid of all civil inhabitants, wher ther are only salvage and brutish men, which range up and downe, little otherwise then the wild beasts of the same...

Thus did the belief in myth allow for the eradication of a people and the taking of their land. It became a justification for racism and for greed permitting these realities to determine the destiny of 500-700 people who did not share, or even understand, the rationale that gave purpose to the Puritan slaughter.

The extermination of the Pequots by the Puritans, on its surface, appears contradictory; why would a group devoted totally to fulfilling the word of God, having formed a "covenant" with Him, having moved from their homeland in England to Holland and thence to America to protect that covenant, enamored of traditional Christian values, accept the mandate of their ministers to eradicate a tribe of people? Even if the "soldiers" who accompanied Endecott were mercenaries, or those regulars who went with Mason acted in accordance with military custom, the consequence of their actions had to be accepted by the Puritan people and their ministers.

Although some argue that opening up southern New England to English expansion would be cause enough, that advantage would not be for those already resident in Massachusetts, but for those yet to come, and they were not privy to the slaughter. It should now be obvious from the above analysis that something inherent in what the Puritans believed, something inculcated in them as an absolute truth, something they could not question, drove this acceptance.

Jennings, in the Appendix to his book, *The Invasion of America*, compares the process of "chartered" conquest in Europe and America. He observes that such a conquest "...was launched ostensibly to reduce heretics or infidels to subjection to a protector or champion of an only true religion...and clerics of the appropriate orthodoxy preceded or accompanied or followed the troops."

Although Jennings' hypothesis sees the use of religion as an "ostensible" tool for intervention and subjection where heretics and infidels are the "game," I believe, in instances where heretics and God's enemies are hunted and burned, as is the case in the Puritan slaughter of the Pequots and in the Papal slaughter of the Cathars, the religious belief precedes the economic advantage and must be employed if the heads of state (the elite) are to maintain their authority and the power they wield. To this end, they will employ the economic "carrot" to motivate others to join their design, offering them the spoils of their efforts.

Economics is, of course, a fundamental cause, but in these instances not the primary one. Maintenance of control through maintenance of that which guarantees control, the myths that control behavior of the masses and ensure power for the elite, is the primary cause. When absorbed in dictatorial activity, the conscious mind responds to no other; the consequence is an obedient servant shackled to ritual, customs, tradition, and rites.

I would posit six characteristics that brought about the destruction of the Pequots and the Cathars, each inherent in the myths that formed the basis of the Puritan and Roman Catholic faiths or were appropriate actions in light of the myths' teachings requiring immediate action. I would also contend that these same characteristics are likely to exist for all similar events recorded in our histories where the actions resulted from fulfillment of myths accepted by that society but destructive of another. The examples are too numerous to record here.

We are witness to this potential in the current conflicts in Israel and Palestine, in Bosnia-Herzegovina, and in Kosovo and our histories have recorded such events in the Conquistador invasion of Central America, in the impact of the Atlantis myths on some of the elite minds in Nazi Germany, in Japan's imperialistic expansion into China in the 1930s and 1940s, and, in ancient times, in the Hebrews' extermination of the Hittites, Amorites, and Canaanites among others.

These are the destructive consequences of adherence to myth. The unquestioned acceptance of absolute right has been the hallmark of humankind's greatest achievements as well as its most loathsome acts.

What does the above analysis teach us? I would suggest that it is possible to identify characteristics of myths as destructive forces. I would recommend that we have much to learn and much to gain if we apply this analysis to current conditions, especially since our Western culture has not altered its adherence to the myths that have determined the events of the past 2000 years. I would also suggest that historians and teachers have to confront these events from a new perspective, one that does not avoid bringing contemporary values and understanding to the analysis; one that does not excuse behavior on the basis that it resulted from commitment to beliefs (an approach that would justify Innocent's eradication of the Cathars, the Puritans' elimination of the Pequots, the Nazis' extermination of the Jews, America's wanton bombing of the Cambodians, and the Terrorists' atrocities that befell America on September 11); one that does not excuse behavior on the basis that it was within the "norms" established by that society; and one that brings the means to analyze the events before all Americans the better to determine what actions should be taken if terrorism is not to haunt us the rest of our lives.

If we extract from the above analysis of the extermination of the Cathars and the Pequots the underlying causes that allowed for the atrocities, we might be able to illuminate the actions of the terrorists that threaten us today. Killing those who are willing to kill themselves for their cause does not eradicate the cause. Addressing the beliefs that become the motivation to action could eliminate the need for terrorist acts. The study of myths, then, becomes a means of acquiring an understanding of people's behavior, and a means of avoiding repetition of destructive behavior.

Events of the past can be recounted, authenticated, and analyzed in light of their contemporary social structures, philosophy, politics, and religious values, but they have little value to us if we cannot learn from them in order to prevent recurrence of past error. By approaching the study of myth as a primary cause of human behavior, we address fundamental truths that have been the foundation of civilizations as they interact one with another. If through this analysis we can predict conditions that will result in the unleashing of destructive forces, we can work to prevent their recurrence.

But the study of the myths that caused the havoc of 9/11 is complicated: we must look at the myths that motivated the perpetrators in the righteousness of their cause and the myths that they believed were the foundations of the West's power that both threatened their culture and oppressed their people. We must analyze the beliefs that Americans and their Western allies accept, versus the reality that exists; a reality that causes the perceptions that give rise to hatred and terrorist acts.

The analysis we have provided of the Roman Church's eradication of the Cathar sect and the Puritan extermination of the Pequots was made possible because

1. An elite group designed myths for purposes of determining human behavior. The Roman Church made Jesus the Messiah and the Pope His voice on earth speaking for the one true Church. In the Puritan instance, this elite group took existing dogma and modified it, codifying in the process, standards of acceptable behavior.
2. The myth(s) contained the seed that allowed for the destructive behavior to flower. That is, there is inherent in the myth a call to action imposed on those who have accepted it as a guidebook for their lives. The dichotomy projected by both denominations of the saved versus the damned, provided the premise for action, and the imaging of the natives as Satan's minions by the Puritan Divines provided the motivation.
3. The myth is exclusionary and restrictive, providing access to its rewards only to the initiate or through him. This characteristic allowed for degrees of punishment to those who would tamper with the accepted doctrines or those unable to accept those doctrines.
4. The culture responding to the myth must be in a state of economic, political, and social ascendancy that requires action to sustain that status. The forces that require action can be economic, for example, land acquisition or fear of loss of existing lands; or political, for example, the opportunity to gain more power or the opposite, the fear that power already acquired is in jeopardy of erosion or loss; or social, for example, the belief that those excluded from participation in the myth must be brought into it or removed as an obstacle of its fulfillment. Each of these conditions existed in the 13th century and in Massachusetts in 1636-37.

5. The nature of the myth does not distinguish between the secular and religious spheres, but rather understands an absolute commitment of life in all its actions to the governing force. We have seen the union of church and civil authority at work in Medieval Europe and in Puritan Massachusetts.

6. A requisite structure is designed and employed, usually hierarchical in nature, to codify, justify, and implement the behaviors called for in the myth. That structure was manifestly evident in the Roman Church's condemnation of the Cathars and in the Puritan community.

I believe an examination of today's terrorist activities reveals that each of the effects that brought about the atrocities of the 13th and 17th centuries as described above exists now. Let's examine the terrorists' perspective first.

Two observations must be addressed: the spasmodic terrorists' acts that have struck various countries around the Mid-East over many years, including those by Palestinians against the Jews, acts that are generally executed by an individual or small groups of people; and the organized business-like operations that seem to be responsible for the destruction of the US Embassies and the atrocities of September 11.

If we reflect on the observations offered by Hedges in his Diary published by *Harpers*, the hatred of the Jewish peoples' oppression of the Palestinians becomes one with hatred of the United States because it is seen as the power behind Israel's strength. The anger must be directed at the Jews because these people have no means to bring their terror to others.

But there are those within Palestine, and similarly in other countries in the Mid-East, who recognize the degree of frustration and hatred and capitalize on it: the "elite" who take power, organize, and manipulate the multitude. They give voice to the anger by giving it a context beyond jealousy and deprivation. The Taliban assumption of control in Afghanistan demonstrates this point. Now the very religion they have practiced for centuries becomes the cause. It, as well as the people it protects, is threatened.

The Satan of the west, with its endless supply of money and military might, threatens to destroy the Arab states and its

Islamic faith. The leaders of Hamas, the various Shite organizations, the Laskar Jihad in Indonesia, the Talibans in Afghanistan, and others throughout the Mid-East have brought together their hoards to fight the infidel as effectively as Innocent III in his conquest of the Cathars and the Puritan Divines in their mission against Satan's "salvages."

The stories in the Islamic faith, interpreted by the elite, allow for the destructive behavior to flower. We've heard the various stories that raise the martyr before the throne of Allah and bring him immediate gratification in eternal life. That promise has been the promise of ages. It blessed the peasant as he followed Simon de Montfort's banner just as it guaranteed salvation to the Puritan fighting Satan's hoards. Not all heed the promise, but to some it is the ultimate idealistic response that gives meaning to their lives, and in most instances, an end to their misery and a reward of eternal bliss. If this is insanity, then our churches have an obligation to ferret out those who use their religion to motivate the few to destroy the many.

But the reward for the individual combatant is not the only reward. For those who take up the cause, there is the victory of righteousness over the forces of evil and the inevitable salvation of the state. These more universal rewards might have greater appeal to the educated who see the world as part of a great design, and their actions as a significant role in that design.

Part of the appeal of any "crusade" or "jihad" rests in its exclusivity. Only the initiate can participate, only the chosen. This appeal to the ego of the individual strengthens resolve, but it also strengthens the directed hatred for the enemy. That which provides the exclusiveness, being part of God's chosen, focuses motivation to condemn those excluded; they become forces in "Evil's" camp or an obstruction in the fulfillment of the grand design that has created the chosen and their set of beliefs. This provides justification for the slaughter of those whom crusaders have never met and whose beliefs they do not know.

Performing an act of self-immolation without involving others, simply to assert the degree of your belief and commitment to an ideal, as the Buddhist Monks did when they set themselves on fire protesting the Vietnam War, cannot be equated to the acts of self-destruction that have taken the lives of others. The latter have responded to the exclusivity of their organization and understand that the enemy, whether civilian or military, is a necessary target to achieve their goal. The Buddhist understands that his act is a sacrifice for others, and in that act, he becomes one with them.

The organizations and nations that support terrorist activities recognize the necessity of undertaking such actions if they are to realize their economic, political, and social goals. Either they have everything to gain or much to lose. The Hamas desire the return of their homeland and hence the need to eradicate the Jewish state. Bin Laden desires a pure Arab State, especially in Saudi Arabia, hence the need to eradicate US forces in his homeland. The Laskar Jihad desires the establishment of a committed Islamic state, thus the need to expel the influence of the West in Indonesia. Inseparable in all three resides the desire for power achievable through the establishment of a state that imposes a monolithic belief system on its peoples. The existence of the belief system ensures the existence of the power. That reality gave Innocent III the power to manipulate monarchs and emperors, just as it gave the Puritan Divines the commitment of its people during the slaughter of the Pequots and following it.

Obviously, the power reflected in the organizations that carry out such devastation must have both political and religious power intertwined. If Hamas and the Jihads could impress or draft combatants, as an independent state can, they would not need the power of the religious beliefs to enlist their forces. But they cannot. They depend, therefore, on instilling a commitment to the righteous cause in their recruits, one that offers the promise of eternal rewards through sacrifice to the God who has chosen them to achieve His end.

And, finally, these organizations contain by design a structure that enables its designers to codify, justify, and implement the behaviors called for in the myth. The elite hierarchy establishes procedures for carrying out the organization's responsibilities. Sacrificial victims see themselves as holy warriors fighting on behalf of their God. They participate in cells where the purposes of the actions and the goals established to fulfill God's will are discussed. They are celebrants. We recognize the ritual that is part of the suicide bomber's sacrifice; it symbolizes the justness of the cause, thus transforming it beyond a series of diverse, random acts of terror.

As we can see, the elements that allow for the destructive forces to mobilize, exist in the terrorist organizations. But they also exist in the West giving credibility to the terrorists' beliefs and giving justification in their minds to their behavior.

Two myths dominate western thought: the belief in Democracy, understood as the power inherent in the individual to determine with their fellow citizens those who will serve them in their government; and the belief in individual empowerment in determining their lifestyle and the economic system that will make it possible.

Neither belief exists in reality. Many have observed the President's comment that the forces of evil desire the destruction of the American way, especially the destruction of the democratic process that allows the citizens to elect their President, when the Supreme Court appointed him to the position. But that is only the most glaring contradiction of the "democratic way."

Watching the Democratic and Republican Conventions dramatically demonstrates the source of power in the country. The power elite, representing the top 1% of the population who own the vast majority of its wealth, control the process. No common citizen could attend the gala events; but those who had contributed upwards of $250,000 had open access. The Party platforms represented the interests of the greatest donors and the most powerful lobbies. The corporate-owned newspapers and TV channels determined who would debate the issues and which candidates would receive coverage. Even the electoral process reflected the willingness of those in power to limit access to the ordinary citizen, as was only too obvious in Florida, where minorities were denied admittance to the polling booth and where the legal system thwarted the very laws that provided for recount of contested votes. This most recent of our elections blatantly demonstrated the power of the monied class to control the "democratic" process. The Bush camp bought the election.

The problem that attends belief in this system exists when the citizens believe our government should impose its perceived values around the world. This gives license to those in power to empower those of like mind in other countries. We have been witness to that system in Chile where our government threw over the legitimately elected President Allende and put in his place the Dictator Pinochet, actions recorded in Christopher Hitchens' book, *The Trial of Henry Kissenger*. His two decades of rule devastated his country, causing an anti-American backlash that lasts to this day. Larry Berman describes in *No Peace, No Honor* how our government took an unknown student out of a New Jersey seminary and made him the first President of Vietnam. It then built a war machine to support his call for US aid to defend his country. The power structure that controlled our government could not let the Communists control the oil in the region and manufactured an attack on a US ship in the Gulf of Tonkin to justify its support of a fabricated nation. Needless to say, hatred of America blossomed.

In 1972, President Nixon needed desperately to show progress toward an "honorable peace" in Vietnam. To force the North Vietnam leaders back to the negotiating table, he ordered the Christmas bombing of Cambodia, Hanoi, and Haiphong. In a little more than 11 days, he devastated Cambodia with whom we were not at war, and all but obliterated the two cities. The people on the ground witnessed the atrocity just as Americans did, watching the slaughter of the innocent in New York City and Washington. Then, to save his political skin for a second term, he sold out the South Vietnamese at the negotiating table by ensuring the presence of the North's troops throughout the South.

Nothing of the above behavior made it to the press or to the American people until long after the events had passed. Three decades after the start of the war, Secretary McNamara unburdened his soul by revealing that the President and the administration knew the futility and injustice of the war. But by then more than 50,000 had sacrificed themselves saving Democracy from communism.

Governments do not mobilize a people by telling the truth; they mobilize through mystery: fear of the unknown that threatens their livelihood, fear of forces that could destroy them, fear that their religious beliefs could be undermined by the forces of evil that accept no religion.

Those that suffered through this war know that once the truth regarding its purpose became known, the peoples' will to sacrifice themselves ceased. Once the government understood it could no longer command the beliefs that motivated the citizens, it attempted desperately to stop the war. To put it another

way, once the elite's myths cease to have credibility, they lose
power or they rearrange the myths to justify an altered policy.

Americans, however, continue to believe that Democracy is
the only acceptable form of government. They retain this belief
in conjunction with the Puritan Divines' belief that this land
should be a "City on a Hill," a phrase that Ronald Reagan used
to justify his war against the "Evil Empire." This is, to all
intents and purposes, America's religion. It justifies our past and
gives credibility to our purpose. We have yet to disassociate ourselves from the Christian belief that God gave this land to us to
illuminate His truths to the world. It does not matter that the
reality of a democratic form of government does not exist here
or that the country is home to countless non-Christian faiths
that do not accept the concepts that reverberate in the call to
establish a "City on a Hill."

As long as the reigning government in Washington, the elite
who choose the President and his cabinet, the members of
Congress and the Senate, and bring financial support to the military; as long as they can appeal to these idealistic beliefs, they can
mobilize the country against external forces characterized as evil.

But if the spread of Democracy has caused ill-will in various
nations around the world, a form of Democracy that imposes a
government friendly to the United States, not one duly elected
by the people, the recognition of that imposed form of government as a puppet of the Capitalistic forces that control the
American Government, causes even greater consternation.

If Democracy recognizes the need to separate church and
state, why do we provide billions of dollars in support of a
theocracy in Israel? If we have no qualms about supporting a
theocracy, why not offer equal support to Islamic nations? If
Democracy recognizes duly elected governments, why does the
US support dictatorships? The answer lies in the need for the
monied forces that control the US to have in power governments that support capitalistic interests.

That reality provided the rationale for production of goods in
Indonesia, China, Korea, and Vietnam, among other nations,
where exploitation of the people resulted in child labor, token
wages, and unsanitary, dangerous working conditions. Nike
Corporation, for example, paid Chinese workers, until recently
and only after a public outcry changed their policy, about $1.50

for making a pair of sneakers that sells for $80.00 to $120.00. In Indonesia, Nike paid 16 to 19 cents per hour. About 40% of Nike's work is now done in China.

This one example illustrates the reality of the "new" industrial revolution taking place across the globe. My visits to China over ten years depicted graphically for me the incursion of the industrial giants into a "new" manufacturing state. During my last visit, ten years after my first, I witnessed the explosion of factories surrounding Bejing. I also witnessed the deep-set smog that fused with the yellow sand that blew through the city and created a pall that ironically foreshadowed the demise from lung diseases of thousands. I took an eight-hour train ride from Yantai City to Jinan watching smoke stacks belch black soot over the countryside. I passed polluted streams that had been a place to swim and fish for my hosts when they were young.

The industrialization of China seems to be following the same agonizing route the British people had to suffer in the decades after 1765 and the Americans had to endure after 1870; each a disastrous route of a hundred years to acceptance of needed, imposed regulations to protect the workers and the environment.

But for the transnational corporations, the bottom line dictates the investment, and without government imposed regulations to protect health, safety, and wages, exploitation of the worker to produce the goods at the cheapest wage, drives the process. Why else would these corporations seek out underdeveloped countries to relocate their plants, except to increase the profit margin? The consequence of this exploitation in each of these countries is an expressed dislike by the ordinary citizen for the industrialized nations that bring about the exploitation, United States included.

Roger Altman has written about the dichotomy that exists between the "Have" and the "Have-Not" nations. He states, "...half of the world's population is increasingly threatened with economic oblivion." But more important, he says, "that is dangerous for world stability, and we should not resign ourselves to it." What happens if the West does not address a redistribution of wealth and the utilization of the earth's resources? Altman responds: "The Fourth World, the least developed parts of Africa and Asia, will become even more fertile territory for brutality, state sponsored terrorism and mass tragedy."

The disparity Altman cites, coupled with the perception of the worker in the exploited nations, breeds resentment against the United States. Yet the average American has no conscious awareness of these issues. They believe that American Capitalism is a benefit to the world's communities, since it provides jobs they would not otherwise have and it gives Americans a cheaper product. To a certain extent they have accepted the need for these "new" industrialized nations to suffer the 100 years it takes to correct the deficiencies that exist at this time. After all, we had to go through that period, why not them? But, once the total picture gets presented, Americans have demanded a change in how these corporations operate. Americans are actually a generous and compassionate people. Once they become aware of inequities, they generally respond positively and force corrections.

However, today Americans lack knowledge of the reality that permeates even their own lives, much less the conditions imposed on other peoples by exploitive companies in their name. Americans do not know that executive pay increased by 571% between 1990 and 2000, not adjusting for inflation, according to the *Washington Post* in September 2001, while the salaries for American workers rose a paltry 5% during that same period, inflation considered. Figures vary slightly, but the typical American household according to Sam Pizzigati, has a paltry $11,700.00 to call its own, down 10% since 1989.

Figures that show the average American household worth at $176,200.00 fail to mention that the top one percent of American households has a worth of $7,875,000.00. That accounts for the dramatic drop in reported value. And more dramatically still is the discrepancy between the "haves" and the "have-nots" in America: the top 1 percent holds more wealth than the entire bottom 95% of American households. Yet Americans generally feel they live well. Why? Because they live far beyond their income; they live on future income through plastic.

The average American has a credit card debt in the neighborhood of $18,000.00. Our economic system has literally forced Americans into an indentured servant relationship with the banks and corporations that manufacture, advertise, and sell the products. That reality has created a lethargic and unquestioning public that must, for its own sanity, believe the system is the best in the world.

Because they have become so invested in the economic system, Americans have a great deal to lose. Any threat to their livelihood evokes fear and retaliation. Thus the atrocities of 9/11, greater in kind than anything yet experienced in the States, awoke the American people to the enormity of the external threat that could destroy their relatively complacent lives. The President responded to these fears initially from an implicitly Christian perspective, seeing the world as divided into the good and the evil, with America as God's force for good leading the world against the forces of evil. He saw the nation's response as a "crusade" against those forces. Calmer minds in the administration corralled these terms by week's end, although the division of the world into those "with America" or "against America" still resounded in his speech before Congress on the September 20.

As we have seen, fear compels obedience. The dualistic division of the world as a ruling principle existed for Pope Innocent III and the Puritan Divines; it exists now. The God of the Old Testament, the Popes leading the Crusades, the Puritan ministers, the Nazi powers, and Imperial Japan, all used fear against the chosen, those protected by God or by genetic right, as the motivating force to mobilize against the enemies that threatened the continuation of the state, a war of good versus evil.

Our President has assumed absolute authority as the leader of all nations against terrorists throughout the world, for he alone is answerable to the American people and is the protector of the American people. That is the mantle Pope Innocent III assumed against the Cathars. He has raised the protection of liberty and freedom as the banner around which the nation will rally, even as he asks Congress to give his administration authority to override civil liberties. Pope Innocent III called upon the faithful to rally in defense of the Church, to liberate it from the forces of evil that threatened its existence. And he imposed the Inquisition to ensure that the one and only true Church would continue to exist.

Our President has demanded of the world's leaders that they choose between the forces of good and evil as defined by the United States. "You are with us or against us," he told the world.

Pope Innocent III menaced the kings of France, Spain, and England that they had to be with God's voice on earth or be forever damned in hell. He excommunicated or laid under anathema the leaders who refused his admonitions and placed their lands under an interdict. He even demanded they "take up the cross." Our President and his administration have threatened other nations with economic catastrophe if they do not join the "war against the terrorists," the crusade that he initially envisioned.

What is comparable here to the religious beliefs that motivate the terrorists, the crusaders of old, or the Puritans? Fear that the American way of life will be destroyed. That way of life, in its first manifestation, offered freedom of opportunity to all in a land that God gave to the founders who came here out of a commitment to their Christian God. The Revolutionary War brought enhancements to that "way of life" by opening the land of opportunity to all peoples, not just Christians. It also proposed that a *laissez-faire* Capitalism offered the only true avenue to fulfillment of that opportunity. America yoked together the freedoms inherent in a democratic form of government—freedom to choose their government, freedom of religion, and freedom of speech—with an economic system that furthered the interests of its peoples to acquire their cherished dreams. This way of life became the only one. What we believed was true should be true for all peoples, and thus we began electing Presidents who would require that our form of government and our economic system be accepted by those nations with whom we would interact and for whom we would provide support.

Most Americans, unfortunately, have not witnessed and have no true perception of how those values are transferred abroad. We are blind to the reality of our own economic condition, the discrepancy between our actual value and our debt. We fail to understand the dichotomy between the "haves" and the "have-nots" in this country, a discrepancy so dramatic that even an economist of the stature of John Kenneth Galbraith has reacted by placing the burden of responsibility on the United States government to set things right: "I have long been persuaded that a rich country such as the United States must give everybody the assurance of a basic income."

But if our recognition of our own condition is lax, our recognition of how other nations view America is almost non-existent. We believe that America is seen as a free society where everyone is equal and has the same opportunities. We believe our government supports true Democracy around the globe; and we believe the capitalistic system provides the best opportunity for all peoples in all nations. But these are myths. In truth, what we believe is what the corporate world wants us to believe and they have the means to make it happen. They own communications—newspapers, television channels, magazines, movie production studios, movie distribution houses, telephone systems, and radio stations. In truth what government supports are governments that will guarantee protection of capitalistic enterprise. They will place in power the necessary government to accomplish that end by whatever means it takes. In truth what Capitalism actually does in the name of the United States is to reap the greatest profits by producing for the least possible cost, regardless of the consequences to the peoples of other countries. These are the realities that turn people against the United States. We do not understand them because we do not see them as others do.

Capitalism, not Democracy, is at fault. As Capitalism has grown in this country, it has saturated over time its primary base, the absolute needs of most of the people for housing, clothing, transportation, and food. Once saturated, new goods had to be designed and new demands for them created. Advertising has taken on that role. But consumption is a never-ending process only as long as there are adequate numbers of consumers. America's population could not absorb the quantity of products the system had to produce to continue profits for investors; consequently, more markets had to be acquired. Russia, after the fall, showed promise. China shows promise now. Unfortunately, as Capitalism moves into countries with huge populations, some of its basic tenets cause problems.

An example will suffice. A department store in the city of Yantai employs hoards of personnel; four girls wait on a single customer buying a sweater with similar numbers at other counters. A conscientious Capitalist would see incredible savings by locating a checkout counter at the exit and laying-off excess personnel. But for China, with a population of 1.3 billion people, finding jobs is a problem. Capitalism's desire to hire as few people as possible to turn out products at the least cost, efficiency

of operation it's called, runs counter to the demands forced on
the government to find jobs for so many people, if only to provide them with a sense of worth and personal dignity.
Capitalism does not want nor can it thrive with a conscience.

Democracy must have a conscience. Capitalism's mobility
across the globe has fostered more hatred for the United States
than any other single cause, either in its support for "friendly"
governments, even if dictatorial, or in its exploitation of the
people. Martin Khor, in his article "Global Economy and the
Third World," describes how such corporations raid resources
and ship them to the wealthiest industrialized nations. New
trade rules imposed with the support of these transnational corporations leave the Third World countries virtually helpless to
protect themselves. Indeed, Ralph Nader and Lori Wallach,
writing about GATT and NAFTA, stated, "Approval of these
agreements has institutionalized a global economic and political
situation that places every government in a virtual hostage situation, at the mercy of a global financial and commercial system
run by empowered corporations." The full power granted to
corporations by these multi-national agreements cannot be fully
appreciated without recognizing that they do not contain regulations of commerce to protect environmental, health, or labor
rights, including prohibitions against child labor. Is it any
wonder other nations hate us?

Khor amplifies the consequences of this intrusion by noting,
"Some corporations are also concentrating their sales efforts on
the markets of the Third World, where they can sell lower-qual-
ity products or products that are outright toxic and thus banned
in the industrialized countries." Is it any wonder America is
hated? But these companies sell more than products; they sell a
culture, a consumer based and valueless culture. Foreign countries despise this erosion of values. They fear loss of a cultural
identity and subsequent loss of values associated with their culture. Richard Barnet and John Cavanagh in a study on
"Homogenization of Global Culture" reflect on the consequences of the globalization of entertainment that sends western
television, film, fashion, and music into virtually every country,
overpowering local stations and media.

Standardization ensues, dominated by the west. They note,
"The strongest remaining ideological barrier to American

music, television, and film is Islamic fundamentalism." That was in 1996. The "values" apparent in this western intrusion into other cultures: huge audiences, fame, and money achieved by costly venues, advertising, and sex. Given Americans' desire to assert family values, the transfer of this pop culture to all peoples seems a perversion of the peoples' values. Is it any wonder that so many hate the United States?

Now that we have confronted the reality behind the myths, it is necessary to reflect on how Americans and their government can respond adequately to the primary cause of the terrorists' acts. The reality the terrorists' see cannot be erased without changing the way the Capitalistic system operates on our behalf. The terrorist knows only that it is America's wealth and that of the industrialized west that manipulates and corrodes their country. They do not know what Americans believe to be true. If America continues to let the transnationals and the power elite control the operations of America abroad, it will continue to suffer from the atrocities terrorists commit. The world has changed, and we have been the instruments of that change. As the Bible says, "They have sown the wind, and they shall reap the whirlwind." [Hosea 8:7]

We have wired the world; they know now how the rest of the world lives. We must recognize that a more equal distribution of the world's resources must be achieved if discontent, deprivation, and hatred are to be assuaged. Our beliefs in what America should be, a melting pot of the world's communities living in tolerance and harmony, reflect desirable and universal values.

Americans must take back control of the government to ensure that those values, and not those of the profit-based transnationals, are the ones seen by peoples around the world. Correction of the myths that motivate one people to eliminate another, will respond to the primary cause that undergirds terrorism.

About the Author

Dr. William (Bill) Cook traces his roots to the first Dr. William A. Cook, honorably discharged by General George Washington from the Revolutionary forces after six years of service.

He, too, battled a despotic George, a madman of his day not unlike our own would-be Emperor, George W. It is in the blood to ensure that Democracy is not denied or stolen!

Prior to dissembling our 43rd President, Bill Cook spent his years managing academic affairs as Chair, Dean and Vice President at seven colleges/universities in five states. He has produced three books in the last four years: *A Time to Know*, *Psalms for the 21st Century*, and now, *Tracking Deception*—in addition to co-authoring with his wife, D'Arcy, *The Unreasoning Mask*, a contemporary tragedy about George W. Bush.

More information is available at his web site, *www.drwilliamacook.com*.

Index

Saddam has defied UN
by not complying
with, 7
the return of Palestinian
refugees, 7
without consequence? 2
Resolution, partitioning of
Palestine by , 87
Security Council, 311
time for Annan to lead the,
116
time for, to assert, 116
to be ridiculed by rogue
nations, permitting the,
277
un-Christian, 277
"war" of terror, 187
World Trade Towers, 266
World War II, 321
Yassin, Sheik, 177
9/11, 82, 93, 97, 110–12,
120, 133–7, 158, 180,
212, 265–6, 270, 273,
282, 305, 307
a deplorable atrocity, 270
actual events of, 135
an excuse to invade? 111
atrocity of, 82, 111, 120,
135, 265
Bush misadventure in Iraq
following, 134
"cleansing", a reason for,
273
consequences of, 180
death rate of American
soldiers in Iraq
comparable to, attacks,
158
death to 3000 Americans
on, 120

forces of evil, catalyst
against the, 266
havoc of, 139, 343
myths that caused, 343
Hiroshima's ashen
landscape, a vision of,
273
horrific morning of, 273
invasion of Iraq
engineered in advance
of, 273
investigation of the
terrorist acts that
resulted in, 212
Iraq, nothing to do with,
305
Iraq supported the,
terrorists, 133
linked Saddam to the,
terrorists, 112
Linking Iraq to, 133
means to bring freedom to
the Mid-East, 282
no part in the disaster
known as, 116
primary causes of the
attacks, 137
revenge against the
perpetrators of, 134
terrorist acts that resulted
in, 212
the day after, 136
Royal family in Saudi
Arabia, 136
audi state, connections
to, 136
9/11 Commission, the, 175,
178, 192, 207, 217
Phillip Zelikow, Director of
the, 192, 217

If You Liked This Book, You Won't Want To Miss Other Titles By Dandelion Books

Available Now And Always Through www.dandelionbooks.net And Affiliated Websites!!

TOLL-FREE ORDERS—1-800-861-7899 (U.S. & CANADA)

Non-Fiction

Prelude to Disaster: The Harring Report – Chronology of the Iraqi War & Complete Official Department of Defense Iraq & Afghanistan U.S. Military Casualty List, by TBR News – tbrnews.org... Actual death toll of the US Military in Iraq... "far more realistic than the government's current official number of 1,800-plus," according to data researcher Brain Harring. Also includes Russian daily military intelligence reports of the Iraqi War from March 17 – April 8, 2003. (ISBN 1-893302-84-9)

Progressive Awareness: Critical Thinking, Self-Awareness & Critical Consciousness, by Norman D. Livergood... How to avoid being manipulated by our emotions and ideas and how to start thinking for ourselves; increase your skills for understanding, critical thinking, self-awareness, critical consciousness, and enlightened discernment. (ISBN 1-893302-80-6)

America 2004: A Power But Not Super, by John Stanton [Foreword by Bev Conover, Editor - onlinejournal.com, Introduction by Karen Kwiatkowski, Lieutenant Colonel, USAF (Ret.)]... Stanton explains how Bush has adroitly fused state, religious (faith-based government) and business interests into one indistinguishable tyrannical mass... his explanation of how this has been accomplished is eye-opening. (ISBN 1-893302-26-1)

America Speaks Out: Collected Essays From Dissident Writers John H. Brand, Meria Heller, John Kaminski, Norman D. Livergood, Wayne Madsen, Kurt Nimmo, Albert D. Pastore, Michael E. Salla, Sherman H. Skolnick & John Stanton... A collection of essays extracted from works recently published by Dandelion Books. (ISBN 1-893302-63-6)

Exopolitics: Political Implications Of The Extraterrestrial Presence, by Michael E. Salla, Ph.D.... According to Dr. Michael Salla and many other experts in the field of ET research, for almost 70 years the

US government has engaged in an extensive "official effort" of disinformation, intimidation and tampering with evidence in order to maintain a non-disclosure policy about extraterrestrial presence. (ISBN 1-893302-56-3)

Stranger than Fiction: An Independent Investigation Of The True Culprits Behind 9-11, by Albert D. Pastore, Ph.D... Twelve months of careful study, painstaking research, detailed analysis, source verification and logical deduction went into the writing of this book. In addition to the stories are approximately 300 detailed footnotes Pastore: "Only by sifting through huge amounts of news data on a daily basis was I able to catch many of these rare 'diamonds in the rough' and organize them into a coherent pattern and logical argument." (ISBN 1-893302-47-4)

Unshackled: A Survivor's Story of Mind Control, by Kathleen Sullivan... A non-fictional account of Kathleen Sullivan's experiences as part of a criminal network that includes Intelligence personnel, military personnel, doctors and mental health professionals contracted by the military and the CIA, criminal cult leaders and members, pedophiles, pornographers, drug dealers and Nazis. "I believe my story needs to be told so that more people will understand how 'Manchurian Candidate' style mind-control techniques can create alter-states in the minds of unwitting victims, causing them to perform deeds that are normally repugnant." (ISBN 1-893302-35-0)

Ahead Of TheParade: A Who's Who Of Treason and High Crimes – Exclusive Details Of Fraud And Corruption Of The Monopoly Press, The Banks, The Bench And The Bar, And The Secret Political Police, by Sherman H. Skolnick... One of America's foremost investigative reporters, speaks out on some of America's current crises. Included in this blockbuster book are the following articles: Big City Newspapers & the Mob, The Sucker Traps, Dirty Tricks of Finance and Brokerage, The Secret History of Airplane Sabotage, Wal-Mart and the Red Chinese Secret Police, The Chandra Levy Affair, The Japanese Mafia in the United States, The Secrets of Timothy McVeigh, and much more. (ISBN 1-893302-32-6)

Another Day In The Empire: Life in Neoconservative America, by Kurt Nimmo... A collection of articles by one of Counterpunch's most popular columnists. Included in this collection are: The Son of COINTELPRO; Clueless at the State Department; Bush Senior: Hating Saddam, Selling Him Weapons; Corporate Media: Selling Dubya's Oil War; Iraq and the Vision of the Velociraptors: The Bleeding Edge of Islam; Condoleezza Rice at the Waldorf Astoria; Predators, Snipers and the Posse Comitatus Act, and many others. (ISBN 1-893302-75-X)

Palestine & The Middle East: Passion, Power & Politics, by Jaffer Ali... The Palestinian struggle is actually a human one that transcends Palestine... There is no longer a place for Zionism in the 20th century... Democracy in the Middle East is mot safe for US interests as long as there is an atmosphere of hostility... Suicide bombings are acts of desperation and mean that a people have been pushed to the brink... failure to understand why they happen will make certain they will continue. Jaffer Ali is a Palestinian-American business man who has been writing on politics and business for over 25 years. (ISBN 1-893302-45-8)

Ben-Gurion's Scandals: How The Haganah And The Mossad Eliminated Jews, by Naeim Giladi... The painful truth about the Zionist rape of Palestine and deliberate planting of anti-Semitism in Iraqi Jewish communities during David Ben-Gurion's political career in order to persuade the Iraqi Jews to immigrate to Israel. (ISBN1-893302-40-7)

America, Awake! We Must Take Back Our Country, by Norman D. Livergood... This book is intended as a wake-up call for Americans, as Paul Revere awakened the Lexington patriots to the British attack on April 18, 1775, and as Thomas Paine's *Common Sense* roused apathetic American colonists to recognize and struggle against British oppression. Our current situation is similar to that which American patriots faced in the 1770s: a country ruled by 'foreign' and 'domestic' plutocratic powers and a divided citizenry uncertain of their vital interests. (ISBN 1-893302-27-X)

The Awakening of An American: How America Broke My Heart, by Meria Heller, with a Foreword by Catherine Austin Fitts... A collection of choice interviews from Meria Heller's world-famous www.meria.net rapidly growing radio network that reaches millions of people daily. Dr. Arun Gandhi, Greg Palast, Vincent Bugliosi, Mark Elsis,

William Rivers Pitt, Mark Rechtenwald, Nancy Oden & Bob Fertik, Howard Winant, Linda Starr, Dave Chandler, Bev Conover, John Nichols, Robert McChesney, Norman Solomon, Stan Goff and Mark Crispin Miller. (ISBN 1-89302-39-3)

America's Nightmare: The Presidency of George Bush II, by John Stanton & Wayne Madsen...Media & Language, War & Weapons, Internal Affairs and a variety of other issues pointing out the US "crisis without precedent" that was wrought by the US Presidential election of 2000 followed by 9/11. "Stanton & Madsen will challenge many of the things you've been told by CNN and Fox news. This book is dangerous." (ISBN 1-893302-29-6)

America's Autopsy Report, by John Kaminski...The false fabric of history is unraveling beneath an avalanche of pathological lies to justify endless war and Orwellian new laws that revoke the rights of Americans. While TV and newspapers glorify the dangerous ideas of perverted billionaires, the Internet has pulsated with outrage and provided a new and real forum for freedom among concerned people all over the world who are opposed to the mass murder and criminal exploitation of the defenseless victims of multinational corporate totalitarianism. John Kaminski's passionate essays give voice to those hopes and fears of humane people that are ignored by the big business shysters who rule the major media. (ISBN 1-893302-42-3)

Seeds Of Fire: China And The Story Behind The Attack On America, by Gordon Thomas... The inside story about China that no one can afford to ignore. Using his unsurpassed contacts in Israel, Washington, London and Europe, Gordon Thomas, internationally acclaimed best-selling author and investigative reporter for over a quarter-century, reveals information about China's intentions to use the current crisis to launch itself as a super-power and become America's new major enemy... *"This has been kept out of the news agenda because it does not suit certain business interests to have that truth emerge...Every patriotic American should buy and read this book... it is simply revelatory."* (Ray Flynn, Former US Ambassador to the Vatican) (ISBN 1-893302-54-7)

Shaking The Foundations: Coming Of Age In The Postmodern Era, by John H. Brand, D.Min., J.D.... Scientific discoveries in the Twentieth Century require the restructuring of our understanding the nature of

Nature and of human beings. In simple language the author explains how significant implications of quantum mechanics, astronomy, biology and brain physiology form the foundation for new perspectives to comprehend the meaning of our lives. (ISBN 1-893302-25-3)

Rebuilding The Foundations: Forging A New And Just America, by John H. Brand, D.Min., J.D....Should we expect a learned scholar to warn us about our dangerous reptilian brains that are the real cause of today's evils? Although Brand is not without hope for rescuing America, he warns us to act fast–and now. Evil men intent on imposing their political, economic, and religious self-serving goals on America are not far from achieving their goal of mastery." (ISBN 1-893302-33-4)

The Perennial Tradition: Overview Of The Secret Heritage, The Single Stream Of Initiatory Teaching Flowing Through All The Great Schools Of Mysticism, by Norman D. Livergood... Like America, Awake, this book is another wake-up call. "It was written to assist readers to awaken to the Higher Spiritual World." In addition to providing a history of the Western tradition of the Perennial Tradition, Livergood also describes the process that serious students use to actually *realize*—bring to manifestation—their Higher Consciousness. "Unless we become aware of this higher state, we face the prospect of a basically useless physical existence and a future life—following physical death—of unpleasant, perhaps anguished reformation of our essence." (ISBN 1-893302-48-2)

The Last Atlantis Book You'll Ever Have To Read! by Gene D. Matlock... More than 25,000 books, plus countless other articles have been written about a fabled confederation of city-states known as Atlantis. If it really did exist, where was it located? Does anyone have valid evidence of its existence – artifacts and other remnants? According to historian, archaeologist, educator and linguist Gene D. Matlock, both questions can easily be answered. (ISBN 1-893302-20-2)

The Last Days Of Israel, by Barry Chamish... With the Middle East crisis ongoing, *The Last Days of Israel* takes on even greater significance as an important book of our age. Barry Chamish, investigative reporter who has the true story about Yitzak Rabin's assassination, tells it like it is. (ISBN 1-893302-16-4)

The Courage To Be Who I Am, by Mary-Margareht Rose... This book is rich with teachings and anecdotes delivered with humor and humanness, by a woman who followed her heart and learned to listen to her inner voice; in the process, transforming every obstacle into an opportunity to test her courage to manifest her true identity. (1SBN 1-893302-13-X)

The Making Of A Master: Tracking Your Self-Worth, by Jeanette O'Donnal... A simple tracking method for self-improvement that takes the mystery out of defining your goals, making a road map and tracking your progress. A book rich with nuggets of wisdom couched in anecdotes and instructive dialogues. (ISBN 1-893302-36-9)

Cancer Doctor: The Biography Josef Issels, M.D., Who Brought Hope To The World With His Revolutionary Cancer Treatment, by Gordon Thomas...Dr. Josef Issels treated more than 12,000 cancer patients who had been written off as "incurable" by other doctors. He claimed no miracle cures, but the success record of his revolutionary "whole person treatment" was extraordinary... the story of his struggle against the medical establishment which put Dr. Issels in prison, charged with fraud and manslaughter. (ISBN 1-893302-18-0)

Fiction

Drifters: The Final Testament, Volume One, by Michael Silverhawk... Within the DRIFTERS trilogy is a powerful secret, a key that unlocks our human potential! Can one man "make a difference" not only in his own life but for everyone else on the planet? Is it possible for a single human to transform chaos into order, darkness into light? (ISBN 1-893302-57-1)

Ticket to Paradise, by Yvonne Ridley...Judith Tempest, a British reporter, is searching for the Truth. But when it starts to spill out in her brilliant front page reportage of Middle East suicide bombing in retaliation for Israeli tanks mowing down innocent Palestinian women and children, both 'Tempest' and 'Truth' start to spell 'Trouble'— with a capital 'T', joke her friends and colleagues. A non-stop mystery thriller that tears along at a reckless pace of passion, betrayal, adventure and espionage. (ISBN 1-893302-77-6)

Synchronicity Gates: An Anthology Of Stories And Poetry About People Transformed In Extraordinary Reality Beyond Experience, by Stephen Vernarelli... An inventive compilation of short stories that take the reader beyond mere science, fiction, or fantasy. Vernarelli introduces the reader to a new perception of reality; he imagines the best and makes it real. (ISBN 1-893302-38-5)

The Alley of Wishes, by Laurel Johnson... Despite the ravages of WWI on Paris and on the young American farm boy, Beck Sanow, and despite the abusive relationship that the chanteuse Cerise endures, the two share a bond that is unbreakable by time, war, loss of memory, loss of life and loss of youth. Beck and Cerise are both good people beset by constant tragedy. Yet it is tragedy that brings them together, and it is unconditional love that keeps them together. (ISBN 1-893302-46-6)

Freedom: Letting Go Of Anxiety And Fear Of The Unknown, by Jim Britt... Jeremy Carter, a fireman from Missouri who is in New York City for the day, decides to take a tour of the Trade Center, only to watch in shock, the attack on its twin towers from a block away. Afterward as he gazes at the pit of rubble and talks with many of the survivors, Jeremy starts to explore the inner depths of his soul, to ask questions he'd never asked before. This dialogue helps him learn who he is and what it takes to overcome the fear, anger, grief and anxiety this kind of tragedy brings. (ISBN 1-893302-74-1)

The Prince Must Die, by Gower Leconfield... breaks all taboos for mystery thrillers. After the "powers that be" suppressed the manuscripts of three major British writers, Dandelion Books breaks through with a thriller involving a plot to assassinate Prince Charles. *The Prince Must Die* brings to life a Britain of today that is on the edge with race riots, neo-Nazis, hard right backlash and neo-punk nihilists. Riveting entertainment... you won't be able to put it down. (ISBN 1-893302-72-5)

Waaaay Out There! Diggertown, Oklahoma, by Tuklo Nashoba... Adventures of constable Clint Mankiller and his deputy, Chad GhostWolf; Jim Bob and Bubba Johnson, Grandfather GhostWolf, Cassie Snodgrass, Doc Jones, Judge Jenkins and the rest of the Diggertown, Oklahoma bunch in the first of a series of Big Foot-Sasquatch tall tales peppered with lots of good belly laughs and just as much fun. (ISBN 1-893302-44-X)

Come as You Are, by Sarah Daniels... "Tongue-in-cheek" entertainment at its wackiest—and most subtle. If anyone ever doubted that sex makes the world go around, author Sarah Daniels will put your mind, and body to test. Non-stop humor, humanness and wisdom are bundled together to deliver one of life's most important unheeded lessons: each of us has a unique destiny to discover, and until we find and embark on that destiny, life may be one bowl of cherry pits after another. Adult language and scenes. (ISBN 1-893302-15-6)

Unfinished Business, by Elizabeth Lucas Taylor... Lindsay Mayer knows something is amiss when her husband, Griffin, a college professor, starts spending too much time at his office and out-of-town. Shortly after the ugly truth surfaces, Griffin disappears altogether. Lindsay is shattered. Life without Griffin is life without life... One of the sexiest books you'll ever read! (ISBN 1-893302-68-7)

The Woman With Qualities, by Sarah Daniels... South Florida isn't exactly the Promised Land that forty-nine-year-old newly widowed Keri Anders had in mind when she transplanted herself here from the northeast... A tough action-packed novel that is far more than a love story. (ISBN 1-893302-11-3)*Adventure Capital*, by John Rushing...South Florida adventure, crime and violence in a fiction story based on a true life experience. A book you will not want to put down until you reach the last page. (ISBN 1-893302-08-3)

A Mother's Journey: To Release Sorrow And Reap Joy, by Sharon Kay... A poignant account of Norah Ann Mason's life journey as a wife, mother and single parent. This book will have a powerful impact on anyone, female or male, who has experienced parental abuse, family separations, financial struggles and a desperate need to find the magic in life that others talk about that just doesn't seem to be there for them. (ISBN 1-893302-52-0)

Return To Masada, by Robert G. Makin... In a gripping account of the famous Battle of Masada, Robert G. Makin skillfully recaptures the blood and gore as well as the spiritual essence of this historic struggle for freedom and independence. (ISBN 1-893302-10-5)

Time Out Of Mind, by Solara Vayanian... Atlantis had become a snake pit of intrigue teeming with factious groups vying for power and control. An unforgettable drama that tells of the breakdown of the priesthood, the hidden scientific experiments in genetic engineering which produced "things" — part human and part animal — and other atrocities; the infiltration by the dark lords of Orion; and the implantation of the human body with a device to fuel the Orion wars. (ISBN 1-893302-21-0)

The Thirteenth Disciple: The Life Of Mary Magdalene, by Gordon Thomas... The closest of Jesus' followers, the name of Mary Magdalene conjures images of a woman both passionate and devoted, both sinner and saint. The first full-length biography for 13 centuries. (ISBN 1-893302-17-2)

ALL DANDELION BOOKS ARE AVAILABLE THROUGH WWW.DANDELIONBOOKS.NET... ALWAYS.

LaVergne, TN USA
05 March 2010
175008LV00003B/3/A